Legal Writing for Legal Readers

ASPEN COURSEBOOK SERIES

Legal Writing for Legal Readers

Predictive Writing for First-Year Students

THIRD EDITION

MARY BETH BEAZLEY
Professor of Law
William S. Boyd School of Law
University of Nevada, Las Vegas

MONTE SMITH
Assistant Clinical Professor of Law
Michael E. Moritz College of Law
The Ohio State University

Cover image: iStock.com/peterschreiber.media

To contact Customer Service, e-mail customer.service@aspenpublishing.com, call 1-800-950-5259, or mail correspondence to:

Aspen Publishing
Attn: Order Department
PO Box 990
Frederick, MD 21705

Printed in the United States of America.

1 2 3 4 5 6 7 8 9 0

ISBN 978-1-5438-3944-9

Library of Congress Cataloging-in-Publication Data application is in process.

About Aspen Publishing

Aspen Publishing is a leading provider of educational content and digital learning solutions to law schools in the U.S. and around the world. Aspen provides best-in-class solutions for legal education through authoritative textbooks, written by renowned authors, and breakthrough products such as Connected eBooks, Connected Quizzing, and PracticePerfect.

The Aspen Casebook Series (famously known among law faculty and students as the "red and black" casebooks) encompasses hundreds of highly regarded textbooks in more than eighty disciplines, from large enrollment courses, such as Torts and Contracts to emerging electives such as Sustainability and the Law of Policing. Study aids such as the *Examples & Explanations* and *Glannon Guide* series, both highly popular collections, help law students master complex subject matter.

Major products, programs, and initiatives include:

- **Connected eBooks** are enhanced digital textbooks and study aids that come with a suite of online content and learning tools designed to maximize student success. Designed in collaboration with hundreds of faculty and students, the Connected eBook is a significant leap forward in the legal education learning tools available to students.
- **Connected Quizzing** is an easy-to-use formative assessment tool that tests law students' understanding and provides timely feedback to improve learning outcomes. Delivered through CasebookConnect.com, the learning platform already used by students to access their Aspen casebooks, Connected Quizzing is simple to implement and integrates seamlessly with law school course curricula.
- **PracticePerfect** is a visually engaging, interactive study aid to explain commonly encountered legal doctrines through easy-to-understand animated videos, illustrative examples, and numerous practice questions. Developed by a team of experts, PracticePerfect is the ideal study companion for today's law students.
- The **Aspen Learning Library** enables law schools to provide their students with access to the most popular study aids on the market across all of their courses. Available through an annual subscription, the online library consists of study aids in e-book, audio, and video formats with full text search, note-taking, and highlighting capabilities.
- Aspen's **Digital Bookshelf** is an institutional-level online education bookshelf, consolidating everything students and professors need to ensure success. This program ensures that every student has access to affordable course materials from day one.
- **Leading Edge** is a community centered on thinking differently about legal education and putting those thoughts into actionable strategies. At the core of the program is the Leading Edge Conference, an annual gathering of legal education thought leaders looking to pool ideas and identify promising directions of exploration.

To my sister, Trish Sanders, and my brother, Mike Beazley.
They piqued my interest in the law at the age of 4,
when they introduced me to *The Bowery Boys*
and inspired me to throw pretend rats at pretend truant officers.

MBB

To my boys, Jonah and Tate, with as much
love as any dad ever felt.

MS

SUMMARY OF CONTENTS

CONTENTS

ACKNOWLEDGMENTS

For this third edition, we particularly thank Ashton Marr, a law student at Ohio State, who used the previous edition of this text as a 1L and then reread it, cover to cover, to identify "areas for growth," major and minor, from a student's perspective. Every one of Ashton's suggestions found its way into this edition.

We also thank the many attorneys who let us seek their wisdom, especially about the role of email in legal practice: Jenna Farrell, Dave Borer, Martha Brewer Motley, Carol Burns, Thommy Butchko, Dave Coyle, Shalini Goyal, Jessica Kim, Audry Klossner, Joanna Medrano, Andy Miller, Joan Rife, Bethany Sanders, Bobby Thaxton, Melissa Wasser, and Rebecca Woods.

Thanks also to Katherine Kelly, who was always ready with reactions and suggestions, even during the busiest time of her year.

Mary Beth thanks the faculty support team at UNLV, especially Maria Campos.

FOREWORD

You are probably a first-year student who is learning to be a legal writer, and you want to know what legal briefs and memos look like. The short answer: they're rectangular. For the long answer, read the book. We have put lots of samples of legal writing in the text and in the top-secret Teachers' Manual that your professor has. We want to tell you a couple of things about the text and the samples so that you can use them more effectively.

- First, please read carefully the samples and the annotations that accompany them. We know that when you are reading for class, it's tempting to skip anything you can. In a legal writing course, though, the samples may be the most important part of the reading. At the very least, you should read them to see if you understand how the sample does and does not follow the guidelines in the text. Sometimes we'll purposely include examples that don't follow the guidelines for good writing, just so you can see how annoying bad writing can be.
- The part of the text that is not samples is not written in formal legal writing style, so don't imitate that style when you write briefs and memos. Legal writing teachers write comments on student papers all the time, and that's the writing style we've used here. We hope it communicates effectively, but we were not trying to sound like lawyers, or even grown-ups, so you shouldn't imitate that style when you are trying to write like a lawyer.
- Don't imitate the samples mindlessly. Some samples are bad on purpose, and some are partly good and partly bad. If you ask the question, "Can I imitate this sample?" the answer is the answer you will hear all the time in law school: "It depends." As you will learn, legal readers need different information depending on their role, on the relevant legal issue, and on many other factors. Some techniques are great in an office memo but not in a brief. Some techniques are great for one client's problem but not another client's problem; some are appropriate for a federal law legal issue but not for a state law question of fact. So when you are debating whether to imitate a sample, consider whether you are in the same rhetorical situation. And by "rhetorical situation," we mean why you're writing, who

you're writing to, the role you are writing in, and what you're writing about.

- Don't rely on the law we cite in the samples. We based almost all of the samples on realistic legal issues, but we didn't update things to make sure the law was still valid. And when we had to choose between using the law precisely and making the sample a useful sample, we went with making a useful sample. Some of the law is obviously fake, because we're citing to the fake states of Vanita or West Montana, and the fake regional reporter of "Region East, Second Series," abbreviated "R.E.2d." (The second half of that sentence has no meaning to you at all if you are a brand-new 1-L, but don't worry about it. You'll understand it when you're older—about 2 months older.) Even when we cite to seemingly real cases, they—or the law we reference—may be fake. So if you find yourself addressing a legal issue that one of our samples addresses, don't rely on the sample. Do your own research.

One more thing. This edition includes some self-testing opportunities. Some of the opportunities are in the text: we will advise you by saying something like, "test yourself by looking for . . ." a certain feature in a sample or in your writing. Developing self-evaluation skills is an important part of becoming a professional. Further, every chapter ends with a set of "Recall and Review" questions. These questions are based on educational research that shows that being asked to recall new concepts is a good way to learn and retain those new concepts. Since the questions will be the very last thing in every chapter, they should be easy for you to find, and we hope they will be easy for you to answer.

Early in the text, most of the Recall and Review questions will test your understanding of new vocabulary words like *jurisdiction* and *elements*. Later, they will ask you to recall foundational doctrines of legal writing, like the elements of a case description or of a CREXAC unit of discourse (we know those words don't mean much now). In later chapters, the questions may ask you to think a little harder or to apply a concept you have learned. Sometimes, your teachers may incorporate the questions into your class, but even if they don't, we recommend that you check to see if you can answer them. In fact, later in the semester, you might want to have another look at the Recall and Review questions from the early chapters, as a way to see if you are retaining the doctrine of legal writing you are working so hard on.

That's all for now. You've just finished the shortest chapter in the book.

CHAPTER 1

INTRODUCTION

You have just gotten home from work, and you have friends arriving soon for dinner. You promised to make crawfish étouffée, which you've never made before. Here are two versions of the recipe.[1] Which one would you rather use?

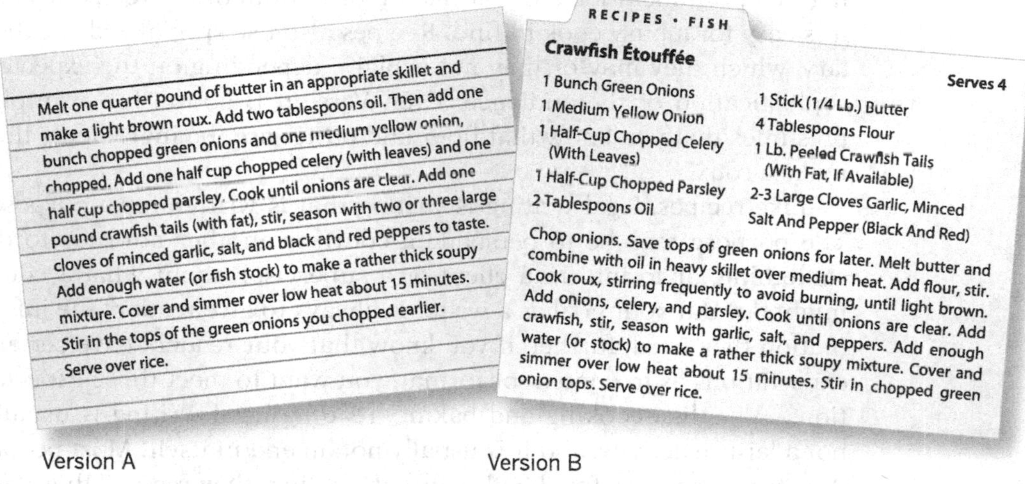

Version A

Version B

We're guessing that most of you would be much more comfortable using Version B than Version A. First, Version B's format meets more of your expectations for a recipe. You can glance at it and know immediately the ingredients that you need to gather. Second, its organization and explanations make it easier to cook from. If you had tried to

1. CajunCrawfish.com, Recipe for Crawfish Étouffée No. 2, http://northcarolinacrawfish.com/Recipes_3XCU.html (accessed May 1, 2014).

follow Version A, you would have had to stop frequently to gather and prepare various ingredients. Further, Version A presumes you know what a "roux" is and how to make one. And if you have never done Cajun cooking or cooked shellfish, you may not know that you are supposed to peel crawfish tails before you add them to a recipe. (And we have no idea where the fat is in a raw crawfish tail or how you are supposed to save it.) When you read Version A, you may have thought that adding "red peppers" meant bell peppers or jalapeno peppers or some other fresh red pepper. But when you look at the list of ingredients in Version B, you see "salt and pepper (black and red)." Seeing "pepper" in that context probably made you realize that the "red peppers" refers to a powdered pepper like chili pepper rather than a fresh red pepper.

What do recipes for crawfish étouffée have to do with legal writing? We think you might have already guessed. Recipes are written for a purpose. Regular readers (and users) of recipes also have certain expectations as to how the information in the recipes will be presented, and what information will be included. When recipes meet readers' expectations, it's easier for readers to use the recipes for their purpose: to prepare particular foods. In baking recipes, for example, the recipe almost always puts the oven temperature and time of cooking in a prominent location, at the top or bottom of the recipe, where it is easy for a busy cook to find. Recipes also use specialized vocabulary, which they may or may not explain, depending on the expected sophistication of the audience. Even Version B above, for example, presumes that you know that flour and butter are the ingredients that make a roux.

Like recipes, legal writing is writing that is written for a purpose. The purpose may be to persuade a court or another attorney to do something, or to inform a client or a supervisor about what a court might do. But your goal as a writer is always to give readers the information they need; further, if you know that your readers have certain expectations as to content or format, you want to meet those expectations. Also, like cooking and baking, reading legal writing is usually not a leisure activity, and it is usually not an end in itself. Most people do not read recipes for the pleasure of reading; they read so that they know what to do. Likewise, when people read legal writing, they are reading so that they can get the information they need to make a decision about a case or about their lives.

This semester, you are beginning your journey as a legal writer. Not coincidentally, you are also beginning your journey as a legal reader. As you read court opinions for your various casebook courses, you may sometimes feel as though you are reading another "Version A" recipe: the court will be using words you don't understand, will not be writing explicitly, and will make important information difficult to find.

The very first case that Mary Beth read in one of her first-year courses (38 years ago) began with the word "assumpsit," and even though she didn't know what it meant, she didn't look it up before class. That case did not do a very good job of meeting her needs as a reader. (Fortunately, the professor called on someone else to define that word.)

We want you to remember how you felt when you read Version A, and how you felt (and feel) when you read court opinions that are badly written or not reader-friendly. It's important to keep your feelings as a reader in mind because empathy for readers is one of the most important tools that a legal writer has. Throughout this text, we're going to ask you to read various versions of the documents that we're asking you to write. We want you to think about how the different versions do or don't help readers use the writing for its particular purpose. You'll notice that whenever we ask you to read a sample, we will tell you the document's purpose, that is, what readers will be using the document for. If you are consistently aware of readers' purpose for reading the documents you write, it will be easier for you to identify the reasons that various documents do and don't meet those needs, and to be a better legal writer.

If you are like most law students, your law school writing class will have some familiar features that some of your other classes don't have. You have probably never studied torts, contracts, or civil procedure, but you have almost certainly taken a writing course. And it's true that at least some of the *writing* part of legal analysis and writing should be familiar, whether you are reading this book for a course titled "research and writing," "legal analysis and writing," "applied legal theory," or just "legal writing." We use the name "legal analysis and writing" because legal writing always encompasses some analytical component.

One of the first things you need to learn about being an effective legal writer is something about readers: readers like *context*. Context helps readers understand new information. In general, you understand new information better when you have some old information (the context) to attach it to. One reason that the Version B recipe is easier to follow is that it uses a title, which gives readers an immediate context for the recipe that follows. And one reason that the first semester of law school is typically so hard is that you're getting lots and lots of new information, and you don't always have old information, or context, to attach it to. So, we're going to try to give you some context right now by explaining what happens when lawyers write and what we're going to try to do in this book.

A *deposition* is a formal interview in which a person swears to tell the truth, like a witness does in court. The questions and answers are recorded orally or in writing, and if the case ends up in court, the attorney can use the information from the deposition.

Generally, legal writing begins with facts. The lawyer may get those facts from a phone call or a client meeting, from documents the client has sent, or from interviews or depositions with the client or others who know about the facts. In a large law firm, a more senior attorney may get initial facts from a client and assign a less-experienced attorney to begin developing the facts.

In addition to telling the attorney the facts, the client will generally ask the attorney some sort of *question*, such as "Can I get money from X because of what he did to me?" Or "Am I going to get in trouble for this?" Or "Can I stop her from doing this?" The attorney's job is then to determine the answer to the client's question by figuring out what the relevant law is and how it *applies* to the client's facts. (Later in this chapter, we'll explain more precisely what lawyers mean when they say "apply law to facts.")

So, let's presume that you are a junior attorney, and a senior attorney just gave you a set of facts and a client's question. What do you do? Generally, after an initial review of the facts, you should develop a hypothesis about what area of law is going to govern the client's facts. That's why you're taking the other classes you take in law school. This class is teaching you legal writing doctrine; those classes are teaching you contracts doctrine, torts doctrine, and so on, so you have some knowledge about the different areas of law that might control various situations. In Chapter 7, we'll talk about developing your hypothesis and planning research.

Case refers to a published court opinion or decision. It also refers to litigation that is in process. Finally, even before a lawsuit is filed, many attorneys refer to a client's situation as that client's "case."

Jurisdiction is a geographical area controlled by a legislature or a court. The term may also refer to a court's authority to hear a particular kind of case.

Once you form a hypothesis about what law might govern the situation, you will do some research in that area, to find statutes and cases that are relevant. Chapter 2 explains in more detail how the American legal system works, but for now you should know that statutes and cases generally contain rules that govern the people and situations in a particular jurisdiction. For example, when the Ohio legislature enacts *statutes* (laws), those statutes regulate behavior that happens within Ohio. *Cases* (court opinions), like statutes, control only behavior that occurs within the relevant jurisdiction. When the Arizona Supreme Court, for instance, issues decisions, those decisions typically regulate only behavior that occurs within or is related to Arizona.

When courts decide cases, they are deciding what will happen to or between the people who are parties to the case. Cases may also regulate future situations, but only when the facts and the legal issues are sufficiently similar. This principle is also known as *stare decisis*, which is Latin for "the decision stands." In general, the phrase is interpreted to mean "like cases are decided alike." Sometimes, a big part of a legal argument will be about whether a case can control a new situation, and the court will analyze whether the authority case is sufficiently "like" the new case. So, a big part of your research is finding cases that are sufficiently like your client's case.

Once you have done some research, you might find that you need more facts. Research and writing can be a recursive process: the facts give you an idea about the relevant law, and then the law tells you what facts you need; so, you get more facts, and they lead you to do more research and get more law. But at some point, you've achieved critical mass: you have enough facts and enough law to begin writing. Now what do you do?

Very broadly, what follows is a two-stage process, which might also be a bit recursive. First, you need to gain your own understanding of how the law governs the facts: you need to be able to answer the question your client asked and to understand how you got to that answer. Second, you need to communicate that answer in writing. This recursiveness doesn't mean you should wait to start writing until you are sure you understand everything. Experts suggest using writing as a way to figure out what you understand and don't understand, and we agree with that suggestion. Creating a working draft, for example, is a way of using writing to flesh out your thoughts and identify areas of confusion.

Once you have a working draft of your legal analysis, you should focus on effectively communicating your analysis to your readers. Like all writing, legal writing is made up of words, sentences, and paragraphs, so you can use what you already know about good writing when you want to create good legal writing. Legal writing is different from many kinds of writing, however, just as swimming across a pool is different from swimming across a lake. You'll be able to use lots of the skills you've already learned, but there are some new skills you will have to master.

First, legal writing demands much more precision than many other kinds of writing. In this text, we'll be talking about common precision issues and how to avoid them. And, of course, you'll be writing in detail about specific areas of the law, subjects that will likely be new to you. This text also talks about how to write effectively about specific aspects of law as expressed in cases and statutes. Further, legal readers have certain expectations that you need to be aware of; your goal as a legal writer is to meet those expectations. The expectations will vary from document to document, but there are some common requirements that recur in most analytical documents. We will talk about several different kinds of documents in this book, and we will explain the requirements for each, and include samples.

One example of an iconic legal writing document is the *office memorandum*, or office memo. A typical office memo is a document from a junior attorney to a senior attorney. The senior attorney gives the junior attorney a set of facts, as reported by the client. The junior attorney must answer one or more questions about those facts, for instance: "Will John be able to recover damages from Mary?" "Will Lisa be found guilty of trespass?" "Do we have a strong enough chance of winning this case to take it on?"

The writer of an office memo finds the relevant law (usually through research) and figures out how the law *applies to the facts*. That phrase may be new to you. When you *apply* lotion to your skin, you touch your skin with the lotion. In the same way, when lawyers apply law to facts, they are determining or explaining whether and how a particular legal rule touches, or controls, the outcome of a legal issue.

For example, if your city has a law forbidding parking near a fire hydrant, you might be surprised to get a ticket for parking a bicycle next to a hydrant. If you asked a lawyer for help, the lawyer would look at the precise words of the ordinance. Imagine that the ordinance reads like this: "No person may park a vehicle on a roadway within ten feet of a fire hydrant." For the ordinance to apply to your fact situation, a court would have to decide that, for purposes of the fire hydrant statute, a bicycle counts as a "vehicle." If the court decides that a bicycle is a vehicle under that ordinance, then it would say that the statute *applies* to your fact situation. If the court decides that a bicycle is *not* a vehicle under that ordinance, it would say that the statute *does not apply* to your fact situation.

An *ordinance* is what we usually call legislation enacted by a city, while we use the word *statute* for legislation enacted by states or by the federal (national) government.

Often, the legislature that passes the law also passes another law that defines terms in the statute. If the legislature that passed the law didn't define the terms, or if a fact situation arises that is not covered by a definition, a court may need to decide what the term means and whether it applies to the new facts.

In the bicycle scenario, the word "vehicle" is what we call the "phrase-that-pays," that is, the word or combination of words that will be the focus of that analysis. Put very simply, if the phrase-that-pays is present in the facts, or is met by the facts, the test is satisfied. Often, your research will be aimed at determining what the phrase-that-pays is and then what the phrase-that-pays means. When you have answered those questions, you know the direction that your analysis will have to take. So, in the bicycle scenario, once the lawyer has answered the question whether a bicycle is a "vehicle" for purposes of the statute, the lawyer will know whether that phrase-that-pays (vehicle) equals bicycle, and the direction of the analysis will be determined.

As we will discuss, just as it is possible for a case to have multiple issues, it is possible for a client's case, or a legal rule, to have multiple phrases-that-pay.

If you were to write an office memo about that issue, you would research the relevant cases and predict how a court would apply the law, capsulized in the phrase-that-pays, to the facts. Although not all law firms request formal office memos nowadays, we believe that the office memo is a great document for first-year law students to write. If you can write an effective formal office memo, you will have mastered many of the skills of effective legal writing.

What follows is a short office memo that presents two very straightforward legal issues. The text in the annotations identifies the legal writing skills that were necessary for the writer to have mastered, and the chapters in this book that will cover those skills.

Presume that you practice law in the fictional state of Vanita. A new client, Wendy Wheelwright, has been arrested for drunk driving. She doesn't understand how she can be found guilty, however. She admits that she failed the blood-alcohol test, but she was not driving at the time of the arrest; rather, she was asleep in her car, which was pulled over on the side of the road. If your supervising attorney asked you to write an office memo analyzing whether Ms. Wheelwright would be found guilty, your memo might look something like this.

Simple Sample Office Memo

MEMORANDUM

To: Aaron Attorney
From: Anne Associate
Re: Case # 13-2534 (Wheelwright); whether being asleep behind the wheel of a parked car constitutes "operating a vehicle" under Vanita's OVI statute. 1.
Date: February 11, 2014

Question Presented 2.

Under Vanita Rev. Code § 4511.19, which forbids "operating a vehicle" with a blood-alcohol concentration (BAC) higher than 0.08%, is a person "operating a vehicle" in violation of the statute if (A) she has a measured BAC of 0.14%, and (B) she is sitting in the driver's seat of a car parked on the side of a road, with the keys in the ignition?

Brief Answer 3.

Almost certainly yes. First, a 0.14% BAC is higher than the 0.08% needed to establish intoxication. Second, Vanita courts have held that someone is "operating a vehicle" when he or she is in control of the vehicle in some way and specifically have found that sitting in the driver's seat with the keys in the ignition constitutes control.

4.

Statute Involved

Vanita Rev. Code § 4511.19 (2014) provides in pertinent part:

> (A) No person shall operate any vehicle, streetcar, or trackless trolley within this state, if any of the following apply:
>
> (1) The person is under the influence of alcohol, a drug of abuse, or alcohol and a drug of abuse;
>
> [or]
>
> (2) The person has a concentration of eight-hundredths of one per cent or more but less than seventeen-hundredths of one per cent by weight per unit volume of alcohol in the person's whole blood.

1. The Re: section describes the memo topic generically and includes an identifying case or file number. (See Chapters 13 and14.)

2. Note the question's three parts. (1) Under relevant law (the DUI law), (2) does legal status ("operating a vehicle") exist, (3) when legally significant facts exist? (See Chapter 13.)

3. Here, the writer directly answers the question and explains the answer by briefly connecting the legal standard(s) to the legally significant facts. (See Chapter 13.)

4. Include a section like this when enacted law governs one or more issues in the memo. (See Chapter 13.)

5\. **Statement of Facts**

6\. Wendy Wheelwright has been charged with operating a motor vehicle while intoxicated after being found asleep behind the wheel of a parked car. The following facts come from a conversation with Ms. Wheelwright and from the police report of the arrest. On September 29, of last year, at about 2:30 a.m., on-duty Officer Pat Perek was driving north on Route 23 when he noticed a car pulled off on the shoulder. He pulled ahead of the car and parked in front of it. He noticed that the car's engine was not running, but the car was still warm. When he reached the driver's side of the car, he saw that the keys were in the ignition and that a woman was in the driver's seat, apparently asleep. Her head was leaning on the door, and her feet were on the floor, although not on the pedals (automatic transmission car). Her hands were in her lap. No one else was in the car.

When Officer Perek knocked on the window, the woman awoke, looking startled. Her eyes were bloodshot. Officer Perek asked her to step out of the car. When she opened the door he smelled a strong odor of liquor. The woman identified herself as Wendy Wheelwright and said that she had pulled over to sleep because she was "tired" and did not want to risk an accident. She admitted that she had been drinking, but denied that she was drunk. Officer Perek conducted two roadside sobriety tests, which Ms. Wheelwright failed. He then arrested her on suspicion of drunk driving and drove her to headquarters, where further tests were administered. These tests revealed that she had a concentration of fourteen-hundredths of one percent by weight of alcohol in her blood.

There is no claim that Officer Perek did not follow correct procedures throughout the apprehension, arrest, and testing of Ms. Wheelwright. Wheelwright has been charged with violating Vanita Rev. Code § 4511.19, "Operating vehicle under the influence of alcohol or drugs."

7\. **Discussion**

8\. A court would probably find Ms. Wheelwright guilty of violating Vanita Rev. Code
9\. § 4511.19 (2014). One way that a person can be convicted of violating this statute is if he or she "operates" a vehicle with a BAC of 0.08% or higher. Ms. Wheelwright will probably be convicted because (1) she had a BAC higher than 0.08%, and (2) she was operating her vehicle under the terms of the statute.

5\. In the fact statement, include the *legally significant facts* (facts that affect the issue) and the *relevant background facts* (facts that help readers understand what happened). (See Chapter 3.)

6\. Begin the fact statement with context; here, the charge against the client. Include the source of the facts if relevant. (See Chapter 3.)

7\. The Discussion section analyzes how the law applies to the facts. (See Chapter 14.)

8\. This introductory material (the "umbrella") gives the reader legal context by providing the "legal backstory" for the governing legal standard. (See Chapter 14.)

9\. The umbrella ends with a roadmap that uses enumeration to tell readers how many points the discussion includes.

I. Blood-alcohol Concentration

Ms. Wheelwright's BAC was higher than that permitted under § 4511.19(A)(2), 10.
which provides that a person may not legally operate a vehicle with a "concentration of 11.
eight-hundredths of one percent or more by weight of alcohol" in her blood. When Ms.
Wheelwright's blood was tested, it showed a concentration of fourteen-hundredths of one 12.
percent by weight of alcohol in her blood. Because this level was almost double the minimum
level needed for conviction, a court could easily find that Ms. Wheelwright met the required 13.
level of intoxication under § 4511.19(A)(2).

II. Operating a Vehicle

A court would almost certainly find that Ms. Wheelwright was "operating" her vehicle. The statute forbids a person with a BAC higher than 0.08% from "operat[ing] any vehicle," and Vanita courts have defined the term rather broadly.

Vanita courts have interpreted the word "operate" in § 4511.19 to include sitting in the 14.
driver's seat of a car that is not in motion. *State v. McGlone*, 101 N.E.2d 355, 365 (Van. 1990). 15.
The defendant in *McGlone* was found to be operating his vehicle when he was sitting in a parked car on a side street with the keys in the ignition. *Id.* at 366. The court found that the
driver was operating the vehicle, noting that "a driver who is in the driver's seat with the 16.
keys in the ignition may start the car and drive away at any time. A person who is under the influence of alcohol should not be in control of a vehicle." *Id.*; *see also State v. Richardson*, 111 N.E.2d 35, 36 (Van. 1992) (intoxicated driver behind wheel of car found to be "operating" when car's motor was running, even though gearshift was in park).

A person in a driver's seat will be found not to be operating only if there is no way that 17.
the car could be in operation at the time of the arrest. *State v. O'Donnell*, 112 N.E.2d 68, 18.
71 (Van. 1993). The defendant driver in *O'Donnell* had been found asleep and intoxicated behind the wheel of a parked car. *Id.* He was found not to be operating a vehicle under § 4511.19, however, because his keys were not in the ignition. *Id.* The *O'Donnell* court specifically concluded that he was not operating the vehicle because the keys were not in the ignition: "Although it may seem to the prosecution that we are splitting hairs, it must be admitted that a driver cannot operate a vehicle while the keys are not in the ignition. Thus,

10. Here is "The" Rule, which defines intoxication. (See Chapter 7.)

11. Here are the legally significant or material facts. (See Chapter 3.)

12. Here, the writer *applies* the law to the facts. (See Chapter 12.)

13. This issue is simple, so the discussion is short. Chapter 10 describes how to decide on depth of discussion.

14. The first sentence of a paragraph must be a good thesis sentence. (See Chapter 16.)

15. This is a *citation.* Citation rules are fussy, but important. (See Chapter 15.)

16. These two paragraphs are the *rule explanation*, which usually describes how the relevant rule has been applied in other similar cases. (See Chapter 11.)

17. The term *operating* is the *phrase-that-pays* for this issue; never use a synonym for the phrase-that-pays. (See Chapter 10.)

18. These sentences are the *case description*, and they help readers understand a case's legal relevance. (See Chapter 11.)

Mr. O'Donnell cannot be found to have been operating a car when the car was unable to be operated." *Id.*

19. Ms. Wheelwright was in the driver's seat and had the key in the ignition, so she
20. was probably "operating" her vehicle under the terms of the statute. Like the defendants
21. in *McGlone* and *Richardson*, she was capable of starting the car and driving away at any time.
Unlike the car at issue in *O'Donnell*, her car was capable of being operated. Thus, a court
would probably find that she was operating the vehicle.

Conclusion

A court would almost certainly find Ms. Wheelwright guilty of violating Vanita Rev.
Code § 4511.19(A)(2). There is no issue as to her intoxication. Further, she was sitting
behind the wheel of her parked car, and Vanita courts have consistently found that this
22. behavior constitutes "operating" a vehicle under § 4511.19(A)(2). Thus, a guilty verdict is
almost certain.

19. Here, the writer applies the law to the facts. (See Chapter 12.)

20. Here, the writer analogizes and distinguishes the cases she cited (not always needed). (See Chapter 12.)

21. Note precise language here. (See Chapter 12.)

22. The conclusion typically synthesizes the results of all significant issues; there may be parallels to the brief answer. (See Chapter 13.)

So now you have some idea what legal writing looks like. At this point, we want to distinguish *legal writing* from *legal drafting*, which is another kind of writing that lawyers do. In general, legal writing is analytical writing; that is, it is writing that analyzes how the law applies to facts.

Some legal writing is *predictive*: it predicts how a court will apply a particular law to a particular set of facts. Examples of this kind of writing include *office memos, opinion letters*, and *law review articles*. Some legal writing is *persuasive*: it advocates, or argues, that a court should apply a particular law to a particular set of facts in a particular way. Examples of persuasive legal writing include documents that are written to courts, which include shorter documents such as complaints and longer documents such as *motion memos* and *appellate briefs*. Attorneys also write some persuasive documents that they send to other attorneys; a *demand letter* is one example.

Motion memos are written to trial courts; they are submitted along with a motion or in opposition to a motion.

Appellate briefs are written to appellate courts, as their name implies. They typically ask courts to affirm or reverse decisions of trial courts or intermediate appellate courts.

We generally use the term *legal drafting* to refer to writing that is not *about* the law but that *is* law. For example, if you were to draft a statute or an ordinance, that statute would be the law for the relevant jurisdiction. A *contract* is also law, but, unlike a statute, it does not govern everyone in a jurisdiction; it is law that applies only to a particular business relationship of the parties who have signed the contract. *Wills* and *trusts* are also examples of legal drafting. A will or trust is law that applies to the distribution of money or other assets of a particular person or entity.

This book focuses on predictive legal writing. We will introduce many of the concepts it teaches briefly and then come back to them later. At other times, we will introduce a concept in depth and then revisit it more briefly. Throughout, as we note above, we will provide samples, and we will ask you to look at those samples through the eyes of a legal reader. By experiencing the reader's perspective, you will be better able to make writing decisions that will help your documents to achieve their goals of communicating the right information to the right person in the right way.

We know that we have given you a lot of information in this short chapter. We hope that it will give you context for the chapters that follow. We are confident that you will be able to master legal writing.

Recall and Review

1. Legal writing is like writing recipes because both are written for a p________.
2. When writing for a purpose, it is important to meet a reader's ex_________ as to content and format.
3. To help legal readers understand new information, a good legal writer begins with "old" information, or c______.

4. The word j__________ refers to a geographical area controlled by a legislature or court, or to a court's authority to hear a particular kind of case.
5. When lawyers justify a decision by relating it to a prior decision that is similar in meaningful ways, they use a two-word Latin phrase that translates specifically as "the decision stands" and loosely as "like cases are decided alike." What is the Latin phrase?
6. Determining or explaining how a particular rule governs the outcome of a legal issue is also known as _______ing the law to the facts.
7. This text refers to the word or combination of words that are the focus of a legal issue as the key terms, or the p____-that-p____.

CHAPTER 2

THE LAW

You have probably come to this class with some sense of what legal writing is about. While you have not written legal documents, and you may not have read them, you have written. Your conception of legal writing may be vague, but it is connected to something you have experienced.

Legal *analysis* is the less obvious part of Legal Analysis and Writing, the title of the course we teach. The course is often called Legal Writing and Analysis, but analysis is really its primary focus. The *writing* part of Legal Analysis and Writing is simply the written embodiment of legal analysis.

You have probably heard people say that one of the main things you will do during your first year of law school is to learn to "think like a lawyer." When we talk about thinking like a lawyer, what we really mean is learning to analyze issues as lawyers do. As we noted earlier, legal analysis begins with *facts* and *law*. You must study the facts to determine which *legal issues* the facts present, and then you must conduct legal research—that is, you must study the law—to determine which *legal rules* determine the outcomes of those issues. You will see many different definitions of the word "rule." We like this one: a *rule* is a statement of the principle or principles that will govern the outcome of a particular issue.

This chapter describes the different sources that make up what we refer to as "The Law" and explains jurisdiction, which is one of the bases for determining whether a particular law or rule applies to a particular set of facts.

A. WHAT IS THE LAW?

We all know that you have come to law school to study the law. Moreover, we all know what laws are. The answer to the question "What Is The Law?" is a bit more difficult.

When we refer to *The Law*, we are talking about more than laws. We are really talking about the body of principles that might constitute legal rules. Legal rules come from many sources. When you took civics in high school, you learned that the United States has three branches of government: the executive, the judicial, and the legislative. Each state and most cities have all three of these branches as well. Each of these three branches can make law. The laws they make go by different names, but they have some things in common.

The legislative branch enacts statutes and ordinances, with which you had some familiarity before coming to law school. We refer generally to laws adopted by legislative bodies as *enacted law*. *Statutes* are typically laws enacted by the Congress of the United States and the legislatures of the states. They govern in the *jurisdictions*, or territories, represented by those legislative bodies. So, statutes enacted by the U.S. Congress apply throughout the United States; the statutes of a particular state apply within the territory of that state. We generally use the term *ordinance* to refer to municipal laws. Ordinances apply within the jurisdiction of a city or other municipality.

The U.S. Constitution and the constitutions of the states are also considered to be enacted law because they were adopted by representative bodies.

The judicial branch does not enact statutes, but courts and judges—which make up the judicial branch—make law when they decide cases. When a legal rule comes from a case, we may refer to it as *judicial law*, *case law*, or *common law*. When we say that a rule may come from a case, what we really mean is this: in deciding legal issues, judges identify rules that are interpretations of enacted law, constitutional provisions, or earlier common law rules. These judges are not really enacting law, and they do not have the power to enact law under the U.S. Constitution or the constitutions of the states. Although the main purpose of the interpretation of the rule is to decide the case before the court, the court's interpretations of enacted law do govern future conduct through *stare decisis*. As we noted in Chapter 1, this term is used to describe the principle that "like cases are decided alike."

Finally, the executive branch creates law by enacting *regulations*. Regulations are created by departments and agencies within the U.S. government, the governments of the states, and the governments of municipalities, counties, and townships. The executive branch does not have the authority to make laws. In enacting laws, however, a legislature will often delegate that authority to an executive agency or department by tasking it with creating regulations to give effect to the enacted law. As long as the regulations are reasonable interpretations of the underlying statutes, the courts will enforce them as laws. In that sense, the regulations are given the force of enacted law by the legislative and judicial branches, even though the regulations are created by the executive branch.

So, as this very brief discussion of the major sources of rules in the United States demonstrates, the term *rules* is broader than the term *laws*. While laws are technically the enactments of the legislative branch, rules encompass pronouncements or statements from all three branches of government. In short, The Law is that set of legal rules that apply within any given jurisdiction. The next section will explain what we mean by jurisdiction.

B. WHERE RULES APPLY: JURISDICTION

We are all aware that some laws apply in limited areas while others govern conduct throughout the country. We know that selling a large quantity of cocaine is *against the law* anywhere in the United States. We also know that a local traffic ordinance creating a 20-mph zone near a school is limited in its scope to the area near a school. These are extreme examples of rules that apply nationally, on the one hand, and extremely locally, on the other.

In fact, every rule has a *scope*. Sometimes that scope is determined by the language of the rule itself. As with the traffic ordinance in the example above, some enacted laws identify their scope explicitly. The school speed limit ordinance likely included such clear limiting language as "within one thousand feet of a school." More often, the scope of a rule is determined by the jurisdiction of the entity that created it.

Why are we coyly using the term *entity* in the last sentence? Remember that rules are created by all three branches of government and at every level of government. So, all of those entities can create rules. The rule-making reach of a governmental entity is known as its *jurisdiction*.

As you will learn in your civil procedure class, the concept of *jurisdiction* refers not only to a geographic area, but also to the authority of a court over certain types of cases or people.

The concept of jurisdiction recognizes the limits on the authority of a governmental entity. Instinctively, we all understand that the General Assembly of Ohio, which is the name given to the legislative branch in Ohio, cannot enact a law that will apply in Oklahoma. No matter what it says in a statute, the legislative branch in Ohio cannot make law outside of Ohio. That is because it has no jurisdiction outside of its own borders. Even if Ohio's General Assembly were to enact a law prohibiting the sale of soft drinks in portions larger than 12 ounces anywhere in the United States, no one would enforce that law outside of Ohio. A legislative body has no jurisdiction outside of the area in which it has power to enforce its laws. We call that power *enforcement power*. The same is true of the U.S. Congress, whose jurisdiction generally does not exceed the national boundaries, and of local legislative bodies, such as city councils.

The jurisdiction of the executive branch when it creates rules in the form of regulations is very similar to that of the legislative branch. Indeed, because the departments and agencies that create regulations are given their authority to do so by the legislative branch, their jurisdiction is coterminous with the legislature's for that function. This means that if a statute applies only to dog owners in Ohio, any regulation created pursuant to that statute will also apply only to dog owners in Ohio.

The most difficult jurisdiction-related concepts are those that determine how broadly a court's decisions apply. As we noted above, the rules articulated or identified in a court's decisions are often referred to as *common law*. The jurisdiction within which a court's common law rules would apply is similar to the jurisdiction of a legislative body in that its statements about the law are applicable only where it has the authority to enforce them. Questions about judicial jurisdiction have been the subject of a great deal of litigation and legislation, however. You will learn about some of the concepts that govern jurisdiction in the judicial sense in your civil procedure classes. For our purposes, just remember that a court's jurisdiction will often have geographical limits (e.g., a state or a defined segment of a state) or legal limits (e.g., a certain category of cases, such as bankruptcy cases).

Everyone lives in many jurisdictions at the same time. You already know that you live in a municipality or township, a county, a state, and a country, and that you are subject to the laws of all four. You may think of each of those entities as having a separate government with an executive branch and a law-making body or legislature. Each of those entities may also have a court system. Many towns and cities have municipal courts; some smaller towns have mayor's courts. The jurisdiction of these judicial bodies is limited to the territory in which they serve, or *sit*. You are subject to their jurisdiction only if you "enter" that territory, directly or indirectly.

We refer to the act of existing, when it is applied to judicial officers, as *sitting*. Some courthouses have gyms in their basements to counteract the effects of all of that sitting.

We use the term *judicial officers* to refer to judges and anyone else who exercises any of the decision-making powers of a judge. Many courts employ magistrates and hearing officers who are authorized by law or by court order to act as judges in some respects. They are not judges, but they are considered to be judicial officers. So, *judicial officer* is a broader term than *judge*.

In the federal court system, the lowest level of courts, or *trial courts*, are known as *United States district courts*. Every state has at least one district; roughly half of the states have multiple districts, depending on a combination of factors, including population, geography, and history. Colorado, for example, is a large state, but it has just one district, the District of Colorado. Ohio is a smaller state, but it is divided into the Northern District of Ohio and the Southern District of Ohio.

As you will learn, most lawsuits that are filed never reach the trial stage. Instead, the parties reach some sort of a settlement, or the court decides the case on a *motion*.

The intermediate-level courts of appeals in the federal court system are called the *United States circuit courts* (see Figure 2.1). Each circuit is comprised of several states. In days of yore, circuit judges would go to the districts, often on horseback or in stagecoaches, to hear cases. They were said to *ride the circuit*. The circuits now have stationary courthouses, but the name has stuck. Appeals to the circuit courts are appeals *as of right*. An appeal as of right is an appeal that the court must consider, as long as certain procedural requirements are met.

Of course, you already know that the highest court in the federal court system is the *United States Supreme Court*. Any party who is unhappy with a decision of a circuit court may appeal to the U.S. Supreme Court. A party may also appeal a decision of a state's highest court to the U.S. Supreme Court, but *only* if the issue is an issue of federal law. Appeal to the U.S. Supreme Court is *discretionary appeal*.

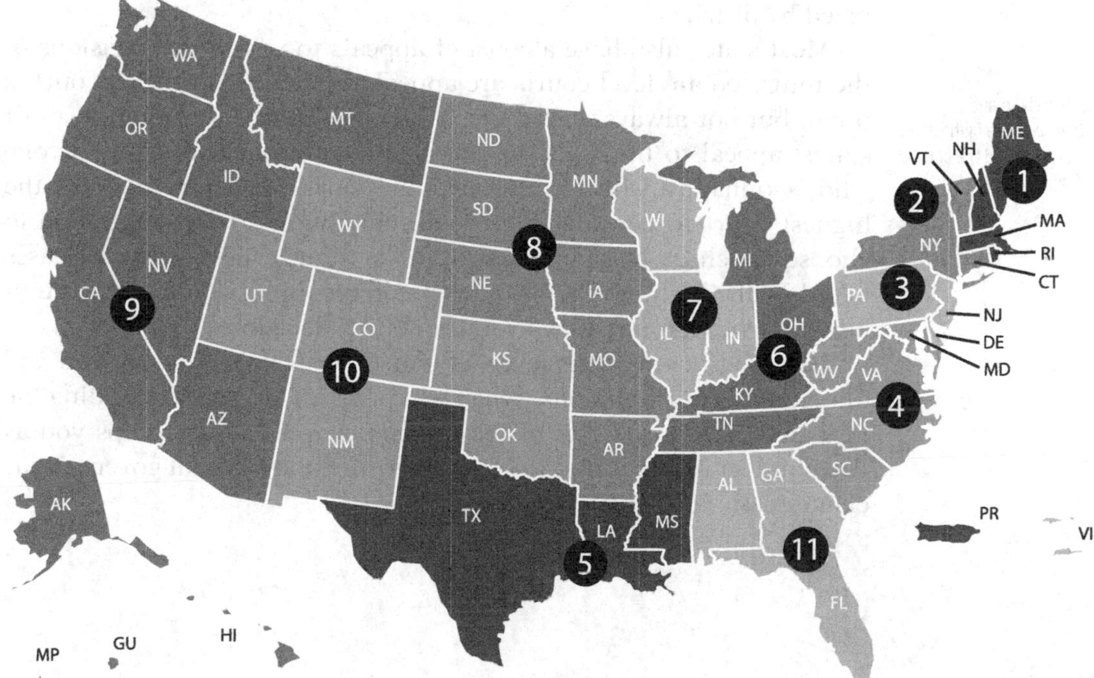

The states use various names for their trial courts. In Pennsylvania, they are the "county courts of common pleas." New York names its trial courts the "supreme courts" (which is very confusing). "Superior court," "circuit court," and "district court" are other common names for state-level trial courts.

That kind of appeal means that the U.S. Supreme Court may exercise its discretion; it chooses which cases it will decide. Discretionary appeal is the opposite of appeal as of right.

Like the federal judicial branch, most states' judicial branches have three levels. The lowest level is always a trial court. Often these trial courts are organized by county, with each county having a trial-level court. In some large counties, these trial courts may be divided into several divisions, including two or more of the following: criminal, civil, domestic relations, probate, juvenile, drug, and environmental. Beyond trial courts are *courts of appeal*. The courts of appeal determine whether trial courts have interpreted and applied the law correctly. Courts of appeal are also called *appellate courts*. They do not conduct trials. If the party who lost at the trial level files an *appeal*, the appellate court considers the arguments of attorneys for each side of the case and reviews the decision of the trial court for errors.

Most states call these intermediate-level appellate courts the "courts of appeals." In New Jersey, however, they are the "superior courts," and in New York, they are the "supreme courts, appellate division" or "supreme courts, appellate term."

In most states, anyone who is unhappy with a trial court's decision may appeal. This type of appeal is called *appeal as of right*. As noted above, *appeal as of right* means that the appellate court must consider every appeal that comes to it. Many states have an intermediate-level court that hears appeals as of right. These intermediate-level courts of appeal are organized regionally. One appellate court might hear appeals from several county-level trial courts. Ohio, for example, has 88 counties, each with its own trial courts, known as the *Courts of Common Pleas*. Ohio has 12 intermediate-level appellate courts, organized by districts.

In Maryland and New York, the highest court is called the court of appeals.

Most states also have a court of appeals to which the decisions of the intermediate-level courts are appealed. This highest-level court is often, but not always, called the *Supreme Court* of the state. In most states, appeal to the highest court is a discretionary appeal. Anyone who is unhappy with an intermediate court's decision may ask the highest court to consider an appeal, but the court has discretion to choose which cases it will hear. In most states, the number of cases heard by the highest court is quite small in comparison with the number of parties left unhappy by lower courts' decisions.

Learning how various levels of courts work helps you to read and understand court opinions. When you practice law, understanding the jurisdictional boundaries of the various sources of law helps you as you conduct research and work to determine the law that governs your client's case.

Recall and Review

1. The three branches of government in the United States are:
2. The concept of j__________ refers to the rule-making reach of a governmental entity. That reach may cover a certain __________ area or certain types of cases or people.
3. Laws made by state and federal (national) legislatures are usually known as s_______, while laws made by municipalities are typically known as ordinances.
4. Laws made by agencies and other executive bodies are typically known as r______s.
5. The rules articulated or identified in a court's decisions are often referred to as c_________ l_______, judge-made law, or case law.
6. Although they go by many different names, the lowest court in both the state and federal judicial system is a ______ court.
7. The lowest court in the federal judicial system is known as the d_________ court.
8. The intermediate courts of appeals in the federal system are divided into _______, typically made up of several states.
9. If a court is required to hear an appeal that meets procedural requirements, we say that those appeals are appeals as of _________.
10. If an appellate court may decide whether to hear an appeal, we say that those appeals are ________ appeals.

CHAPTER 3

RULES, FACTS, AND READING CASES WITH A PURPOSE

Are you reading this book for pleasure? Don't let us stop you. The chances are awfully good, however, that you are reading it because your professor assigned it. You therefore are reading with a purpose other than your own enjoyment. That purpose will influence the way you read.

As you have no doubt already discovered, law school requires a lot of reading. We are sure that much of it seems more difficult than reading you have done in the past. We suspect, however, that in some ways it is similar to reading you have done in your academic past. For example, you have probably read many novels for pleasure, but you have probably also had the experience of being *required* to read a novel. When you were assigned a book to read, your manner of reading was probably quite different than when you were reading for pleasure.

In the reading-for-pleasure scenario, you might have stolen short blocks of time to read partial chapters, stopping wherever your time ran out. Maybe you read at the end of the day, sticking the bookmark between the pages just before you fell asleep and then having to find the last paragraph you remembered reading the next time you picked up the book. Maybe you accepted that you had missed a few minor events and assumed that you would be able to figure out what you had missed as you read on. In any event, the fact that you would not be quizzed on the details of the book allowed you the freedom to read at your own pace, to skim over the boring parts, and to absorb as much or as little of the story as you chose.

When the book was part of an assignment, however, your approach was probably quite different. You would have attempted to memorize characters and plot points, major and minor. You may have taken notes, highlighted and reread important passages, and reviewed the details before class. Any pleasure you took in reading the book was secondary to your main purpose: to learn whatever you believed the instructor intended for you to learn in order to take a quiz or write a paper.

This book is not a novel, and you will probably complete law school without ever being assigned a novel. Shed a tear if that makes you sad. On the other hand, you will read an enormous quantity of written words during the course of your law studies. Early on, most of those words will be in judicial opinions, either in casebooks or online. Later, you may read law review articles, statutes, regulations, legal briefs, legal encyclopedias, and legislative history. In each instance, your purpose in reading will influence how you read. If you read any of these documents as you would read a novel for pleasure, you will likely not achieve that purpose.

A. THE JUDICIAL OPINION EXAMPLE

For most of you, the beginning of law school was the first time you had read a judicial opinion. Early in the experience, your understanding of the purpose for which you were reading those opinions was negligible. Because you did not know what you were supposed to be learning from the opinions, you likely pored over them, trying to memorize the facts and understand the law the court was discussing. You may have highlighted everything because you didn't know which parts of the opinion were important.

Let's use the *Case of the Thorns* to illustrate the type of reading that this new genre requires. From 1466, the *Case of the Thorns* is one of the earliest English torts cases. It has been preserved in various forms, including as a summary in a later English case, *Bessey v. Olliot & Lambert*, T. Raym. 467 (1681):

> A man brought a writ of Trespass *quare vi et armis clausum fregit, & herban suam pedibus conculcando consumpsit* in five Acres. The Defendant pleads, that he hath an Acre lying next the said five Acres, and upon it a hedge of Thorns, and he cut the Thorns, and they, against his will, fell upon the Plaintiff's Land, and the Defendant took them off as soon as he could, which is the same Trespass; and the Plaintiff demurred; and adjudged for the Plaintiff; for though a Man doth a lawful Thing, yet if any damage do thereby befall another, he shall answer for it, if he could have avoided it. As if a Man lop a Tree, and the boughs fall upon another against his will yet an Action lies. If a Man shoot at the Butts, and hurt another unawares, an Action lies. I have Land through which a River runs to your Mill, and I lop the Sallows growing upon the Riverside, which accidentally stop the Water, so as your Mill is hindered, an Action lies. If I am Building my own house, and a Piece of Timber falls on my Neighbour's house and breaks Part of it, an Action

> lies. If a Man assault me, and I lift up my Staff to defend myself, and in lifting it up hit another, an Action lies by that Person, and yet I did a lawful Thing. And the Reason of all these Cases is because he that is damaged ought to be recompensed. But otherwise it is in Criminal Cases, for there *actus non facit reum nisi mens sit rea.*

You may have been assigned this opinion very early in your torts or property course. At that time, you may have still been reading for everything. So, you would have done your best to memorize the facts that the defendant owned five acres with a thorn hedge abutting the plaintiff's land, that he cut the thorns, that they fell onto the plaintiff's land, that the defendant did not intend for them to fall onto the plaintiff's land, and that the defendant removed the thorns as soon as he could.

Next, you might have attempted to identify the issue presented by these facts. You likely would have concluded that the issue was whether the plaintiff could recover from the defendant for the damage caused by the thorns falling onto the plaintiff's property. You might also have identified the rule as "for though a Man doth a lawful Thing, yet if any damage do thereby befall another, he shall answer for it, if he could have avoided it." Finally, you would probably have made note of all of the other scenarios the court identified in order to illustrate the rule.

In the process, you should have ascertained the definitions of the Latin phrases, learning that "trespass *quire vi et armis clausum fregit, & herban suam pedibus conculcando consumpsit*" means "without permission entered upon the land of another, trampling and damaging the vegetation," and that "*actus non facit reum nisi mens sit rea*" means "an act does not make one guilty unless there be a guilty mind." The act of defining the Latin terms would have helped you to understand that, without intending to, the defendant had caused some actual damage to the plaintiff's property: he had trampled and damaged the plaintiff's vegetation. That clarification of the facts would enable you to clarify the rule with the additional understanding that a plaintiff is entitled to recover for damage actually caused by the otherwise lawful action of the defendant. At the end of this exercise, you probably wondered how you would ever get through a 900-page casebook if it took you two hours to read one paragraph.

Soon, you probably discovered that the professor would ask for only a brief overview of the critical facts, the ones that affected the court's decision. We call those the *legally significant facts*. In future reading, you might have paid slightly less attention to the facts, making certain only that you understood the scenario in which the legal issue arose. Your focus was refined by the purpose for which you were reading the opinion: to identify the legally significant facts, the legal issue, the rule the court identified, and the court's reasoning.

So, turning back to the *Case of the Thorns*, you might have written one sentence in your notes indicating that the defendant had entered onto the plaintiff's property and caused some damage by accident. You would have spent the remainder of your energies on identifying the rule. The illustrations of the rule included in the opinion would have helped you to state the rule as "a tort is a lawful action, taken without criminal intent, that causes damage to someone else, and the actor is liable to that other person for that damage." By the time you were ready to take the final exam, that rule may have been all that was left of the *Case of the Thorns* in your outline, and, if it was, you were probably adequately prepared to use the case in response to an essay question. The title of the case alone might have been sufficient to remind you of the one sentence you might write about the facts.

Maybe you are in your first semester, or even your first week, of law school, and you are not yet ready to read "efficiently." Eventually, however, you will reach the point in reading judicial opinions at which you will allow yourself to streamline your focus on the facts in deference to whatever the court has to say about the law. You will learn that your purpose is *not* to memorize the facts of the very limited set of cases the casebook author chose to include. You will also learn that when you are reading opinions in a casebook, your primary purposes are (1) to trace the development of the law and (2) to understand its nuances and permutations. Your task will be easier, in most instances, because the opinions included in your casebooks are heavily edited to eliminate anything that might distract you unduly from achieving those purposes. For example, if a court has addressed two issues, or three, the casebook's author may have edited the opinion to eliminate all but the issue that the particular section of the text is focused on. If the case presented a civil procedure issue and a property issue, an author who included that case in a property casebook would most likely edit out the facts relating to the civil procedure issue.

Consider this special notice in the front of a typical civil procedure casebook: "We have edited cases and articles for the sake of smoother reading. Deleted material is indicated by ellipses. . . ."[1] You will find that most of your casebooks include similar notices. This sort of editing keeps casebooks from being thousands of pages long, and it helps you to achieve the purpose for which you are reading the opinions. The authors know that slogging through three pages of facts relating to a civil procedure issue will not help you to understand the law of property, so they have saved you the effort.

---

1. Linda J. Silberman & Allan R. Stein, *Civil Procedure: Theory and Practice* xxvii (Aspen 2001).

When you are a law student, reading this type of edited case is fine. When you are a lawyer, however, you will rarely read a judicial opinion for the *sole* purpose of learning what a rule is. And no one carefully edits judicial opinions to fit a particular lawyer's particular purpose for reading the opinion. A lawyer does not ask a search engine to provide only the portions of an opinion that will be helpful to understanding a narrow issue of law. So, as you develop your legal *reading* skills, you will be your own editor according to your own purpose. You will have to decide which parts of the opinion you must read carefully because they are significant and which parts you can skim over or ignore. As we will explain in a moment, that purpose will almost always include more than learning a rule with a sentence of context.

B. WHY LAWYERS READ JUDICIAL OPINIONS

Although lawyers read many kinds of documents, we begin our discussion of legal reading with judicial opinions because you are already generally familiar with them, and you have already read them with one purpose in mind: learning the law and, perhaps more importantly at this stage of the game, not being embarrassed when you are called on in class. Lawyers sometimes read for that purpose as well. More often, however, a lawyer reads an opinion because the lawyer has a problem to solve and wants to determine whether the opinion will help to solve the problem.

1. It Starts with a Problem

Almost everything a practicing lawyer does starts with a problem. A client has a problem: it may be a dispute, or it may be a plan. In either event, the client seeks the lawyer's assistance in solving the problem. A judge has a problem: someone has filed a lawsuit, and the judge must resolve it. We call the situations that these problems arise from the *facts*.

When a potential client comes to a lawyer with a problem, he or she brings a set of facts. When a party files a lawsuit, the lawsuit begins with a *complaint.* A complaint is a set of *allegations,* which are facts from the perspective of one side of a dispute. The problem, in either scenario, is based in facts. The lawyer's first two tasks, therefore, are (1) to understand the facts and (2) to identify the law that is relevant to those facts.

The problem may be a desire to open a new business or a desire to enter into a prenuptial agreement, in which case the lawyer may begin to identify the applicable law by looking at statutes and regulations. When the problem is a dispute, however, judicial opinions will be a major source of the law that will govern the resolution of that dispute. What will be the lawyer's purpose in reading those opinions?

2. A Sample Problem

Suppose that a potential client has come to you because the fence surrounding her yard was knocked down when a car backed into it. The car was being operated by a person who had attempted to turn around in a neighbor's driveway. Your potential client wants to know whether her neighbor is liable to her for the damage to the fence.

Had your client's fence been damaged after thorns fell from her neighbor's tree, you might conclude that the neighbor is liable. You might do so, of course, because that precise factual scenario was presented in the *Case of the Thorns*, which you have read.

Your client's facts are different, however. So, you may understand that the problem is a torts issue because you read the *Case of the Thorns* in torts class. You may also understand that the rule from the *Case of the Thorns* has some relevance because your client's fence suffered damage when someone trespassed onto her property without an apparent criminal motive. You are not likely to believe that the *Case of the Thorns* resolves the problem, however.

Your hesitation has several sources. The first, if you are smart, is that the *Case of the Thorns* was decided by an English court. Even if you have not yet studied jurisdiction, you are probably reluctant to rely on an English case to resolve an American dispute. The second is that the opinion is more than 500 years old. Your instinct tells you that the law may have changed, or at least been refined, in the ensuing centuries.

Let's say, however, that the *Case of the Thorns* is a brand-new opinion from the highest court in your state. You are still reluctant to believe that it resolves your client's problem, not because the law may not be current or applicable but because the facts are different.

This is where reading judicial opinions for the purpose of learning the law is completely different from reading judicial opinions for the purpose of resolving disputes. The first purpose requires only a cursory understanding of the facts and is performed with no particular problem in mind. The reader's interest in the facts is academic. The second purpose requires a careful study of the facts in the judicial opinion with another set of facts, the problem facts, in mind. When you are reading an opinion in a casebook, you will pay careful attention to what the court said about the rule because you will know that the casebook author purposely made sure that language stayed in the opinion. When you are reading an opinion for the purpose of resolving a dispute, you will still be somewhat interested in what the court says, but you will be much more interested in what the court did, in how the court disposed of the legal issues.

Lawyers often use the word *disposition* to refer to how a court decided a particular issue or a case. It may help you to think of a court getting rid of, or disposing of, that issue or case.

3. Why the Facts Matter

The judicial opinions in law casebooks are a bit misleading in one respect: the opinions are often included because they reflect a change in the law or a new legal principle. Because many of the opinions in your casebooks are landmark decisions, you may have the impression that every judicial opinion breaks new legal ground. In fact, the opinion that alters the law is a rarity.

If you were to look at every opinion addressing the same narrow point of law, such as liability for damage to property occasioned by actions on a neighbor's property, you would likely find the same rule stated in the same or similar terms over and over. If your focus were on the rule only, as it is when your purpose for reading the opinion is to identify the rule, your body of knowledge about the rule would not increase much, no matter how many of those opinions you read.

We have already established, however, that identifying the rule does not give you much certainty in answering your client's question about her fence. That purpose requires a different kind of reading. What could expand your knowledge about the rule in such a way that you might feel more confident about answering your client's question? One way to expand your knowledge about a rule is to gain an understanding of how the rule has been applied in various factual scenarios, some like yours and others different in a variety of ways. This knowledge would allow you to begin to identify the contours of the rule. As you know, *stare decisis* dictates that like cases are decided alike. A big part of what lawyers do is make arguments that certain cases are like, or not like, certain other cases. When lawyers make those arguments, they often focus on the facts.

Let's consider four fictional opinions applying the rule from the *Case of the Thorns*.

Opinion 1: A child of a landowner has rolled a ball onto a neighbor's lawn, damaging a bed of prize roses. The landowner is liable.

Opinion 2: A guest of a landowner has set off fireworks, one of which has damaged a neighbor's roof. The landowner is liable for the guest's actions because the landowner invited the guest to set off fireworks.

Opinion 3: A piece of siding from a landowner's house has blown into a neighbor's light post, breaking it. The landowner is liable.

Opinion 4: A stranger who was not authorized to be on the defendant-landowner's property started a fire, and the fire destroyed a neighbor's tree. The landowner is not liable: the court concluded that the landowner had no responsibility for the damage because he had not authorized the fire and had not invited the stranger to be on his property.

Notice that the descriptions of these four opinions say very little about the rule the courts applied. The general rule was known before the reading began. It is essentially the rule from the *Case of the Thorns*. The purpose for reading the opinions was not, primarily, to identify the rule but to learn how it had been applied to facts that are like those of your case, and not like those of your case, in various ways.

So, how do you achieve that purpose? The potential client has presented a scenario in which someone who was on her neighbor's property took an action, not criminal in nature, which caused damage to the client's property. That scenario has elements in common with the scenarios described in each of the four opinions.

Each includes damage to the property of a neighbor. That element is present even in the fourth scenario, where liability was not found; thus, it is not a basis for distinguishing a successful tort claim from an unsuccessful one.

In the scenario in Opinion 1, a child of the landowner propelled the item (a ball) that caused the damage, suggesting that liability applies when a member of the landowner's family takes an action that causes damage to a neighboring property. Had you stopped reading there, you might have concluded that the rule requires that the landowner or a member of the landowner's family have caused the damage in order for liability to apply. By reading Opinion 2, however, you would have learned that your conception of the rule was too narrow. In Opinion 2, a landowner was held liable for damage caused by the action of a guest (setting off fireworks). So, your conception of the rule is now broadened to include damage caused by the action of a person on the landowner's property.

Now, however, your conception of the rule is both too broad and too narrow. How is it too narrow? In Opinion 3, the court found the landowner liable even though the wind, not a person, caused the harm (by blowing a piece of the landowner's siding onto the neighbor's property). The court found liability nevertheless. So, human action is not required for liability. How is your conception of the rule too broad? Remember that after reading Opinions 1 and 2, you believed that a landowner is liable for the action of anyone on the landowner's property who causes damage to a neighboring property. Opinion 4, however, gives the lie to that statement of the rule.

Opinion 4 is the one opinion in which liability was not found. In that scenario, a human on the landowner's property started the action (a fire) that caused the damage to the neighbor's property. Your conception of the rule after reading Opinions 1 to 3 would have made the landowner liable for the damage, but the court issuing Opinion 4 said otherwise. So, your conception was too broad: not all damage caused by human action on the landowner's property leads to liability.

Can you identify the *legally significant* difference in the facts that may explain the difference in the outcome? In Opinion 4, the landowner had not authorized the person whose action caused the damage to be on the landowner's property. A trespasser had come onto the landowner's property and started a fire, which spread to the neighbor's property and caused damage. So, the lack of authority or permission from the landowner appears to be a *legally significant* factual distinction between the scenario in Opinion 4 and the other three opinions.

Some courts and some writers use the word *material* to mean the same thing as *legally significant*.

We called the factual distinction between the facts in Opinion 4 and the other opinions a *legally significant distinction*. That distinction was not the only factual difference among the scenarios, of course. The scenarios were different in a variety of ways, including the identity of the object causing the damage (a piece of siding, a ball, fireworks, and a fire) and the types of harm (a broken lightpost, damage to a flower bed, damage to a roof, and a burned tree). None of the other differences explained the difference in the outcomes in the opinions, however. They were factual distinctions, but they were *not legally significant*. The difference in authorization is *legally significant* because it is the reason the court gave for reaching a different conclusion.

Those who describe legally significant facts as material would describe facts that are not legally significant as immaterial.

Of course, if you were really the attorney for the fictional client, you would probably do more research to confirm that you had identified the legally significant distinction *and* that it was the only one. For the sake of completing our analysis, however, let's assume that we have identified the only legally significant factual distinction among the four opinions. We earlier identified the rule from the *Case of the Thorns* as follows: a landowner-plaintiff is entitled to recover for damage to his property actually caused by the otherwise lawful action of a neighboring landowner. Our reading of the four opinions in which the courts applied that rule enlightens us as to the interpretation of the second half of the rule, "actually caused by the otherwise lawful action of a neighboring landowner." If the damage was caused by an action not taken by or authorized by the neighboring landowner or a member of the landowner's family, the court will not impose liability on that landowner, even if the damage was caused from her property or by an action taken on her property.

In the potential client's situation, the neighbor was not driving the car that caused the damage. That fact is not *legally significant*, however, because a landowner can be liable for the actions of others on the landowner's property. The *legally significant* fact, according to our research to date, is that the person who was driving the car was *authorized* by the neighbor to drive into the neighbor's driveway.

Now that you know the legally significant fact, can you answer the client's question? What fact is missing? From the facts that the client gave you, you know that the person in the neighbor's driveway was there to turn his car around. You do not know the relationship, if any, between the driver and your client's neighbor. You could have asked, but at the time you talked to the client, you did not know enough about the law to know which facts would be important, or legally significant, to your answer.

Your research indicates that if the driver was a stranger to the neighbor and just using the driveway as a convenient place to turn around, we might predict that a court would not impose liability on the neighbor. On the other hand, if the neighbor had invited the driver to his home or if the driver was in the process of making a delivery requested by the neighbor, we might predict that a court would impose liability.

We now know that a legally significant fact is missing from the version of events presented by the potential client and that our prediction about the outcome of a claim against the neighbor will turn on that fact. We cannot predict the outcome without that additional fact, but we know much more about how the rule will apply than we would have known if our focus in reading the four opinions had been primarily on the rule, rather than on the application of that rule to the unique facts of each case.

4. Now You Try It: Exercise 3.1

Presume that you live in Pennsylvania. A potential client has come to you to seek representation. He is a salesperson who drives a car provided by his employer. His employer permits its employees and their licensed family members to drive company cars. It also provides insurance coverage for all legal drivers in the employees' families. We'll call the potential client "Peter."

Peter has a 17-year-old son. We'll call Peter's son "Junior." Junior often drives Peter's company car to evening football practices.

Recently, Peter's company car was in the shop for maintenance, and he was driving a rental car provided by his employer. The rental agreement provided that Peter was covered by insurance on the rental car but prohibited anyone other than Peter from driving the car.

Peter often drives rental cars provided by his employer when his company car is out of service. Junior has driven some of those rental cars to football practices with Peter's knowledge. Peter has never told Junior that he may drive the rental cars, and he has not told him that he may not.

One evening, Junior took the latest rental car to a movie and wrecked it. Junior had not asked Peter for permission to use the rental car on this occasion, and Peter did not know that Junior was driving the rental car on the evening of the accident. A passenger in the rental car at the time of the accident was injured, and she has sued Junior and Peter. Peter wants to know whether the insurance on the rental car will cover the injuries and legal fees.

Suppose that you know the general rule that governs this type of insurance coverage question in Pennsylvania: *coverage extends to the insured and to any other person driving the insured's car with the insured's permission*. This is the rule of *Beatty v. Hoff*.[2]

Would you be comfortable advising Peter on the basis of the general rule? If not, chances are good that your hesitation results from your uncertainty about whether the circumstances that led to Junior's using the rental car would constitute *permission*. Very often, the focus of a legal argument is the meaning of a word or a phrase in the relevant rule. Some writers call that word or phrase the "key term"; as you know, we refer to it as "the phrase-that-pays." In the case about the car turning around in the neighbor's driveway, for example, the word "authorized" was the phrase-that-pays. Identifying a phrase-that-pays can help you to focus both your analysis and your writing.

Consider the facts of these Pennsylvania cases, together with the court's decisions. What do the courts say—or what do the dispositions indicate—about the meaning of the word *permission*, which is the phrase-that-pays in this exercise? What are the legally significant facts on which the decisions seem to turn? What advice would you give Peter?

Exner v. Safeco Insurance Co. of America[3]

The instant action was brought in Lehigh County against the father's insurance carrier to recover under the omnibus clause in the policy, the insurer having refused payment. The complaint is based

---

2. 114 A.2d 173 (Pa. 1955).

3. 167 A.2d 703 (Pa. 1961). The facts and the court's decision are edited for clarity.

on the original verdicts against Jacoby [, the son of the insured]. The jury found for the plaintiffs, but the court below, on motion, entered judgment [] for the defendant [insurance company].

The case spins on the point of paternal permission to use the car, and since they won the verdicts the plaintiffs are entitled to the favorable facts and inferences.

The father, Gangewere, lived with his mentally incompetent wife in Allentown, Lehigh County. He also owned and maintained another home about four miles away, which he visited almost every day and where his mistress lived with their several children, one of whom was Robert Jacoby, the driver in the accident. The day of the accident was Sunday, December 18th, and Gangewere arrived at the Jacoby house early. The jury might have inferred that Gangewere would have been happy to have the day there alone and that his son knew it.

Relations between father and son were good. The boy had a car of his own and the father did for him as well as he could: he expected, for example, to give him a present of waxing the car on the instant occasion. Jacoby had previously used his father's car, with permission, for several small commissions, such as twice taking his mother to market, polishing the car, making minor repairs, getting a newspaper for his father, and taking it to a nearby filling station to put on chains. On these errands he had not strayed beyond the geographical limits of the task in hand.

On this occasion he seemed to have an ulterior motive, for on the day before he laid the groundwork for waxing the car by arranging to meet a friend. On Sunday morning he told his father that he would wax the car and was told that the keys to it were in the pocket of his father's coat, which appeared to be hanging in a closet. Permission was given to wax and polish, and nothing was said about where to do it or about what else the son might or might not do.

At about one o'clock Jacoby called for his friend. As it was Sunday, the nearby filling station was closed. Jacoby knew a girl in the town of Jim Thorpe, thirty-seven miles away, and they drove past her house there, but not seeing her went on to a back road where they waxed and polished half the car. As it was then growing dark they drove past the girl's house again but again failed to see her and started back to Allentown. Halfway there the accident occurred. The instant action was brought by the driver of the other car in the accident against Gangewere.

* * *

[This case] involves only the fact and breadth of permission to drive under an insurance policy.

A subsidiary question is whether there was a substantial deviation when Jacoby tried to drive to and from a town thirty-seven miles away.

* * *

Jacoby found the nearest filling station closed and then went on a rather long way, but he did then do a substantial part of the thing for which permission had been given him. We cannot say as a matter of law that he should have hunted other filling stations at slowly increasing distances from Allentown. The case was, rather, for the jury under all of the circumstances. Permission may be either express or implied.

* * *

Judgment reversed. The record is remanded with instructions to enter judgment on the verdicts [against the father and his insurer].

General Accident Insurance Co. of America v. Margerum[4]

The record reveals that Hricko is the owner of a roofing company in Bristol, Bucks County. His business equipment includes two vans insured by General Accident. In December 1981, he hired Margerum to work as a laborer. At that time, Margerum lived with his parents in Cornwell Heights, Bucks County, approximately three miles from the roofing company. Hricko considered Margerum a dependable employee and was concerned that Margerum had no means of arriving at work other than hitchhiking. In mid-January, with the onset of unfavorable winter weather, Hricko offered a van to Margerum with the following restrictions: that it be used solely for commuting between home and work, that Margerum not drink and drive, and that the van not be used for personal reasons.

On January 22, 1982, approximately one week after Hricko permitted Margerum to begin using the van, Margerum requested permission to leave work early to attend his sister's wedding in Newtown, Bucks County. Hricko granted the request but specifically instructed Margerum not to take the van to the reception

4. 544 A.2d 512 (Pa. Super. 1988). The facts and the court's decision are edited for clarity.

and not to consume alcoholic beverages while driving the van. Margerum drove the van home to his parents' and then received a ride to the wedding reception. He left the wedding at approximately 12:30 a.m., and his father drove him back to Cornwell Heights. Margerum then packed his work clothes for the next day, put them in the van and commenced driving about seven miles to his fiancée's residence in Fairless Hills, Bucks County, where he intended to spend the night. As his fiancée's residence was about four miles from the roofing company, his parents' residence and his fiancée's residence were approximately equidistant from his work place. While driving to his fiancée's and still about a mile away from her residence, Margerum struck and killed a pedestrian walking on the side of the road.

The police report in the record reveals that the violations indicated include driving while intoxicated. The trial court specifically found that during the course of the evening, Margerum imbibed steadily. Margerum did not present evidence to contradict his intoxicated condition at the time of the accident.

* * *

The parties do not contend that there was an implied permission. Rather, the issue is whether Margerum's use of the van to drive to his fiancée's was within Hricko's express permission. We look to whether Margerum's use of the van was a substantial deviation from permission to determine coverage under the insurance policy.

Hricko's instructions on what constituted commuting and personal use were not highly specific. He did not demand that Margerum travel a particular route or that Margerum continue to reside with his parents. In packing his work clothes and taking them to his fiancée's, Margerum was generally conforming to Hricko's instruction to use the van for commuting. It is not clear that Margerum's use of the vehicle was exclusively for personal reasons. Therefore by driving to his fiancée's and planning to commute to work from her residence, Margerum did not substantially deviate from Hricko's permission.

Nevertheless, by driving under the influence of alcohol, Margerum violated the express specific restriction on his use of the van. Since Margerum violated an express specific restriction of Hricko's permission to use the van, his deviation in use from Hricko's express permission was a substantial deviation. As a result, Margerum is not an insured under General Accident's policy with Hricko.

Loftus v. Allstate Insurance Co.[5]

Sean P. Loftus has brought this action, seeking to have the court determine his status and rights under an automobile insurance policy issued to one Joseph Butch. Both Loftus and Butch are defendants in an action to recover for personal injuries filed by Samir Salah, arising out of an automobile accident which occurred on August 21, 1982.

As Loftus is not a resident relative of Butch, the named insured, to become a beneficiary under the policy, he must show that at the time of the accident he was using the insured vehicle with Butch's permission. Permission may be given either expressly or impliedly.

We have little difficulty in finding that Loftus was not given express permission to drive Butch's car on August 21, 1982. On this point, the evidence is that Loftus and Butch had spent that Saturday afternoon at the residence of Loftus's brother, playing a drinking game called "quarters" with two of Loftus's friends. The object of the game was to bounce quarters into a cup and the successful party would pick another player to drink an entire beer. It was a warm day and Butch was wearing gym shorts and a cut off T-shirt. As he had no pockets, he kept the keys to his car, which were on a key ring, on his finger. After two or three hours of playing quarters, Loftus became drunk and Butch, either through fatigue (he had worked the night before) or drinking or a combination of the two, became sick. It was at this point that the alleged permission was given. According to Butch, he placed his keys on the table and said to plaintiff, "Watch my keys; I'm going upstairs to be sick." According to Loftus and his friend Holzworth, Butch said, "Here are my keys; I'm going upstairs to be sick." The automobile which Butch had parked in front of the house was not mentioned in the key transaction. Butch went upstairs, where he slept for several hours. When he recovered, his car and Loftus were missing.

In the absence of an unequivocally expressed permission, in order to prevail Loftus must show some relationship or course of conduct or other circumstance in which the parties have mutually acquiesced, which implies permission to use the vehicle, i.e., that the named insured did or said something in reference to the insured's car leaving the impression that the ensuing use was with permission.

With regard to use of the insured's automobile, Loftus admits that the 1976 Pontiac Firebird was Butch's "pride and joy" and that

5. 42 Pa. D. & C.3d 254 (Pa. Common Pleas Phila. 1986).

> he hardly ever entrusted it to anyone. Notwithstanding, Loftus says that prior to the August 21 incident, he had used the car three or four times. He corroborated its use on May 22, 1982 by presenting a ticket he had gotten for speeding, and he testified that on several occasions after a night on the town in Atlantic City, Butch asked him to drive the car on their return trip home. Butch admits that on one such trip he entrusted the operation of the car to Loftus because he himself was tired. He denied that he ever gave the car or permission to use it to Loftus at any other time, and showed genuine surprise to Loftus's evidence of the speeding ticket. He remembered the incident of May 22, 1982; he and Loftus had been at a diner and he had met a girl, whom he walked to her car at the rear of the parking lot. He left the keys in the ignition of his car so that his erstwhile friend could listen to the radio, and when he returned 20 minutes later, the car was right where he had left it. He learned for the first time at trial that Loftus had used the car in his absence and had gotten a ticket.
>
> This evidence is insufficient to establish a course of conduct acquiesced in by the parties which would indicate that Loftus had permission to use the insured's car for his own pleasure on August 21, 1982. Indeed, the inferences are to the contrary. The vehicle was the insured's pride and joy and he steadfastly refused to permit even his closest friends to use it. The one time he permitted Loftus to drive it, he was present and the operation was for their mutual purpose, not Loftus's individual pleasure. There is nothing in the prior relationship between the parties in reference to the use of the car that would have led Loftus to believe that he had permission to use it the late night of August 21, 1982 for a drunken frolic of his own.

Once again, here are the questions: What do the courts say—or what do the dispositions indicate—about the meaning of the word *permission*, which is the phrase-that-pays in this exercise? What are the legally significant facts on which the decisions seem to turn? What advice would you give Peter?

Recall and Review

1. Facts that could affect the outcome of a legal issue are called ____________ ________ facts.
2. A lawsuit begins with a set of factual allegations called a __________.

3. When lawyers talk about how a court decided, or "got rid of," a legal issue, they refer to it as the __________ of the issue.
4. In real life, most court opinions do/do not break new legal ground or change legal rules significantly.
5. While you may read cases in casebooks to understand how law develops, most lawyers read cases to see how courts have ________ rules to various factual scenarios.
6. When the focus of a legal argument is on the meaning of a word or a phrase in the relevant rule (as it very often is), we call that word or phrase the ________________.

CHAPTER 4

DECIPHERING OPINIONS

Now that you have some understanding of the very important role of judicial opinions in The Law, we want to delve deeper into the elements of an opinion. This chapter will introduce you to some of the vocabulary that lawyers use to describe the parts of an opinion. Knowing and understanding this vocabulary will help you understand how the parts of an opinion fit together to identify, clarify, and interpret rules. Recall that when we refer to the *common law*, we are referring to the body of rules whose sources can be traced to judicial opinions. An *opinion* is the written embodiment of a court's decision, and an opinion will almost always include an explanation of that decision. We will define and illustrate some of the important vocabulary and then give you a chance to test your understanding of the terms.

If your casebook professors have asked you to prepare "case briefs," the elements listed below may be useful in developing a case brief format—or a series of case brief formats. You might want to include different elements in briefs for different courses, depending on which aspects of an opinion a particular professor emphasizes. In addition, understanding the elements of a judicial opinion may help you to take effective notes on the cases you read and to organize those notes effectively. Even if you don't prepare formal case briefs, understanding the elements of a judicial opinion will help you to read and understand court opinions more effectively and more efficiently.

The word *brief* typically has two meanings in law. In law school, case *brief* usually means an organized set of notes about a court opinion. In legal practice, *brief* usually refers to an argumentative document that an attorney files with a court, particularly an appellate court.

A. THE ELEMENTS OF A JUDICIAL OPINION

There are many different ways that you can categorize opinions: by court, by date, by area of substantive law addressed, and the like. The explanations below will refer to two sets of particularly significant categories: criminal opinions and civil opinions, and trial opinions and appellate opinions.

In a criminal case, a governmental entity (e.g., a city, state, or federal government) *files charges* (e.g., via an indictment) against someone for violating a *criminal statute*. In a civil case, one or more persons or entities *file a lawsuit* (e.g., via a complaint) against one or more persons or entities under *civil law*. In the definitions below, we will explain important differences between criminal opinions and civil opinions.

As we explained in Chapter 2, almost all cases begin in trial courts, and the decisions of a trial court are called *trial court opinions* or, occasionally, *lower court opinions*. If the losing party files an appeal, the case may proceed to an appellate court. The opinions of an appellate court are called *appellate opinions* or *appellate decisions*; a court of last resort (that is, the highest court in a jurisdiction) may also refer to an intermediate appellate court decision as a *lower court opinion*.

1. Caption

The *caption* is the name of the case. The caption usually includes the name of the party who brought the lawsuit and the name of the party against whom the suit was brought. *Party* is a useful term because it encompasses people, corporations, governmental entities, civic groups, and others. Cases often involve multiple parties on either side. Although a formal caption would include the names of all parties, in most situations it is appropriate to reduce the caption to one party per side, usually the first one named in the initial complaint. If that party is a person, we use only the last name. So, in the famous case *Brown v. Board of Education of Topeka*, we know that the surname of the plaintiff listed first in the complaint was Brown. Few of us know that his first name was Oliver or that he was one of 13 plaintiffs named in that complaint.

Later, we will explain the very fussy rules for citation form. Even if you are using the wrong citation form, readers need to know these five things about a case.

2. Citation

The *citation* is the "address" of an opinion. It provides information that readers use to find the case in a library or an electronic database *and* to help assess the relevance of the opinion to future cases. A case citation (or "cite") should tell readers five things: (1) the name; (2) where readers can find the case; (3) the particular page being cited to, if any; (4) when the case was decided; and (5) which court decided it.

As lawyers move from hardcopy text to digital text, citations are changing, too. Some citations will require you to cite to the paragraph rather than (or in addition to) the page. The traditional cite form shown here is a citation to a book. Citations to online resources may follow different formats.

Example
Brown v. Bd. of Educ. of Topeka, 98 F. Supp. 797, 800 (D. Kan. 1951).

Brown v. Bd. of Educ. of Topeka: The caption.

98 F. Supp. 797: The reader can find the case at Volume 98 of the *Federal Supplement* reporter, beginning on page 797. (Of course, it would also be available on the web.)

800: The part of the case the writer is referring to can be found on page 800.

We call this a *pinpoint* citation. Some people use the phrase *pin cite* or *jump cite* to mean the same thing.

(1951): The case was decided in 1951.

(D. Kan.): The court is the United States District Court for the District of Kansas.

3. Parties

Most courts use the following procedural labels for parties: In a civil case, the party that brings the action is called the plaintiff, and the other side is called the defendant. In a criminal case, the person being charged is also called the defendant. As for the entity doing the charging, the federal government is usually referred to as "the United States," while other governmental entities are typically referred to as "the People," "the State," or "the City." In addition or in the alternative, they may be referred to more specifically, as in "the Commonwealth of Kentucky" or "New York."

Appellate courts use the label "appellant" for the party that brings the appeal and "appellee" or "respondent" for the party that responds to the appeal. Some courts use the term "petitioner" for the party who brings the appeal, especially if that court's procedures require the party to file a "petition" to seek the appeal.

To identify the *parties*, you need to determine who initiated the case and who the case was brought against. In a civil case, you must determine who was sued and who is being sued. In a criminal case, you must ask who the government has charged with a crime, and which unit of government is doing the charging. As noted above, some cases have more than one party on one side or on both sides. In addition to names, try to identify the *procedural categories* that each party falls into (i.e., appellant or appellee, plaintiff or defendant). If you are reading an appellate opinion, each party will have at least two procedural categories. For example, the party who lost at the trial court and appealed is generally called the *appellant*. In the trial court (presuming a civil case), the party was probably either the plaintiff or the defendant.

After you identify the procedural categories, try to identify the *legally significant factual categories* for each party, as well (e.g., employer or employee, husband or wife, driver or passenger). The procedural categories will be pretty similar from case to case (almost every trial has a defendant, for example), while the factual categories will vary depending on the facts and issues that each case presents.

Generally, after you complete this list of labels, you will want to refer to the parties by their *legally significant categories*. Sometimes the procedural category can be legally significant (especially in courses like civil procedure, where you are addressing procedural issues). More often, though, what is significant is that the person was a homeowner or a driver or a landlord. If that category label isn't handy, you may decide to use another label. Names, of course, are almost never legally significant.

4. Prior Proceedings

The phrase *prior proceedings* refers to the court proceedings that have already occurred in this particular legal dispute. You must determine how this case advanced through the court system from the initial complaint or indictment to the current point. For a civil case, you must determine who sued whom, in what court, and on what basis. For a criminal case, you must determine what charges were filed against the defendant, by what governmental entity, and in what court. In either kind of case, you must determine whether any *motions* have been made and ruled on. If you are reading an appellate decision, you must identify the precise decision that was made at the trial court. For a civil case, you must determine whether the court found in favor of the plaintiff or the defendant, and the basis for the decision. For a criminal case, you must determine whether the court found that the defendant was guilty or not guilty. (No one is found "innocent," despite what they say on the news.) You must also determine whether there was another appellate decision after the trial court and before the case came to this court (i.e., a decision of an intermediate appellate court).

A *motion* is how parties (usually through their attorneys) get the court to do something. Some motions are very routine (e.g., "a motion to continue trial" will postpone the trial to a later date). Other motions are called *dispositive motions* because they can dispose of the case, at least temporarily (e.g., a *motion to dismiss* asks the court to dismiss the case from the court system).

5. Facts

The *facts* of the case are what happened "in the world" that got the case into court. For a civil case, this usually means identifying why the plaintiff sued the defendant—what did the defendant (allegedly) do wrong, or what did the defendant allegedly fail to do? Is there anything relevant about the personal or professional relationship between the parties? In a criminal case, identify what the defendant (allegedly) did wrong that got the defendant arrested and charged with a crime. You should also determine whether the defendant alleges that the police did something wrong in the way they arrested or interrogated the defendant.

The facts you include in your fact section will vary depending on the issues before the court in the case you are reading. Broadly speaking, legal questions concern two main kinds of issues: *merits issues* and *procedural issues*. In a criminal example, if Josie is accused of murder, a merits question is whether Josie committed the murder. Another merits question might be whether Josie had the requisite intent to commit the murder. Procedural issues might be whether Josie's arrest and confession were handled appropriately by the police. In a civil example, presume that your client's front porch swing broke, injuring his children. He is suing the manufacturer of the swing on the basis of products liability, claiming that the company was negligent in the manufacturing process. A merits issue would be whether the company was actually negligent. Another merits issue would be whether the company's negligence caused the swing to break. A procedural issue would be whether the manufacturer is a resident of Ohio for purposes of jurisdiction. The facts that the court includes—and that you focus on—will be different, depending on the issue before the court and on whether it is a merits issue or a procedural issue.

When you are taking notes for a case brief or for a writing project, the facts you incorporate will generally include some combination of the legally significant facts and the relevant background facts. *Legally significant facts* are facts that, if they were different, might mean that the outcome of the case would be different. *Relevant background facts* are facts that help you understand, organize, or think about the legally significant facts. We think of background facts as the facts that help you tell the story. For example, in a case about failure to construct a new office complex, it is probably not relevant that one party to the construction contract was a doctor and another was a hairdresser. Those identifiers, however, might be helpful in keeping the parties straight in the story.

6. Issues

An *issue* is a legal question that the court answers. Generally, a formal issue statement will include three elements: (1) the legal context (usually the area of law that is relevant, and maybe a particular statute or other enacted law), (2) the narrow legal question (a yes-or-no question), and (3) the factual context. A less formal issue statement will just identify the narrow legal question and perhaps some facts. Thus, a formal issue statement might be: "Under Ohio's dog owner liability statute, which allows an owner to escape liability for a dog's bite if the victim was 'committing a trespass or other criminal offense,' [legal context] can an owner avoid liability [narrow legal question] if the victim was committing a civil trespass when he was bitten? [facts]" A less formal issue statement might omit the context and say, for example, "Can a dog owner avoid liability for her dog's bite if the victim was committing a civil trespass when he was bitten?" Sometimes, a court will be so informal as to fail to state the issue as a question at all. The issue may be inferred from the court's discussion of the facts and the law. In that situation, you can identify the legal issue(s) by identifying the question(s) the court has answered. Even when the court has not articulated the issue, it can be helpful for you to do so, especially if your professor calls on you to ask you to recite it.

7. Holding

Some people use the word *holding* to describe how the court disposed of the case; for example, "the court held for the defendant."

Others use the term more formally to mean "the rule of the case"—in other words, the legal rule in the context of the facts of this case. Often, a more formal holding will have the same elements as a formal issue statement (stated as a pronouncement rather than as an issue or question, of course). Thus, a formal holding might say, "Under the dog owner liability statute, a dog owner can avoid liability for a dog bite when the victim was committing a civil trespass at the time of the attack because civil trespass is included in the meaning of the phrase 'trespass or other criminal offense.'" Trying to identify the holding, or to articulate it in this way (even when the court has failed to do so) will help you to focus on the narrow legal issue(s), and to identify the rule(s) the court used to decide the issue.

8. Rule

As we have already noted, scholars debate the precise meaning of the term *rule*, but in this context, we use the term to mean the governing legal principle. In other words, a *rule* is a statement of the principle(s) that will govern the outcome of a particular issue. All statutes are rules, for example, but the rule governing a particular issue may not be the statute at issue in the case: the court may be using a different rule to decide the meaning of a particular word or phrase within the statute. In some cases that you read, you will probably see references to many different kinds of rules. Your job will be to distinguish the rules that are relevant but tangential from the rules that articulate the legal principles that govern the court's analysis of each issue and sub-issue.

In addition to statutes and other enacted law, you should look for common law rules. Statutory law and common law rules often interact: some rules that originate in the common law are later made statutes, and some statutes are interpreted using common law rules. On the other hand, some cases are solely about common law rules. For example, many states have a common law rule that says that employers must provide their employees with a "safe workplace." An employee might bring a lawsuit trying to enforce that rule, and a court might apply that rule to the case, as well as other rules about what a "safe workplace" means, or about what types of legal remedies an employee might be entitled to if he or she proves that the workplace is unsafe. Even if the case were mostly about the types of remedies available to the employee, you will help your own understanding of the case (as well as your readers' understanding) if you start by identifying the rule that underlies the lawsuit—in this example, the rule about employers providing safe workplaces.

You should be aware of one other factor when looking for the rule. Many students read phrases like "the rule in this area has always been thus-and-so" and presume that they have found the rule. Unfortunately for these students, they may miss the sentence a few paragraphs later in which the court says, "we now hold that the old rule is unconstitutional (or wrong, or irrelevant, or whatever)." Thus, Professor Linda Edwards advises that students look to see whether there is an "inherited rule," that is, the "old" rule that has always been applied in cases like this.[1] She then advises that students look to see whether the court has changed the inherited rule into a new rule, which she calls the "processed rule."[2] You shouldn't necessarily skip over an "inherited rule" because identifying the inherited rule may help you understand the court's reasoning.

Rules are the building blocks of legal analysis, and we will explore finding them and using them throughout this text.

9. Reasoning

The court's *reasoning* is its description of how it moved from the issue to the holding. Sometimes, the court will divide one legal issue into sub-issues. Sometimes the court will mention issues that the parties identified, but then, in its reasoning, it will identify other issues as the basis for its decision.

To analyze the court's reasoning, the best way to start is by looking for the rules the court used. In addition, look to see how it applied those rules to the facts and the methods of reasoning it used. For example, the court might analogize the current case to or distinguish it from previous cases. It might rely on relevant policy arguments to help it choose between two or more logically possible options. It might modify the original rule to get the result.

First, identify the issues that the court actually *analyzed*, not just the issues it refers to. You want to identify the issues or sub-issues on which the court reached a conclusion by using the law and the facts. After you identify the issues that the court actually analyzed, look for three elements for *each* issue you have identified: (1) the rule (or governing legal principle), (2) the court's explanation of what that rule means, and (3) how the court applied the rule to the facts of the case.

When beginning to analyze the reasoning, first make sure you understand the legal context in which the case is set (you should have begun this task when you articulated the issue). Generally, if there is a statute, a constitutional provision, or other enacted law at issue, you

---

1. Linda H. Edwards, *Legal Writing: Process, Analysis, and Organization* 40-43 (5th ed., Aspen 2010).

2. *Id.*

should begin there. If the court is applying that enacted law to this situation, look to see whether there is a dispute about what certain words or phrases within the enacted law mean. For example, in a Fourth Amendment case, the court might be analyzing what "unreasonable search and seizure" means. In doing so, however, it might consider a sub-rule that says that a search and seizure is reasonable if it does not violate a "reasonable expectation of privacy." In that situation, the phrase-that-pays would be "reasonable expectation of privacy" because the court would likely focus its analysis on the meaning of that term and use that analysis to decide whether the search was reasonable or unreasonable. Nevertheless, you would begin your description of the reasoning with the language of the Fourth Amendment and then move to the narrower rule.

After you have identified the rule, look to see how the court explained the rule's meaning. In simple cases with uncontroversial rules, a court can apply a rule to the facts of the case without providing much (or any) explanation of the rule's meaning. As we noted in an earlier chapter, some courts reach a conclusion without even stating the rule. Most cases are not that simple, however. Thus, to understand the court's reasoning, you will try to identify how the court explained what the rule means. If the court moved from an inherited rule to a processed rule, for example, look for reasons the court gave for doing so. Perhaps the old rule is out of date in light of rules from analogous cases or changes in the law or in society. If the court did not change the rule, it may have changed the interpretation of the rule (e.g., by broadening it to include a new category of people or situations that other courts may not have considered). Again, look for the reasons the court gave for doing so. Even if the court did not change the rule, it may still spend some time explaining what the rule means, usually by talking about other cases in which it has been applied, about hypothetical cases in which it might be applied, or about the policies behind the rule.

After you have found any rule explanation, look for rule application. When a court applies law to facts, it shows how the rule connects or doesn't connect to the facts of the case. Some people say *apply the facts to the law* to mean the same thing. In some cases, the application is obvious once the knotty legal problem of what the words mean has been solved, and so the court may spend little time on application. In other cases, the "fit" of the case facts and the rule may be the heart of the issue, and so the court will spend more time on it. In these cases, the court may analogize or distinguish the facts of the case before it, comparing those facts to facts in previous cases or to facts in hypotheticals. Sometimes the court will use these analogies and distinctions as part of its explanation of the rule's meaning.

Focusing on the factual details the court includes in its opinion can help you to identify legally significant facts. Try to note which facts it ties to any phrases-that-pay. Doing so can help you to understand the court's reasoning.

10. Policy

Generally, a *public policy* is a strongly held societal belief or understanding that supports a rule. When these societal beliefs change, rules change. For example, in the *Mad Men* days of the 1960s, people smoked almost anywhere, and few laws governed smoking. As society began to understand the dangers of secondhand smoke, rules of law changed to restrict the places in which people were allowed to smoke; this change was based on a public policy in favor of public health. When analyzing a court's reasoning, look to see whether the court justified itself by referring to *a societal belief or understanding about human behavior, the role of law, the role of certain institutions in society*, and the like.[3]

Sometimes, an issue is susceptible to two logically plausible results. The court may well make its decision (consciously or unconsciously) based on which decision best promotes public policy. Where competing policies argue for different outcomes—a decision in either party's favor would support some kind of public policy—the court must decide which policy is more important in the given situation. For example, a court might decide that protecting the health of nonsmokers is more important than protecting the freedom of choice of smokers.

11. Disposition

The disposition is how the court *disposed* (or got rid of) of the case. Did it affirm, reverse, reverse and remand, vacate? Did it grant the motion or deny the motion? To *affirm* is to leave the lower court's disposition intact. To *reverse* is to change the disposition. To *remand* is to send the case back to a lower court to deal with the case again, perhaps with a new rule or with specific directions as to which issue(s) to address. To *vacate* is to nullify a lower court's decision. These precise procedural terms are important because they have significance to legally trained readers. For example, motions are *granted* or *denied*, not *upheld* or *overturned*. An appellate court *reverses* or *affirms* or *vacates* or *reverses and remands* a decision submitted to it for review. It does not *strike down* or overrule the decision submitted to it.

The word *overrule* has at least two meanings in the law. In the trial setting, courts either *sustain* or *overrule* objections. In the appellate setting, *overrule* is most often used when a decision explicitly changes, or overrules, the rule articulated by a previous decision in a *different case* in the same court (or a lower one).

3. *See generally* Ellie Margolis, *Closing the Floodgates: Making Persuasive Policy Arguments in Appellate Briefs*, 62 Mont. L. Rev. 60 (2001).

12. Dicta

Dicta means statements or analyses by the court that are not needed for the court to arrive at its holding. Generally, dicta includes the court's comments on issues that are not currently before it. "This case is about dogs. If it were about cats, we would reverse, but because it is about dogs, we will affirm." In a future case about cats, a court would not be obligated to follow this court's hypothetical rule about a cat case. Of course, if the court finds the hypothetical rule persuasive, it may always decide to adopt it.

In your casebook courses, your professors may or may not ask about dicta. Recognizing it can be useful when you argue for clients, however. You may be able to persuade a court that it need not follow a rule propounded by your opponent because it is dicta.

B. A LABELING EXERCISE: EXERCISE 4.1

Below is a short opinion from the Ohio Supreme Court. What is the caption? What is the citation, and what five things does the citation tell you? Who are the parties, including any relevant categories? What were the prior proceedings?

In the margin of the opinion, label each of the following elements: the facts, the issue(s), the holding, the rule(s) (if you find both inherited and processed rules, identify them as such), the reasoning, the explanation, the application, and the disposition. If you find a mention or suggestion of a policy, identify it as such. Identify any dicta you find.

Sample Opinion

68 Ohio St.2d 53, 428 N.E.2d 410, 22 O.O.3d 259
Supreme Court of Ohio.

The STATE of Ohio, Appellant,
v.
FOX, Appellee.
The STATE of Ohio, Appellant,
v.
CUSTER, Appellee.
The STATE of Ohio, Appellant,
v.
FREEMAN, Appellee.

Nov. 18, 1981.

CLIFFORD F. BROWN, Justice.

The common law and statutory rule in American jurisprudence is that voluntary intoxication is not a defense to any crime. *Long v. State*, 109 Ohio St. 77, 86 (1923). An exception to the general rule has developed, where specific intent is a necessary element, that if the intoxication was such as to preclude the formation of such intent, the fact of intoxication may be shown to negative this element. See 8 A.L.R.3d 1236, Modern Status of the Rules as to Voluntary Intoxication as Defense to Criminal Charge. In such a case, intoxication, although voluntary, may be considered in determining whether an act was done intentionally or with deliberation or premeditation. *State v. French*, 171 Ohio St.501, 502 (1961), *cert. denied*, 366 U.S. 973 (1961).

R.C. 2923.02, which in conjunction with R.C. 2903.02 defines the offense of attempt to commit murder,[1] prohibits any person from purposely engaging in conduct which, if successful,

---

1. R.C. 2903.02 provides as follows:

(A) No person shall purposely cause the death of another.

(B) Whoever violates this section is guilty of murder, and shall be punished as provided in section 2929.02 of the Revised Code.

R.C. 2923.02 reads, in part, as follows:

(A) No person, purposely or knowingly, and when purpose or knowledge is sufficient culpability for the commission of an offense, shall engage in conduct which, if successful, would constitute or result in the offense.

Relevant to the application of these two statutes is R.C. 2901.22, which in part provides:

(A) A person acts purposely when it is his specific intention to cause a certain result, or, when the gist of the offense is a prohibition against conduct of a certain nature, regardless of what the offender intends to accomplish thereby, it is his specific intention to engage in conduct of that nature.

would constitute the offense of murder. Thus, the instant offense is a specific intent crime, for which evidence of voluntary intoxication may be taken in order to show defendant was thereby precluded from forming the necessary "purpose" to commit murder. The trial court correctly permitted introduction of evidence of defendants' intoxication on the evening of August 17, 1979.

Given the admissibility of evidence of intoxication, the issue is whether the trial court erred by refusing to go further and charge the jury on the possibility intoxication negated formation of the specific intent to attempt murder.

This court first addressed this precise issue in *Nichols v. State*, 8 Ohio St. 435 (1858). In that case Caleb Nichols was tried by jury for attempted murder.[2] On appeal, Nichols claimed, among other errors, the failure of the trial court to instruct that drunkenness should be considered by the jury in determining the existence of the malicious intent charged. After "somewhat anxious deliberation," we concluded that "a proper regard to the public safety in the practical administration of criminal justice" mandated introduction of the evidence of intoxication, "to show that the accused did not at the time intend to do the act which he did do." *Nichols, supra*, at 439. But we refused to require a jury instruction to be given on the question, stating as follows:

> . . . (W)hen we admit evidence of intoxication to rebut . . . a charge of deliberation and premeditation, . . . we think we have gone far enough; and that, looking to the practical administration of the criminal law, a due regard to the public safety requires that the mere question of malice should be determined by the circumstances of the case, aside from the fact of intoxication, as in other cases.

Id.

This court's denial of a right to a jury charge in *Nichols* was based on a deep seated distrust of the reliability of such evidence:

"Intoxication is easily simulated. It is often voluntarily induced for the sole purpose of nerving a wicked heart to the firmness requisite for the commission of a crime soberly premeditated, or as an excuse for such crime." *Id.* Rather than impose a strict rule of criminal procedure, we left the trial judge with discretion to handle the evidence and submit it to the jurors in the appropriate manner.

2. The indictment contained two counts: the first, for maliciously stabbing, with intent to kill, one Zachariah Riley; and the other, for maliciously stabbing, with intent to wound, the said Riley. *Nichols, supra*, at 436.

Subsequent cases decided by this court have recognized the appropriateness of a special jury charge on the effect of intoxication on formation of intent when that issue is properly raised by the evidence.[3] But this court has never found it necessary to promulgate a rule to regulate judges in this matter. Nor is this court well suited to make such a rule. This matter is best left to the discretion of the experienced trial judge.

The evidence in the case *sub judice* that the defendants were intoxicated was coupled with extensive evidence arguably incompatible with such a condition. Defendants testified in detail to the events leading up to the shooting at chief Rich's home. Nor did any defendant testify that at the time of the offense any of them were influenced by alcohol in their actions, although they did testify to consuming more than two six-packs of beer among themselves. But taking the evidence as a whole, we cannot say it was error for the trial judge to refuse to instruct on intoxication. The trial judge had a better opportunity to observe the demeanor and physical characteristics of the defendants, and was inherently better qualified than an appellate court to decide whether sufficient evidence was introduced to charge on the issue here. Out of a concern for the "practical administration of justice," we conclude, with the trial judge here, that not enough evidence was introduced to warrant the requested instruction.

Accordingly, the judgment of the Court of Appeals is reversed.

Judgment reversed.

CELEBREZZE, C.J., and WILLIAM B. BROWN, LOCHER and KRUPANSKY, JJ., concur.

SWEENEY and HOLMES, JJ., concur in the judgment.

---

3. *Long v. State*, 109 Ohio St. 77 (1923); *State v. Vargo*, 116 Ohio St. 195 (1927); *State v. French*, 171 Ohio St. 501 (1961).

Recall and Review

1. The body of rules that comes from judicial opinions is known as the c_______ l____.
2. In a _________ case, a governmental entity files charges against a person or entity. In a _________ case, one or more persons or entities files a lawsuit against one or more other persons or entities.
3. In a criminal case, the defendant is found guilty or ______________.
4. When parties in a case want the court to do something, they file a ___________.
5. The issue of whether a particular court is the correct court to hear a case would be one example of what could be called a p__________ issue.
6. The issue of whether a defendant violated the statute the defendant is accused of violating would be called a m_________ issue.
7. Laws forbidding smoking in public places are an example of laws based on the p_________ p_________ or social guideline that people shouldn't needlessly harm the health of others.
8. When an appellate court decides that the lower court decision was correct, we say that it ________ the decision.
9. When an appellate court decides that the lower court decision was incorrect, we say that it ___________ the decision.
10. When an appellate court sends a case back to a lower court, we say that it ________ the case.

CHAPTER 5

MORE ABOUT RULES (JUST AS WE PROMISED)

First, let's define our terms: As we hope you remember, a *rule* is a statement of the principle(s) that will govern the outcome of a particular issue. In law, as in life, a rule describes a consequence that results when a certain variable occurs or a certain condition is met. For example, parents often impose rules on their children like "you can eat your dessert if you finish your vegetables," or "you have to go in timeout if you hit one of your siblings." In both of those examples, the consequence was an action: a reward or a punishment. In law, the consequence is typically a punishment, a requirement to act, or some kind of legal status. For example, "you have to get a license if you want to drive in this state," "you can receive a sentence of up to ten years if you commit an aggravated burglary," "you can be held liable in a civil lawsuit if you violate the Americans with Disabilities Act," or "you meet the first part of the negligence test if you have a legal duty to another." An easy way to identify whether something is a rule is to see if you can create an *if-then* statement from it:

> **If** you can create an if-then statement, **then** that statement is a rule.
> **If** you eat your vegetables, **then** you get dessert.
> **If** you hit your brother or sister, **then** you have to spend ten minutes in timeout.

In law, then, we can phrase a generic rule as in the following examples. **If** a certain condition occurs or is met, **then** a certain legal consequence results, as in these examples:

> **If** your negligent actions were the legal cause of harm to someone you owed a duty to, **then** you meet one part of the causation element of the negligence test.

> **If** your blood-alcohol level measures higher than .08, **then** you have met the intoxication element of Vanita's Driving While Intoxicated statute.
> **If** you are convicted of violating Vanita's Driving While Intoxicated statute, **then** you can be sentenced to time in prison.

The *legal consequence* may be an easily identifiable legal status like "guilty" in a criminal case or "liable" in a civil case. In the alternative, the legal consequence may be that a person, thing, or situation is within or not within the definition of a particular legal concept (e.g., an "employer" under Title VII). Sometimes the legal consequence may be a punishment or other mandate; it might also be merely the fact that meeting the condition means that a party has satisfied a particular element or factor of a test.

The *condition* part of the rule may be what the two sides in a case are arguing about. A statute may read, for example,

> **If** a vehicle enters an intersection after the traffic signal has turned red, **then** the driver of that vehicle is guilty of a misdemeanor.

If you are the attorney for a driver who says that the signal turned red as he entered the intersection, you and the prosecutor may be arguing about what the statute means by "after." In the alternative, the driver may report that only his front bumper was in the intersection. In that case, you and the prosecutor might argue about what the statute means by "enters an intersection." In either situation, you are arguing about whether the facts meet the conditions that the rule sets.

A. IDENTIFYING "THE" RULE

One of the questions that haunts law students is "what is the rule here?" We can solve your problem. The answer is *it depends*. The first thing it depends on is the legal issue you are focusing on. The second thing it depends on is whether you're being asked the question in a casebook course, or you're trying to answer the question yourself as you analyze a legal issue in a legal writing memo, a brief, or another document for a fictional or real-life client.

If you're in doubt as to what that one legal issue is, consult the table of contents or the title of the chapter or chapter section: if it's a section on breach, "the rule" the professor is asking about is almost certainly the breach rule.

In your casebook courses, the casebooks help you to find the rule. As you know, the cases in your casebooks are typically edited to focus on only one legal issue, even if the court may have dealt with several issues as it made its decision. Thus, when your casebook professor asks you "what's the rule in this case?" your answer should probably be the rule that the court used to decide that one legal issue.

When you are reading a case to help a real or fictional client, however, you will often have to articulate "the rule" for more than one relevant issue, and the cases you read may address many issues. Sometimes, one court opinion will contain "the rule" for each of your issues. At other times, one of "the" rules will be stated explicitly, while you have to read several cases to synthesize "the" rule for other issues.

As you have probably noticed, legal writing is full of rules—i.e., sentences or parts of sentences that can be transformed into if-then statements. Some may be rules about procedure (e.g., whether it's appropriate for a case to be in a particular court, or whether law enforcement officers followed the law), while others may be rules about the merits of the case (e.g., whether certain types of behavior are or are not illegal).

Law students are often confused by the multiple rules they encounter in legal writing. If you want to know what "the rule" is, it can be overwhelming to try to figure out which rule is "the rule" in an opinion that may contain dozens of sentences that could qualify as "a" rule. Understanding the roles that those many rules fulfill may help you to separate "a" rule from "the rule."

In general, there are two reasons that statutes and court opinions contain many rules. The first reason is that it's very common for a rule to have sub-rules that create exceptions to or further define concepts in the overall or main rule. The second reason is that lawyers sometimes need guiding rules to tell them which rule to apply.

1. Sub-Rules

In law, a rule may have many sub-rules, each of which can be thought of as "a" rule on its own. For example, an entire statute may be thought of as a rule: *if* your behavior meets all of the provisions of a criminal statute, *then* you can be found guilty of violating it. But a statute may also have many sub-rules. For example, a so-called drunk driving statute usually provides that if you meet the *condition* of operating a vehicle while under the influence of an intoxicant, then you face the *legal consequence* of being guilty of drunk driving. But the typical drunk driving rule has many explicit or implicit sub-rules as well. For example, in most states, many different *conditions* can lead to the *legal consequence* of being deemed "intoxicated" or "under the influence." These conditions might include having a certain percentage of alcohol by weight in your blood or a certain percentage of designated intoxicants of other kinds. Each of these ways to establish the legal status of "intoxication" could be thought of as a separate rule.

Further, intoxication alone does not violate the statute: a driver must be intoxicated *and* operating a vehicle. Thus, a lawyer prosecuting a drunk driving case must establish that the person charged had the legal status of being intoxicated *and* had the legal status of operating a vehicle at the time. The lawyer may need at least two separate "rules" from the statute to analyze these issues.

Likewise, a common torts rule states that a person is liable for negligence if the person had a duty, breached the duty, and caused damages to another person through the breach. Meeting each element of the negligence standard—duty, breach, causation, and damages—can be thought of as a separate legal consequence, and thus establishing whether a person or situation meets that element can be articulated as part of a separate rule. Thus, there could be at least four separate rules that a lawyer must analyze to establish that a person is liable for the tort of negligence.

2. Guiding Rules

Sometimes, rules are connected to each other without the obvious connection of rule and sub-rule. It's hard to put a label on this relationship; you might think of some of these rules as guiding rules or helper rules or clarifying rules.

Below is an excerpt from the court's opinion in *Hurd v. Williamsburg County*.[1] In that case, the plaintiff sued for negligence after he was hit by a car while crossing a highway. He had exited a city bus at a non-designated stop and crossed the street to get to a popular diner; the bus company had recently created a designated stop on the opposite side of the road (a little further along the same route) to avoid the problems caused by people running across the highway to the diner. Here is a paragraph from the section of the opinion in which the court analyzed the causation issue; see how many rules (either explicit or implicit) you can find; we have numbered the non-citation sentences for ease of discussion:

> (1) In a negligence action the plaintiff must prove proximate cause. *Rush v. Blanchard*, 310 S.C. 375, 426 S.E.2d 802 (1993). (2) "Ordinarily, the question of proximate cause is one of fact for the jury and the trial judge's sole function regarding the issue is to inquire whether particular conclusions are the only reasonable inferences that can be drawn from the evidence." *McNair v. Rainsford*, 330 S.C. 332, 349, 499 S.E.2d 488, 497 (Ct. App. 1998). (3) Proximate cause requires proof of both causation in fact and legal cause. *Oliver v. South Carolina Dep't of Hwys. & Pub. Transp.*, 309 S.C. 313, 422 S.E.2d 128 (1992). (4) Causation in fact is proved by establishing the plaintiff's injury would not have occurred "but for" the defendant's negligence. *Oliver*, 309 S.C. at 316, 422 S.E.2d at 130. (5) Legal cause is proved by establishing foreseeability.

1. 611 S.E.2d 488, 492 (S.C. 2005)

Id. (6) An injury is foreseeable if it is the natural and probable consequence of a breach of duty. *Trivelas v. South Carolina Dep't of Transp.*, 348 S.C. 125, 558 S.E.2d 271 (Ct. App. 2001).

We can change each of those sentences into an if-then statement (and one of them into two if-then statements), indicating that they could each function as a rule (citations are omitted):

(1) If a plaintiff wants to succeed in a negligence action, then the plaintiff must prove proximate cause.
(2) A. If proximate cause is at issue, then the jury must decide the issue as a question of fact.
(3) B. If proximate cause is at issue, then the trial judge's sole function regarding the issue is to inquire whether particular conclusions are the only reasonable inferences that can be drawn from the evidence.
(4) If a plaintiff establishes both causation in fact and legal cause, then the plaintiff has established proximate cause.
(5) If a plaintiff proves that the relevant injury would not have occurred "but for" the defendant's negligence, then the plaintiff has established cause in fact.
(6) If a plaintiff establishes foreseeability, then the plaintiff has established proximate cause.
(7) If an injury is the natural and probable consequence of a breach of duty, then that injury is foreseeable in the context of establishing causation in fact.

In a way, each new sentence articulates a principle that clarifies a concept in one of the previous sentences. Some of them meet our definition of a sub-rule, but not all of them do. The first sentence mentions proximate cause, and the second sentence articulates the rules about how the judge and jury must decide proximate cause. The third sentence lays out sub-rules, describing the elements for establishing proximate cause. The fourth sentence focuses on the rule for establishing cause in fact, and the fifth sentence lays out the rule for establishing legal cause. Finally, the sixth sentence clarifies the legal cause rule by defining what "foreseeability" means in this context.

3. Using Rule Application to Identify The Rule

One of the things that makes legal writing and legal reading challenging is that sometimes "a rule" from one issue is "the rule" in another, because the condition it names is the nub of the controversy. Likewise, sometimes either the overall rule *or* an exception can be "the rule." To identify "the rule," look at how the court opinion uses the various rules it articulates. A rule serving as "a rule" may be helpful, it may be meaningful, it may be relevant, and it may even be necessary. But "the rule" is the one that the court applies to the specific facts at issue in your case. And yep, we just articulated "the rule" for finding "the rule":

> **If** you can apply a rule to case facts without articulating another guiding rule or sub-rule, **then** that rule is "the rule."

So, are any of those rules we listed above "the rule"? They are each a "governing principle" in that they are rules that lead you from the legal issue—was the proximate cause finding correct in the decision below?—to the analysis of that issue. Reading further in the opinion will help you answer the question. In the very next paragraph, the court applied the rules articulated in sentence four and sentence six to the facts of the case. The court used a phrase-that-pays from each of those rules and showed how it connects to the facts of the case. Therefore, each was "the rule" for its relevant issue:

Here, the court connects the "but for" language to the facts: but for the bus pulling out at that moment, the plaintiff would not have been injured.

Here, the court connects the concept of "foreseeability" to the facts.

> We conclude Hurd presented evidence of both factual and legal causation. Hurd presented evidence that "but for" the bus pulling out concurrently with Hurd attempting to cross the road, Hurd would not have been struck by the oncoming car. Hurd also presented evidence that the vehicle-pedestrian accident was foreseeable. Pressley's testimony is evidence suggesting (1) the Transit Authority knew that the location of the accident was dangerous to pedestrians; (2) the County constructed the Park and Ride to minimize known dangers at this intersection; (3) the Transit Authority implemented a policy that all drivers were to use the Park and Ride rather than the shoulder of the Highway; (4) the Transit Authority violated its own safety policy by discharging Hurd and the other passengers on the side of the highway; (5) the Transit Authority issued the bus driver a warning for violating the safety policy on the date of the accident; and (6) the starting of the bus prevented Hurd from hearing or seeing traffic on the highway.

The same guideline applies when looking at rules from statutes. For example, in a drunk driving case, the typical issues are whether the person was "intoxicated" under the statute's definitions, and whether the person was "operating" the vehicle. If the person charged in your case was intoxicated with alcohol, "the rule" for the intoxication issue would be the part of the statute that defines intoxication by alcohol, because the court would need to apply that standard to the blood-alcohol level of the defendant in that case.

In legal writing, you must work with many rules other than The Rule. Of course, you must determine what The Rule is when doing research, but when you write, you will often provide context for your reader by including sub-rules, overall rules, or guiding rules. Thus, it's important to identify all of the relevant rules and to understand how they relate to each other. Identifying rules and understanding their relationships is the first step toward organizing legal analysis.

In this text, we will usually refer just to *rules*, even when those rules may also be thought of as sub-rules or guiding rules. We will try to make it clear when we are articulating a principle that applies only to how you use The Rule.

B. DIVIDE AND CONQUER: IDENTIFYING RELATIONSHIPS BETWEEN AND WITHIN RULES

A rule that has two or more sub-rules may be described as a "test." Sometimes, you will have to prove that every element of a test has been met. A test that requires all elements to be met is known as a *conjunctive* test.[2] To remember what a conjunctive test is, remember that *and* is a conjunction, and that part of *conjunction*, the syllable *con-*, comes from the Latin for "with." With a conjunctive test, you have to prove one part, *and* another part, *and* another part, and so on to establish that the test has been met.

For example, as noted earlier, a person cannot be held liable for negligence unless the plaintiff establishes that the person had a duty *and* breached the duty *and* that the breach caused harm *and* that the harm resulted in compensable damages. So, that is a conjunctive test.

On the other hand, some tests are *disjunctive* tests.[3] To remember what a disjunctive test is, remember that *dis-*, the first syllable of *disjunctive*, comes from the Latin for "apart." With a disjunctive test, you have to prove one part of the test *or* another part *or* another part to establish that a test has been met. For example, as indicated above, a person is usually considered to be "under the influence" for purposes of a reckless operation statute if he or she has in his or her bloodstream a certain amount of alcohol *or* cocaine *or* marijuana *or* another controlled substance. So, the test for intoxication can be thought of as a disjunctive test.

A conjunctive test for one party may be a disjunctive test for the other. For example, the prosecutor has to prove that a drunk driving defendant was (a) intoxicated *and* (b) operating a vehicle. A defendant, however, can get a not guilty verdict by proving that the prosecutor has not established one of the two parts of the test, *either* intoxication *or* operation of a vehicle. Thus, the prosecutor is facing a conjunctive test, but the defendant faces only a disjunctive test.

---

2. Linda H. Edwards, *Legal Writing: Process, Analysis, and Organization* 19 (5th ed., Aspen 2010).

3. *Id.*

A third kind of test is a *factors* test.[4] With a factors test, the court considers several different ways that a rule could be met, but no particular set of elements is required to be met; instead, the court makes a judgment after reviewing the factors. For example, in criminal law, a court may look at "the totality of the circumstances" to determine whether a police officer should have secured a search warrant before searching a defendant's car. It considers a variety of factors that generally occur in similar situations.

A particular client's case may present rules with conjunctive, disjunctive, and factors tests. When analyzing the case, your job is to look at the facts, conduct legal research, and determine what statutes and cases govern the situation. Then you must determine how the pieces of the law operate with one another. Must all of the elements be proved to establish guilt or liability? Then you may have a conjunctive test. Are there alternate paths to the same result? Then you may have a disjunctive test. Sometimes, a case may present more than one kind of test. For example, in a drunk driving statute, you have a conjunctive test: you must prove that the defendant was (a) under the influence *and* (b) operating a vehicle. However, you may have a disjunctive test to determine "under the influence": the defendant may have the legal status of "under the influence" if he or she had a certain blood level of alcohol *or* amphetamines *or* cocaine *or* some other designated drug. Thus, the various parts of the statute provide alternative ways of establishing the requirement, or element, of intoxication.

C. IDENTIFYING CONTROVERSIES

After you have identified the rules that govern your client's case and analyzed the tests that are part of those rules, you should identify which tests are relevant to your analysis. Sometimes identifying elements that might be in controversy can help you with this task. For example, most statutes apply to "persons," and usually whether someone is a "person" is uncontroversial and need not be analyzed. However, if a corporation is sued, the plaintiff may first need to establish that the corporation is a "person" under the statute.

To take another example, if you are prosecuting a person who has been arrested for driving while intoxicated when that person was sitting in a parked car, you must argue that the person met the standard for intoxication *and* that sitting in a parked car constitutes "operating a vehicle." In contrast, if the person was arrested for drunk driving

4. *Id.*

while riding a bicycle, you must establish that a bicycle constitutes a "vehicle" under the statute. Suppose the person was arrested after being found lying in the road on top of a bicycle after having obviously fallen off the bicycle. In that situation you would need to prove (1) that the person was "intoxicated" under the statute, (2) that a bicycle is a "vehicle" under the statute, and (3) that evidence that the person was lying on top of the bicycle would be sufficient to establish that the person was "operating a vehicle" under the statute.

Thus, after you have found the relevant legal rules, analyze them to determine what the parties must prove to successfully prosecute or sue or to defend against a prosecution or a suit. Then determine how the rules operate: do they present conjunctive tests, disjunctive tests, factors tests, or all of the above? Finally, note which elements are relevant or controversial given your facts. Completing these tasks moves you toward an organization for your legal analysis.

D. SOME RULE-OUTLINING EXERCISES

Once you have identified a rule, outlining it is usually pretty simple. For example, Ohio's assault statute[5] provides that

> (A) No person shall knowingly cause or attempt to cause physical harm to another or to another's unborn.
>
> (B) No person shall recklessly cause serious physical harm to another or to another's unborn.

The statute is written in the disjunctive; a person who violates either (A) or (B) is guilty of assault. The outline of the rule embodied in the statute would look something like this:

> A person who does any of the following is guilty of assault:
>
> (1) knowingly causing physical harm to another person;
>
> (2) knowingly attempting to cause physical harm to another person;
>
> (3) knowingly causing physical harm to the unborn of another person;
>
> (4) knowingly attempting to cause physical harm to the unborn of another person;
>
> (5) recklessly causing physical harm to another person; or
>
> (6) recklessly causing physical harm to the unborn of another person.

---

5. Ohio Rev. Code § 2903.13 (Westlaw, current through Files 29, 30 of the 134 th GA (2020-2021)).

Note that this outline shows you all of the sub-rules. To identify The Rule, you would have to know the issue(s) in your case.

Exercise 5.1

How might you outline the rule from this statute in the Laws of New York?

> **§ 155.05 Larceny; defined.**
> A person steals property and commits larceny when, with intent to deprive another of property or to appropriate the same to himself or to a third person, he wrongfully takes, obtains or withholds such property from an owner thereof.

Exercise 5.2

As we have already discussed, rules may be embodied in judicial opinions as well as statutes. This excerpt from a 1982 opinion[6] sets out the rule for proving that consumers are likely to be confused by competing use of similar trademarks. How would you outline that rule?

> Here, since equitable relief is sought, only the likelihood of confusion need be shown, and not proof of actual confusion as was required by the District Court.
>
> * * *
>
> Under § 43(a) of the Lanham Act it is not necessary to show that any false description or representation is willful or intentional. *Parkway Baking Co. v. Freihofer Baking Co.*, 255 F.2d 641, 648 (3d Cir. 1958). All that is required is that the representation or descriptions either be "false" or such as is "tending falsely to describe or represent the goods or services in question." *Ames Publishing Co. v. Walker-Davis Publications, Inc.*, 372 F. Supp. 1, 11 (E.D. Pa. 1974). Thus, liability is not restricted solely to descriptions which are literally false, but extends to instances where the defendant creates a false impression. *Id.*
>
> * * *
>
> [E]ight factors[] are helpful in demonstrating that there is a likelihood of confusion among consumers:

6. *Frisch's Restaurants, Inc. v. Elby's Big Boy of Steubenville, Inc.*, 670 F.2d 642, 647-51 (6th Cir. 1982).

> 1. strength of the plaintiff's mark;
> 2. relatedness of the goods;
> 3. similarity of the marks;
> 4. evidence of actual confusion;
> 5. marketing channels used;
> 6. likely degree of purchaser care;
> 7. defendant's intent in selecting the mark;
> 8. likelihood of expansion of the product lines. . . .
>
> In assessing whether there is likelihood of confusion, a court first considers [those] factors and then, based thereon, determines whether there exists a likelihood of confusion.

Exercise 5.3

Sometimes outlining a rule is not simple at all. For a bigger challenge, read the statute below and make a list showing what a defendant would have to prove to use section (A) of the statute to defend against a charge of animal cruelty. Then, make a list showing what a plaintiff would have to prove to use section (B) of the statute to sue a dog owner for injuries caused by the dog. Be able to explain how the different items on the list relate to each other.

> **§ 955.28. Dog may be killed for certain acts; owner liable for damages**
>
> (A) Subject to divisions (A)(2) and (3) of section 955.261 of the Revised Code, a dog that is chasing or approaching in a menacing fashion or apparent attitude of attack, that attempts to bite or otherwise endanger, or that kills or injures a person or a dog that chases, injures, or kills livestock, poultry, other domestic animal, or other animal, that is the property of another person, except a cat or another dog, can be killed at the time of that chasing, approaching, attempt, killing, or injury. If, in attempting to kill such a dog, a person wounds it, he is not liable to prosecution under the penal laws which punish cruelty to animals.
>
> (B) The owner, keeper, or harborer of a dog is liable in damages for any injury, death, or loss to person or property that is caused by the dog, unless the injury, death, or loss was caused to the person or property of an individual who, at the time, was committing or attempting to commit a trespass or other criminal offense on the property of the owner, keeper, or harborer, or was committing or attempting to commit a criminal offense against any person, or was teasing, tormenting, or abusing the dog on the owner's, keeper's, or harborer's property.

Recall and Review

1. A statement of the principle(s) that will govern the outcome of a particular issue is a r_______.
2. A rule that governs whether certain plaintiffs are allowed to join a class action, or whether it's appropriate for a particular case to be heard in a particular court, are examples of p_______ rules.
3. A rule that governs whether certain types of behavior are or are not illegal is a m____ rule.
4. One way to identify whether something is a rule is to see if you can create what kind of statement from it?
5. In a court opinion, you can often identify The Rule because that is the rule that the court _______ to the _________.
6. Legal writers include rules, sub-rules, overall rules, or guiding rules to provide _______ for their readers.
7. A test that requires a party to meet all of its elements is called a c_________ test.
8. A test that allows a party to succeed by proving only one element is called a d_________ test.
9. A test whose requirements may vary depending on the facts of a case is called a f_________ test.
10. Understanding the relationships between and among all of the relevant rules is the first step toward ________ing legal analysis.

CHAPTER 6

USING AUTHORITY TO FIND RULES

Hierarchy and Rule Synthesis

As a lawyer, you will frequently be asked to apply law to facts. Your clients will usually provide the facts, but you must provide the law. On television, lawyers often seem to know the law off the top of their heads. On *Law and Order*, the prosecuting attorneys sometimes talk about case authority, but you seldom see them doing the research needed to find that authority. There's at least one reason for that: legal research doesn't provide a lot of visuals. Most of the action is going on inside your head, and action inside your head doesn't make for very good television. It does, however, make for good lawyering.

As a lawyer, what you will frequently be doing is listening to a client's story, developing a hypothesis about what category of law might apply, and then doing research to check your hypothesis. Eventually, your research will narrow your focus, until you find (or articulate) the rules that govern your client's situation.

To develop a hypothesis about your client's situation—and then to test that hypothesis—you have to develop certain kinds of *knowledge* and *skills*. First, you have to develop the *knowledge* of the hierarchy of authority, knowing which jurisdiction's rules will apply and where to begin looking for rules. You must understand the hierarchy of authority so that you know where to focus your research. Second, you have to develop the *skill* of being able to discern and express a rule that a court may apply to decide your issue. Third, you have to acquire *knowledge* about methods of legal research and develop the *skill* of using databases, books, and other search methods to find—and recognize—the relevant law. Fourth, you must gain the *skill* of applying law to facts in a variety of contexts. Finally, you need to acquire *knowledge* about the doctrine of legal writing and develop the *skill* of using this doctrine to analyze how law applies to facts and to communicate it effectively to the appropriate audiences. In this chapter, we will begin the discussion of the first type of knowledge, an understanding of the hierarchy of authorities, and the first skill, discerning and expressing rules.

A. WHAT IS LEGAL AUTHORITY?

When we talk about legal authority, we are talking about a very broad body of sources and resources that contain law, discuss law, interpret law, and cite law. These sources have widely varying influence in how courts will decide whether the law applies to any particular set of facts or issues. A nomenclature, or system of names, has developed to help lawyers to distinguish between the various types of sources. While it is helpful, this nomenclature does not answer all of the questions you will encounter about how influential a certain source will be when you need to resolve an issue you are analyzing. To fill in the gaps, lawyers must rely on experience and judgment.

In this section, we will identify four categories of authority: *primary*, *secondary*, *mandatory*, and *persuasive*. You should know at the outset that these are not mutually exclusive categories. For example, a source may be both primary and persuasive authority or both primary and mandatory authority. We will also begin to explore how lawyers use experience and judgment to determine which sources will be more influential than others in the resolution of a particular issue.

1. Primary Authority

In Chapter 2, we reminded you that rules come from a variety of sources. Those sources have varying levels of authority. When a source produces or contains rules that are The Law in a given place, we call that source a *primary authority*. Primary authority is the law if it is valid law and if it covers the particular set of facts at issue in the appropriate jurisdiction. Applicable decisions of the U.S. Supreme Court that have not been superseded are primary authority, as are the rules contained in the U.S. Constitution, statutes passed by Congress, and regulations promulgated by executive agencies and departments when those regulations have been given the force of law. The comparable sources from within each state's system are also primary authority. These are not the only sources of primary authority, however.

Within both the federal and state governments, many smaller jurisdictions also have the power to make or identify law. For instance, within the federal court system, the intermediate appellate courts, known as the circuit courts of appeal, identify rules, and their decisions may also be primary authority. Likewise, within each state, decisions of intermediate appellate courts may be primary authority. Ordinances enacted by counties (or parishes), municipalities, and townships are primary authority too. Within state and local governments, agencies and departments are sometimes given authority to make regulations or rules that have the force of law, and those regulations and rules are primary authority.

Perhaps the easiest way to understand primary authority is to think of it like this: primary authority is The Law somewhere.

You may already be thinking, "But some of those sources of primary authority have no jurisdiction where I live." And you would be right. The fact that an authority is The Law somewhere, and thus primary authority, does not mean that it is The Law everywhere. So, we need another term to identify an authority that is The Law in a particular jurisdiction. That term is *mandatory authority*.[1]

2. Mandatory Authority

Mandatory authority is any rule that a court must follow. You will hear lawyers refer to mandatory authority as "binding." To be binding, mandatory authority must, of course, be relevant to the legal issue (think *stare decisis*). More importantly, it must be from the appropriate jurisdiction, whether federal or state.

a. Issues of federal law

When any court, federal or state, analyzes an issue of federal law, it is required to follow the decisions of the U.S. Supreme Court. We would say, therefore, that decisions of the U.S. Supreme Court are mandatory authority everywhere in the United States as to questions of federal law. The U.S. Constitution, federal statutes, and federal regulations that have been given the force of law are also mandatory authority everywhere in the United States as to questions of federal law. Those federal sources are also mandatory authorities for state courts as to issues of federal law. When a federal trial court (U.S. district court) addresses issues of federal law, it is also required to follow the decisions of the U.S. Supreme Court and of the U.S. court of appeals for the circuit in which it sits. As you may know, the United States is divided into about a dozen circuits, drawn along state lines. The Sixth Circuit, for example, includes the states of Michigan, Ohio, Kentucky, and Tennessee. Any federal district court in Kentucky, therefore, is required to follow

The principle of *stare decisis* is relevant to how much a mandatory authority controls another case. A court must follow a decision from a mandatory court only when the two cases are sufficiently "alike." Very often, counsel for the two sides of the case will not agree on whether two cases are sufficiently alike and will focus much of their attention on that question.

When an authority case is from a higher court in the appropriate jurisdiction and meets the standards of *stare decisis*, it is "binding authority." Courts sometimes say that they are *bound* by these decisions.

1. *E.g.*, Linda H. Edwards, *Legal Writing: Process, Analysis, and Organization* 56 (5th ed., Aspen 2010).

the decisions of both the U.S. Supreme Court and the U.S. Court of Appeals for the Sixth Circuit.

When a State Court Interprets Federal Law, What Courts Are Mandatory?

You have asked an interesting question, grasshopper. The short answer is that a state court always must follow the U.S. Supreme Court, and that it is likely to follow federal courts that happen to share its geographical area.

Let us presume that a person charged with a crime in a state court in Ohio has claimed that the police officers violated his rights under the Fourth Amendment to the U.S. Constitution. In analyzing this question of federal law, the Ohio court would be obligated to follow the U.S. Supreme Court. But what if the U.S. Supreme Court had not yet decided the narrow issue, but the Sixth Circuit had? Would that Ohio court be obligated to follow the Sixth Circuit? The answer is that the Ohio court would not be *obligated* to follow the Sixth Circuit. That court has no authority over the Ohio court; it's not the "boss" of the Ohio court in any way. The Ohio court, however, would be very likely to respect the expertise of the Sixth Circuit and to follow any decision it has made about the Fourth Amendment.

The takeaway is that if you are arguing a case to a state court and there is a federal issue that hasn't been decided yet by the U.S. Supreme Court, it would make sense to look to other federal courts, particularly those in nearby federal jurisdictions.

A Kentucky district court, however, is *not* required to follow the decisions of the U.S. Court of Appeals for the Seventh Circuit, or for any other circuit but the Sixth Circuit.

In summary, on issues of federal law, all federal and state courts are required to follow the U.S. Constitution, federal statutes, federal regulations that have the force of law, and decisions of the U.S. Supreme Court. A federal district court is also required to follow decisions of the intermediate-level appellate court (the U.S. Court of Appeals) for the circuit in which it sits.

b. Issues of state law

On issues of state law, every court, whether federal or state, is required to follow the decisions of the highest court of the state whose law it is applying. We would say that those decisions are mandatory authority everywhere as to questions of that state's law. A state's constitution, statutes, and regulations that have the force of law are also mandatory authority everywhere as to questions of that state's law. Typically, a state trial court is also required to follow the decisions of the state's intermediate appellate court for the district or division of the state in which it sits as to questions of that state's law.

Note that states may have differing rules on how appellate courts are binding on trial courts. In California, for example, trial courts are obligated to follow the decisions of any appellate court that has decided the issue in the state. It is important to know the rules of mandatory authority in any state in which you practice.

This rule operates in state courts in much the same way that it operates in federal courts. In many states, for example, the state appellate districts include certain counties. A trial court located within the fourth appellate district, for example, would be required to follow the decisions of the fourth appellate district and of the state's highest court, but would probably not be required to follow the decisions of appellate courts in other districts in the state.

Federal courts may also be required to follow the decisions of state courts. For example, presume that a Michigan federal district court is hearing a state law case that was filed in federal court due to diversity of citizenship between the parties. When it is interpreting a Michigan statute, the federal court is required to follow the rulings of the Michigan Supreme Court. If the Michigan Supreme Court has not yet decided the issue, the federal court is obligated to interpret the statute in the way that it predicts the Michigan Supreme Court *would* decide the issue. The court may make this prediction by considering the decisions of Michigan intermediate appellate courts, by considering other Michigan Supreme Court decisions, or by some combination of the two.

Federal law allows a party to file a state claim in federal court if the party's opponent is a citizen of a different state. The basic reason for this law is to avoid any bias for the local party that might exist in state courts. *See* 28 U.S.C. § 1332 (2012).

In summary, when interpreting a state law issue, all courts, federal and state, are required to follow that state's constitution, statutes, and regulations that have the force of law, as well as the decisions of that state's highest court. Typically, a state trial court is also required to follow decisions of the intermediate-level state appellate court for the district or division in which it sits on questions of that state's law.

In summary, the following authorities are mandatory:

On Questions of Federal Law

Federal statutes

Federal regulations (where Congress has given them the force of law)

Decisions of the United States Supreme Court (and the United States Court of Appeals for the local circuit but only in federal cases)

On Questions of State Law

Statutes of the state whose law is in question

Regulations of the state whose law is in question (if they have force of law within that state)

Decisions of the highest court of the state whose law is in question

In state cases in some states, decisions of the intermediate appellate courts of the state whose law is in question (check state law within the jurisdiction state)

You may test your understanding of these mandatory authority concepts by taking the quiz at the end of this chapter.

3. Secondary Authority

We have explained the concepts of primary and mandatory authority. Their mere names suggest that other types of authority exist. And they do: *secondary authority* and *persuasive authority*. We'll start with secondary authority because it's easier to explain.

If primary authority is any authority that is The Law somewhere, *secondary authority* is any authority that is not The Law anywhere. A good way to think about secondary authority is that, very often, a secondary authority consists of analysis of The Law. The types of secondary authority that you are most likely to encounter are hornbooks, treatises, legal encyclopedias, law review articles, and legislative history. When executive branch agencies and departments interpret statutes, and their interpretations are not given the force of law, those interpretations are also secondary authority. In short, a secondary authority says something about what the law is and how it might be interpreted and applied, but it is not The Law. No one is required, or *bound*, to follow it.

Lawyers often rely on secondary authority to help them to understand some aspect of the law. They rarely cite that authority to a court, however. A court is not likely to rely on secondary authority as a basis for a decision, although it may find the explanation or interpretation offered by the secondary authority to be helpful in the absence of any primary authority on the issue. This is especially true of legislative history, which may offer the court some guidance about how the legislature intended for a statute to be applied. Because secondary authority is never mandatory authority, however, the court is not required to adopt the interpretation suggested by the legislative history.

4. Persuasive Authority

The term *persuasive authority* suggests that the concept will be as simple as the secondary authority concept. Alas, simplicity is somewhat elusive in this instance. One aspect of persuasive authority is easy to understand: all authority that is not mandatory authority is persuasive authority. If mandatory authority is any primary authority that a particular court must follow, persuasive authority is all other authority. The simple concept is that all secondary authority is persuasive authority; it is persuasive because by definition it is not The Law, and an authority that is not The Law can never be mandatory authority. When it comes to primary authorities, however, things get a little more complicated. Sometimes, a court decision may be mandatory authority to one court and persuasive authority to another court. Illustrations will make the concept easier to grasp.

A decision of the Michigan Supreme Court is primary authority no matter where you are. It is The Law as to questions of Michigan law. In any court interpreting Michigan law, that decision is mandatory authority. If, on the other hand, an intermediate-level Michigan appellate court were to decide the same issue, its decision is mandatory authority within its jurisdiction and persuasive authority everywhere else.

Decisions of trial courts may be quite helpful to other trial courts, and even to appellate courts, facing similar issues. They are primary authority because they are The Law to the parties to that particular case, but no court is required to follow that decision in a future case—not even the court that originally issued it. Therefore, they are persuasive authority everywhere.

A decision by the U.S. Court of Appeals for the Sixth Circuit is primary authority because it is The Law as to questions of federal law in the Sixth Circuit. In a U.S. district court in Michigan, that decision is also mandatory authority because Michigan is in the Sixth Circuit. In a U.S. district court in Indiana, however, the same decision is persuasive authority because Indiana is in the Seventh Circuit.

From these illustrations, we can distill a couple of important principles. First, if an authority is primary, it is primary everywhere. A decision's status as mandatory or persuasive authority is not static, however. The same decision is mandatory authority in some courts and persuasive authority in others. Second, geography does not determine whether an authority is mandatory or persuasive. The determinant is the nature of the question the court is addressing: if the issue is a federal issue, only federal authorities can be mandatory; if it is a state law issue, only courts and laws of that state can ever be mandatory.

5. How Persuasive Is That Persuasive Authority?

Once the mandatory versus persuasive question is answered, a second question may arise. If an authority is merely persuasive, how persuasive is it? The "how persuasive" question is as much a matter of judgment and psychology as it is a matter of law. In fact, it isn't really a question of law at all. Unless an authority is mandatory for a particular court on a particular question, that court is not required to follow that authority. The legal part of the "how persuasive" question ends there. In general, primary authority is almost always more persuasive than secondary authority. This may be because primary authority is more likely to address specific issues that a court faces, while a secondary authority may talk more generally about issues.

Still, courts often do seem to follow authority that is not mandatory. If the U.S. Court of Appeals for the First Circuit is answering a question of federal law for the first time, and all of the other circuit courts have answered the same question uniformly, the First Circuit is very likely to reach the same decision. It is likely to find the decisions of the other circuit courts to be very persuasive. We might be tempted to say that it will "follow" the decisions of the other circuits. "Follow" would be a deceptive verb choice in that instance, however, because it suggests that the First Circuit is applying the other circuit courts' decisions as law. In fact, the action of the First Circuit is better described as "adopting." It is interpreting the law in a manner suggested by the decisions of the other courts and adopting their reasoning, even though it is not required to do so.

If you were a lawyer in the case described above who was preparing to argue the unresolved question before the U.S. Court of Appeals for the First Circuit, you would rely on your judgment and what you know about psychology to estimate the likelihood that the court would adopt the reasoning of all of the other circuit courts. Most lawyers would estimate that likelihood to be very great. A court will find multiple decisions by its peer courts, all speaking with one voice, to be very, very persuasive. It will depart from their reasoning only if (1) something about the applicable law has changed since all of the other circuit courts issued their decisions, (2) it sees an error in the reasoning of all of those courts, or (3) it is convinced that all of the other courts are wrong, and it is bold enough to go in a different direction.

Now suppose that none of the circuit courts had answered the question. In fact, only one court has ever considered it, and that court is a state trial court in New Mexico in 1962. Let's further suppose that the New Mexico court did not explain the reasoning behind its decision but simply held for one party or the other. The U.S. Court of Appeals for the First Circuit is not likely to find that decision to be persuasive.

On the other hand, if there is a recent law review article that directly addresses the legal issue, analyzes possible ways to apply the law to the facts, and makes a recommendation as to how courts should resolve the issue, a court could decide to adopt the reasoning of the law review article. Legally, the law review article, the New Mexico court's decision, and the unanimous decisions of the U.S. circuit courts all have the same weight. The First Circuit is under no obligation to follow any of them. We assume, however, as a matter of judgment and psychology, that the First Circuit is least likely to pay much attention to an aged trial court decision with no explicit reasoning and that it would be most likely to adopt the reasoning expressed in the unanimous circuit court decisions.

As this distinction illustrates, the identity of the source of the authority, the authority's age, and the depth and quality of its reasoning are three important factors in the persuasive force of the authority. Some additional factors affect the persuasive value of an authority: the extent to which other courts have adopted its reasoning or cited it favorably, the similarity of the facts in the authority case and the facts before a subsequent court, and whether the decision represents an emerging trend in the law. A court is likely to find another court's decision to be very persuasive if several other courts have adopted its reasoning when they were not required to do so. Likewise, a court is more likely to find another court's decision to be persuasive if it is consistent with the direction in which the law in a particular area is developing. As a lawyer, you will never be certain that a court will find a particular nonmandatory authority to be especially persuasive, but you can make an educated guess based on these factors.

A few other factors may occasionally affect an authority's persuasive value. The decisions of a few extraordinarily respected judges are unusually persuasive to some courts. You should be very cautious about overrelying on a judge's reputation, however. While nearly every court will recognize that Learned Hand was an unusually wise judge, his reasoning must convince the court before it will adopt it. Your argument will not carry the day simply because you have cited one of Judge Hand's decisions.

A court is somewhat more likely to adopt the reasoning of another court in its own jurisdiction when the issues presented are similar to those the sister court considered. A couple of reasons explain this phenomenon. First, judges in a jurisdiction are much more likely to know one another personally and to trust one another. They are less likely to disagree if they can avoid doing so. A court will not blindly follow the decision of another court in its jurisdiction, of course, but it may be more likely to attempt to reconcile differences. Second, when possible, a court will attempt to minimize the uncertainty that would result within the jurisdiction from conflicting resolutions of the same or very similar issues. A court will never ignore its own firm conviction that a sister court is wrong, however.

6. Nonprecedential Authority and Its Persuasive Value

You know that the decisions of certain courts constitute mandatory authority depending on the jurisdiction in which your case is filed. For example, if you intend to file a complaint in a federal district court in Illinois, decisions of the Seventh Circuit Court of Appeals will be mandatory authority in your case. You may not know that only *some* decisions from that court are mandatory, however. In fact, the majority of Seventh Circuit decisions are persuasive at best. Why?

All decisions of the U.S. Supreme Court and most decisions of the states' highest courts are reported.

A decision of a federal circuit, for example, is mandatory authority only if it is "reported." The concept of reporting a decision has lost most of its practical meaning because virtually all federal court decisions are now "reported" in that they are published somewhere. Before LEXIS and Westlaw, however, federal decisions were published only in bound case reporters, the *Federal* and *Federal Supplement* series. The court issuing the decision could choose to send it to the publisher of the reporter, and it would be published in the bound volume, thereby becoming a "reported" decision. Only reported decisions had precedential value, and only reported decisions constituted mandatory authority.

Many lawyers still use the term *reported* to refer to decisions that constitute mandatory authority. Because most decisions are published, or "reported," somewhere, however, the better term is *precedential*. The court issuing the decision still determines whether it will be reported and, thus, mandatory. If it is not reported, we may refer to it as *nonprecedential authority*.

In Chapter 11, we will tell you about how to determine whether you may cite a nonprecedential authority at all. The rules vary by jurisdiction. Here, the focus is on the persuasive value of authority that is not mandatory.

As you might guess, a federal district court is likely to find a nonprecedential decision from the court of appeals in its circuit to be quite persuasive. It provides an indication of how a panel of circuit judges viewed a rule or applied that rule to a set of facts. In the absence of a precedential, or mandatory, decision from that same court, the nonprecedential decision is a reasonable basis on which to formulate an educated guess about how the same court would decide another similar case. It is not foolproof, however, and when possible, you should avoid relying solely on nonprecedential authority.

The most obvious drawback to relying on nonprecedential authority is that it is nonprecedential. No one, including the judges who issued the decision, is obligated to follow it. You may be able to gain some additional confidence in the nonprecedential authority, however, if other indicators suggest that it is a reliable indication of the likely view of the court.

One possible indicator of reliability is a series of similar nonprecedential decisions from the same court. Suppose you find that several panels of the same court of appeals have issued nonprecedential decisions in which they have interpreted or applied a rule in the same fashion. The consistency within that series of opinions should give you greater confidence that they are a reliable indicator of what the court would do in a precedential decision. On the other hand, your confidence will be weakened by nonprecedential decisions from the same court in which the rule is explained or applied differently.

Another source of confidence in the reliability of a nonprecedential decision may be consistent precedential decisions from other courts, especially in the absence of contrary authority. For example, assume that your circuit court has issued only nonprecedential decisions on the interpretation of a particular federal statute. If those decisions are consistent with the precedential decisions of every other circuit court that has considered the issue, you may be more comfortable relying on the nonprecedential decision from your circuit.

One final indicator that a nonprecedential decision is likely to be a reliable indicator of the court's view is citations of that decision in precedential decisions from the same court. Sometimes, a court will cite its own nonprecedential decisions in later cases. If the court has done so, it is signaling its satisfaction with at least one aspect of that nonprecedential decision. The same court could later disagree, of course, with some other aspect of that same nonprecedential decision, but it is slightly less likely to do so after having cited it for some purpose.

In the end, nonprecedential authority will never be mandatory. Mandatory authority will always be preferable. In the absence of mandatory authority, however, a nonprecedential decision may be your best source for a prediction of what a court is likely to do with your case.

7. Two Other Important Considerations

A rule is not mandatory or persuasive authority if it is no longer valid law. Legislatures can amend, repeal, and supersede statutes, and courts can find them unconstitutional. Courts can reverse lower courts' decisions. Later decisions can specifically or effectively overrule earlier ones. Never rely on a source for a rule until you have ascertained that it is still *good law*.

You can ascertain that a statute is still good law by making sure you have the most recent version of the statute and that you have verified that no court has invalidated the statute. You can verify that a case is still good law in two ways. First, enter the relevant citation into what is called a "citator" such as Shepard's or KeyCite, on the computer research databases. Second, search the key terms from the law and the facts to make sure courts have not implicitly overruled the rule that you want the court to apply. See Chapter 7 for more information.

The principle of *stare decisis* may also come into play in your assessment of the likelihood that a court will consider another court's decision to be persuasive. In American jurisprudence, *stare decisis* is the principle that a settled issue should remain settled. If any court, whether it is a trial court, the Supreme Court, or a circuit court, decides a matter in one case, it has the power to decide differently, or to overturn its own precedent, if a similar issue comes before it again later. Respect for *stare decisis*, however, causes most courts to hesitate before overturning earlier decisions. Courts value stability and predictability in the law. So, in assessing how likely a court is to deviate from its own decisions, you should take the principle of *stare decisis* into consideration and understand that a court may, but is unlikely to, deviate from settled law.

B. WHERE DO I FIND LEGAL AUTHORITY?

When we talk about *finding the law*, we're generally talking about finding the *rules* that govern your client's situation. You have to find the rules because lawyers generally engage in rule-based reasoning. The rules come in a variety of packages. This chapter will discuss some of the different kinds of rules that lawyers use and how to find those rules when researching.

1. Rules from Statutes

The most obvious place to find legal rules is in statutes. Statutes are written as rules, with the expectation that the affected persons within the relevant jurisdiction will follow those rules. The same is true of constitutional provisions and regulations. All three of these kinds of rules are *enacted laws* that are put into place by legislative bodies or by executive agencies acting with the authority of those legislative bodies. For example, here is a rule about obeying red lights:

> (c) Steady Red Indication
>
> (1) Vehicular traffic facing a steady red signal alone shall stop at (a) a clearly marked stop line, (b) if no stop line, before entering the crosswalk on the near side of the intersection, or (c) if no stop line or crosswalk, before entering the intersection. Traffic must remain standing until an indication to proceed is shown except as provided in subsections (c)(2) and (3) of these ordinances.

If any type of enacted law applies to an issue you are analyzing, you should discuss rules that come from the enacted law first, before moving on to other types of rules.

2. Rules from Cases; Synthesizing Rules by Looking at Facts

In addition to rules based on enacted law, lawyers look to common law rules, or rules that courts have articulated and developed when deciding specific cases. This kind of law is also known as *case law*. Common law rules develop in a few different ways. Often, courts will articulate a rule based on the facts and issues of the case before them or adapted from earlier versions of common law rules, as in this case about a dispute between a landlord and a tenant:

> First, we must determine whether the lease expired in October 2007 or remained in effect on the date the Carbajals gave notice of exercise of the option [to continue the lease]. The general common law rule provides that "[a] tenant who remains in possession of the premises after termination of the lease occupies 'wrongfully' and is said to have a tenancy at sufferance." *Bockelmann v. Marynick*, 788 S.W.2d 569, 571 (Tex. 1990). "Under the common law holdover rule, a landlord may elect to treat a tenant holding over as either a trespasser or as a tenant holding under the terms of the original lease." *Id.* We look to the terms of the lease to determine whether the terms of the lease continue in the event of a holdover tenancy. *See id.* at 571-72.[2]

Sometimes, courts articulate common law rules that they have adopted from another source such as a law review article or, as in this case, a Restatement of the Law:

> Under Indiana's common law, Dollahan was required to establish three elements to recover on a theory of negligence: (1) a duty on the part of City to conform its conduct to a standard of care arising from its relationship with the Dollahan; (2) a failure of City to conform its conduct to the requisite standard of care required by the relationship; and (3) an injury to Dollahan proximately caused by City's breach. *Mayfield v. Levy Co.*, 833 N.E.2d 501, 505 (Ind. Ct. App. 2005).
>
> Indiana has adopted the Restatement (Second) of Torts, which provides:
>
> > A possessor of land is subject to liability for physical harm caused to his invitees by a condition on the land if, but only if, he
> >
> > (a) knows or by the exercise of reasonable care would discover the condition, and should realize it involves an unreasonable risk of harm to such invitees, and
> >
> > (b) should expect that they will not discover or realize the danger, or will fail to protect themselves against it, and
> >
> > (c) fails to exercise reasonable care to protect them against the danger.
>
> Restatement (Second) of Torts § 343.[3]

---

2. *Taylor v. Carbajal*, 304 S.W.3d 585, 588 (Tex. App. 2010).
3. *City of South Bend v. Dollahan*, 918 N.E.2d 343, 352 (Ind. App. 2009).

However, in other cases, courts make decisions without explicitly articulating the rule on which the courts are relying. They may do this when they articulate a rule that governed similar situations in the past and then issue a decision that is inconsistent with that old rule. A court may or may not articulate the "new" rule that it is implicitly using to make its decision.

Part of your job as a lawyer is to identify rules that courts have used or relied on, even if they have not stated the rules explicitly. Doing so may require that you read between the lines of court opinions in order to reason by analogy or by induction or deduction. First, look at what the court did: what did it hold as to a particular issue? How did it apply the rule to the facts? Next, look at the rule or the case that the court said it relied on. If possible, look at the similarities and differences between the *legally significant* facts of the old case and the facts of the case you are reading. If the outcome is the same, what connections can you draw between the facts of the case you are reading and the old case? If the outcome is different, what differences can you see?

In a 2005 Florida case, for example, the court analyzed whether a landlord had a duty to warn a tenant about possible dangers posed by another tenant in the complex.[4] The court analyzed the cases cited by the parties; many of the cases involved situations in which someone had been injured by a third party, and the victim had sued a person who had prior knowledge that the third party might be dangerous. The court looked at these cases and noted analogies and distinctions between the knowledge that each party had before the incidents occurred. It also noted analogies and distinctions based on the relationships between and among the parties within the cited cases and the case before the court:

> The major difference between the cases cited by Regal Trace and T.W. and K.W. centers on superior knowledge. In *Gross* and *Shurben*, the university and the rental car company were aware of the potential for criminality at the internship site and on the streets, while the students and tourists were not. This fact distinguishes *Attardo*, because the theory of negligence in that case related to inadequate lighting and security, and not to any claim of superior knowledge of foreseeable criminal activity. *Adika* is also distinguishable on this basis, because although the claim was partly about failure to warn of ocean conditions which the hotel would be more aware of than tourists, it was determined that the hotel had in

4. *T.W. v. Regal Trace, Ltd.*, 908 So. 2d 499, 501 (Fla. App. 2005).

> fact verbally warned the tourists of the dangerous conditions. *K.M.* is more difficult to distinguish because it most certainly addresses a scenario in which the employer had superior knowledge that one employee who was babysitting for another had a criminal record of sexual battery on a minor, a fact that the employee-mother did not know. Despite this fact and the existence of a special relationship regarding the claims of the employee (although not the child), this Court found that the employer did not have a duty to protect or warn against the eventual sexual assault occurring off the premises. Given this, there remains a key distinction between *K.M.* on the one hand and *Gross* and *Shurben* on the other hand: a university is in the business of arranging internships for students and a rental agency is in the business of providing cars to tourists, but a grocery store is not in the business of arranging for babysitting services between employees. As such, the course of the relationship in *K.M.* does not give rise to a duty, although because of the activity involved rather than its location.[5]

Note how the court analyzed the similarities and differences between *K.M.* and *Gross* and *Shurben*. As noted above, in all three of those cases some sort of special relationship existed between the plaintiff and the defendant. In *Gross* and *Shurben*, the plaintiff was harmed in a situation that related to the special relationship between the plaintiffs and the defendants—within the internship and while in the rented car, respectively. In *K.M.*, however, the defendant's special relationship to the plaintiff did not reach the situation in which the victim was harmed: the victim worked for the defendant, but the victim was not harmed while at work. Accordingly, the court determined that the duty arises not based on the location of the harm alone or on the relationship of the parties alone, but on whether a special relationship existed *and* whether the harm occurred in a situation that was directly tied to the special relationship between the plaintiff and the defendant.

The kind of reasoning that the Florida court used in the paragraphs above is often referred to as *rule synthesis*. The court looked at several decisions and noted the ways in which the facts were consistent and inconsistent with each other and with the situation before it. The court was, in essence, articulating a rule that provides that a person who has a certain legally recognizable relationship to another person (such as a landlord's relationship to a tenant) may owe a duty to warn that person of a harm that is appropriately connected to that relationship in both location and activity.

5. *Id.* at 505.

3. Synthesizing by Looking at How Authorities Have Articulated the Rule

Lawyers must often use rule synthesis. Frequently, when doing research, you will find some cases that address one facet of your fact situation and others that address another facet. Similarly, your client's case may be governed by a statute, but certain terms within the statute (e.g., the term "operate" in a drunk driving statute) may have been interpreted by the courts. Your job will be to read the law—whether the law exists in cases alone or some combination of enacted law and cases—and to identify the rule implicit in the relationship between and among those authorities.

When synthesizing a rule from two or more sources, it is important to look at both the facts (in cases in which the rule has been applied) and at the law (i.e., the language in the rule itself, as articulated by courts, legislatures, or both). The rule synthesized in the example above depended heavily on looking at the facts that resulted in specific holdings. But sometimes the language of the rule is just as important.

For example, State's drunk driving statute makes it a crime for a person to "operate" a vehicle while intoxicated. Presume that your client, Biff Borer, got drunk at a party. When he tried to drive home, his friend Heidi Wright confiscated his keys and drove him home. Unfortunately, Biff sat in the front seat. While Heidi was driving, Biff grabbed the wheel several times, trying to steer. Heidi was able to keep control of the car, but their struggle caused the car to weave into the wrong lane several times. Fortunately, the road was wide and no other cars were anywhere nearby, so they did not crash. Heidi was pulled over by the police. Heidi appeared to be sober (and was sober), and when the officer asked what had happened, she told him the truth. The officer then conducted field sobriety tests on Heidi and Biff. Biff failed the tests, and the officer charged him with operating a vehicle while under the influence of alcohol.

When you finished researching Biff's situation, you had five relevant sources. The first two sources were the statutes governing OMVI (operation of a motor vehicle while intoxicated), which provide in relevant part as follows:

> § 2511.19(A)(1): "No person shall operate any vehicle . . . within this state, if, at the time of the operation . . . [t]he person is under the influence of alcohol."
>
> § 2511.01(DD): "As used in this chapter of the state code . . . 'Operate' means to cause or have caused movement."

The other three sources were cases, summarized as follows:

State v. Bondsman **(2012)**
Both defendant-passenger and defendant-driver had been drinking all afternoon. The facts show that as they drove away from a party, the passenger grabbed the steering wheel and turned it to the right. The driver tried to steer back to the left, but lost control of the vehicle. The vehicle hit a guardrail, then a light post and street sign, before coming to rest nose-end in a ditch. Both driver and passenger were charged with operation of a vehicle while intoxicated. In finding the passenger guilty, the court said as follows:

> The plain meaning of § 2511.01(DD) does not limit the state to a single prosecution for each alcohol-related accident but permits two or more impaired occupants to be "operating" the same vehicle, at the same time, when their combined actions caused movement of the vehicle. Under the undisputed facts, Bondsman's conduct caused movement of the vehicle and the driver's loss of control when Bondsman grabbed the steering wheel and caused the vehicle to crash. Accordingly, her conduct fit within the unambiguous statutory definition of "operate" in § 2511.01(DD).

State v. Newhart **(2007)**
Drunken passenger and sober driver were in the front seat of a car. The drunken passenger grabbed the wheel, and the sober driver lost control of the vehicle, crashing it into a low wall on the side of the road and narrowly avoiding several pedestrians. In finding the drunken passenger guilty of OMVI, the court said as follows:

> The statutory definition of "operate" in § 2511.01(DD) is unambiguous and broad enough to encompass Newhart's actions. From the word's plain meaning, "operate" includes causing dangerous movement of a vehicle, and it is not limited to drivers. Certainly, this definition can encompass a person in the vehicle whose conduct causes the driver to crash a vehicle by grabbing the steering wheel and changing the vehicle's direction of movement.

State v. Buster **(2014)**
Police officer pulls a vehicle over after observing it run a red light, speed up and slow down, and bump into the curb twice. Defendant driver is intoxicated and is alone in the vehicle. The driver is found guilty of violating the OMVI statute.

In synthesizing these five sources, you learn that people can be convicted if they are "operating" a vehicle while intoxicated. *Bondsman* and *Newhart* indicate that intoxicated passengers, as well as intoxicated drivers, can be convicted of operation. In both of those cases, intoxicated passengers grabbed the wheel of a car and caused the car to crash. If you focused too much on the facts under which those defendants were found guilty, you might synthesize the rule as follows:

> *Inaccurate Rule Synthesis*
> An intoxicated passenger can be convicted of "operating" a vehicle in violation of the OMVI statute if he or she grabs the steering wheel of a vehicle and causes that vehicle to crash.

That rule synthesis would be ineffective because the fact that each vehicle crashed was probably not material, or legally significant, even though each court mentioned it as part of its rule application. Two of your sources can clarify that crashing the vehicle is not necessary for a conviction. First, § 2511.01(DD), the statute that defines "operate," provides only that the person must "cause movement" of a vehicle. It does not mention any consequences other than the movement itself.

If you were still uncertain after consulting this statute, you might consult other cases in which the court found people guilty of "operating" in violation of § 2511.19. When you consulted the *Buster* case, you saw that the defendant in that case was found guilty even though his vehicle never crashed, doing nothing more harmful than bumping into a curb. After consulting these sources, you would revise your rule synthesis as follows:

> *More Accurate Rule Synthesis*
> An intoxicated passenger can be convicted of "operating" a vehicle in violation of the OMVI statute if he or she grabs the steering wheel of a vehicle and causes that vehicle to move in any way.

The statute does not use the words "in any way," but your synthesis does so because the sources indicate that any type of movement of the vehicle is sufficient to establish operation.

Accordingly, to conduct effective rule synthesis, consult the language of the relevant statute(s) and rule(s), the facts of relevant cases, and the results of those cases.

Before you can use rule synthesis, of course, you have to find the sources that you will synthesize the rules from. In the exercise below, we have found the sources for you. Later, we will talk about how to find the law for yourself.

C. EXERCISES

Exercise 6.1

Assume that your client believes that her employer discriminated against her in violation of the Americans with Disabilities Act (the "ADA"). If you were to file suit, the action would be in the United States District Court for the District of Nevada (which is in the Ninth Circuit). An issue in the case will be whether your client was *qualified* for the job she sought. Her employer discharged her on the apparent belief that she was not qualified because she could not perform one essential function of her job: occasionally lifting objects weighing ten pounds. But her personal physician had certified that your client could lift up to ten pounds safely as of the date when her employer discharged her from her position.

Eighteen months after her employer discharged her, your client saw a vocational therapist as she prepared to apply for disability benefits. The vocational therapist opined that your client could lift only five pounds as of the date on which the therapist examined her.

You want to know whether a court would consider the vocational therapist's opinion as evidence of your client's ability to lift up to ten pounds *as of the date when her employer discharged her*. You have found the following authorities. Review them. Then, synthesize a rule for the admissibility of the vocational therapist's opinion.

Federal Rule of Evidence 401

Evidence is relevant if:

(a) it has any tendency to make a fact more or less probable than it would be without the evidence; and

(b) the fact is of consequence in determining the action.

Federal Rule of Evidence 403

The court may exclude relevant evidence if its probative value is substantially outweighed by a danger of one or more of the following: unfair prejudice, confusing the issues, misleading the jury, undue delay, wasting time, or needlessly presenting cumulative evidence.

***Cleveland v. Policy Management Systems Corporation*, 526 U.S. 795 (1999)**

The Supreme Court held that a person may pursue an ADA claim and another type of disability claim provided that the person can provide a reasonable explanation for any inconsistencies between the two claims. An ADA claim, in which a plaintiff claims to be able to perform the essential functions of a job, is not inherently inconsistent with a different claim in which the same person claims to be disabled from working.

***Anthony v. Trax International Corporation*, 955 F.3d 1123 (9th Cir. 2020)**
The plaintiff claimed total disability and later sued her employer under the ADA, claiming that she was qualified for the position from which her employer had discharged her. The employer introduced evidence suggesting that the plaintiff had not been qualified for her position, even while she was employed, because she lacked the degree required for the job. The Ninth Circuit held that the plaintiff could not prove that she was qualified, for ADA purposes, at the time of her discharge.

***Bowers v. National Collegiate Athletic Association*, 475 F.3d 524 (3d Cir. 2007)**
The plaintiff sued under the ADA and claimed to be *qualified*. The defendant learned of illegal drug abuse by the plaintiff years after the alleged ADA violation and argued, on that basis, that the plaintiff could not prove that he was qualified for ADA purposes. The Third Circuit held that the issue in an ADA case is whether the plaintiff was qualified at the time of the alleged discrimination. The court reasoned that a person may be qualified and later become unqualified and concluded that evidence of illegal drug use at a time after the alleged discrimination was irrelevant to the ADA claim.

***Smith v. Clark County School District.*, 727 F.3d 950, 957 (9th Cir. 2013)**
The plaintiff sued her employer under the ADA after the employer insisted on transferring her to a position that she could not perform because of her physical limitations. The plaintiff claimed that she was qualified for and could have continued to perform her previous job. After the employer refused to keep the plaintiff in the job for which she alleged she was qualified, the plaintiff applied for benefits for total disability. The employer argued that the plaintiff's representations in her application precluded her from proving that she was qualified for any job with the employer. The Ninth Circuit, applying the reasoning of the Supreme Court in *Cleveland*, held that

the plaintiff could still prove that she was qualified, for ADA purposes, by explaining the apparent discrepancies to a jury. The court observed, specifically, that evidence of a person's physical qualifications at one time do not necessarily prove the same person's physical qualifications at a different time.

Exercise 6.2

Review the following case summaries from the fictitious state of Vanita. First, articulate the rule that each case suggests about when a landowner has a duty to provide security to people on his or her property. When you are done, synthesize the rules to create one rule that encapsulates Vanita's current law on the topic.

Rodriguez v. Slade **[Vanita Supreme Court, 1948]**
Rodriguez, a tenant of Slade's apartment complex, was assaulted in the courtyard of the complex by a person from outside the complex. The neighborhood had no known history of criminal activity. Rodriguez sued Slade for failure to provide adequate security. The court held that as a basic principle of law, a property owner has no duty to protect one on his or her premises from criminal attack by a third person. Even though one's negligence may be a cause in fact of another's loss, he or she will not be liable if an independent, intervening, and unforeseeable criminal act also causes the loss. Slade has no duty to Rodriguez in this case.

Quirrell v. State **[Vanita Appellate Court, 1969]**
Quirrell, a student at State U, is abducted and killed while returning from a night class. Parents sue the Board of Regents for failure to provide adequate security. Neighborhood has a history of criminal activity, but there have been no incidents on campus. Court holds that State U is immune due to sovereign immunity, but notes that the school could have been held liable because the criminal activity was foreseeable. Court noted that criminal history of campus neighborhood constituted actual or constructive notice that criminal activity on campus was foreseeable.

Regis v. Lupin **[Vanita Appellate Court, 1988]**
Tenant Regis was assaulted in her apartment complex by an intruder and sues Lupin, the landowner, for failure to provide

adequate security. Neighborhood has a well-known history of criminal activity, including assaults and burglaries in surrounding apartment complexes, but there has never been an assault in the plaintiff's complex before this incident. Court holds that Lupin has no duty to protect from unforeseeable criminal activity by third persons, noting that it must be borne in mind that a landowner is not an insurer of the safety of his or her tenants and is not required to take precautions against a sudden attack from a third person that he or she has no reason to anticipate. A landowner's duty to protect an invitee from a criminal act arises only when he or she has actual or constructive knowledge of similar criminal actions committed on his or her premises. Because the other assaults in the neighborhood were not committed on the landowner's premises, the criminal activity was not foreseeable. Thus, Lupin had no duty to protect Regis from this assault.

In general terms, a *licensee* is a person who comes on land for his or her own purposes, and not for the economic benefit of the landowner. An *invitee* is a person who is on the premises of another for purposes in which the landowner has an economic interest.

Bueller v. Rooney **[Vanita Supreme Court, 1993]**
Bueller is waiting for Parker in the lobby of Parker's apartment building. He plans to ask Parker for a date when she returns from work. Bueller is assaulted in the lobby. He sues the landowner, Rooney, for failure to provide adequate security. There have been previous assaults in the neighborhood, but not within Rooney's apartment building. Court holds that Rooney owes no duty to Bueller because Bueller is a licensee, not an invitee.

Arabella v. Hagrid **[Vanita Supreme Court, 1996]**
Arabella, tenant, is assaulted in the laundry room of her apartment complex and sues landlord, Hagrid, for failure to provide adequate security. The complex's laundry room, like other common areas of the apartment complex, is not protected by locked doors. The complex's neighborhood is known as a high-crime neighborhood; two months earlier, a tenant had been assaulted in the apartment complex across the street, and several burglaries and assaults had occurred in apartment buildings on the next block within past year. The court held that Hagrid was on notice that criminal activity was foreseeable and thus had a duty to Arabella to provide security from this type of foreseeable criminal activity.

Efta v. Farb **[Vanita Appellate Court, 2005]**
Tenant Efta was assaulted in apartment building's common area. Efta sues Farb, the landowner, for failure to provide adequate security. Several burglaries had occurred in the building over the past two years, but never an assault. Court finds that the assault was foreseeable. Court states that a landowner has a duty to protect tenants from foreseeable harm and that previous burglary on the premises made an assault foreseeable because a burglar, when surprised, may turn into an assailant.

Recall and Review

1. A source that produces or contains rules that are The Law in a given place is a source of ___________ authority.
2. True or False: Federal district courts (trial courts) are required to follow applicable decisions of the United States courts of appeals for any circuit.
3. True or False: If a federal court is interpreting Arkansas law, it must follow applicable decisions of the Arkansas Supreme Court.
4. Materials such as treatises and legal encyclopedias, which are not The Law anywhere, are known as __________ authorities.
5. A decision that is published online but not published in an official reporter is known as a non_______ authority.
6. True or False: Statutes, constitutional provisions, and regulations are all types of enacted law.
7. A Virginia state court contemplates the meaning of the word "child" in a Virginia statute. Which of the following authorities are mandatory (if good law that addresses the question)?

   a. the Virginia state constitution
   b. a decision of United States Court of Appeals for the Fourth Circuit
   c. a Virginia statute
   d. a federal statute
   e. a decision of the United States Supreme Court

8. A United States District Court contemplates the meaning of the word "child" in a Virginia statute. Which of the following authorities are mandatory (if good law that addresses the question)?
   a. the Virginia state constitution
   b. a decision of United States Court of Appeals for the Fourth Circuit
   c. a Virginia statute
   d. a federal statute
   e. a decision of the United States Supreme Court

9. A Virginia state court contemplates the meaning of the world "child" in a federal statute. Which of the following authorities are mandatory (if good law that addresses the question)?
   a. the Virginia state constitution
   b. a decision of United States Court of Appeals for the Fourth Circuit
   c. a Virginia statute
   d. a federal statute
   e. a decision of the United States Supreme Court

10. A United States District Court contemplates the meaning of the word "child" in a federal statute. Which of the following authorities are mandatory (if good law that addresses the question)?
    a. the Virginia state constitution
    b. a decision of United States Court of Appeals for the Fourth Circuit
    c. a Virginia statute
    d. a federal statute
    e. a decision of the United States Supreme Court

CHAPTER 7

HOW DO I FIND LEGAL AUTHORITY?

Planning and Recording Research

The short answer to "How do I find the rules that govern my client's case?" is research. A longer answer follows. Although this text is not meant to teach you details about how legal research works, a few practical guidelines can help you to conduct your research more effectively. You must develop both the ability to find relevant authorities and the ability to recognize that the authorities are relevant.

The three basic steps in the research process are most simply expressed as follows: (1) formulate the research question, incorporating as much as you know about the relevant area of law and the legally significant facts; (2) learn how your jurisdiction treats the relevant area of law; and (3) determine whether mandatory authority answers your question directly. If mandatory authority does not answer your question directly, your plan will go to a fourth step: look for the most helpful persuasive authority. Along the way, keep track of where your efforts have taken you and what you have found there. Now, let's slow down and go through those steps in much greater detail.

A. FRAMING THE RESEARCH QUESTION

There are many ways to begin researching a legal issue. One method is to analyze the facts that you have at hand and begin to identify possible search words and possible legally significant categories.[1] Then,

1. *See, e.g.*, Mary Barnard Ray & Jill J. Ramsfield, *Legal Writing: Getting It Right and Getting It Written* 258-62 (2d ed., West 1993) (citing Christopher Wren & Jill R. Wren, *The Legal Research Manual: A Game Plan for Legal Research and Analysis* (2d ed., Adams & Ambrose 1986)).

create "research questions" based on what you know about the client's situation so far.

Like all statements of legal issues, your research questions should be focused on how the relevant law applies to the legally significant facts. A popular structure for these questions is the so-called under-does-when structure.[2] The "under" part of the question identifies the law that governs the legal issue, the "does" part (which won't necessarily begin with the word *does*) identifies the narrow, yes-or-no legal question that you are trying to answer (whether it is about liability, guilt, or some other legal consequence, legal status, or form of legal responsibility), and the "when" part (which might start with *include* instead of *when*) identifies the legally significant facts that relate to the legal issue. Thus, a format for the research question is "Under relevant law, can legal status result when legally significant facts exist?" Put another way, you could ask, "Under relevant law, does legal status include this set of legally significant facts?"

Before you write your research question(s), you may want to do a quick search to give yourself some general understanding of the area of law. Often the best way to begin researching a new legal issue is by looking for secondary authorities such as law review articles or legal encyclopedias. If you are uncertain about the correct rule or even area of law, reading secondary sources can help focus your search, and it can even help you find good phrases-that-pay to use as search terms. Sometimes Google can be a good place to begin, because many law firms put short essays on their websites about legal issues that they commonly work on. You should never cite these types of authorities (just as you should rarely cite any secondary authority), but reading them can help give you useful background information on the relevant law and may help you craft your research question(s).

After you have identified your research questions, begin your research, looking for authorities that are relevant to the governing law, relevant to the "legal status" (i.e., to the issue), and relevant to the facts. We use the word *relevant* rather than *legally significant* on purpose. It is best if you do not try to look for cases that are *identical* to the fact scenario you have before you. Instead, look for cases that are similar categorically in legally significant ways.

Many legal writers use a theoretical device called the *abstraction ladder* to help them identify relevant categories. The abstraction ladder

2. *See, e.g., id.* at 243-44; Laurel Currie Oates, Anne M. Enquist & Kelly Kunsch, *The Legal Writing Handbook* 118-23 (2d ed., Aspen 1998). Although your research questions may be similar in format to questions presented, you should not expect that the research questions will be identical to the formal question presented.

is based on the concept that everything in the world can be thought of at various levels of abstraction or concreteness.

First, let's define our terms. The word *abstract* has several meanings and is sometimes hard for people to understand. In this sense, art is abstract if two people could see different things in the same painting. A word is abstract if two people could perceive two (or more than two) different meanings from the same word.

For example, if someone asked you what you did before you came in to school or work this morning, you might answer, somewhat abstractly, "I ate." Different people might conjure up different mental images of what kind of food you had from your rather abstract reply. You might be a little less abstract and say, "I had breakfast." Even with this description, some people might picture yogurt, while others would think of bacon and eggs. Or you could be a little more concrete and say, "I had some cereal." Or even more concrete and say, "I had some Cheerios." Or you might be even more concrete and say, "I had one and one quarter cups of multi-grain Cheerios and three-quarters of a cup of skim milk." Thus, the words you use to describe something can be placed on a ladder between the extremes of "most abstract" and "most concrete." You might think of the ladder growing wider as it grows taller; the more abstract something is, the more other things share the same rung.

Moving in the other direction, from most concrete to most abstract, you can think of a cow by thinking of Bossy, a particular cow. Or you can be a little more abstract and think of a Holstein. Or you can be a little more abstract and just think of cows in general. Or you could move up the abstraction ladder—or several abstraction ladders—and think of farm animals, or mammals, or farm property, or assets, or wealth. At the top of this (and every) abstraction ladder, you can think of a cow as a "thing."[3]

This concept is important to legal analysis because abstract reasoning helps lawyers to identify analogous authorities. Once you recognize that facts and issues can be put into broader, more abstract categories, you may be better able to see legal similarities between your client's situation and relevant authorities. Very frequently, the tension in a legal issue is about whether a rule applies to a broad category that includes a certain person, thing, or event, or whether the rule applies to a narrower group that excludes a certain person, thing, or event. You can use the abstraction ladder to identify both legal and factual categories that may be significant to your analysis.

3. S. I. Hayakawa, *Language in Thought and Action* 155 (4th ed., HBJ 1978) (discussing the abstraction ladder in general and the cow example in particular).

The good news is that if you move up the abstraction ladder high enough, you can almost always identify some connection between two sets of facts. For example, you could analogize a cow to a horse because they are both farm animals. Or you could analogize a cow to a wheat field because they are both income-producing property for farmers. You could even analogize a cow to a tractor because they are both farm property. Or you could analogize a cow to a pet dog because both are mammals.

The bad news is that after asking whether there is an analogy, you must then ask whether the analogy is legally significant. For example, if a rule governs licensing of pet dogs and cats, that rule will probably not apply to cows on a dairy farm even though cows, dogs, and cats are all mammals. If, however, a common law rule governed additives to cow feed, you might be able to argue that this rule should also apply to fertilizers on wheat fields because both cow feed and wheat field fertilizer may affect food that consumers purchase. One hint about using the abstraction ladder: try to go "up" (i.e., to a more abstract level) only as far as you need to go in order to find a legally significant analogy and no farther. For example, a goat and a cow are both mammals, but their more legally significant connection in most situations could well be lower on the abstraction ladder: They are both animals that produce milk that may be sold for human consumption.

Thus, before you begin your research, look at your client's situation and at your research question(s) and decide what types of authorities you're looking for. For example, if your client were a tenant who wanted to sue the landlord of her apartment building, your first stop might be to look for cases about apartment building landlords. But you might also want to broaden your horizons and look for landlords of rental houses or office space. You might even look for cases and statutes describing duties that building owners have toward people who use their buildings or for cases describing duties based on "special relationships" between parties.

Broadening your horizons in this way can make the research process easier because you will be more attuned to the cases that are relevant and helpful even though they are not 100 percent on point. By being more realistic about the potential results of your research, you will be more likely to recognize relevant authorities.

In addition to assessing whether authorities are relevant, you must decide whether they are *valid*. Because each case is decided based on the legal rules within its jurisdiction and on the facts and issues unique to it, the validity of an authority can vary depending on both the court you are arguing to and the facts of the case before the court. Therefore, when assessing the validity of authorities during your research, keep several different aspects of authorities in mind.

1. The Relevance of the Facts

First, consider what types of facts might be relevant, and look for authorities that relate to those types of facts. Some cases with similar facts will be easy to recognize, but be sure to consider the different levels of similarity. This is where the lessons of the abstraction ladder become important: thinking about your facts at various levels of abstraction can help you to recognize facts from other cases whose relevance is not apparent. For example, if you are arguing about the validity of a drunk driving checkpoint, you might be able to compare it to cases in which someone has challenged the use of a metal detector. Thinking more abstractly, you would see that both the checkpoint and the metal detector are set up to detect things that might affect safety—drunk drivers and weapons—and in both situations, those affected may be able to choose to avoid the situation: by not driving on the street with the checkpoint or by not going into the building.

Another technique to use is to look at the facts of your client's situation from a few different angles. For example, you should consider (1) the behavior at issue itself, (2) the people or things involved in the behavior, and (3) the context in which the behavior occurs. Each of these facets of the fact situation can help you to identify analogous authorities.

For example, suppose you are defending the decision of a police department to conduct a roadblock to seek information about a recent incident in the community.[4] If you consider the *behavior* at issue, you could look for cases in which citizens were questioned for information about crimes for which they were not the suspect. You might analogize this situation to cases where police go door to door to seek witnesses to a crime. If you consider the *people or things* involved in the behavior, you would be considering police officers, drivers, and cars. This angle might lead you to discover cases in which courts discussed privacy interests in cars or other consensual encounters between police officers and drivers, such as traffic control. Thinking more abstractly, you might also consider analogies to vehicles other than motor vehicles or to police-citizen encounters rather than police-driver encounters.

Finally, if you considered the *context* in which the incident occurred, you might consider the physical location (e.g., urban or rural) or the time of day (e.g., day or night) to look for cases in which courts analyze how different factors can affect whether police have a right to impose burdens on people in order to further an investigation.

It might be helpful to think of each facet or category as a circle in a Venn diagram. The more overlap there is, the more likely the authority

4. *E.g., Illinois v. Lidster,* 540 U.S. 419, 425 (2004).

case will be analogous. For example, a case about drunk driving roadblocks would be more useful (because it would involve drivers and police officers and cars) than a case that is just about police officers asking questions of people on the street.

Thinking more broadly about the facts will help you to be more creative and more successful in your research.

2. The Relevance of the Legal Issues

In addition to considering the facts, consider what types of legal issues might be relevant. If your issue involves the meaning of a statute, for example, cases interpreting the statute would certainly be relevant. But you might also consider looking for cases that have interpreted other statutes that either use similar language or govern similar legal problems. If your client has sued under the Americans with Disabilities Act, for example, you might search for cases interpreting similar aspects of Title VII or the Family and Medical Leave Act. If your client's situation involves a state statute, you might look at how courts have interpreted similar statutes from different states. Some annotated statutes will aid your research by including cross-references to similar statutes in other states.

If your client's situation has several possible sub-issues, authorities that address a sub-issue might be highly relevant for that sub-issue, even though they might not be relevant to every issue in your client's situation. For example, if you are analyzing an issue involving consent to search, you might be able to analogize it to cases involving consent to interrogation.

3. The Relevance of the Sources

Finally, consider what types of sources might be relevant. One obvious source for legal authority is a court of law, but some courts' decisions will have more validity with the reviewing court. The simple rule is that mandatory authorities from the relevant jurisdiction will have the most validity with the court. Thus, if you are writing to an Indiana Court of Appeals, opinions of the Indiana Supreme Court would have high relevance.

If you find no mandatory authority exactly on point, find out how close your jurisdiction has come to the relevant issue and build your argument on those authorities. If the mandatory jurisdiction has not yet considered the precise legal issue in your client's situation, or if nonmandatory decisions are much more on point than any mandatory decisions, you may wish to go beyond cases from the mandatory court. If you do cite to nonmandatory authorities, however, you will increase

For a discussion of whether you may cite a particular nonprecedential (unreported) decision, see Chapter 11.D.

the validity of those authorities if you tie them to mandatory authorities or to rules from mandatory authorities.

Thus, if you find few opinions addressing the issue in your client's situation, and none that are on point, first find the opinions in your mandatory court that are most on point. If you also wish to cite to a nonmandatory authority, begin your discussion of that issue by citing to the mandatory authority. Only then should you cite the nonmandatory authorities, noting perhaps that the courts in those cases are applying the mandatory rule or (for cases from other jurisdictions) are applying rules that are consistent with or very similar to the mandatory rule. Although, as you know, the court is not obligated to follow or adopt the rules from these cases, you have laid groundwork that will help the court to find the authorities valid.

Assessing the possible relevance of the facts, the legal issues, and the sources of the authorities you plan to cite can help you to predict which authorities the court will find more valid and to decide where and how to concentrate your research.

4. What Is a Case That Is "On All Fours"?

Cases that are similar to a client's case are often referred to as *on point* or *on all fours*. A case that is on all fours is highly similar; we would say that a case is on all fours when it is similar as to the law, the facts, the issues, and the jurisdiction. A case does not have to be on all fours to be useful. Of course, the more similar a case is, the more likely it is that a court will follow it or find it to be mandatory authority if it is from a mandatory court. But a court may well adopt a case's reasoning even if it is on point as to only one aspect of the case. Further, *all fours* does not cover all of the facets of a case that you should consider when determining whether a case is useful.

Figure 7.1 illustrates the facets of a case that might make it useful as to a particular issue. The best cases would include the items on all of the brighter daisy petals: the court would be the highest court in your jurisdiction (the mandatory court), and it would be addressing the same issue as the issue that faces your client; the court would apply the rule that you want your court to apply; the phrase-that-pays would be the same; the policy would be the same; and so on.

Figure 7.2 shows how a case can still be useful authority even if it is not identical in every way. Behind every "best" petal is a "good enough" petal that shows how a non-identical case can still be useful. A best case will include detailed reasoning on the relevant decision. A case can still be very useful, however, if the court has made a relevant decision without explaining its reasoning. Remember, you can use a case for something other than its main holding or its main point.

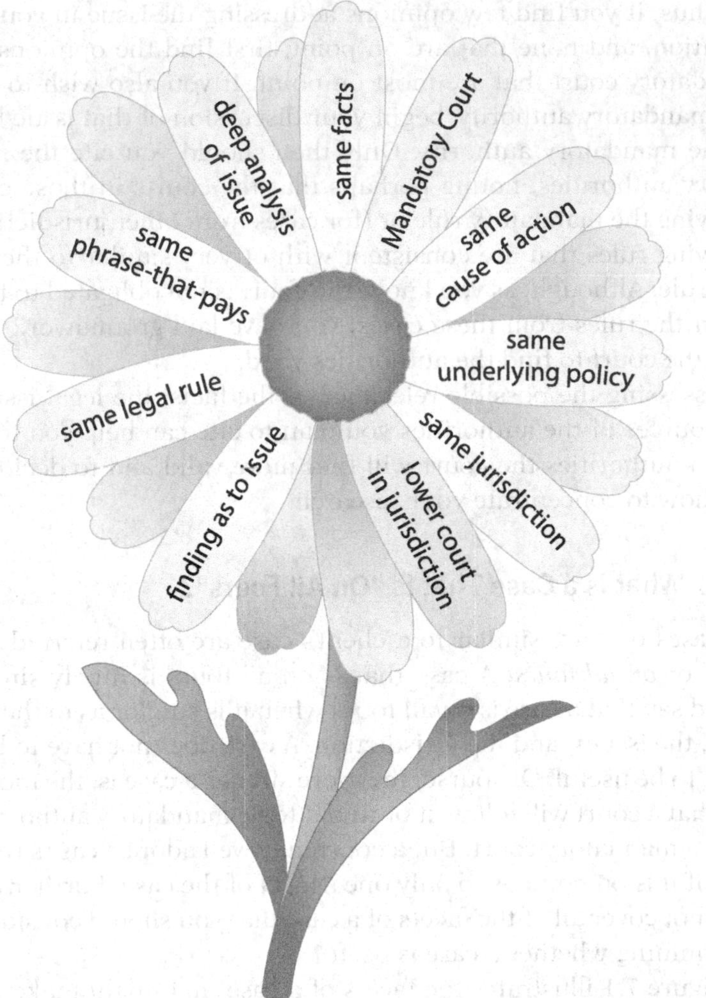

Figure 7.1

Likewise, the best case would include a decision on the merits. A case can be useful, however, even if the court made a decision to reverse or affirm a motion to dismiss due to relevant facts or issues. Even a difference in jurisdiction does not make a case worthless, although, as the illustration shows, a difference in jurisdiction is a more significant difference than the others. In Ohio, for example, courts have used a federal test when analyzing the "causation" element in state wrongful discharge cases based on Ohio's public policy exception to the employment at will doctrine. Ohio courts have used a

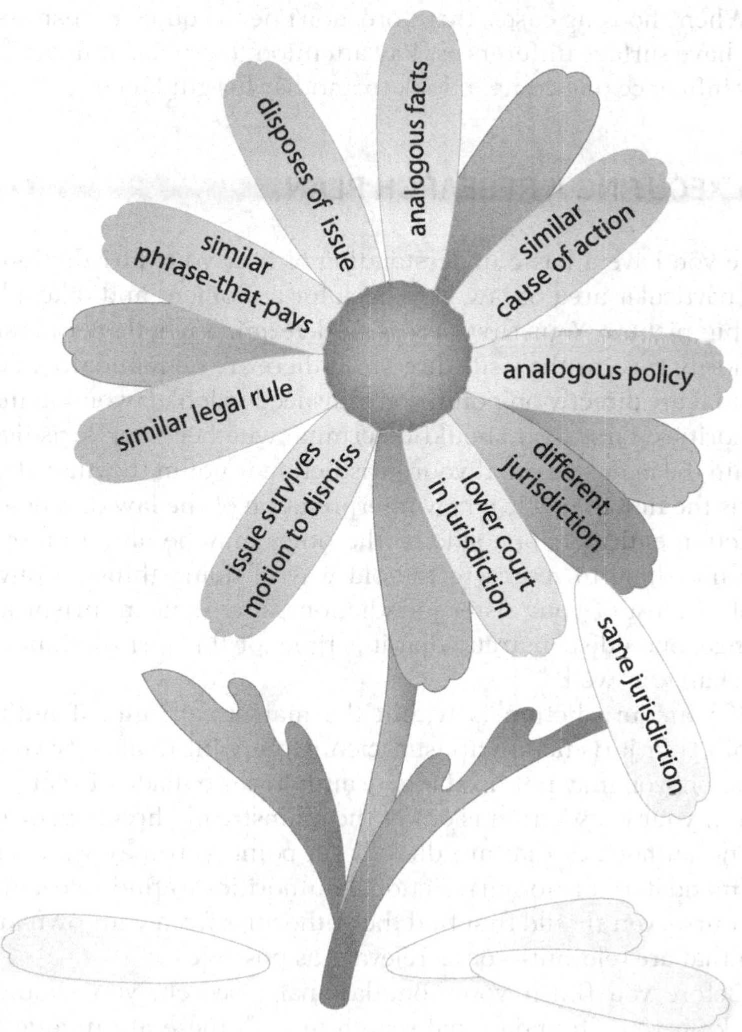

Figure 7.2

burden-shifting test applied by federal courts when determining "causation" in federal Title VII retaliation claims, finding it helpful because both tests analyze whether an improper motive caused the employer's behavior and whether the employer had an alternative proper motive for the behavior.[5] In other words, because the federal cases were using

5. *E.g., Sells v. Holiday Mgt. Ltd.*, 2011-Ohio-5974, ¶ 22 (10th Dist. Franklin No. 11AP-205) (citing *McDonnell Douglas Corp. v. Green*, 411 U.S. 792 (1973)).

a similar rule to analyze the same phrase-that-pays, they were good enough to be useful to those state courts.

When choosing cases, therefore, don't be too quick to dismiss cases that have surface differences. Pay attention to crucial similarities that may influence one court to look to another for guidance.

B. EXECUTING A RESEARCH PLAN

Once you have a basic understanding of how your jurisdiction treats this particular area of law, step back for a moment and take a look at the big picture. Your first task is to determine whether a mandatory authority governs the issue directly. If there are no mandatory authorities that are directly on point, you may need to look beyond mandatory authorities. First, you should determine whether your jurisdiction is within the mainstream. If your jurisdiction is not in the mainstream—if it is the first to tackle a new interpretation of the law or a new cause of action entirely—one side or the other may be able to argue that it is now time to return to the old way of doing things. Conversely, if all or most of your sister jurisdictions have made a jurisprudential change, one side can argue that it is time for this jurisdiction to make the change as well.

If your jurisdiction is within the mainstream and if authorities within your jurisdiction are sufficiently on point to answer your legal question, you may not need to cite authorities outside of that jurisdiction. If your jurisdiction is out of the mainstream, however, or if there are no authorities that are directly on point, you may want to go to nonmandatory or nonjurisdictional authorities to find relevant cases. Of course, you should first find the authorities from your own jurisdiction that are relevant—or as relevant as possible.

Before you finish your foundational research, you should do a check on your "foundational search terms": these are unique statute numbers or legal phrases that will be certain to pull up authorities that are on point, if any exist. They may also pull up authorities that are not useful, but your search process should include a broad search like this to ensure that you have identified the most recent authorities that are on point, as well as the most relevant authorities from the highest court in your jurisdiction.

For example, presume you are researching whether your client can be found guilty of "operating a vehicle" under Ohio's drunk driving statute (Ohio Rev. Code § 4511.19). Your client was found asleep in a parked car. You used the annotated version of the Code, and you think you have found all of the cases. To check your research, you identify a foundational search term, "4511.19." You first plug that term into the

Ohio cases database, and you find out that you have more than 3,000 hits. So you use a field restriction, and you limit your search to cases from the Ohio Supreme Court. This step reduces the number to about 130. You review the cases from within the last two to five years and determine that none of them are on point as to your issue. So you consult your "under-does-when" research question to help narrow your search. Since you are trying to find out how broadly or narrowly the courts have interpreted the statute's word "operate," you then use the "find" or "locate" function of the search engine and search just those 130 or so cases for the term ["operat!"]. If you check each use of the word "operate" or "operation" in the Ohio Supreme Court cases that have also cited § 4511.19, you will be almost certain to find any discussions that are relevant to your analysis. If you wanted to narrow your search a bit, you could decide to use a Boolean search and hunt for ["operat!" w/5 (word or term or interpret! or mean!)].

When we conduct Boolean searches, we first try to conjure a sentence—or a couple of sentences—that would appear in an on-point case. Then we try to identify the unique terms in that sentence or those sentences to help structure our search. In this situation, the ideal sentence we were thinking of was, "In this case, we are asked to interpret the meaning of the word 'operation' as that term is used in Ohio Rev. Code § 4511.19." As it turned out, one of our hits contained this sentence: "The principal issue presented by these cases involves an interpretation of the word 'operate,' as that term is used in R.C. § 4511.19."

By using your foundational search terms in this focused way, you would be able to find the most recent cases in which the court has discussed the issue that you are researching. You may simply find other references to cases you have already found in your initial search, but you are also finding reassurance that your search has been as complete as possible.

Some people say that you are never really "done" with your research, but it is helpful to use a concrete method to measure your progress and update your authorities. One way to check your research is to use a citator like Shepard's or KeyCite (available in the major commercial legal research databases) to check your case authorities. If you put a case citation into a citator, it will show you what cases have cited the cited case, often allowing you to check for cases that have cited certain significant paragraphs from the case you entered. Citators will also tell you if a court has reversed the decision or specifically overruled a rule from the case. Citators have limits, however. If the law has evolved less dramatically, courts may have never explicitly overruled prior decisions. Likewise, if the case you put into the citator is less significant, a court overruling a case with the same rule would not have cited your case.

People call this method of checking research by a variety of names, including "updating," "cite-checking," and "Shepardizing" (because Shepard's was the first commercial citator).

Thus, when updating your research, you need to be sure that you understand the current state of the law as to the relevant legal issue. Be sure that you have identified the most recent decision in your jurisdiction—at any level—in which the court addressed your direct issue and any issue that is tangential to your issue. Identify the same for the highest court in your jurisdiction. In other words, for our drunk driving example, you would want to find the most recent case in which any Ohio court addressed § 4511.19, and the most recent case in which any Ohio court addressed the meaning of the term "operate" as used in that statute. You would want to do the same for the Ohio Supreme Court; that is, identify the most recent case in which that court addressed § 4511.19, and the most recent case (if any) in which it addressed the issue of operating a vehicle. Of course, these cases are not the *only* cases that you should find in your research; in fact, you may not even cite them. Rather, this method is a check to perform near the end of your initial research. If these cases are consistent with the rest of the research you have done, you should feel some confidence that your research is valid.

If you find relevant authorities in your jurisdiction but no authorities that are sufficiently on point, try plugging variations of your foundational search terms into nonmandatory databases and databases outside your jurisdiction. In this way you may be able to discover any 100 percent on-point cases that can serve as persuasive authority. While these cases would be a *source* of analysis rather than an authority for it, courts often find on-point authorities to be persuasive, even when they are from another jurisdiction.

C. SUMMARY OF BASIC RESEARCH STRATEGY

Before you research, get to know the facts of your client's situation by analyzing the facts and identifying the questions that your research must answer. When searching for authorities and assessing their validity, use the abstraction ladder to identify those that address analogous facts and issues. Weigh the validity of the source of the authority, be certain to update your authorities, and take steps to get a complete picture of the relevant area of law. Set a deadline for research that allows you sufficient time to work on the actual writing of your document. The process of writing may reveal gaps in your research; by giving yourself time to write, you create opportunities for finding any research gaps.

D. CREATING A RESEARCH LOG

A research log is a tool that attorneys and law students can use to keep track of their research. Creating a research log allows you to have a written record of every search you have made for answers to the legal questions raised by a set of facts. The log has no official or standard form, and attorneys and law students have developed countless methods for keeping track of their research efforts and their results. The form you develop should be the one that best allows you to document your work and catalog the results for future reference (by you and often by others). These documenting and cataloging functions are the two main reasons for creating a research log.

1. Why Create a Research Log?

If you have a good memory and little experience with conducting research on a complicated set of facts over an extended period of time, you may believe that your memory is up to the challenge of retaining the searches you have performed and the results of those searches. Even perfect recall will not serve some of the purposes for which attorneys create research logs, however. Further, no one can remember every fruitless search in sufficient detail to ensure that future efforts do not repeat past efforts and that the research has followed every potentially productive path.

The immediate users of the research log will be the attorney who has conducted the research and other legal professionals working on the same project. This group needs to efficiently use the time available for research and to have a record of research results. So, the most obvious reason for creating the log is the ability to keep track of searches that have been conducted and their results, whether fruitful or not. The written log is far superior to the memory of the researcher because it is accessible to anyone else who needs to know what the researcher has found.

Another immediate reason for maintaining a log is the ability to quickly pick up a research path that has been pursued to a point short of exhaustion. Sometimes, an attorney or a law student will do a quick search to educate him- or herself about an unfamiliar area of law and to identify some general governing principles. The researcher may abandon that search once those two basic, early-stage goals are achieved. The search may, nevertheless, have identified some viable paths for more detail-oriented research. The log allows the researcher to identify the limitations of the initial search and to highlight ways in which picking up the search at a later stage may yield authority for explanations of governing rules or support for the researcher's conclusions about how those rules will apply to a particular set of facts.

If the researcher will be presenting or discussing the results of research with other legal professionals or with clients, a well-organized log will allow the researcher to identify the research paths taken (and the results found) without having to refer to volumes of printed opinions or to rely exclusively on memory. If the researcher has made a note in the log about why unproductive searches were abandoned as dead ends, questions about whether the researcher has explored particular avenues of research can be easily answered. Perhaps another attorney will look at an abandoned search and see a use for it that the first researcher overlooked. A record of the limitations of that search will allow the second researcher to pick the search back up without duplicating past efforts.

When the writing process begins, the well-organized research log will provide an outline for the analysis and a quick reference tool for useful language or reasoning from authority cases. Without having to return to the authorities themselves, the writer will be able to identify, cite, and discuss the authorities. The carefully constructed research log is, therefore, also a very useful blueprint to the analysis. If the log includes nothing on an essential point, that gap in the legal support for the writer's analysis will be obvious during the research stage rather than when the writer reaches that part of the analysis during the writing process.

Finally, a good research log is a useful tool for the researcher's own future use and for the use of other legal professionals who may encounter similar facts or legal issues. The practice of law requires that lawyers develop efficiencies that benefit both the clients' wallet and the attorney's sanity. No one wants to reinvent the wheel every time a new research project begins. A record of past research in the same, or a closely related, area of law will yield efficiency benefits. In other words, you will thank yourself later for taking great care in the preparation of the research log now.

2. What Should the Research Log Include?

As is true of nearly everything an attorney does, the work on a research log could continue until the end of time. The more detailed and inclusive the log is, the greater the number of potential future uses it will have. The attorney who invests a great deal of thought and time in the creation of the research log will be more efficient in future research and in the writing process.

On the other hand, the creation of the research log is not the end goal. It is like the outline a law student prepares in anticipation of a final exam. The outline is a tool; it is not the end product. The research log should include everything that is, or may become, useful, but it should not become a treatise on the law in the area. Finding the right level of inclusiveness and methods for economically presenting elements of the log will be an ongoing process, and the log for one type of project will differ from the log for another. In general, a good research log should contain two parts: a record of the research process itself and a record of the useful results of that research. You may want to label these parts the "research record" and the "research results," but of course, you should create whatever labels are useful to you.

a. Research record

The researcher's immediate reason for creating the research log, you will recall, is the ability to document research work and catalog the results for future reference by the researcher and often others. The first essential part of the log, therefore, is a record of each search. That record should include (1) the identity of the database, electronic or otherwise, where the search was conducted; (2) the jurisdiction searched; (3) the initial search terms; and (4) the results of the search. If the result of the search is that it uncovers no documents *or* that it uncovers so many documents that an immediate revision of the search is required, that fact should be included. Then, the record should include any changes to the search terms or the jurisdiction. That information can be presented in narrative or bullet-point format. A word-processing document is an entirely appropriate format for keeping a list of searches and refinements. If your research database keeps such records automatically, you may use that record as your database, but remember that some databases delete search information after a certain number of days or weeks. If the database does not store the record of searches automatically or if you want a permanent record of the search, you may print the record or store it elsewhere electronically. Even if the database does keep track of searches conducted, you may want to supplement that information with comments about the type of cases that you found or did not find. As noted earlier, recording this information at the moment of the search will help you later when you are deciding how best to pick up your research.

b. Research results chart

When a search yields useful documents, a research log should include information about each of those documents. This research results chart should probably be a separate document from the research record addressed above. In general, the information in this results-focused chart includes, at a minimum, the citation, the jurisdiction, the claim(s) or issue(s) (and, sometimes, the element(s) of the claim(s) or the sub-issue(s)) to which the document relates, and as much information about the document as will be necessary in order to prevent the researcher's having to pull up the document again to remember why it is helpful. For this level of information, a word-processing document will present frustrating limitations. A more interactive format will be much more useful.[6]

If the document is a case, the citation information will allow users to quickly grasp the case name, the deciding court and its jurisdiction, and the date of decision. The recorded information should also usually include the facts, the disposition of the relevant issue(s) or sub-issue(s), the court's statements about the rule, and something about

6. A well-drafted chart can have many uses. *See, e.g.,* Tracy McGaugh, *The Synthesis Chart: Swiss Army Knife of Legal Writing*, 9(2) Persp: Teaching Legal Res. & Writing 80, 80 (2001).

the court's reasoning. If the case is a source for a rule, the researcher should include any information about the case that will be helpful in determining the breadth of the rule. The chart should also include anything enlightening or unusual about the case that might have some bearing on future research, even if the researcher has not thought through why the information is useful. That last piece of information could also be preserved in a separate part of the chart for possible future areas of inquiry.

If the document is a statute or a regulation, the information will include the statute's citation and its key language. If the document is a secondary source, the researcher will chart the citation and any information from the document that helps to answer questions about the law. Again, possible areas for future inquiry should be documented. For cases and statutes, the chart should include a reference to the date the writer last cite-checked or Shepardized the authorities.

The organization of information about cases, in particular, will affect the later usefulness of the chart. Ideally, the researcher will use a format that permits the input of information as it is obtained and the reorganization of that information in various ways for later use. A spreadsheet that includes multiple columns will allow the researcher to later reorganize information by claim, issue, element, or jurisdiction. Organizing in that fashion allows the researcher to quickly identify gaps in the research. It also provides a visual outline to the available authority. Learning to use spreadsheet technology or other formats that allow reorganization and re-reorganization by element or factor will be a worthwhile investment of time and mental energy.

Figures 7.3 and 7.4 show excerpts of the two parts of a research log: the research record and the research results chart. As indicated above, when taking notes for your research results chart, take those notes in a way that allows you to separate the discussion of different issues within the same case. Doing so will make it easier for you to organize your analysis around issues and to support your analysis with the best authorities.

E. AM I DONE WITH THE FIRST STAGE OF MY RESEARCH OF A LEGAL ISSUE?

One of the most difficult phases of any research and writing project for a law student is after some research is completed but the full analysis is not yet obvious. Students often keep researching, looking for the one case that will answer every question. They frequently ask, "How do I know when I'm done?"

Excerpt from Sample Research Record

(1) Westlaw search in Sixth Circuit Court of Appeals cases: "elements" and "Title VII retaliation"

102 results; 4th case led to *Nguyen*; went there and stopped looking at results

Nguyen v. City of Cleveland, 229 F.3d 559, 563 (6th Cir. 2000): "In order to establish a *prima facie* case of retaliation, a plaintiff must establish that: (1) he engaged in activity protected by Title VII; (2) the exercise of his civil rights was known to the defendant; (3) thereafter, the defendant took an employment action adverse to the plaintiff; and (4) there was a causal connection between the protected activity and the adverse employment action." *See Harrison v. Metropolitan Gov't*, 80 F.3d 1107, 1118 (6th Cir.1996) (citing *Wrenn v. Gould*, 808 F.2d 493, 500 (6th Cir.1987))."

(2) Westlaw search in Sixth Circuit Court of Appeals cases: "title vii retaliation" w/50 "protected activity"

53 results add "and complain!"

52 results add "informal complain!" or "oral complain!"

2 results (added to results log): *Sampson v. Vanderbilt U.*, 359 Fed. App'x 562 (6th Cir. 2009); *Delisle v. Brimfield Twp. Police Dep't*, 94 Fed. App'x 247 (6th Cir. 2004)

(3) Same search in Sixth Circuit federal cases

11 results (3 added to results log): *Adkison v. Procter & Gamble Co.*, 2011 WL 6371084 (S.D. Ohio Dec. 19, 2011); *E.E.O.C. v. Rocket Enters.*, Inc., 2008 WL 724613 (E.D. Mich. March 18, 2008); *Burns v. Jacor Broad. Corp.*, 128 F. Supp. 2d 497 (S.D. Ohio 2001)

Figure 7.3

While you will probably continue to do targeted research throughout the writing process, you can consider yourself "done" with the primary research phase if you are able to answer "yes" to the following questions:

A. Do I have a general understanding of how courts in my jurisdiction have addressed this issue?
B. Do I know whether my jurisdiction is within the mainstream? That is, do I know generally how courts outside of the jurisdiction have addressed this issue (or, for issues of state law, an analogous issue), and do I understand how my jurisdiction compares to others?
C. For each rule I am asking the court to apply, do I have appropriate "rule authority"? That is, have I identified a statute or a case from the highest court in which the rule is articulated?

Excerpt from Sample Research Results Chart

Inducing Panic Cases								
Element	Issue	Case Name, citation	Mandatory/ Persuasive	Facts	Reasoning	Rule	Useful holding (or dicta)	Analogize/ Distinguish Our Facts
1	What is a "cause"?	*State v. Jordan*, No. 05CA16, 2006 Ohio App. LEXIS 330 (4th Dist. Ct. App. January 18, 2006)	P	Defendant placed 911 call, reporting burglary in progress; dispatcher dispatched police to reported site.	Implicit: police respond to report, so report "caused" response.	Implicit: when police respond to report, their actions are "caused" by report.		School officials evacuated school in repsponse to McGee's signs
3	What is protected speech?	*State v. Loless*, 31 Ohio App. 3d 7 (1986)	P	Defendant made threats to blow up bridges in order to make a political point.	Threats are not protected under the First Amendment.	When a person's threats induce panic, the First Amendment does not immunize from prosecution.	Clear threat is not subject to interpretation based on speaker's intent.	McGee's signs are subject to interpretation as a threat but also to a more innocent interpretation.

Figure 7.4

D. Do I know how the highest court in my jurisdiction has addressed this issue? Can I name the most recent case in which the issue has been addressed by the highest court?
E. If the issue has not been addressed by the highest court, have I identified one or more cases in which the highest court has addressed similar issues or sub-issues?
F. Can I name the most recent case in which the issue has been addressed by any court within my jurisdiction?
G. Do I have appropriate "illustrative authority"? That is, have I found one or more cases that are similar enough to mine (e.g., factually and beyond) to serve as good illustrations of situations in which an appropriate court found that the standard in the rule has been met, and in which an appropriate court found that the standard in the rule had not been met?
H. If I do need to cite nonmandatory authority, have I chosen it appropriately? That is, am I using nonmandatory or nonjurisdictional sources only as needed for one of the two following reasons? (1) They are so close factually (or in some other significant way) that they are a particularly effective way to illustrate a point I want to make. (2) Cases from the mandatory courts and/or the jurisdiction do not address the issue in sufficient depth or in a sufficiently similar context.

In Chapter 11, we will discuss the use of nonmandatory authority in greater detail.

Recall and Review

1. In the "under" clause of a research question, describe in general the relevant __________ in order to provide legal context.
2. True or False: The "does" (or *is* or *can*) clause of a research question should be a yes or no question.
3. In the "when" (or *includes*) clause of a research question, you should list the __________.
4. An intellectual device that helps you identify legally significant categories is the __________ ladder.
5. A good way to give yourself background information on the relevant area of law is by beginning your research with s__________ authorities.
6. True or False: A case that addresses one of your sub-issues in a different context can never be useful; the legal context must always be identical.
7. How do you verify that a case you are citing has not been reversed by a higher court?
8. What is one way you can verify that a legal rule you found in an old case is still a valid legal rule in your jurisdiction?

CHAPTER 8

STATUTES AS AUTHORITY

You already know that statutes are *primary* authorities and that they are *mandatory* authorities within the jurisdictions in which they are enacted. If a statute governs the legal question you are analyzing, you will not have to look far to find the starting point for your research. The language of the statute is rarely the ending point, however.

In this short chapter, we will identify some of the methods you will pursue to enlighten yourself and your readers when you are working with the mandatory authority of a statute. Those methods include (A) conducting exegesis, or analysis, of the *plain meaning* of the language; (B) interpreting the words and phrases used in the statute by reference to definitions in statutory and case law; (C) clarifying the meaning of the statute by observing how it has been applied by courts; (D) examining legislative history to ascertain the intent of the legislature that enacted it; (E) looking for analogous statutes and interpretations; and (F) considering the policy underlying the statute.

A. WHAT DOES *PLAIN MEANING* MEAN?

The starting point for the interpretation of any statute is its *plain meaning*. Courts routinely say that they give effect to the plain meaning of the statute when that meaning is evident from an ordinary understanding of the words and phrases chosen by the legislative body that enacted it. When you interpret any statute, you should begin with an analysis of the ordinary understanding of those words and phrases. Often, you will have a clear, general understanding of what each of those words and phrases means as a layperson would interpret them.

A lay interpretation of the text, however, rarely ends the inquiry for a court, and it should never end your inquiry as you conduct research into the proper interpretation and application of the statute. You already know from your limited experience reading cases that words and phrases in statutes often don't mean what they plainly seem to mean. As an easy example, "knowledge" suggests active awareness to most people. As it is used in statutes, however, "knowledge" often includes the presence or availability of facts that might have led a person to active awareness, even if those available facts did not lead to actual awareness. In those instances, courts define "knowledge" to include a state of actually knowing something, as well as a state of having had an opportunity to know something. So, "knowledge" becomes knowing or not knowing when one had the opportunity to know. Courts sometimes express this concept by saying that a defendant "knew or should have known" some piece of information, and they are often interpreting the single word "knowledge" when they make this statement. This understanding of the word "knowledge" is both exactly the plain meaning of the word and its near opposite.

Whenever you are analyzing a statute at issue, you should read the complete "law" that contains the statute. Often, an isolated statute is just one section of a chapter or other grouping of statutes that makes up a law. The federal "Civil Rights Act," for example, is made up of numerous statutes, beginning at 42 U.S.C. § 1981. If you read only one isolated statutory section, you may not obtain a sufficiently complete understanding of the law.

Thus, even if you believe that you understand exactly what a statute means upon carefully considering its language, your inquiry cannot stop there. The interpretation of the statute will often lead to an understanding of the words and phrases that is very different from the plain meaning. Accordingly, your task is to determine what those words and phrases mean as they are used in the statute. You will look to various sources to identify those as-used definitions. The first two are (1) definitions within the statute or surrounding statutes and (2) definitions from judicial explanations of the statute.

First, as suggested here, reading the complete set of statutes may reveal definitions. Just as important, however, reading the complete set of statutes may reveal enforcement provisions and other facets of the law that may be crucial to your analysis or your argument.

B. FINDING DEFINITIONS IN STATUTORY AND CASE LAW

The first place to look for definitions of statutory language is within statutory law. A helpful legislature will define the words and phrases it uses. If you are very lucky, the legislature that enacted the statute you are analyzing will have included definitions within the very statute in which they are used. You should not stop your search for statutory definitions there, however, because legislatures more frequently enact separate definitional sections at the beginning or the end of a chapter or section of a code or other grouping of statutes. Those definitions often apply to all provisions within that chapter or section. A court will hesitate significantly before concluding that a word or phrase in a statute does not mean what the enacting legislature has explicitly said it means. When a legislature has used a definitional section to indicate how it intends a statutory term to be interpreted, you should presume that a court will interpret the language of the statute as the legislature has mandated.

Unfortunately, you will be unlucky in this regard more often than you will be lucky. There are many reasons why a legislature may not have included defining statutory language. Sometimes legislatures are able to reach sufficient agreement to enact a statute but are unable to come to agreement on the meaning of the words and phrases they have chosen. Sometimes, different legislators prefer different interpretations and, in the absence of agreement, are willing to settle for vague or ambiguous language that may be interpreted in various ways. Sometimes, the legislature runs out of time or steam and does not get to the tedious work of defining the words and phrases it has chosen. In any of those instances, your best hope is that a mandatory court will have defined those words and phrases. When a statutory term is defined in a court decision, the definition is known as a *case law definition*.

We use the phrase *mandatory court* to mean a court whose decisions constitute mandatory authority in the jurisdiction where any statute or other rule is being interpreted. Obviously, the courts that are mandatory courts will vary from issue to issue or from case to case.

Your search for case law definitions begins with a search for cases from mandatory courts. You will look for cases in which the court has interpreted and applied the language of the statute and where its interpretation is essential to the resolution of the issues before it. If the court has been helpful to you as a future user of its work, it will have cited the statute by number so that you will find its decision easily in your research.

Statute numbers are usually wonderful search terms. As we have noted, in Boolean searching your goal is to think of a sentence or sentences that would appear in the document you are looking for. (See Chapter 7.) Of course, if the statute is often referred to by a common name in addition to a number, you should add that name as an alternative to the number.

If the highest court in the jurisdiction has interpreted the very language that is the subject of your research, and if its decision is good law, your search for the definition of that language has ended. You will check the citation of the case to make certain that the enacting legislature has not acted to correct the court's interpretation of the statute, and, if it has not, you will apply the definition the court has provided. In the absence of a definition from the jurisdiction's highest court, you will look to other case law authority that is mandatory for you.

When mandatory authority is elusive, your search will move to persuasive authority interpreting the language. You will treat that authority as you would any other persuasive authority: it may be helpful, in varying degrees, but a court may choose to ignore it. Whether or not you find persuasive authority that provides definitions, you will also look at the ways in which courts have applied the language in order to clarify its meaning.

C. GAINING CLEARER UNDERSTANDING OF THE MEANING OF A STATUTE BY OBSERVING HOW COURTS HAVE APPLIED IT

Even when a court has not defined the words and phrases in a statute, you can gain clearer understanding of their meaning by observing how the court has applied the statute. As always, the most helpful case law authorities will be mandatory ones. Your target cases will be mandatory cases in which the courts have applied the word or phrase you are examining in a manner that is consistent with a particular meaning and inconsistent with any other. Consider for example, a statute that requires "knowledge" but does not define it. Suppose you find a decision from a mandatory court in which the court has found that the defendant was not liable and gave as its reason the fact that the defendant did not actually know about the critical event or fact. If the decision is good law—that is, if it has not been superseded by other authorities—you may rely on that decision as authority for the proposition that liability under the statute requires actual knowledge.

As you gain more experience, you will gain more confidence in your ability to ascertain the meanings of words and phrases from court opinions. At first, you may feel comfortable only when the court has been explicit about its reasoning by saying something like this: "The statute requires knowledge, and the defendant cannot be held liable because he did not have actual knowledge." In time, you will learn how to take a court's application to its logical conclusion. When you find an application that would not be consistent with one possible interpretation of a word or phrase in the statute, you will reason by negative implication that the other interpretation must therefore be correct. Suppose that the defendant had received a notice in the mail but had not opened it. Further, suppose that the court finds no liability because the knowledge element is not satisfied. You could be comfortable with the interpretation of "knowledge" to mean actual knowledge because the court's decision would be inconsistent with any other interpretation.

When judicial applications clarify the meaning of a statute to a degree that allows you to be confident in your understanding, your inquiry may be finished. If you have found several consistent applications, and none that are inconsistent, you will likely stop looking for guidance about how to interpret the statute. If the case law does not give you the answers you seek, however, you may turn to other sources for help.

Remember that legislative history is secondary authority. While courts often find it to be persuasive, a court is never required to follow it. You may find it helpful in understanding the law and in constructing an argument, but you should not presume that it will carry the day if your client's case goes to court.

D. HOW LEGISLATIVE HISTORY MAY ENLIGHTEN YOU

A court will always begin its analysis of a statute with the plain meaning of the words and phrases used by the legislature. As we have established, however, the inquiry rarely stops there, either for the court or for you. When statutory and case law definitions are unavailable, and the courts have not interpreted the language clearly or consistently, a court will often turn to the legislative history of the statute to glean some understanding of the legislature's intent in enacting it.

Legislative history consists of documents and records generated or gathered by the legislature and its staff in the course of considering proposed legislation. It may take the form of reports by committees or staff, testimony of witnesses before the committee or the full legislature, and statements of legislators. Legislative history also includes the changes in a statute as it is amended over time. Those amendments are often persuasive evidence of how the legislature intends the statute to be interpreted or applied. Legislative history is most reliable when it is included in the official legislative record.

Note that you need not always conduct your research in the full legislative record. Try searching cases or law review articles to see if others have discussed the legislative history relevant to your issue. As you may have guessed, in a Boolean search, you could look for the phrase "legislative history" within the same sentence as your statute number or common name. Of course, if that search fails, you may need to turn to the full record.

Legislative history rarely provides the clarity that courts and lawyers desire when they are attempting to define words and phrases within statutes. In many of your searches, you will find no legislative record. On the other hand, you may find the legislative record but find nothing that relates to the part of the statute you need to interpret, or you may find that the record contains contradictory statements or testimony. It may contain documents or statements that are directly on point but show no indication of agreement by the legislators. In short, while you may find some guidance as to what the legislature intended when it enacted the statute, the legislative history will rarely be definitive. In many instances, you will find yourself on safer footing when you rely on the policy underlying the statute, even when that policy is not explicit in the statute or the legislative history.

You are probably most familiar with legislative history as it relates to federal statutes. Some states provide similarly complete legislative history, but not every state does. Ohio, for example, does not publish any legislative history.

E. LOOKING FOR INTERPRETATIONS OF ANALOGOUS STATUTES OR STATUTORY LANGUAGE

Just as you look for analogies when considering common law rules, you can look for analogies when considering the meanings of statutes. When enacting statutes, legislatures often save time by adopting or adapting language from statutes, or pieces of statutes, that address similar issues. When enacting the Family and Medical Leave Act, for example, Congress looked to other civil rights statutes to find language that defines who constitutes an "employer." Likewise, when a state legislature is drafting a new law, it may consult federal statutes, similar statutes within its own code, or statutes enacted by other states.

The concept of mandatory and persuasive authority is relevant here, of course. An interpretation of statute A would not be mandatory authority to a court that is interpreting statute B. Nevertheless, courts frequently look to interpretations of similar statutes, or of similar language or issues within statutes, and they often find them to be persuasive. Federal courts, for example, have adopted interpretations of provisions of Title VII when they have interpreted other antidiscrimination statutes, such as the Americans with Disabilities Act or the Age Discrimination in Employment Act. Although the contexts in which the statutes apply are not exactly the same, the courts have developed similar tests for assessing claims under all of the federal antidiscrimination statutes, and they often adapt standards from one statute when they are analyzing another, especially when the language of the statutes themselves does not make clear that Congress had a contrary intention.

F. CONSIDERING POLICY TO CLARIFY THE MEANING OF A STATUTE

A legislator who introduces a bill may be motivated by one or more policy objectives. Other members of the legislature may support the same bill for their own policy reasons. These reasons may be explicit in the language of the eventual statute or in the legislative history, but more often they will not be. Whether explicit or implicit, these policy foundations may be useful tools in the interpretation of the statute.

In the absence of mandatory authority that specifies a particular interpretation, a court will generally try to interpret a statute in a manner that serves the policy that motivated its enactment. When a court perceives that the policy underlying the statute was the broadening of a right, the court is likely to interpret the statute in such a manner that the right is broadened. When the policy is the protection of innocent civilians, the court will likely interpret the statute in a way that advances the protection of civilians.

You may already be thinking that the policy underlying a statute will often appear to be different to different observers. You are right, of course. Statutes that criminalize behavior almost always serve a public-protection policy. That policy may suggest a broad application. When the same statute provides minimal penalties, however, a second possible policy may be narrow application. A prosecutor may rely on the broad public-protection policy to argue that the court should apply the statute to behavior that does not quite fit within the statute's plain meaning, while a defense attorney may argue that the narrow application policy would not support any application other than those spelled out explicitly in the language. The good news for you as a lawyer is that you will almost always be able to conceive of a policy that supports your position. The bad news is that your opponent is likely in the same position. So, plain meaning, statutory and case law definitions, and case law applications, all of which are less susceptible to competing interpretations, are far more reliable guides to statutory meaning.

Like many research trails, considering policy brings us back to case law. When you identify a policy that your interpretation of a statute would advance, you cannot just present your bald assertion of that policy to your supervisor or to a court. Rather, you should look for cases in which the court has mentioned that policy as being significant. The ideal case would be a decision by a mandatory court in which that court cited the policy as a reason for interpreting the relevant statute in the way that you want it to be interpreted. Of course, as we have observed, courts do not always cooperate by writing opinions that are tailored to your precise research needs.

Even if there is not an opinion that is directly on point, however, you can reason by analogy when looking at policy issues in the same way that you reason by analogy in other contexts. For example, if you are trying to argue that a statute that contains minimal penalties is a statute that should be interpreted narrowly, you could look for cases interpreting other statutes that impose minimal penalties. If courts have stated that they have interpreted those statutes narrowly because of their minimal penalty provisions, you could cite those opinions as support for your argument that the court should do the same in your case.

G. SUMMARY

After learning about the malleability of common law rules, you may believe that statutory rules will be easier to apply and interpret. But, alas, statutory language is just the first stop in interpretation, and once statutory language has been interpreted by a court, it has many of the features of a common law rule. Just as you will use a variety of techniques when researching and interpreting common law rules, you must expect to use a variety of techniques when researching and interpreting statutory rules.

Recall and Review

1. When courts interpret statutory language, the first thing they consider is the statute's ____________.
2. Name two places you can look to find definitions of statutory language.
3. True or False: You should read all statutory provisions that make up a law, even if your issue focuses on only one provision.
4. When searching for cases that have interpreted a statute, one of the best search terms is the statute's _______________.

5. We use the term ________________ to refer to documents and records generated or gathered by the legislature and its staff in the course of considering proposed legislation.
6. True or False: When looking for rules about how language in a statute should be interpreted, it is appropriate to look at similar language in other statutes, even if those statutes are not perfectly analogous.
7. True or False: Policy arguments are one of the rare occasions when it's best to make an argument without citing to authorities.

CHAPTER 9

ORGANIZING AN ANALYSIS

By now you have probably encountered quite a few rules. You have encountered them in statutes, and, in your reading of cases for this class or others, you have attempted to find the rules identified by courts. You may have outlined some of those rules or otherwise broken them down to their individual components, also making note of the relationships between those components. By breaking down a rule, you have begun the process of organizing an analysis of any issue that might arise with respect to that rule.

As you know from a previous chapter, some rules have *elements,* which are components that must be met or established in order for a rule to apply. Other rules have *factors,* which are a set of components that a court may consider when deciding whether a rule does or does not apply. We will use the term *component* to include *elements* and *factors,* as well as any other label that could apply to a part or facet of a legal rule or sub-rule.

In order to answer a legal question, a lawyer must identify every component of the applicable rule that may be in controversy, as you have done when you have outlined a rule. The lawyer then analyzes each controversial component individually.

In this chapter, we will discuss how to use a rule outline to help you organize an analysis of a legal issue. We will also discuss how to use the outline to connect the sources that you find in research to the parts of your analysis.

A. THE STRUCTURE OF LEGAL ANALYSIS

If you have ever taken a creative writing course or a poetry course, your teachers may have told you to "think outside the box" or to "try something different!" If you have ever taken a technical writing course, however, you probably got a very different message. Your technical writing teacher probably didn't tell you to "be creative." Instead, you were probably told to figure out what information your readers needed and when they needed it and to organize the information to make sure that your readers received the right information at the right time and in the right order. The two recipes in Chapter 1 show what a difference it makes when information isn't organized or presented effectively, or when it doesn't include everything the reader needs.

As you might expect, legal writing is a lot more like technical writing than it is like creative writing. Later, we will try to convince you that the guidelines for legal writing leave room for creativity: it takes creative thinking to recognize relationships that no one has ever recognized before. It took a creative lawyer to argue that heat escaping from a building is like garbage abandoned at a curb, and that each could be observed by police without a search warrant.[1] And it took another creative lawyer to argue that garbage is intentionally abandoned but that heat is not and that the thermal imaging devices that measure that heat are measuring personal information from inside the "sanctity" of the home.[2]

But there is a time and a place for creativity, and there is a time and a place for understanding and meeting your readers' needs and expectations. Legal audiences have a fairly rigid set of expectations. As to any legal issue that they hear or read about, they expect to know what rule governs the issue, what that rule means, how it applies or doesn't apply to the current situation, and how the application of that rule affects the case as a whole.

B. BEGINNING WITH AN OUTLINE

All legal analysis includes a question or set of questions, thoughtful discussion of the question, research of some kind, thoughtful discussion about the results of the research, some structure or organization,

1. *United States v. Myers*, 46 F.3d 668, 670 (7th Cir. 1995) (citations omitted) ("Moreover, society has been unwilling to protect as reasonable 'waste products intentionally or inevitably exposed to the public' such as the garbage left at the curbside, the smoke rising from a chimney, and the scent of drugs emanating from luggage. We conclude that society is similarly not willing to protect as reasonable an expectation of privacy in the wasted heat emitted from a home.").

2. *See generally* Br. for the Petr., *Kyllo v. United States*, 2000 WL 33127872 15 (U.S. Nov. 13, 2000). The *Kyllo* Court found that the information from the thermal imaging report was the "product of a search." *Kyllo v. United States*, 533 U.S. 27, 34-35 (2001).

and a result. The result may be communicated orally, communicated in writing, or never communicated. Whatever its end form, legal analysis is easier when you begin with a working outline.

1. Finding Structure

At this stage, you have identified a rule or set of rules that you plan to use in analyzing and making a prediction on the outcome of a legal question or set of legal questions. You have outlined the rule and understand something about how its components relate. For example, you might know that the plaintiff must prove three mandatory elements or that the court will consider a list of eight factors in deciding whether the plaintiff has made its case. You may have located the rule in a case or a series of cases, but effective legal analyses are usually best organized around issues, rules, and arguments rather than around cases. Of course, you may describe cases at some point—to illustrate or explain rules that you identify—but the *rules,* rather than the cases, should be the focus of your analysis.

Let's begin this discussion of structure with one of the rules that you may have outlined in Chapter 5. To prove that a person is guilty of assault in Ohio, the state must prove that the defendant did one of the following:

1. knowingly caused physical harm to another person;
2. knowingly attempted to cause physical harm to another person;
3. knowingly caused physical harm to the unborn of another person;
4. knowingly attempted to cause physical harm to the unborn of another person;
5. recklessly caused physical harm to another person; or
6. recklessly caused physical harm to the unborn of another person.

We know that the state is required to prove only one of these alternatives because the rule is disjunctive. If each of the elements of the rule were joined with the conjunction *and,* then the state would be required to prove all of them.

As we indicated in a previous chapter, the first purpose for outlining a rule is to identify points of controversy. In order to do that, you will want to have the outline of the rule in front of you. You may also find that turning the components of the rule into individual questions makes it easier to determine whether that component is a point of controversy. So, let's turn the outline of the Ohio assault rule into six questions:

1. Did the defendant knowingly cause physical harm to another person? or

2. Did the defendant knowingly attempt to cause physical harm to another person? or
3. Did the defendant knowingly cause physical harm to the unborn of another person? or
4. Did the defendant knowingly attempt to cause physical harm to the unborn of another person? or
5. Did the defendant recklessly cause physical harm to another person? or
6. Did the defendant recklessly cause physical harm to the unborn of another person?

If you were a criminal defense attorney whose client had been charged with assault in Ohio, you might use those six questions as a guide to identifying the points of controversy in your client's case. Suppose, for example, that the charge arose from a fight in which your male client grabbed his brother by the arm and broke it. You could quickly determine that the third, fourth, and sixth questions are not points of controversy. Your client's brother was probably not carrying an "unborn" at the time of the fight. You have just reduced from six to three the components of the rule that require further analysis.

Having determined which components of the rule may be controversial in your case, you have identified the sub-issues that will require further analysis. While an overall rule has helped you to identify the elements of the assault charge, separate rules, often called *sub-rules*, will help you to interpret each controversial component. You can begin to think of your analysis as having multiple individual components.

The next step in your analysis is to determine how you will begin to answer the question posed by each of the three components of the assault rule that may be controversial. One way to accomplish this task is to look for each component's *key terms*[3] or, as we call them, the *phrases-that-pay*. We use this term to label the word or phrase that is the focus of a controversy about whether or how a rule applies. If you devote a *unit of discourse* to each controversial phrase-that-pays and then organize those units of discourse effectively, you will be able to understand your analysis and communicate it to others effectively.

Although the term *unit of discourse* could refer to any word or set of words, from a single word to a book, we use the term *unit of discourse* to describe the analysis of a single point of controversy or sub-issue.

A quick method for finding the phrase-that-pays is to ask yourself what words or phrases opponents might pick fights over. For example, the Ohio assault rule provides that a person commits assault when he or she "knowingly cause[s] or attempt[s] to cause physical harm to another person." You can imagine that your client might argue that he did not know that his actions would cause physical harm to his brother.

3. *See, e.g.*, Laurel Oates, Anne Enquist & Kelly Kunsch, *The Legal Writing Handbook* 539 (2d ed., Aspen 1998).

You can also imagine your client arguing that he was not attempting to cause physical harm to his brother when he confronted him. Accordingly, the terms "knowingly" and "attempt" could be phrases-that-pay in your client's case.

The other potential point of controversy for your client is the third element: "Did the defendant recklessly cause physical harm to another person?" There, the phrase-that-pays is likely to be "recklessly" because your client is likely to argue that he was not behaving recklessly when his brother was hurt. On the other hand, it is unlikely that either party will dispute that your client's actions "caused" the broken bone, so "cause" is *not* a phrase-that-pays in this situation because cause will not be in controversy.

By looking at each component of the rule and asking yourself which terms are likely to be the phrases-that-pay in your case, you have quickly identified the sub-issues that will require further analysis in order for you to determine whether your client is likely to be convicted of assault. You have identified three of them: "knowingly," "attempt," and "recklessly." You will begin by analyzing those three sub-issues. Because each sub-issue will be the subject of its own unit of discourse, you can anticipate that your analysis will include three units of discourse.

We do not mean to suggest that these are the only possible phrases-that-pay under the Ohio assault statute. For example, a defendant could admit to forcibly cutting his brother's hair, thus eliminating any controversy about whether his actions were knowing or an attempt. In that scenario, the parties are more likely to argue about whether a forced haircut is "physical harm." The phrase-that-pays, and the term that will be the focus of the analysis, would be "physical harm."

2. Using the Phrases-That-Pay to Organize an Analysis

You can use phrases-that-pay as an effective organizing principle: focus on one phrase-that-pays at a time, and you will ensure that you are giving attention to each potentially controversial component. By doing so, you will be more likely to understand how the parts of your overall analysis fit together, and you will make it easier for readers to understand your later written analysis (you may also make it easier to write). Thus, you can begin to structure your analysis by identifying the phrases-that-pay from the rules that govern your case.

You can often identify phrases-that-pay by turning each component of the rule into an if-then statement, even though you will not necessarily articulate the rule this way in the memo. As you know, an if-then rule says, in essence, "if a certain condition exists, then a certain legal consequence results." The phrase-that-pays is almost always the "condition" that you are trying to prove the existence (or nonexistence) of. Thus, look for (or put) the phrases-that-pay in the "if" clause; that clause usually contains the narrow point that the writer is trying to explain or prove. For example, one sub-rule for the assault memo we have been discussing would be "if a person 'recklessly' causes harm to another person, that person is guilty of assault."

To take another example, let us presume that you are representing Bob Boyfriend, who wants to sue Larry Landowner after he was assaulted in the lobby of his girlfriend's apartment building, which Larry owns. Although Bob does not pay rent at the apartment building, he visits constantly, often overnight. On Bob's behalf, you will want to establish that Mr. Landowner had a duty to provide better security in his apartment building. After doing some research, you discover that landlords are often found to have a duty to provide security to invitees when harm to the invitees is foreseeable. You might find yourself articulating an if-then rule such as this:

An *invitee* is a person who enters premises that are open to the public or who enters private premises with the owner's permission.

> *If* harm to invitees is foreseeable, *then* a landowner has a duty to provide security.

In your analysis, you would be trying to determine whether Bob was an invitee and whether the harm Bob suffered was foreseeable; thus, "invitee" and "foreseeable" would be your phrases-that-pay. It would then be easy to divide the analysis of this rule into two parts:

1. Is a guest of an apartment building's resident an "invitee"?
2. Was harm to invitees "foreseeable" in this situation?

After you have identified each phrase-that-pays that relates to your client's facts, your next task is to determine how courts have interpreted that phrase-that-pays. You are looking for the rule or sub-rule that defines or clarifies your phrase-that-pays. In the example above, for instance, you might do some research to determine how "foreseeability" has been analyzed by the courts. Let us presume that the courts in your jurisdiction have found that foreseeability exists when a landowner is "on actual or constructive notice that similar criminal activity had occurred within the recent past on the landowner's premises or within sufficient proximity." This judicial analysis creates another rule:

> *If* a landowner has actual or constructive notice that identical or similar criminal activity has occurred within the recent past on the landowner's premises or within sufficient proximity, *then* the foreseeability element of the duty test has been met.

Looking at this new rule reveals several possible new phrases-that-pay and thus, several possible issues. Here are some examples:

What is "constructive notice"?
What constitutes "similar criminal activity"?
What amount of time qualifies as "the recent past"?
What does "sufficient proximity" mean?

To determine which of these phrases-that-pay is in controversy, look to your facts again. For example, let's presume that Mr. Landowner lives in the building that he owns. There have been assaults and burglaries in many of the surrounding apartment buildings within the past year, the most recent being four days ago. All of the crimes have received normal publicity, that is, they have been reported in the relevant police documents and have been mentioned in news sources and other media. Fortunately, none of these crimes occurred in Mr. Landowner's building. Thus, you might make the following list of possible issues to analyze:

1. Was Boyfriend an "invitee"?
2. Was harm to invitees "foreseeable"?
   A. Do normal police records and news and other media accounts of an event give Landowner "actual or constructive notice" of crimes in the neighborhood?
   B. Did the assaults in the neighborhood constitute criminal activity that was sufficiently "similar" to the assault of Boyfriend?
   C. Did assaults and burglaries that occurred four days ago occur "within the recent past"?
   D. Did the assaults that happened in neighboring apartment buildings occur "within sufficient proximity" to put Landowner on notice that crime was possible in his building?

Note how the phrases-that-pay appear in quotation marks in the outline above. Although you do not need to use quotation marks each time you use the phrase-that-pays within a given analysis, doing so in the outline (and the first time you mention the phrase-that-pays in your discussion) can help both you and your readers to focus on the components of your analysis.

In analyzing the issues, you might think that the fact that both kinds of crimes were "assaults" means that you do not have to conduct an in-depth analysis of point 2.B because Bob Boyfriend was also assaulted. At this stage of your legal career, however, it is difficult to decide how much effort to devote to any particular issue. So, you should explore any potentially controversial components. Later, we will help you to determine how much analysis to provide for the various kinds of issues that a case may present.

3. Using the Outline of Phrases-That-Pay to Help You Identify Authorities

An outline can help you to isolate issues; it can also help you to identify which authorities are relevant to each issue. Thus, as you make your outline, you can and should annotate it by noting which cases, statutes, or other sources contain arguments or other information relevant to each point. Thus, you might annotate the outline above as follows[4]:

1. Was Boyfriend an "invitee"?
   Bueller v. Rooney (Vanita Supreme Court, 1993)
   Kobacker v. Wagner (Vanita Appellate Court, 2005)
   Totino v. Montague (Vanita Appellate Court, 2008)
2. Was harm to invitees "foreseeable"?
   A. Did police, newspaper, and media accounts give Landowner "actual or constructive notice" of crimes in the neighborhood?
   Quirrell v. State (Vanita Appellate Court, 1969) (dicta)
   Arabella v. Hagrid (Vanita Supreme Court, 1996)
   Russ v. Cummins (Vanita Appellate Court, 2001)

   B. Did the assaults in the neighborhood constitute criminal activity that was sufficiently "similar" to the assault of Boyfriend?
   Russ v. Cummins (Vanita Appellate Court, 2001)
   Efta v. Farb (Vanita Appellate Court, 2005)
   Fuerst v. Roche (Vanita Supreme Court, 2006)

   C. Did assaults and burglaries that occurred four days ago occur "within the recent past"?
   Fuerst v. Roche (Vanita Supreme Court, 2006)

   D. Did the assaults in neighboring apartment buildings occur "within sufficient proximity" to the landowner's building to put Landowner on notice that crime was possible in his building?
   Regis v. Lupin (Vanita Appellate Court, 1988)
   Arabella v. Hagrid (Vanita Supreme Court, 1996)
   Kobacker v. Wagner (Vanita Appellate Court, 2005)
   Totino v. Montague (Vanita Appellate Court, 2008)

Notice a couple of things about this annotated outline. First, notice how the enumeration shows the relationships between and among the issues. The plaintiff must establish A, B, C, and D in order to establish that 2 has been established. Second, notice how some cases are

---

4. In this instance, all of the authority cases come from the fictional jurisdiction of Vanita.

repeated a few times. Some students get the idea that they must use a case only once or that, if it is particularly good for one issue, they should "save" it for that issue and not use it for any others. Put that idea out of your head. Just as your client's case might present several issues, it is unsurprising that some authority cases will be useful for more than one issue.

Once you have identified authority for each part of your outline, you are probably ready to begin the writing task (if that is the form that you will use to report the results of your research). This is not the end of your outline, however. It will also serve as your guide as you begin writing. The time and effort you put into the outline will be well worth the investment as you begin to write; the more care you exercise now, the more time you will save yourself later. Including pinpoint citations, for example, may save you time later, and your future self will thank your current self.

Recall and Review

1. A component that must be met or established in order for a rule to apply is called an ______.
2. A set of components that a court may consider when deciding whether a rule does or does not apply is called a set of __________.
3. True or False: After you have outlined the rule and identified all possible phrases-that-pay, you should give each phrase-that-pays its own separate unit of discourse.
4. True or False: If you address multiple issues in an analytical document, you should never use the same case in multiple units of discourse.
5. If you restate your rule as an if-then proposition, is the phrase-that-pays more likely to be in the *if* clause or the *then* clause?

CHAPTER 10

TURNING YOUR OUTLINE INTO A WRITTEN ANALYSIS

You have an outline, and you have identified authorities that will help you to answer each component of that outline. In this chapter, we will show you how to make decisions about how to fill in your outline. And then, ready or not, we will show you how you can put your analysis into writing.

Because it's sometimes difficult for new legal writers to know how much information to provide about each issue, this chapter will explain how to decide how much time you should spend on each component of your outline. Your "discussion" of some parts of your outline can be very short; for other parts, you will need to provide a complete "unit of discourse." This chapter will help you write units of discourse by giving you a formula you can use to make sure you have given your readers all of the information that they need. At the end of the chapter, we include a sample unit of discourse. Don't worry if you don't understand all of the details included in the sample; consider it a sneak preview.

A. DECIDING HOW MUCH ATTENTION EACH SUB-ISSUE DEMANDS

After you have identified the issues or possible issues that your case presents, you must decide how much time (or, more accurately, how many words) to devote to each. Figure 10.1 shows the four possible levels of discussion for each issue or sub-issue.

1. When to *Ignore* an Issue

Some issues are obviously not relevant to the analysis or are quite obviously not controversial. These issues can be ignored. In the Bob

Boyfriend example, you might find a case that says that landowners have no duty to protect trespassers from harm by third parties. Bob Boyfriend was not a trespasser, and no reasonable attorney would argue that Bob was a trespasser: he was invited onto the property by a tenant. Therefore, the trespassing issue is not relevant, and you would not need to address it in your analysis.

Other issues are relevant to your analysis but are obviously not controversial. Readers do not need even one sentence discussing these types of issues. For example, suppose that your state's statute forbidding texting while driving contains this language:

> A person shall not drive a motor vehicle while using a handheld wireless communication device to manually write, send, or read a text-based communication.

Let us presume that your client, Dora Driver, was charged with violating this statute when she was arrested after crashing her car, a Chevy Impala, into a light pole. Her phone records revealed that she had sent and received several text messages within the 15 minutes before the accident. To find Dora guilty of violating this statute, the state would have to prove the following elements (words signaling possible phrases-that-pay are italicized; brackets separate adjacent phrases-that-pay):

> Defendant is a person who used a [*handheld*] [*wireless communication device*] while *driving* a [*motor vehicle*] to [*manually*] *write, send,* or *read* a *text-based communication*.

We'll explain below how to use this acronym to remind you to construct your analysis by stating the Conclusion, the Rule, the EXplanation, the Application, and the Connection-Conclusion

As we will explain below, "CRAC" stands for "Conclusion, Rule, Application, Conclusion."

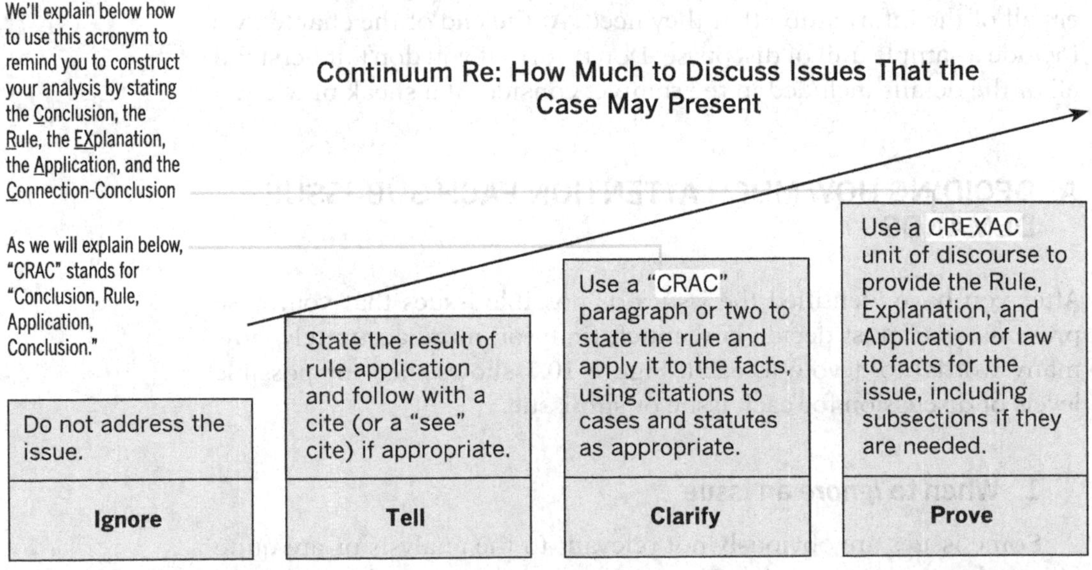
Continuum Re: How Much to Discuss Issues That the Case May Present
Do not address the issue.
Ignore
State the result of rule application and follow with a cite (or a "see" cite) if appropriate.
Tell
Use a "CRAC" paragraph or two to state the rule and apply it to the facts, using citations to cases and statutes as appropriate.
Clarify
Use a CREXAC unit of discourse to provide the Rule, Explanation, and Application of law to facts for the issue, including subsections if they are needed.
Prove

Figure 10.1

In your written analysis, you would not spend any time explaining that Dora, as a human being, is a "person" under the statute. Likewise, you would not spend even a sentence to say "a Chevy Impala, an automobile, is a 'motor vehicle' under the statute." These elements are so obviously met that there could be no doubt in any attorney's mind that they are satisfied in this case. Therefore, you should ignore them.

Do not let yourself be lulled into a false belief that an issue is not controversial, however. For example, you might presume that "driving" a vehicle requires the car to be in motion and that you could conclude that Dora was not driving when she sent her texts while she was stopped at a red light. Your research, however, might well reveal that "driving" includes having control of a motor vehicle that is in gear, even if it is not moving at the time of the offense.[1] Thus, you will usually want to conduct some research before deciding to ignore an issue.

2. When to *Tell* Readers About an Issue

The answers to some issues are so straightforward that you can just *tell* readers the answer, with only minimal justification (e.g., a citation or a few words of explanation). There are two kinds of *tell* issues. The first kind is an issue that is relevant but is *not* controversial. Unlike an *ignore* issue, however, with a *tell* issue, a reasonable attorney might not immediately understand that the issue is not controversial. Accordingly, after you discern how the law applies to the facts, you tell readers the outcome of that analysis in your document, with a supporting citation as appropriate.

For example, suppose that you have been asked to write a memo explaining whether your client, Lou Carey, will be able to recover damages from Rob Barker. Rob's dog, Pricey, bit Lou while Lou was on Rob's yacht. Rob was not on the yacht at the time, and Lou was there without permission. The dog-bite statute in your jurisdiction says that a dog owner is not liable if the victim of the dog bite was committing a trespass or other criminal offense "on the property of the [dog] owner" at the time of the dog bite. At first, you wonder whether a yacht counts as "property" under the statute. You anticipate that the term "property" means only "real property" and does not include other kinds of property. You discover, however, several cases in which dogs attacked people who were involved in various kinds of criminal activity on or around boats, and the courts in your jurisdiction have consistently held that a boat constitutes "property" under the statute. Thus,

1. *See, e.g.*, *State v. Mailman*, 242 P.3d 269, 271 (N.M. 2010) (we have interpreted the word *drive* to mean either "driving a motor vehicle" or being "in actual physical control whether or not the vehicle is moving") (citations omitted).

you decide that it would not be worth arguing about whether Lou was on Rob's "property" at the time of the attack. Even though you would not recommend arguing about the point, however, it is still a required element of the analysis, and you should still tell readers the resolution of the issue:

> A boat is considered "property" for purposes of the statute. *E.g., Speigh v. Gnooter*, 105 R.E.2d 2446 (Van. 2004) ("Vanita courts have consistently held that boats constitute 'property' under § 1055.28.").

The second kind of *tell* issue is an issue that is not relevant. With this kind of *tell* issue, however, a reasonable attorney might believe that the issue is relevant and might be expecting you to address it. Accordingly, after your research reveals that the issue is not relevant, you simply tell your readers why you will not be addressing the issue, citing authority that establishes that the issue is irrelevant.

For example, suppose that your client, Jay Methuselah, contacts your office after having been terminated from his job. His new supervisor, who made the decision to fire him, had made several comments about Methuselah's age—Methuselah is 61 years old—in the weeks since the supervisor's arrival (and thus the weeks leading up to Methuselah's discharge). You are aware of federal and state statutes that ban age discrimination in employment, and you hypothesize that these will be your governing authorities, so you start your research there. The state statute seems to apply. Upon reading the federal statute, however, you discover that it applies only to those employers who have 20 or more employees. Methuselah's employer, Old Testament Publishers, has only 16 employees, so the Federal Age Discrimination in Employment Act will not apply to Methuselah's employer. You realize that the attorney who will be reading the memo may not remember the exact number of employees required for coverage under the federal act and may wonder why you did not address the issue. Accordingly, you tell your readers why the issue is not relevant, citing appropriate authority:

> Methuselah cannot bring a cause of action under the Federal Age Discrimination in Employment Act because Old Testament Publishers has only 16 employees. 29 U.S.C. § 630 (Westlaw, current through Jan. 13, 2022) (requiring 20 or more employees to qualify as "employer").

Deciding whether your readers will expect you to address an issue can be difficult. If your initial hypothesis led you to believe that an issue (or a governing rule) was relevant, that is a good sign that your readers will believe so, too, and that you should address the issue quickly to relieve your readers' curiosity.

3. When to *Clarify* an Issue

A *clarify* issue is similar to a *tell* issue, but it is a shade more complex. We use the term *clarify* to describe an issue that requires you to include just a little bit more information—law, facts, or both—for readers to understand either why the issue is not controversial or why the issue is not relevant.

For example, let's presume that your firm's client, Mickey McPherson, was bitten by a dog when she went to deliver cookies to her customers, the Thurbers. Mickey has been selling cookies to the Thurbers for years, and she was delivering cookies that they had ordered. You are assigned to write a memo analyzing the chances of Mickey being able to recover damages for her injuries from the Thurbers. After conducting some research, you find the following statute:

> The owner of any dog which shall bite a person while such person is on or in a public place, or lawfully on or in a private place, including the property of the owner of the dog, shall be liable for such damages as may be suffered by the person bitten.

You might need to clarify how you know that Mickey was "lawfully" on the Thurbers' property:

> Mickey was "lawfully" on the Thurbers' property. Courts have consistently held that a person is "lawfully" on another's property when on the property upon the owner's "express or implied invitation." *E.g., Entrikin v. Neumann*, 117 R.E.2d 102, 106 (Van. 2016). Further, the Vanita Supreme Court has specifically found that a person delivering a previously ordered product is on the orderer's property "by implied invitation." *Lysaght v. Pillion*, 112 R.E.2d 116, 123 (Van. 2011). Because Mickey was delivering cookies that the Thurbers had ordered, she was "lawfully" on the property under this standard.

It is difficult to give an exact formula for deciding whether to tell or clarify the outcome of an issue. You may presume that "more is always better," but that is not always true. You will needlessly annoy some readers by giving a paragraph of analysis where a sentence plus citation will suffice. As you gain more experience in written legal analysis (and experience with various readers), you will develop your own sense of judgment as to depth of analysis. In the meantime, there are a few factors you can consider. For example, is the language in the rule abstract or highly technical? The harder the rule is to understand on its own, the more likely it is that your readers will benefit from a clarify analysis. Are you writing about an area of law that some or all

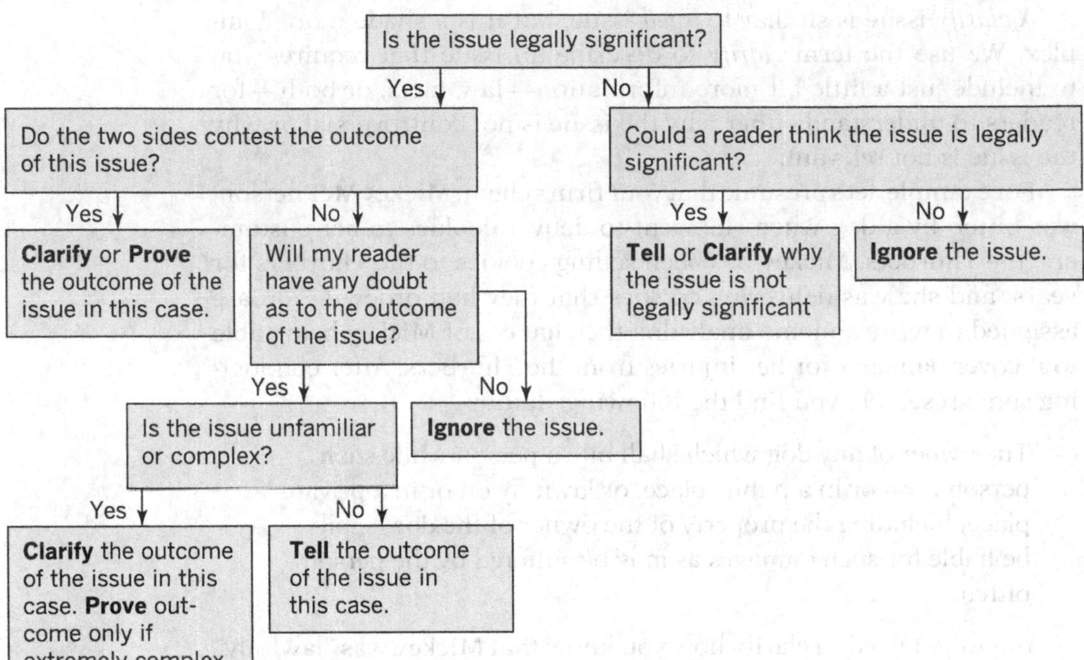

Figure 10.2

of your readers may be unfamiliar with? If so, it may be worth the extra sentence or two to clarify the outcome of the issue. Figure 10.2 is a flow chart that may help you to decide how much time to spend on an issue. At this stage in your career, seek guidance (from a flow chart or a mentor) when making your decision; when in doubt, err on the side of giving too much information rather than too little.

4. When to *Prove* the Outcome of a Legal Issue

We use the word *prove* to describe the most in-depth type of legal analysis.[2] You should prove the outcome of your legal issues if (1) the issue concerns a required element of the analysis, and (2) the issue is either controversial or complex.

To analyze a *prove* issue, you should use a CREXAC unit of discourse. This concept is described and illustrated in Section B below.

2. In their text, Professors Neumann and Tiscione use the term *rule proof* in much the same way that this text uses the term *rule explanation*. RICHARD K. NEUMANN, JR. & KRISTEN KONRAD TISCIONE, LEGAL REASONING AND LEGAL WRITING ch. 12 (7th ed., Aspen 2013).

Once you have analyzed all of the applicable rules, identified their phrases-that-pay, and determined which phrases-that-pay are in controversy in your case, you can draft a working outline of your analysis.

As you identify the relevant components of the relevant rules, identify which components you can ignore and which components you need to address in some way. Notice how the following sample outline suggests a plan for the written version of each component: the writer specifies whether she plans to tell, clarify, or prove the outcome of her rule application.

B. USING PRIVATE MEMOS TO QUIET YOUR INNER DEMONS AND PREVENT WRITER'S BLOCK

Even with a strong outline, you may still face writer's block at this stage of the process if you worry so much about avoiding mistakes or leaving something important out that you are afraid to write a word. You may hear a critical voice yammering away inside your head: "What about the *recklessness* issue? Do I have enough cases on this point? Shouldn't that second issue come before this one?" and so on. These types of critical voices can make you freeze, and writing comes to a stop.

Hearing your critical voice is not a bad thing in itself. After all, as cognitive scholars have told us, writing is a method of thinking and of learning. While you write, that critical voice may help you discover avenues of research, aspects of your case that you hadn't noticed before, or even whole areas of analysis that didn't occur to you while you were researching or outlining. That's why it's important to leave yourself enough time to write: you should presume that your first couple of drafts will be "thinking drafts" or "learning drafts" that will teach you a lot about your case.

If you stop writing every time your critical voice reminds you of something, however, you may never finish a draft. Instead, allow yourself to write an imperfect first draft and record the questions or criticisms that occur to you. Instead of freezing up, use a method we call private memos, or sidebars. As the critical voices chatter in your head, drop a footnote and write down what those voices are saying: "Do I need more research here?" "Should I talk about the other issue first?" In this way, you can silence your critical voice by preserving the concern that you're worried about, but you avoid writer's block because you don't interrupt your writing process. Plan to review your private memo footnotes during the rewriting stage of your writing process. You may find some points were irrelevant after all; on the other hand, some of the private memos may lead you to new and more effective analysis.

Anne Lamott advises writers to let themselves write what she calls "shitty first drafts" and to have confidence that they will be able to improve these rough attempts. Anne Lamott, *Bird by Bird: Some Instructions on Writing and Life* 22 (Anchor 1995).

Although of course you must delete your private memos before you submit a document to a court or a client, they may be helpful reading for your teacher or supervisor. You can use these private memos as

Sample Annotated Outline

Name: Jo Student

Issue:

Under Title VII, does an employee have a cause of action for sex discrimination when she was terminated in a reduction in force on the basis of lower performance evaluation scores than those given to male colleagues whose responsibilities were less difficult and who reported to different supervisors?

Overall Rule:

In this circuit, a Title VII sex discrimination claim based upon unequal treatment requires that the plaintiff prove the following : (1) that she is a member of a protected class, (2) that she was qualified for the position in question, (3) that she suffered an adverse employment action, and either (4a) that she can produce direct evidence of discrimination or (4b) that she can demonstrate that similarly-situated non-protected employees were treated better.

See, e.g., Ercegovich v. Goodyear Tire & Rubber Co., 154 F.3d 344, 350 (6th Cir. 1998).

First Element

Rule Explanation

42 U.S.C.A. § 2000e-2 (Title VII protects women and racial minorities, among others).

Rule Application

Tell: Plaintiff is a woman, so first element is met.

Second Element

Rule Explanation

Wexler v. White's Fine Furniture, Inc., 317 F.3d 564, 575-76 (6th Cir. 2003) (a plaintiff can show that she is qualified by showing that her qualifications are at least equivalent to minimum objective criteria for employment in the field, skills, education, experience).

Rule Application

Clarify: Plaintiff had been performing the job for many years with excellent performance evaluations. She is qualified on a prima facie basis, so second element is met.

Third Element

Rule Explanation

Mitchell v. Toledo Hospital, 964 F.2d 577, 582 (6th Cir. 1992) (termination of employment is an adverse employment action).

Rule Application

Tell: Defendant terminated Plaintiff's employment, so third element is satisfied.

Fourth Element

(a) Rule Explanation

Geiger v. Tower Automotive, 579 F.3d 614, 624 (6th Cir. 2009) (plaintiff may prove fourth element through direct evidence of discriminatory motive).

Id. (evidence of discriminatory motive must be direct and not based on inferences).

Rule Application

Tell: Plaintiff has no direct evidence of discriminatory motive.

(b) Rule Explanation

Ercegovich v. Goodyear Tire & Rubber Co., 154 F.3d 344, 352 (6th Cir. 1998) (to show disparate treatment without direct evidence, employee must show that she was treated less favorably than an employee who is not part of her protected class and is otherwise similar in all relevant respects).

Mickey v. Zeidler Tool and Die Co., 516 F.3d 516, 522-23 (6th Cir. 2008) (relevant respects are those that relate in some fashion to the basis for the adverse employment action).

Mitchell v. Toledo Hospital, 964 F.2d 577, 583 (6th Cir. 1992) ("relevant respects" may include same supervisor and same performance standards).

Rule Application

Prove: Plaintiff identifies two male managers as having been treated more favorably than she was in the reduction in force. Those managers worked in different departments, had different supervisors, and received better evaluations for employee management than Plaintiff did.

a way to ask for specific guidance on a problem or to make sure that your mentor notices a particular concern that you have. Most supervisors (and most writing teachers) are so busy that they may not notice every problem on every draft. Use private memos to draw attention to particular concerns.

C. DRAFTING THE DISCUSSION SECTION

The typical research memorandum has a few basic parts: first comes the *question* or *questions presented*, followed by the *brief answer*. Next is the *statement of facts*. At the end of the research memo, most writers include a *conclusion*, in which they summarize their answers to all of the issues and sub-issues that the case presents.

At the heart of the research memorandum, however, is the *discussion* section. In this section, the writer analyzes all of the issues and sub-issues, taking each one and describing how the law dictates a particular result in the client's case. The best way to organize the discussion section is to use an analytical formula to help guide your analysis—and your presentation of that analysis.

Technically, two kinds of formulas can help you to draft your discussion. The first is a substantive formula: the formula of issues and sub-issues that you identify as necessary to answer the questions that your case presents. Previous chapters (and Section A of this chapter) were meant to help you to craft that formula, to decide how to structure your analysis of the issues and assertions relevant to your discussion. That formula is unique to this set of facts and issues in this jurisdiction at this time; you might be able to reuse certain elements in the formula, but you will never write another memorandum with that identical set of questions and assertions. It is for one-time-use only.

The second kind of formula is an analytical formula that can help you to draft your discussion, and it is far from unique: it can be recycled forever, for as many times as you need it. Similar formulas go by their various acronyms, including CREAC, IREAC, and CRuPAC. We call the formula CREXAC, and it can be used whenever you organize and write a *unit of discourse* to analyze a legal point. In analytical writing, a *CREXAC unit of discourse* refers to a section or subsection in which you use the CREXAC analytical formula to analyze the truth or validity of a legal assertion.

CREXAC is adapted from a syllogistic formula that many first-year law students learn as a method of organizing legal analysis. The acronym for that formula is IRAC, which stands for Issue-Rule-Application-Conclusion. IRAC and similar formulas can be helpful because they can serve as heuristics—or formulaic sets of questions—that guide writers to answer vital questions about their analyses. Your outline has identified the issues that you think are relevant to your analysis. For each of those issues, you must answer four questions, questions that IRAC alone won't answer:

1. What rule governs this issue?
2. What does this rule mean?
3. How should this rule be applied (or not applied) in this case?
4. What impact could that application have on a court's decision in this case?

We can illustrate how we need to adapt IRAC by beginning with a familiar syllogism:

Issue:	Is Socrates mortal?
Rule:	All human beings are mortal.
Application:	Socrates is a man.
Conclusion:	Socrates is mortal.

You may notice a problem in this syllogism. The rule application (aka the minor premise) must be connected to the rule itself (aka the major premise), but that connection is not obvious in this example. So we move beyond the syllogism to create a formula that asks the writer to explain what the rule means in this context:

Issue:	Is Socrates mortal?
Rule:	All human beings are mortal.
Explanation:	Human beings include men and women.
Application:	Socrates is a man.
Conclusion:	Socrates is mortal.

Thus, the rule explanation is a gap-filler that enables the writer to show readers how the rule about mortality connects to the facts about Socrates. Admittedly, rule explanation gets more complicated when we move beyond the question of simple mortality. Nevertheless, the formula remains the same, with two minor adaptations for analytical writing. Instead of beginning the analysis by stating the legal issue as a question, most analytical writers state the issue as an assertion or a conclusion. We sometimes call it a *conclusion-thesis*, because in a way it articulates the thesis of that unit of discourse. We change the second "conclusion" to "connection-conclusion" to distinguish it from the first conclusion and to remind us that, at the end of the formula (and thus at the end of each CREXAC unit of discourse), we should connect our analysis to the point we are making in that section of the discussion, and sometimes to our overall thesis. Therefore, our formula changes from IRAC to CREXAC, and it now looks like this:

Conclusion-thesis:	Socrates is mortal.
Rule:	All human beings are mortal.
Explanation:	Human beings include men and women.

Application: Socrates is a man.
Connection-conclusion: Socrates is mortal.

Thus, for each point that we need to establish in our discussion section, we will write a CREXAC unit of discourse, or "a CREXAC." Each element of the CREXAC formula is explained more fully below.

1. State Your Issue as a Conclusion

In the first conclusion element of the formula, the writer begins a unit of discourse by identifying the specific issue that is being addressed or the problem (or part or subpart of the problem) that is being analyzed in this section of the document. For example, a person writing a memo about the Bob Boyfriend problem above might begin one section as follows:

> The next issue to be decided is whether assaults that occurred in neighboring apartment buildings were "within sufficient proximity" to establish foreseeability.

Although this method effectively tells readers the issue, effective legal writers articulate the issue by stating it as a conclusion:

> A court would probably find that assaults on the landowner's premises were foreseeable.

The word "because" is not magical, and an effective writer can identify the reason for a conclusion without it. For example, another version of the same conclusion would be "A court would probably find that recent assaults in neighboring apartment buildings were 'within sufficient proximity' to the landowner's premises to make assaults there foreseeable."

A writer should remember to include the reason for the conclusion, with or without the word "because."

The conclusion-thesis tells readers even more about the direction the coming analysis will take when it includes a simple version of the reason for the writer's prediction. You may think of that part of the conclusion-thesis as the *"because"* clause:

> A court would probably find that assaults on the landowner's premises were foreseeable because they were "within sufficient proximity" to neighboring apartment buildings where assaults had occurred in the recent past.

Notice that the "because" clause includes the phrase-that-pays, "within sufficient proximity," that the writer associates with the issue of foreseeability. So, this version of the conclusion-thesis implies the issue, predicts the outcome, and identifies the phrase-that-pays that will be central to the analysis.

Note that if the issue is more complicated, the conclusion may be longer than just a simple sentence. The writer may need to provide legal or factual context to help readers understand how the conclusion fits into the analysis. In any event, by stating the issue as a conclusion, the writer begins to focus readers not only on the issue that will be addressed in that section of the analysis, but also on the result that the analysis of the issue will reveal and the reason for that result.

2. Articulate the Rule

After the writer has focused readers' attention on the issue being addressed, it's time to articulate the rule that governs the issue. If the rule comes from a statute or a well-established common law test, stating the rule may be simple. If the rule is derived from a statute or other enacted law, the writer may simply quote or paraphrase the pertinent language, as in this example:

> Under Van. Rev. Code § 1055.28, a dog owner is not liable for injuries caused by the dog if the person injured was "committing or attempting to commit a trespass or other criminal offense on the property of the owner" at the time of the attack.

Similarly, if the rule is a well-accepted common law rule derived from a well-known authority, the writer simply articulates the rule in its familiar language:

> A landowner's duty to protect an invitee from a criminal act arises only when he or she has actual or constructive knowledge of similar criminal actions committed on his or her premises or "within sufficient proximity" to those premises. *Arabella v. Hagrid*, 107 R.E.2d 1223, 1225 (Van. 1996).

If the case is more complex, however, stating one rule may not give readers enough context. As noted in an earlier chapter, sometimes it is appropriate to include "guiding rules" in a "rule cluster" as a way to give the reader sufficient information about the law before providing the rule. A "rule cluster" often starts with a well-accepted general rule and moves to one or more narrower rules or related rules, each of which governs an aspect of the issue presented by the writer's facts. The sample below is from a case in which one controversy was whether police needed a warrant to enter a house after dispatchers had received a 9-1-1 "hang-up" call and did not get a response when they called the number back. Notice how the writer of this excerpt moves from a general rule about the Fourth Amendment to the specific rule about whether a warrant is needed in this type of situation:

> The Fourth Amendment's reasonableness requirement mandates that police obtain a **warrant** "based upon a judicial determination of probable cause prior to entering a home." *Thacker v. City of Columbus*, 328 F.3d 244, 252 (6th Cir. 2003). "Exigent circumstances" are one of the many **exceptions to the warrant requirement.** *See Mincey v. Arizona*, 437 U.S. 385, 390 (1978). Courts have repeatedly recognized four situations that may rise to the level of exigency : "'(1) hot pursuit of a fleeing felon, (2) imminent destruction of evidence, (3) the need to prevent a suspect's escape, and (4) a

> risk of danger to the police or others.'" *Thacker*, 328 F.3d at 253 (quoting *United States v. Johnson*, 22 F.3d 674, 680 (6th Cir. 1994)). The Supreme Court has also recognized that another "exigency obviating the requirement of a warrant" is "the need to assist persons who are seriously injured or threatened with such injury." *Brigham City v. Stuart*, 547 U.S. 398, 403 (2006).

Thus, although the paragraph lists several rules, the final rule alone is the focus of this writer's analysis. The writer includes the earlier, guiding rules to provide sufficient context, moving readers from the general rule to the specific rule at issue in the client's case.

This discussion began with a rule from a single authority. Often, a single authority will not provide a rule that governs the writer's issue. In the portion of Chapter 6 devoted to rule synthesis, we discussed how to articulate a rule from multiple authorities. A review of that rule synthesis discussion may help you now if your task includes articulating a rule from more than one authority.

However you articulate your rule, be sure to articulate it early in your analysis and to cite appropriate authority from your jurisdiction for the rule. If you have used quotations longer than a few words, be certain that you have articulated the final rule in very clear terms.

3. Explain the Rule

After the writer has articulated the rule, it's time to provide the reader with any needed explanation of the rule. Before explaining the rule, however, the writer must decide which component of the rule is the focus of the particular subsection of the analysis. Usually, controversies about whether or how a rule applies will focus on certain key words or phrases-that-pay that are at the heart of the controversy regarding that rule. As you know, by focusing on one phrase-that-pays within each section or subsection of the discussion section, the writer makes sure to focus on one issue or sub-issue at a time. Thus, after articulating the rule, the writer must be sure to identify the word or phrase within that rule that is the phrase-that-pays for that section of the discussion. In almost all circumstances, each CREXAC unit of discourse in a Discussion section of a memo will have a different phrase-that-pays.

Identifying the phrase-that-pays is important because writers often explain rules by defining the phrase-that-pays, by showing how it has been applied in the past, or both. Thus, identifying a phrase-that-pays for each section of your document can aid focus: once the writer has identified the phrase-that-pays, it is easy to test the analysis in each section of the formula to make sure that it relates somehow to that phrase-that-pays.

When deciding how much explanation to provide for the phrase-that-pays in any particular section of your discussion, writers must consider two questions: (1) How ambiguous is the language of the phrase-that-pays? (2) How controversial is the application of the phrase-that-pays to the facts of this case? The more ambiguous and controversial the phrase-that-pays is, the more detailed the explanation should be.

Usually, the best way to explain the meaning of a phrase-that-pays is by illustrating how it has been applied in one or more authority cases. For example, presume you have a client, Mr. Honeycutt, whose dog had bitten a man who had trespassed by mistake on the dog owner's property. Presume the man had entered Honeycutt's house, thinking it was his brother's house. In that case, the victim might believe that only those who committed a *criminal*, as opposed to a *civil*, trespass would be unable to recover. When analyzing the issue, you would have to explain the rule in sufficient depth so that readers would understand that both civil and criminal trespasses are included in the exception:

> For purposes of § 1055.28, the term "trespass or other criminal offense" includes civil trespass. *Enns v. Kelly*, 112 R.E.2d 7, 8 (Van. App. 2011). In that case, a UPS driver was bitten by a homeowner's dog while delivering a package. *Id.* at 9. The dog was within a fenced yard labeled with a "No Trespassing" sign, but the driver testified that he did not see the sign, and he entered the yard. *Id.* Although the driver's action was not criminal, the appellate court reasoned that the legislature intended to include civil trespass within the scope of § 1055.28(B)'s affirmative defenses. *Id.* at 13. The court noted that innocent landowners should not be held liable to people who come onto their property uninvited. *Id.*; *see also Simmons v. Merritt*, 116 R.E.2d 567, 588 (Van. 2015) (noting that "for decades, Vanita courts have interpreted § 1055.28(B) to include both civil and criminal trespass").

Writers should almost always avoid using an intensifier such as "clearly" or "obviously." If you believe that its use is justified, you should—as the writer does here—include information that shows why your conclusion is "clear" or "obvious." Here, the parenthetical serves that purpose.

In this case, the rule explanation raises another possible issue. We now know that the statute prevents both civil and criminal trespassers from recovering. We know that the plaintiff is not a criminal trespasser, because he had entered the property by mistake. To explain whether the plaintiff could recover, the writer must apply the rule about civil trespass to the client's facts. As with any other issue, the writer must decide whether the issue is an *ignore, tell, clarify*, or *prove* issue. If it were a *prove* issue, the writer would need to create another CREXAC unit of discourse to address it, and the writer might want to do so even if it is a *clarify* issue. Because the issue of civil trespass is a *tell* issue in this situation, however, the writer can just address it in the same rule explanation section:

> Mr. Traveler's behavior obviously constitutes "civil trespass" as defined by Vanita courts. *See, e.g.*, *Lipman v. Cuyahoga*, 114 R.E.2d 105, 109 (Van. 2013) ("the classic example of a civil trespasser is one who enters another's property by mistake").

The writer uses the *see* signal here because she is drawing an inference from the case. The *Lipman* case did not discuss Mr. Traveler's behavior; rather, its holding provided the basis for the writer's legal conclusion. The writer uses the *e.g.* signal because this concept is so common that she could have cited to one of many cases.

The length of the rule explanation will vary depending on how abstract and/or controversial the rule is. Probably the best way for a writer to fully illustrate the meaning of a rule is to describe at least one case in which the court found that the case met the standard of the phrase-that-pays and at least one case in which the court found that the case *did not meet* the standard of the phrase-that-pays.[3] (Of course, for best results, these cases should be cases that are as close as possible to the client's situation.) Although not every issue will allow this sort of rule explanation (as the example above illustrates), good legal writers strive to find at least one case on each side of the issue they are analyzing. Illustrating what the phrase-that-pays means and does not mean sets the boundaries of the phrase-that-pays and gives the application of law to facts more validity.

The rule explanation example on the previous page includes just one paragraph. It explains a rule derived from a single authority, the trespass statute. As you know, however, a writer's *rule* is often synthesized from components of rules from multiple authorities. Usually, a synthesized rule requires multiple paragraphs of rule explanation, at least one for each component of the rule.

To examine this principle, consider this synthesized rule from the second exercise at the end of Chapter 6:

> Evidence of a person's qualifications at a significantly different point in time from the time of the alleged discrimination is irrelevant, and a court will exclude it, unless it has some tendency to prove that the person was not qualified when the discrimination occurred. To the extent that the evidence is probative of the person's qualifications at the time of the alleged discrimination, the court will still exclude and disregard it if its probative value is significantly outweighed by the risk of unfair prejudice, confusing the issues, or misleading the jury.

Of course, if any of these phrases-that-pay turn out to be significantly controversial, the writer might decide to divide the discussion of this rule into sub-parts and give any controversial phrases-that-pay a separate CREXAC unit of discourse.

The writer of that rule has synthesized the rule from components of two rules of evidence and at least one case. The rule explanation is likely to include at least one paragraph explaining the phrases-that-pay "irrelevant" and "probative value is significantly outweighed" from Federal Rules of Evidence 401 and 403. The rule explanation is also likely to include at least one paragraph explaining the phrase-that-pays "significantly different point in time."

3. *See also* Laurel Oates, Anne Enquist & Kelly Kunsch, *The Legal Writing Handbook* 134 (2d ed., Aspen 1998).

The Thesis Sentence

Look back at the first sentence of the quoted paragraph about § 1055.28 two pages back. Do you notice how that one sentence encapsulates the information about the rule that the entire paragraph is designed to convey? It is a one-sentence statement of the new information about the rule. The remainder of the paragraph supports it, elaborates on it, and provides authority for it. A skimming reader would be able to gain the critical information by reading just that one sentence, however. In that sense, it is a very effective thesis sentence.

In a well-written rule explanation, the first sentence of each paragraph will be a one-sentence statement of the new information about the rule that the entire paragraph is designed to convey. That *new information* will usually be either a phrase-that-pays associated with a component of a synthesized rule or a clarification of the phrase-that-pays that was the subject of the previous paragraph.

The remainder of the paragraph will support and elaborate on that sentence. You could extract the first sentences from each paragraph of the rule explanation, and a reader would have the basic necessary information about the rule. In fact, we suggest that you do that when you have completed a draft of a rule explanation. Is each piece of new information about the rule included in a thesis sentence? Is each thesis sentence focused on the rule, rather than on an authority? Could a reader learn the basic necessary information about the rule that you are explaining by reading just the thesis sentences? If the answers to all three questions is "yes," you have crafted effective thesis sentences.

When you have finished your explanation, evaluate whether it is so complicated that readers may have lost track of the rule you are explaining. For example, a rule explanation that includes two or three descriptions of cases in which the rule has been applied will have included some discussion of the facts of other cases. These "alien" facts may fill readers' short-term memory, crowding out the rule itself. To combat this problem, and to help readers to understand your rule application, it may be appropriate to end the rule explanation section of a CREXAC unit of discourse by restating the rule in a way that clarifies what facets of the rule are particularly relevant to the client's case. We call that restatement of the rule just before turning to application a *rule summary*. It will generally occupy only a sentence or two because the explanation should have already simplified the rule to the greatest extent possible.

In Mr. Honeycutt's case, for example, a rule summary could show how the rule explanation had clarified the meaning of the term "trespass":

> Accordingly, a dog owner cannot be held liable to either civil or criminal trespassers.

Although not every rule explanation needs a rule summary, it is probably a good default rule to include one. Most rules have many different facets. Using a rule summary allows the writer to highlight the facets of the rule that are relevant to your client's case.

4. Apply the Rule to the Facts

After the writer has articulated and then explained the rule, it's time to apply the rule to the facts (some legal writers say "applying the facts to the rule" to mean the same thing). In this step of the analysis, the writer shows readers how the phrase-that-pays intersects with the facts. How do the required elements or factors exist (or not exist) in the case? Note that you should never substitute synonyms for the phrase-that-pays, but this guideline is particularly important in the application section.

The application section should begin by stating affirmatively how the rule does or does not apply to the facts. It should *not* begin the application by drawing analogies; analogies support the application of law to facts, but they do not substitute for it. Essentially, the writer begins the application by saying, "Phrase-that-pays equals (or does not equal) our case facts." If the case is not controversial, a short passage might be enough:

> In this case, Mr. Traveler was "committing a trespass" under the terms of the statute. Although Mr. Traveler did not enter the property intentionally, his behavior meets Vanita's definition of civil trespass. Thus, under Van. Rev. Code § 1055.28, Mr. Honeycutt cannot be held liable to Mr. Traveler for any injuries he suffered from the dog bite.

This writer showed readers how the rule intersected with the client's facts by stating that civil trespass "equals" a "trespass" under Van. Rev. Code § 1055.28.

If the issue is at all controversial, the application should also provide details about how the facts support the statement about how the law applies to the facts. In this example from a memo about a similar issue, the writer is trying to analyze whether there is sufficient evidence that a dog is "vicious":

> In this case, the dog's behavior made evident that he was a "vicious dog" as required under the statute. Several neighbors testified that the dog growled and bared its teeth at every person who entered the

> house. Two neighbors testified that Mr. Slupe had paid for medical costs resulting from dog bites in the previous six months.

Sometimes, it's appropriate to draw analogies or distinctions between the client's case and the cases cited for authority in the explanation section:

> Like the UPS driver in *Enns*, Mr. Traveler entered a dog owner's property uninvited.

Note that drawing analogies or distinctions is not always necessary. For more complex or controversial issues, however, analogizing and distinguishing relevant authorities can help to cement readers' understanding of how a rule does or does not apply to the client's case. In Chapter 12, we will explain in more depth how to use the application section, analogies, and distinctions.

5. The Connection-Conclusion

After applying the rule to the facts, the writer connects the application to the analysis by articulating a connection-conclusion. The connection-conclusion need not begin a new paragraph if the application has been brief and the connection-conclusion is straightforward:

> Therefore, because Mr. Traveler was committing a civil trespass when he was bitten, Mr. Honeycutt cannot be held liable for his injuries under Van Rev. Code § 1055.28.

Stating a connection-conclusion explicitly at the end of a CREXAC unit of discourse is an important part of the analytical formula. Even though the unit of discourse began with a conclusion-thesis, the connection-conclusion at the end of the analysis serves a different purpose. It makes readers aware of the conclusion, yes, but it also tells them that the analysis of this issue is finished and that the discussion will soon be moving on to another point.

Furthermore, as its name implies, the connection-conclusion shows readers how this part of the analysis fits into, or connects to, the discussion as a whole. If a section of the discussion is about a dispositive point, the connection-conclusion should clarify the connection between that point and the ultimate result sought or the client's ultimate question. At the very least, the connection-conclusion should connect the analysis of the phrase-that-pays to the point that was at issue in that section of the analysis:

> Thus, a court would probably find that Mr. Traveler was "committing a trespass" under § 1055.28.

If appropriate, the connection-conclusion may also connect that section of the discussion to the ultimate issue that the memo is addressing:

> Thus, a court would probably find that Mr. Traveler was "committing a trespass" under § 1055.28, and Mr. Honeycutt will not be held liable.

This connection-conclusion connects the writer's point about the phrase-that-pays of one section—"committing a trespass"—to the writer's larger point: whether Mr. Honeycutt can be held liable.

D. SUMMING IT ALL UP

Before you can analyze your client's case, you have to identify the rules that govern the situation and the controversial issues that those rules present. After you have analyzed the kinds of issues that your case presents, you will be better equipped to draft a working outline. Before you can create a working outline, you must (1) conduct research to identify relevant rules and (2) look both to your case facts and to the courts' analyses to identify the phrases-that-pay that are relevant to your analysis by looking for new rules that interpret the phrases-that-pay of the rules you identified in step (1). Once you have identified the possible controversies, decide whether you need to ignore, tell, clarify, or prove each one, and then draft a working outline. You can leave an issue out of your outline if you plan to ignore it, but other issues should be included. If you plan to dispose of an issue in introductory material to a section or as an aside within another section, you should indicate that decision in the outline as well.

Even after you have carefully followed this guidance, you are likely to receive substantial feedback from your professor or supervisor. Think of that feedback in two positive ways. First, it allows you to see where you are on the learning curve. How well are you applying what you have learned so far? Second, feedback often guides your next steps in that learning process. So, the reader's comments may indicate that you have applied what you have learned accurately and you are ready to do more.

When you write up your analysis, use the CREXAC formula to help make sure that you provide a complete analysis of every needed element in your discussion section and thus give readers the information they need to understand your analysis.

E. EXERCISE 10.1: LABELING THE PARTS OF A CREXAC UNIT OF DISCOURSE

To get a better understanding of how the parts of the CREXAC fit together in a single unit of discourse, please label the five components of the CREXAC unit of discourse in this example. In addition, identify the rule summary within the rule explanation:

> Lisa Lagos is not likely to be able to prove that Bank Two treated her less favorably in the management restructuring

than male employees who were similarly situated in all material respects. *See McDonnell Douglas Corp.*, 411 U.S. at 802. She is unlikely, therefore, to succeed on her Title VII claim based on the termination of her employment.

To satisfy the *similarly situated* element of the disparate treatment claim, the plaintiff must allege that the identified employee was "nearly identical" to the plaintiff. *Pierce v. Commonwealth*, 40 F.3d 796, 804 (6th Cir. 1994). In determining whether a demotion violated Title VII, the court in *Pierce* looked at nonprotected employees and concluded that they were not similarly situated to the plaintiff in all material respects. *Id.* at 801. The plaintiff in *Pierce* had significantly different job duties than the employee he identified as comparable. *Id.* at 802. The court concluded, therefore, that the plaintiff had failed to meet his burden of pleading a Title VII claim. *Id.* at 804.

If an aspect of the plaintiff's job is materially different from the comparator employee's job, then the two may not be similarly situated. The Sixth Circuit has applied the "similarly-situated-in-all-material-respects" standard in more recent cases, most notably *Mazur v. Wal-Mart, Inc.*, No. 06-2485, 2007 WL 2859721 (6th Cir. Oct. 3, 2007). In *Mazur*, the court restricted consideration of employee similarity to those employees who were subject to the same supervisor and held to the same standards, with no differentiating or mitigating circumstances. *Id.* at *5. In other words, when some aspect of the other employee's job was different in a material way, that employee was not similarly situated in all material respects and could not serve as a comparator for purposes of establishing liability.

You should avoid using unreported decisions for rule authority. The writer cites this case as an illustrative authority rather than as a rule authority.

In the age discrimination context, a plaintiff need not prove "exact correlation"; plaintiffs must, however, establish "relevant similarity," that is, similarity in all material respects. *Ercegovich v. Goodyear Tire & Rubber Co.*, 154 F.3d 344, 352 (6th Cir. 1998). In *Ercegovich*, the court held that a Coordinator in Human Resources Development who was denied an opportunity to relocate during a reorganization was similarly situated to a Manager of Human Resources and a Personnel Development Specialist who were relocated because the differences in their positions were not relevant to the ability to relocate. *Id.*

Again, this unreported case is being used as illustrative authority rather than as a rule authority.

One district court, applying the "same supervisor" standard from *Mitchell*, considered when differences in supervisors will prevent an employee from proving similarity. *See Duncan v. Koch Air, L.L.C.*, No. Civ. A. 3:04CV-72-H, 2005 WL 1353758, *3 (W.D. Ky. June 2, 2005). Plaintiff, who was female, was fired for missing work without prior notice. *Id.* at *1. A male employee was not fired for violating the same rule. *Id.* The supervisor who fired the plaintiff did not make the decision to retain the other employee, however. *Id.* at *3. The court concluded that the plaintiff could not prove similarity because her claim was based, at least in part, on her supervisor's actions, and the employee to whom she compared herself reported to a different supervisor. *Id.* Because of the difference in supervisors, the differences in the employees' treatment could not be evidence of discrimination. *Id.* (citing *McMillan v. Castro*, 405 F.3d 405, 413-14 (6th Cir. 2003); *Mitchell*, 964 F.2d at 583).

Accordingly, to establish Bank Two's liability under Title VII for terminating her employment, Ms. Lagos must be able to prove that the male managers to whom she compares herself were similar in all material respects. Plaintiff is not likely to be able to meet this standard.

Ms. Lagos has alleged that Mr. North and Mr. South are similarly situated male coworkers whom Bank Two treated more favorably than it did Ms. Lagos when it allowed them to retain their jobs and terminated Ms. Lagos's. Lagos, North, and South were all similarly situated in that Bank Two hired all three at the same time. Furthermore, Bank Two evaluated all three using the same system for each year of their employment. The three worked at the same management level, reported to their respective departmental vice presidents, and supervised other employees. The similarities end there, however. Ms. Lagos is not similar to North and South as to the aspects of their employment that are material to her claim.

Mr. North and Mr. South worked in the International Transactions Department of Bank Two, while Ms. Lagos worked in the Commercial Lending Department. Plaintiff reported to a different supervisor. That different supervisor assigned her lower performance evaluation scores, which resulted in her lower salary. Performance evaluation scores and salaries were the critical factors in Bank Two's decision about which managers would be retained; these scores and salaries, therefore, were material to the decision. Because Ms. Lagos's scores and salary were set by a different person, she was, unquestionably, *dissimilar* from North and South in a *material* respect

Ms. Lagos's responsibilities were different in another material respect because she supervised a different type of employee than did Mr. North and Mr. South. Further, Mr. North and Mr. South performed more effectively in supervising and retaining their employees than Ms. Lagos did. Her performance in these areas was a critical factor in her annual evaluation scores. It was, therefore, material to the termination decision and another respect in which Ms. Lagos was not *similar* to Mr. North and Mr. South.

Like the plaintiff in *Pierce*, Ms. Lagos had different job duties than did North and South. She supervised a nonprofessional group of employees, while they supervised professional employees. Her performance evaluations reflected those differences. She was not, therefore, similarly situated in a material respect to North and South.

Lisa Lagos is like the plaintiff in *Duncan*, who could not establish that her employer discriminatorily applied the same rule differently to two different employees because she could not demonstrate that the same supervisor had interpreted and applied the rule to each of them. Lisa Lagos has not suggested that the Bank Two vice president who evaluated her performance also supervised the male employees to whom she compares herself. Accordingly, like the plaintiff in *Duncan*, Lisa Lagos will be stifled in her effort to establish that the termination of her employment resulted from discrimination in her performance evaluations.

Plaintiff is unlikely to be able to demonstrate that she, Mr. North, and Mr. South were similar in all material respects as regards the management restructuring. Even if she is able to establish all of the other elements of the *prima facie* case, therefore, she is not likely to succeed on her Title VII claim based on the termination of her employment.

Recall and Review

1. What are the five components of a CREXAC unit of discourse?
2. What are the four categories to consider when deciding whether to address an issue or how much time to spend addressing it? I_____, T_______, C_________, and P______.
3. If your client's case has three controversial phrases-that-pay, you would expect your discussion to include how many CREXAC units of discourse?
4. In general, the more ambiguous and controversial the phrase-that-pays is, the (longer or shorter?) the rule explanation will be.
5. If rule explanation has been lengthy and/or complicated, it's good to include what optional component before shifting to rule application?
6. True or False: Rule application should begin with a statement that translates to "phrase-that-pays equals [or does not equal] legally significant facts."
7. A ________ sentence at the beginning of each rule explanation paragraph focuses on introducing the phrase-that-pays or on telling readers what they will learn about the phrase-that-pays from the paragraph.
8. True or False: You should always include analogies when applying law to facts.
9. In what component of a CREXAC unit of discourse would a writer state the conclusion as to that issue and perhaps show how that conclusion affects the ultimate issue being addressed in the memo?

CHAPTER 11

USING CASES IN THE RULE EXPLANATION

Legal analysis, whether predictive or persuasive, is built on rules, which are the "R" in CREXAC. Whether those rules come from statutes or common law, the legal writer almost always uses cases to explain (the "EX" in CREXAC) those rules to readers. Thus, writing about cases will be a significant part of most legal writing projects that you tackle.

When using cases in a legal memorandum, your first concern should be choosing the best cases possible. As we discussed in Chapter 6, when you analyze a client's situation, you should use authorities from mandatory courts whenever possible. The problem, of course, is that courts do not always cooperate in this endeavor; they may stubbornly refuse to provide you with the case authority that you seek. In those situations, you must cite decisions from nonmandatory courts, taking care to acknowledge the court to which you are citing. Even when you are able to cite a decision from a mandatory court, however, you must do more than merely cite it; your description of the case must show readers why the decision is relevant.

Accordingly, this chapter will discuss how to write about and cite case authority. In general, you will be citing cases for one of two reasons. The first reason is as authority for the existence of a rule. The second, and more frequent, reason for citing a case is to use it as *illustrative authority*—that is, authority that illustrates how a rule has been or could be applied. While mandatory authority is still preferred even in this circumstance, nonmandatory authorities are more acceptable as illustrations than as sources for the rule itself.

Whenever possible, you should use mandatory authority for rule authorities. If you cannot cite to a mandatory authority, cite to a nonmandatory authority that is as similar as possible to the client's case.

To write about rule authorities and illustrative authorities effectively, you must include both substantive information about the authorities and appropriate citation information. These two kinds of information serve different roles: the substantive information should allow any reader to understand the cases' significance. The citation information should allow the cases to be located easily so that readers can assess their validity.

At least some of your readers, however, may never read the complete opinions of many of the cases that you cite. Depending on the level of supervision that you receive—and on how good a job you have done on your previous assignments—the office memo reader may review most, some, few, or even none of those cases. Although a few of your readers may go so far as to conduct independent research to verify your work, others may evaluate the validity of the authorities you cite—and of your analysis—based only on the information you include in the memorandum. Accordingly, your memo should include enough information about the cited cases to be useful to those who want to go beyond the memo and to be understandable and credible to those who do not.

Judges are more likely to conduct their own research or to have law clerks do so, but they, too, may rely on your descriptions of cases to some extent.

With these concerns in mind, you should pay attention to three aspects of using case authority: (1) you must provide readers with an appropriate amount of information about the cases you cite; (2) you must provide that information in the clearest and most helpful way possible, being especially careful about how you use quotations; and (3) you must use the best available authority, justifying your use of authority that is not mandatory.

Use of case authority is so important that we can't fit it all into one chapter. See Chapter 15 to learn about quoting, paraphrasing, and citing, with a special focus on case authority.

A. CASE DESCRIPTIONS

Analyzing authority cases is an essential part of effective rule explanation. Many legal writers neglect this important task, presuming wrongly that citations alone provide adequate support for the assertions they make. They seem to have the mistaken impression that lawyers have all of the needed law at their mental fingertips and that the legal writer needs only to allude to some of the relevant authorities, drop in some favorite quotations, or provide a string cite of the cases that might have some bearing on the case. Almost all readers, however, need more information than the citation can give.

While the depth of your case descriptions may vary depending on whether you are using the cases as rule authorities or illustrative authorities, you should plan to provide some description for every case you cite. As a former deputy solicitor general has noted, "[e]very case that is worth citing . . . is worth discussing sufficiently to show why it is particularly on point or sheds analogous light on the question at hand."[1]

1. James van R. Springer, *Symposium on Supreme Court Advocacy: Some Suggestions on Preparing Briefs on the Merits in the Supreme Court of the United States*, 33 Cath. U. L. Rev. 593, 601 (1984). The author was a deputy solicitor general of the United States from 1968 to 1971.

The question remains, what is "sufficient" discussion? Usually, when you are citing a case, you have some language in mind to quote or some holding to point out. That's fine. But in addition, make sure that readers can glean four elements from your case description:

1. the relevant issue,
2. the disposition of that issue,
3. the relevant facts, and
4. the relevant reasoning.

Notice that we say that readers should be able to *glean* these four elements. We are not saying that you must devote a sentence to each of these elements or even that you must state each one directly. Your decisions as to which elements to state directly and which to leave unstated will depend, as do most decisions, on the context in which the case descriptions appear.

1. Elements of a Description

With that warning, here is a description of each element.

a. The relevant issue

Be sure that readers can identify which of the case's many issues and sub-issues you are using the case to illustrate. You should also provide the legal context in which the court analyzed that issue, *if it is different from the context of your client's case or the cases under discussion in that section of your memo*. If you will be analogizing or distinguishing the case based on some particular facet of the legal issue, be sure to provide sufficient detail so that readers can understand that facet of the issue.

In most situations, the issue should be obvious from the case description, as it is in this example in which the writer is explaining the meaning of the term "tormenting the dog" in a dog-bite statute:

> Under normal circumstances, merely picking up a dog may not constitute "teasing or tormenting." *See Walton v. Hamner*, 99 N.E.2d 322, 329 (Ohio App. 2004). The plaintiff in *Walton* was on the dog owner's property for a party; the dog bit him when he picked up the dog to pet it. *Id.* at 325. The dog was healthy, and the dog owner had not warned the guests against petting or touching the dog. *Id.* at 324. The court reversed the decision of the trial court, which had granted a motion to dismiss in favor of the dog owner. *Id.* at 330. The court indicated that in most circumstances, picking up a small dog is an appropriate act and is not abusive, noting that the plaintiff was making a "friendly

gesture" and that the dog may have been "ornery," but it was not "in pain." *See id*.

The use of quotation marks around the word "tormenting" signals readers that the court in the *Walton* case was discussing the same statute that was at issue in the client's case. Suppose, however, that the writer found a case in which a court analyzed the meaning of the word "torture" as it is used in an animal cruelty statute as opposed to a dog-bite statute. A case like that might not be 100 percent on point, but it could still be useful to a court and therefore useful in your memo. In that situation, however, the writer must signal to readers that the issue is arising in a different context, as in this example:

> A court analyzing the meaning of Ohio's animal cruelty statute has held that even minor physical contact may constitute "torture" if the contact inflicts pain on the animal. *Beazley v. Smith*, 104 N.E.2d 355, 359 (Ohio App. 2009).

Unless you specify otherwise, readers will presume that the issues in cases you describe in a given section are situated in the same legal context as the client's issue. Be aware of that presumption so that you can correct it if needed.

b. The disposition

Make clear how the court disposed of that narrow issue and, if relevant, how it disposed of the entire case.

The point of the rule explanation section is to show readers how a particular rule has been applied in cases that are similar to or dissimilar from yours in legally significant ways. One of the most effective ways to accomplish that goal is to tell the results of rule application in cases that you cite. Too often, the rule explanation section consists merely of several different iterations of the same rule. You will frustrate your readers if you talk generally about a court's statement of the rule or about its reasoning without addressing the outcome of the issue:

> ***Bad Example***
> Another court has also analyzed the meaning of "taking charge" as it relates to establishing a duty. *Albert v. Shepard*, 199 N.E.2d 422, 429 (Ohio App. 2007). The *Albert* court noted that "taking charge requires an affirmative act for the benefit of another." *Id*. at 425. The court indicated that the act must be voluntary. *Id*.

This description does little more than restate the rule, and it leaves readers wondering whether the court made a finding as to the defendant in the *Albert* case and, if so, what facts that finding was based on. A better case description would make the finding explicit:

Better Example
A defendant may "take charge" if he takes steps to promote the safety of a helpless person. *Albert v. Shepard*, 199 N.E.2d 422, 429 (Ohio App. 2007). In *Albert*, the court held that the defendant had taken charge of the plaintiff when he took away the plaintiff's car keys, telling others that plaintiff was "too drunk to get behind the wheel." *Id.* at 425. The court noted that taking away car keys was an "affirmative act" that was meant to promote the defendant's safety. *Id.* at 429.

It is sometimes useful for readers to know the disposition of the entire case as well as the disposition of the relevant issue. There is no hard and fast rule about when to include the disposition of the entire case. If you decide to do so, however, you can often accomplish your goal by adding only a few words to the case description:

A defendant may "take charge" if he takes steps to promote the safety of a helpless person. *Albert v. Shepard*, 199 N.E.2d 422, 429 (Ohio App. 2007). The *Albert* court found that the defendant had taken charge of the plaintiff, when he took away the plaintiff's car keys, telling others that plaintiff was "too drunk to get behind the wheel." *Id.* at 425. In holding the defendant liable, the court noted that taking away car keys was an "affirmative act" that was meant to promote the defendant's safety. *Id.* at 429.

This phrase shows the disposition of the relevant issue.

This phrase shows the outcome of the entire case.

Knowing what a court said about a legal rule may be helpful, but it is almost always more helpful to know how the court decided, or disposed of, a particular issue when it applied the rule to the facts.

One more note about the disposition: it is easy to articulate the disposition when a court makes a finding on the merits. You can simply note that the court found that the phrase-that-pays was met or not met. Many cases you find in your research, however, will not include a finding on the merits. A significant number of appellate cases are reviews of decisions on *dispositive motions*, particularly motions to dismiss and motions for summary judgment. The trial court did not make a finding on the merits, so the appellate court is addressing a slightly different issue, such as whether the pleadings were sufficient to prevent a court from granting a motion to dismiss, or whether there were issues of material fact that would prevent a court from granting a motion for summary judgment.

Dispositive motions are those that can allow a court to "dispose" of a case by granting a motion to dismiss or a motion for summary judgment. As we explain below, we often refer to appellate cases that address dispositive motions as "kickback cases." We call them this because the appellant in those cases is typically asking the court to reverse and remand, i.e., kick the case back to the trial court.

In describing the disposition of an issue in a situation like this, the writer's main job is to be precise: don't misrepresent the disposition by saying that the court made a finding on the merits when it did not. In this excerpt from a court opinion, the court explains why it is reversing a partial grant of summary judgment:

> In the present action, DOT provided deposition testimony from an accident reconstruction expert, as well as the state trooper who witnessed the accident. Each opined that Trivelas's inattentiveness and failure to properly reduce his speed was the proximate cause of the collision between the DOT truck and Trivelas's van. Additionally, Trooper Lynn stated in deposition that following the accident, Trivelas told him he was distracted and was not observing the traffic directly in front of him when the accident occurred. Viewing the evidence in the light most favorable to DOT, we find there are genuine issues as to material facts in regard to "proximate cause " and "comparative negligence " precluding the grant of summary judgment. Concomitantly, we rule the trial court erred in granting partial summary judgment in favor of the plaintiffs.[2]

In describing the disposition of the comparative negligence issue, an effective legal writer should focus on the precise finding, taking care to be describe it accurately:

> ***Bad Example***
> The *Trivelas* court found that testimony from a state trooper about the driver's failure to reduce his speed and that the driver had admitted that he was "distracted" at the time of the accident showed that the driver was comparatively negligent. 558 S.E.2d at 278.

This description of the disposition misrepresents the court's holding as a finding on the merits. The following example is accurate:

> ***Better Example***
> The *Trivelas* court held that testimony from a state trooper about the driver's failure to reduce his speed and that the driver had admitted that he was "distracted" at the time of the accident were sufficient to create a question of material fact as to the comparative negligence issue. 558 S.E.2d at 278.

Some writers dislike precision because they believe that the case description is useless unless it includes a finding on the merits.

2. Trivelas v. S.C. Dept. of Transp., 558 S.E.2d 271, 278 (S.C. Ct. App. 2001).

It's true that a case with a finding on the merits is preferred. The *Trivelas* example, however, at least informs the reader of the kind of evidence that may constitute proof that a driver was comparatively negligent.

c. The facts

An effective case description should include enough of the legally significant facts for readers to understand how the court applied the law to reach its holding on the issue and how the case is analogous to your client's case. If you plan to draw an analogy to these facts or to distinguish your case based on its facts, be sure to provide sufficient detail to lay the foundation for that analogy or distinction.

When you are analyzing a question of fact, you can expect to provide more details. For example, suppose that you are writing a memorandum in a case in which an employee was arguing that he had been wrongly discharged based on age, in violation of Ohio's public policy exception to the employment at will doctrine. One way to establish causation (one of four elements in the relevant test) was to look at comments made by the defendant. An *ineffective* case description would merely refer to the comments that a court analyzed:

> ***Bad Example***
> An employer's comments about age can be direct evidence that age-related animus caused the discharge. *McGuffin v. Stewart*, 671 N.E.2d 145, 152 (Ohio 1996). The employee in *McGuffin* sued after he was terminated and replaced with a much younger worker. *Id*. The court found that causation was established because the employer's comments "showed an intent to discriminate based on age." *Id*. at 154.

The description above is ineffective because it does not include the factual details that will help readers to understand what kinds of comments would meet the standard. The example below gives the needed details:

> ***Better Example***
> An employer's comments that connect age and employment decisions can be direct evidence that age-related animus caused the discharge. *McGuffin v. Stewart*, 671 N.E.2d 145, 152 (Ohio 1996). In *McGuffin*, the Ohio Supreme Court found evidence of causation in an employer's statements that "I don't want old marathoners in my sales organization[;] I want young sprinters," and that the employee was "too old to grasp the concepts that he was looking for." *Id*. at 153. These statements particularly proved

that the employer had the intent to apply his age-related bias to employment decisions. *Id.*

Some writers include all of the facts from a case in a case description because they are unsure about which facts are *relevant* to the purpose for which they have included the case description. The result is an unfocused and unhelpful case description like this one:

Bad Example
Another court also found evidence of age discrimination. *See Zampierollo-Rheinfeldt v. Ingersoll-Rand de Puerto Rico, Inc.*, 999 F.3d 37 (1st Cir. 2021). The plaintiff's supervisor, who was older than the plaintiff, had just retired. *Id.* at 43. Soon, a much younger person became the supervisor. *Id.* Departments were eliminated, and a new structure was imposed on the organization. *Id.* at 43-44. A reduction in force accompanied the reorganization. *Id.* at 44. The plaintiff's supervisor chose the plaintiff for termination and told the plaintiff that he wanted to "rejuvenate" the company. *Id.* at 52. The court concluded that the plaintiff had carried his burden of identifying direct evidence of discrimination. *Id.*

Looking to the language of the rule will help you determine what the facts are. For example, the rule about "taking charge" has been interpreted to require that the defendant "affirmatively acted" to take charge of the plaintiff (or other victim). This requirement tells you that you must look for facts consisting of human behavior that shows that a person took some affirmative action. On the other hand, one rule of statutory construction provides that a specific statutory provision trumps a general statutory provision. (*See, e.g.*, Ohio Rev. Code § 1.51; *Meyer v. UPS*, 909 N.E.2d 106, 110 (Ohio 2009).) That requirement tells you that you must look for facts consisting of words in statutes that show that a provision is either more general or more specific than another provision.

This case description clutters the reader's mind with needless information. A good case description focuses on the case facts that were relevant to the disposition of the issue related to the phrase-that-pays.

If you are including a case description within a discussion of a question of law, you may need less detailed discussion of the facts; the court's decision in that case may be based more on policy reasons than on particular facts in the case. You should also be aware that the definition of *facts* may be broader than you realize. If you are analyzing an issue of statutory construction, for example, the facts may be legislative facts rather than real-world facts. Likewise, the facts relevant to an issue of contract law may be the real-world facts of who said what in regard to offer and acceptance, or they may be the less tangible facts of what words are in the contract.

Further, whether you are addressing a question of fact or a question of law, the facts included in the case description should be only those that are relevant to the issue under discussion. For example, part one of the four-part test used to analyze the Ohio public policy exception requires plaintiffs to establish the existence of a relevant and "sufficiently clear" public policy established in "constitutions, statutes, or the common law." A case description in this section of the document would not be helpful if it spent time giving details about why and how the employee had been terminated.

Question of Law

Courts often treat questions of law differently than they treat questions of fact. In general, a question of fact is a question that must be settled by looking at what someone did or said or wrote. For example, to determine whether a defendant's behavior caused injury to another, a court would look at the rule about causation and would then look at evidence about the behavior of the defendant to decide the question.

A question of law is often more focused on legal decisions about how certain established facts will be treated. For example, presume that the court must decide whether police had valid consent when one roommate consented to a search and one roommate objected to the search. In that situation, the court would not be asking who said and did what. Nor would it be asking whether the behavior did or did not meet the definition of legal consent; that question would be a question of fact. Instead, the court will be asking the legal question of what "legal consent" means: does it require both roommates to agree? Does the objecting roommate control, or does the consenting roommate control? This issue is a question of law because the court is deciding what the law is.

Bad Example

> A sufficiently clear public policy can be found when an employee is discharged for protesting unsafe working conditions. *Pelehach v. Clare Prods., Inc.*, 761 N.E.2d 385, 388 (Ohio 2002). In *Pelehach*, an employee was discharged after complaining to his employer about working conditions that he believed threatened employee health and safety. *Id.* at 386. The employee was a truck driver, and he noted that the company was violating rest-period requirements and other safety provisions. *Id.* at 388. The employee was fired two days after making a written complaint. *Id.* The Supreme Court of Ohio found that the "sufficiently clear public policy element" had been met. *Id.* at 387.

The details about the termination do not help readers understand how or why the court found the existence of a sufficiently clear public policy. Instead, the writer should give more information about that decision, giving only enough information about the discharge to show the relevance of the public policy:

> *Better Example*
> A sufficiently clear public policy can be found when an employee is discharged for protesting unsafe working conditions. *Pelehach v. Clare Prods., Inc.*, 761 N.E.2d 385, 388 (Ohio 2002). In *Pelehach*, an employee was discharged after complaining to his employer about working conditions that he believed threatened employee health and safety. *Id.* at 386. The Supreme Court of Ohio looked to the Constitution of Ohio and Ohio "safe workplace" statutes before concluding that "Ohio public policy favoring workplace safety" met the sufficiently clear public policy requirement. *Id.* at 387 (citing Ohio Rev. Code Ann. §§ 4101.11, 4101.12 (Westlaw current through Mar. 9, 2010)).

This example is better because it focuses on the facts that the court used to determine whether the phrase-that-pays ("sufficiently clear public policy") was met: Ohio has constitutional provisions and statutes that show that Ohio has a public policy favoring workplace safety.

d. The reasoning

Most case descriptions will be more effective if they include enough information to give readers a basic understanding of the court's reasoning, showing why the court decided the issue in the way that it did. If either the case or the reasoning behind the court's decision is significant, try to provide more detail. It is sometimes difficult to separate facts from reasoning because courts may use facts to articulate the reasons for their decisions. Don't worry about drawing a clear line between facts and reasoning; focus on giving readers the information needed to understand why the court reached the decision that it did. In this drunk driving case, the court addressed the defendant's claim that the lower court had erred by finding that the officer had probable cause to stop the defendant on suspicion of drunk driving:

> Here, the trooper testified that he observed Appellant travel left of center two times. The video from the cruiser showed at least one left of center violation. The trial court, based upon the testimony and a review of the video, found that there was a "substantial, like I would say more than a foot left of center and a relatively jerky correction which I'm sure is what got the officer's attention." Based upon these facts and findings we find that the trial court reasonably concluded that probable cause existed for Appellant's stop and, as a result, we find Appellant's first assignment of error to be without merit.[3]

3. *State v. Gunther*, 2005-Ohio-3492 (Ohio App. July 5, 2005).

If you were writing a case description of this case, you should not just restate this entire paragraph. Instead, you should identify and include only the crucial aspects of the court's reasoning. Not surprisingly, in this fact-dependent inquiry, your discussion of the reasoning will necessarily include facts:

> In Gunther, the court found that an officer who observes a driver traveling left-of-center twice in short succession has probable cause to stop the driver on suspicion of drunk driving.

Here are the facts.

Here is the disposition.

Here is the issue.

This reasoning is tied inextricably to the facts, and so the reasoning is implicit in the other aspects of the case description: the finding of probable cause was valid because those facts existed. On the other hand, if the issue is more of a legal question, the reasoning will focus less on the facts and more on the policies behind the court's legal conclusion.

In a 2003 case, for example, the Eleventh Circuit addressed the question of whether a community college president and dean were entitled to qualified immunity in a case in which they had been accused of not acting on knowledge of same-sex sexual harassment.[4] The court observed that the defense would be unavailable only if freedom from same-sex sexual harassment were a "clearly established constitutional right."[5] To answer this question of law—which was not dependent on any behavior of any harassers or of college officials—the court spent nine paragraphs analyzing the development of the rule against same-sex sexual harassment and whether it was sufficiently "clearly established." The court eventually found that the college officials were entitled to qualified immunity because the right was not sufficiently clear. We will not repeat those paragraphs here, nor should a legal writer include those paragraphs in a case description. Rather, that writer should identify the nugget of reasoning that is most useful to his or her analysis, as in the following textual description:

> Public officials cannot use the defense of qualified immunity if the complaint alleges the violation of a clearly established constitutional right. *Snider v. Jefferson State Cmty. Coll.*, 344 F.3d 1325, 1327 (11th Cir. 2003). The plaintiffs in *Snider* had alleged same-sex sexual harassment in violation of the equal protection clause. *Id.* The court found that same-sex sexual harassment was not "clearly established" as a violation of the constitution, noting the "bewildering" array of decisions and finding that a rule forbidding this behavior in private, rather than public,

This sentence contains the only necessary "facts" for the issue of qualified immunity. The rule asks whether the alleged violation was clearly established, so the facts are, of necessity, facts about what was alleged.

4. *Snider v. Jefferson State Cmty. Coll.*, 344 F.3d 1325, 1327-1330 (11th Cir. 2003).
5. *Id.*

employment settings was the only clearly established rule at the time of the alleged incidents. *Id.* at 1330.

When writing a case description, presume that you need to include all four of these elements. Admittedly, on some occasions, it may be permissible to include only three of the four elements. At times, the facts may be omitted in a section devoted to an issue of law, particularly in a situation in which the writer cites two or more cases with similar fact situations. Likewise, when an argument turns on a question of fact, it may be permissible to omit a court's reasoning. At this stage in your career, however, a good rule to follow when in doubt is to include all four elements.

Note that including these four elements in a case description is not all that the effective writer must do. To ensure that the case description is effective, make it as succinct as possible, use parenthetical case descriptions effectively and appropriately, and be sure that the case description is accurate.

2. Writing Succinct Case Descriptions

Including the issue, the holding, the facts, and the reasoning in a case description may seem to require a long description. Actually, all four of these elements can often be conveyed in a parenthetical description, and they can certainly be conveyed in a textual description of two sentences. Of course, if the case is significant or the argument is controversial, your case description may be lengthier.

There are two keys to succinct case descriptions. The first key is *focus*. You must understand the focus of the issue you are addressing and make sure that the case description has that same focus. The second key is *efficient use of language*. Too many case descriptions begin with a wasted sentence that does little more than announce that the case exists. Use your subjects and verbs with care to convey the most information in the fewest words.

a. Focus

The case descriptions below are from a memorandum in an Americans with Disabilities Act (ADA) case. An employee is entitled to the protections of the ADA only if the employee can prove a disability, as defined under the ADA. Notice how these descriptions efficiently include each of the necessary case description elements:

These words signal the issue.

These words signal the disposition.

These words signal the significant facts.

Good Example

The Ninth Circuit determined that employees were not disabled under the ADA in spite of their monocular vision because they did not have an impairment that substantially limited them in any major life activity. *EEOC v. United Parcel Service*, 306 F.3d 794, 803 (9th Cir. 2002). The evidence demonstrated that the employees could drive, read, use tools, and play sports. *Id*. The court concluded, therefore, that they were not substantially limited in the major life activity of seeing. *Id*.

These words signal the reasoning.

This sentence includes more facts.

This sentence includes more of the court's reasoning.

One method you can use to test the focus of your case descriptions is to look for the phrase-that-pays for that section of the document. If your case description includes the phrase-that-pays, chances are good that you have at least focused the description on the right legal issue. The phrase-that-pays in the example above is "substantially limited in any major life activity." The case description is well focused because that phrase-that-pays appears prominently in the case description.

In the following example, from an analysis of the meaning of the "otherwise qualified" element of the same case, the writer discusses cases in which courts have determined that disabled employees were "otherwise qualified" for their positions because they had been successfully performing the duties of the positions in spite of their disabilities. Note how the writer took care to connect the phrase-that-pays, "otherwise qualified," to both of the case descriptions (the phrase-that-pays is underlined).

Good Example

A disabled employee may prove that he is <u>otherwise qualified</u> for his position by demonstrating that he has been performing the position successfully in spite of his disability. *See, e.g., Fouraker v. Publix Super Markets, Inc.*, 959 F. Supp. 1504, 1507 (M.D. Fla. 1997) (employee with cerebral palsy was <u>otherwise qualified</u> for his position as a grocery service person because he had been successfully performing the position for 17 years).

Where the employee has been successful in the very position from which he was discharged, evidence of his success in that position is sufficient to prove that he is <u>otherwise qualified</u> for it. *See Montegue v. City of New Orleans*, No. 95-2420, 1996 WL 531830, *4 (E.D. La. Sept. 3, 1996). The employer in *Montegue* argued that a drug-addicted employee was no longer qualified to be a firefighter because of his drug addiction. *Id*. The court observed, however, that the employee had been a successful firefighter, never having been reprimanded or disciplined. *Id*. The condition upon which the disability claim is based (drug addiction) cannot be the

> basis for concluding that the employee is not otherwise qualified, the court held, because the presence of a disability is a separate issue under the ADA framework. *Id*. The employee is otherwise qualified if he can perform the essential functions of the position; his past success in the position is sufficient to prove that he is otherwise qualified. *Id*.

If a court has not been thoughtful enough to use the phrase-that-pays that you have identified for that section of the argument, you can make the connection yourself, as long as you do it honestly. If you do make the connection yourself, be sure to justify the connection in the way you describe the case or with language that you quote. The word *apparently* is often helpful when describing a connection that is implicit rather than explicit, as in this description of a court's reasoning:

> ***Good Example***
> The court apparently believed that the employee was otherwise qualified for a position as a driver, even though his epilepsy prevented him from obtaining a commercial driver's license, because when it found that the employee had been discriminated against, the court specifically noted that he had been a successful driver before the employer added the commercial driver's license requirement. *Smith v. Medical Devices, Ltd.*, 101 F.3d 101, 105 (E.D. La. 1996).

A writer who failed to recognize that the court in *Smith* had applied the *otherwise qualified* concept without naming it might reject *Smith* or describe it without connecting it to the phrase-that-pays:

> ***Bad Example***
> The court found that the employer discriminated against a driver whose epilepsy prevented him from obtaining a commercial driver's license because he had been a successful driver before the employer added the commercial driver's license requirement. *Smith v. Medical Devices, Ltd.*, 101 F.3d 101, 105 (E.D. La. 1996).

A thoughtful writer will recognize that the *otherwise qualified* concept is present and identify the concept in the case description, even though the court has not done so explicitly.

When trying to decide how much detail to give readers, first assess how you are using the case. If you are using the case as rule authority and plan to discuss it in depth in your explanation section, you may give only a naked cite. On the other hand, you may be using a case as rule authority only because it is from a court of mandatory jurisdiction or it is well known as the source of a particular rule, rather than because of its relevance to your client's case. (Presumably, you plan to use other cases to illustrate the rule.) If that is the situation, you should provide a parenthetical description, as shown above with the writer's use of the *Fouraker* case. Parenthetical case descriptions are also illustrated below.

When you believe that you have completed the case description, you may want to test its usefulness to the reader by employing the following technique. Cut and paste the case descriptions to a separate document so that you can read them in isolation. Does each description provide enough context so that the reader can easily ascertain how the relevant issue arose and how the court resolved it? Is the court's reasoning clear? Does the description provide enough context to make the relevance of the case clear? Is the description sufficiently focused, or does it include extraneous information that does not help the reader understand why the reader has included it? Reading the case description out loud as you contemplate these questions may help you to find weaknesses. When you are satisfied with the answers to these questions, the description is ready.

After testing the following case description's usefulness, a writer would likely determine that it is too detailed to effectively focus the reader's attention on the *otherwise qualified* analysis:

> ***Bad Example***
> The court considered several questions, including whether the employee could perform the essential functions of the position, whether a reasonable accommodation would have enabled the employee to perform the essential functions of the position, and whether the employer discriminated by failing to engage in an interactive process with the employee to identify a reasonable accommodation. *Anthony v. Trax Int'l Corp.*, 955 F.3d 1123, 1127-34 (9th Cir. 2020). The court agreed with the employee that a person who can perform the essential functions of the position may be qualified for the position. *Id.* at 1134. The court also concluded that the employee was not qualified because she lacked some of the educational qualifications for the position, so she could not have overcome the lack of qualifications, even if the employer had attempted to accommodate her disability. *Id.*

The same writer would probably determine that the next case description suffers from the opposite weakness; it includes insufficient information to be useful:

> ***Bad Example***
> One court held that assistance from coworkers, which the plaintiff had requested, was not a reasonable accommodation, so the

plaintiff was not otherwise qualified. *Gardea v. JBS USA, LLC*, 915 F.3d 537, 542 (8th Cir. 2019).

b. Using language effectively

Even when you are using a textual case description or when you must give readers more detail, do not make your case description needlessly long. Provide only the information that readers need about each of the four elements. The description of the *Montegue* case above is somewhat lengthy, but its length is concentrated in the facts and the reasoning. The "otherwise qualified" element is fact specific, and thus the details about cases in which that element was or was not established were particularly important in that case.

In many case descriptions, writers run into trouble in the first sentence. One way to avoid this trouble is to concentrate on the subject-verb combination. The first sentence you write about a case should tell readers something that the court did or something about why the court did what it did. It should *not* tell readers what the case *involved, regarded,* or *concerned*, or what the court *addressed, considered, examined,* or *dealt with*. Notice how the first sentence in the following case description wastes readers' (scarce) time and energy:

> ***Bad Example***
> The court in *Gilbert v. Frank*, 949 F.2d 637, 639 (2d Cir. 1991), examined the issue of when an employee is "otherwise qualified."

This description tells readers that the court examined an issue, but it leaves them in suspense as to what happened as a result of the examination. Suspense is the enemy of good legal writing. Instead of saying only that the court "examined" the issue, the writer should say something about a court's ultimate ruling or, if relevant, a particular finding in the case. Verbs such as *held* and *found* are more likely to get your readers to the point of the case:

> ***Good Example***
> In 1991, the Second Circuit held that an employee was not "otherwise qualified" to perform a position for which he had applied when his disability prevented him from carrying out the job's essential functions. *Gilbert v. Frank*, 949 F.2d 637, 639 (2d Cir. 1991).

The bad example told readers only the issue that the court addressed in *Gilbert*. The good example, on the other hand, tells readers the issue, the legally significant facts, and the disposition of the issue. In later sentences, the writer can add more facts (if needed) or reasoning.

c. Verb tense in case descriptions

Many writers get confused as to the appropriate verb tense when describing cases. This confusion results when courts mix legal rules that are currently in force—properly stated in the present tense—with case facts, findings, and holdings—properly stated in some form of the past tense.

Within a case description, use an appropriate form of past tense to describe events that happened before the case began as well as events that happened in the case. The court's holdings as to specific parties should also be described using the past tense, but statements about rules that are currently in force should be stated in the present tense:

Good Examples

The plaintiff claimed that he was otherwise qualified for the position from which he was discharged.

The position description had not included lifting heavy objects.

Defendant had questioned Plaintiff about her frequent illnesses.

The plaintiff alleged . . .

The defendant argued . . .

The court found . . .

The court reasoned . . .

The court held that the employer had violated the ADA when it discharged Mr. Ogakor even though he had been performing his job successfully without accommodations.

The court held that performance in a previous job can be used to provide evidence of a plaintiff's qualifications.

The correct verb tense may not make or break your argument, but using the wrong verb tense distracts readers at best. At worst, it confuses them and slows down their comprehension.

3. Writing Effective Parenthetical Descriptions

The case descriptions we have shown so far are known as *textual* descriptions because they occur within the text. Most writers, however, also learn to use parenthetical case descriptions so they can, when appropriate, give readers information about authority cases more

The skill of succinct case descriptions—perhaps best exemplified in parenthetical case descriptions—is particularly useful when writing short-form office memos such as E-memos. See Chapter 16.

efficiently. Parenthetical descriptions can save both space and readers' time, and they are often a good choice. However, it is just as important to keep the principles of focus and completeness in mind when writing parenthetical descriptions as it is when writing textual descriptions. Ineffective parentheticals tend to give only a snippet of information. Often, unfortunately, the snippet does not contain enough information to make the case useful to readers, who must decide whether the cited case provides authority for a ruling in the case at bar:

> ***Bad Example***
> *Arline*, 480 U.S. at 278 (explaining who is "otherwise qualified"); *Gilbert*, 949 F.2d at 639 (employer complained that employee's disability meant he was not "otherwise qualified").

These parentheticals identify a potential issue (whether an employee is "otherwise qualified"), but they do not tell readers which facts were relevant to the court or how the issue will apply to particular facts. This type of snippet parenthetical may be effective, but only if the surrounding text—usually the text before the citation—supplies sufficient context. For a parenthetical to be effective, either the parenthetical alone *or* the parenthetical and the preceding text will give readers information about at least three, and preferably four, of the required elements: the issue, the disposition, the facts, and the reasoning. In the first example below, the text before the citation provides the disposition, the issue, and the reasoning; the parenthetical, therefore, need include only the legally significant facts. In the second example, which has no introductory text, the parenthetical includes all four elements:

Issue indicated here.

Reasoning indicated here.

Issue and disposition indicated here.

Facts indicated here.

Issue and disposition indicated here.

Facts and reasoning indicated here.

> ***Good Example***
> Courts have defined an otherwise qualified individual as one who is capable of meeting all of a position's essential requirements. *E.g., McGuffin v. Ifeduba Enters., Inc.*, 101 F.3d 104, 111 (6th Cir. 2001). They have indicated that employees may be discharged when their disabilities prevent them from performing those essential responsibilities on the ground that they were not otherwise qualified. *See, e.g., Arline*, 480 U.S. at 288 (if plaintiff's tuberculosis prevented her from being at work, she was not otherwise qualified because an essential requirement of her teaching position was presence in the workplace); *see also Gilbert*, 949 F.2d at 641-42 (employee could not prove that he was otherwise qualified because his illness prevented him from performing the lifting requirement of his postal worker position).

As with textual descriptions, using language effectively and focusing on the phrase-that-pays can make parenthetical descriptions more useful. Be aware of length when writing parenthetical case descriptions. If a parenthetical description requires multiple sentences or complex single-sentence structures, you should use a textual case description instead.

Knowing how to write effective parenthetical case descriptions is important, but the writer must also know *when* to use a parenthetical description. Deciding whether to use a textual or a parenthetical description for a cited case is really a question about how much detail to provide. If little detail is needed, as when you are citing a case only for rule authority, you can easily use a parenthetical description. Ultimately, your decision will be based on the answers to two questions:

1. How is the case significant to the analysis?
2. What information do readers need to understand the case's significance?

The more significant an authority case is, and the more important it is for readers to understand its facts and reasoning, the more detail you need to provide *in the rule explanation.* If the issue or the authority case is more straightforward, on the other hand, you can provide a shorter textual description *or* a parenthetical description. Note that you should generally *not* provide both a parenthetical and a textual description for the same case. You may appropriately have a sentence with introductory text that precedes a citation with a parenthetical description. Generally, however, you should not follow a parenthetical case description with further textual description.

4. Making Case Descriptions Accurate

It should go without saying that legal writers should not misrepresent any of the four case description elements. Say it we must, however. When we chat with judges and law clerks and quiz them about their legal writing pet peeves, many mention wordiness and poor organization. Almost all of them, however, complain about attorneys who misrepresent the facts or the law. Law clerks describe the many times that they have read in a brief that a case stands for one proposition, only to consult the case and find that it stood for some wholly unrelated point or, worse, contradicted the very point the attorney was using the case to make.

Remember: someone will be checking your work when you submit a document to a court. This fact is still important if you are writing an office memo, because many office memos are later turned into briefs and submitted to courts. Don't be tempted to misrepresent case law, either through negligence or willfulness. The momentary satisfaction of presenting analysis with a veneer of validity is not worth the cost in reputation and future credibility. Further, you may face sanctions; ABA Model Rule of Professional Conduct 3.3(a) provides that a lawyer shall not knowingly "make a false statement of fact or law to a tribunal. . . ."

There is even less reason to misrepresent case authority when working on an in-house document; doing so may lead to unemployment. Your employer should not have to check your work to verify its accuracy. Accordingly, let us presume that you are not going to knowingly misrepresent cases; how can you avoid doing so negligently? First, avoid two common shortcuts that often lead to mistakes; second, be careful to avoid characterizing dicta as holdings, particularly when describing certain categories of cases.

One shortcut to avoid is relying on how others have characterized cases. If you read a memo, brief, or court opinion that characterizes a case in a certain way, it is tempting to repeat that characterization yourself. Certainly, you may reason, that attorney or that judge would not have misrepresented the law. Resist the temptation. Take the time to click through to the cited case and to read it yourself to verify that it says what you think it says. Further, be sure to use *Shepard's*, KeyCite, or another citator and conduct further research to verify that the case is still valid law. Even if the judge or attorney did not misrepresent the law, more recent authorities may affect the validity of that case.

Lexis and Westlaw have recently updated their databases to provide visual cues that indicate when you are reading text that is not in the majority opinion. Whatever format you are reading a case in, be sure you know which part of the opinion you are reading.

Another shortcut to avoid is using a case as authority when you have read only an isolated paragraph or two. Modern computer research can often send legal researchers on a cavalcade of clicking, jumping from one source to another to another. If you are not careful, you can end up citing a dissenting opinion as authority. If you don't take the time to discern the relevant issue, disposition, facts, and reasoning, you may not discover that you are reading something other than the majority opinion.

Dicta in this context is anything that a court has said about a rule that it did not have to say to resolve the dispute before it. To determine whether a statement about a rule is dicta, ask yourself whether that statement was a factor in the court's analysis of the issue it was deciding. If not, it is dicta.

If you need that statement about the rule for your own analysis, the court may have helped you by citing an authority in which the statement is *not* dicta, so don't lose hope.

The second way that writers may negligently misrepresent the law is by failing to distinguish dicta from holdings, especially in what we refer to as *kickback cases.* A kickback case is a case that comes to a court of appeals after the trial court has granted a motion to dismiss or a motion for summary judgment. If the court of appeals reverses and remands the decision, it in essence "kicks back" the case to the court below. But a decision to reverse and remand does not necessarily mean that the court made any *findings* as to the merits regarding how the law applies to the facts. In reversing a grant of a motion for summary judgment, the court may be doing no more than finding that a dispute exists as to the legally significant facts. When reversing a grant of a motion to dismiss, the court is merely finding that the pleadings were sufficient to state a claim, not that the pleadings were true or that the plaintiff will necessarily succeed in his or her cause of action. It is particularly important to remember that the standard of review for a motion to dismiss requires a court to presume that a complaint's factual allegations are true; in a motion for summary judgment, a court generally draws any inferences in favor of the nonmoving party. These presumptions do *not* mean, however, that the allegations are in fact true or that the plaintiff will be able to establish at trial that they are true.

For example, in a Florida case, *Holley v. Mt. Zion Apartments*,[6] an apartment owner was sued by the estate of a woman who had been killed in her apartment. The plaintiff alleged that the landlord had negligently failed to provide adequate security in the building's common areas. The trial court had granted the defendant's motion for summary judgment, but the appellate court reversed and remanded, finding that there were "substantial fact issues" that prevented a finding of summary judgment for the defendant.

In general terms, courts will grant a *motion to dismiss* if the alleged facts create no possibility for relief; they will grant a *motion for summary judgment* if (1) there are no issues of "material" fact and (2) the moving party is entitled to judgment as a matter of law.

A careless writer, trying to explain the rule about a landlord's duty, might misrepresent the court's holding by quoting a partial sentence with a misleading introduction:

> ***Bad Example***
> The court held that "the landlord's duty to keep the common areas reasonably safe required that a guard or other security measures be provided at the complex." *Holley v. Mt. Zion Terrace Apts., Inc.*, 382 So. 2d 98, 99-100 (Fla. Dist. Ct. App. 1980).

The *language* is quoted accurately; the context, however, is not accurate. A supervisor (or worse, an opponent or a judge) who read the decision would find that some words missing from the sentence create a vastly different impression of the case (the emphasis is added):

> *[A] jury could properly find that* a discharge of the landlord's duty to keep the common areas reasonably safe required that a guard or other security measures be provided at the complex.

The court did not hold that the landlord's duty required the guards; rather, it found that it would be reasonable for a jury to conclude that the plaintiff had a valid argument as to this point. This finding required it to reverse summary judgment in the defendant's favor, but it did *not* constitute a finding as to the truth of the plaintiff's pleadings, nor did it constitute a finding that the plaintiff would definitely win that legal argument. In contrast, notice how the writer in the example below accurately portrays the disposition of the issue and uses the word "may" to indicate the lack of a legal holding:

6. 382 So. 2d 98 (Fla. Dist. Ct. App. 1980).

> *Good Example*
> A landlord's duty to keep common areas reasonably safe may require that the landlord provide guards or other security measures. *See Holley v. Mt. Zion Terrace Apts., Inc.*, 382 So. 2d 98, 99-100 (Fla. Dist. Ct. App. 1980) (reversing summary judgment in landlord's favor and finding that jury could properly find such a requirement).

Thus, you can still cite a kickback case; you must, however, accurately portray the issue and its disposition in any case description.

Accurately describing authority cases is one of the best ways to educate a court about the meaning of the law. You will increase your chances of doing so both effectively and accurately when you

1. provide sufficient information about the issue, disposition, facts, and reasoning;
2. focus the information on the issue currently under discussion;
3. use language efficiently to avoid unnecessary wordiness;
4. use parentheticals as needed for rule authorities or less significant cases; and
5. take care to avoid misrepresenting the cases you cite.

B. COUNTERANALYSIS

When we begin our search for the rule that governs any legal issue, we first assume that a clear rule exists and that our tasks are simply to identify that rule and to explain it so that readers will understand how it applies to our facts. Often, that assumption is more or less correct. Sometimes, however, our research will lead us to a variety of rules from different courts or the same court. Sometimes two or more rules arguably apply to the legal issue we are addressing. Sometimes these various rules are substantially the same but use different words. And sometimes they conflict with each other, in part or in whole. When no highest-level mandatory authority has resolved any apparent conflict among those competing rules, our task in articulating and explaining the rule may include *counteranalysis*.

Counteranalysis is a discussion of the weaknesses of any interpretation of the rule that differs from the writer's. Counteranalysis is not necessary in all cases, but a careful writer will always think about whether an opposing attorney would articulate or explain the rule differently. If so, the writer should consider including counteranalysis in the rule explanation section of an analysis or argument. Note that counteranalysis never takes the *place* of a full explanation of the rule

Counteranalysis may also occur in the application section of an analysis. In that context, the dispute is over how a clear rule will apply to certain facts, rather than on the identity of the rule itself. (See Chapter 12.)

as the writer has identified it. Rather, when the writer has finished explaining the identified rule, the writer turns to an explanation of why a competing view of the rule is incorrect or less secure.

The writer's goal in including counteranalysis is to convince readers that the writer has accurately identified and explained the rule. The goal is not to cast aspersions on the other side. So, an appropriate thesis sentence to begin the counteranalysis would be "X, rather than Y, is the rule governing this question," consciously keeping the focus on the preferable rule. The alternative, while not legally incorrect, shifts the focus: "The other side says that the rule is Y, but that is wrong."

On some occasions, you might even devote a CREXAC unit of discourse to analyzing which rule is appropriate, using a rule that determines which rule to apply. This method is used often when the constitutionality of a statute is challenged. In that circumstance, the rule could be phrased as "If a statute implicates a fundamental right, then the court must use the 'strict scrutiny' standard to analyze the statute's constitutionality." The issue would be whether the right at issue was a "fundamental right."

The counteranalysis will rarely be as long or as detailed as the writer's explanation of the rule. It should be long enough to point out the flaw or to convince readers that the writer has been accurate and careful in identifying and explaining the rule. The example below shows a rule explanation that includes counteranalysis. Notice how the writer first explains the correct, more stringent rule and then follows with counteranalysis that explains why a less stringent rule is not appropriate:

Good Example

An adverse inference is an inference a court indulges against a party that has destroyed evidence. *E.g., McGuffin v. Norris*, 144 F.3d 201, 209 (9th Cir. 2020). The court draws, or instructs a jury to draw, some conclusion against the destroying party. For nearly two centuries, negligent spoliation of evidence has not merited an adverse inference instruction. *The Pizzaro*, 15 U.S. 227, 241 (1817). A court will grant a party that discards relevant evidence an opportunity to explain the circumstances that led to the destruction of evidence, and only bad faith will give rise to an adverse inference. *The Olinde Rodrigues*, 174 U.S. 510, 528-29 (1899). This is true even when individuals discarding the relevant documents knew of a legal cause to keep the documents. *Id.*

In *The Olinde Rodrigues*, a ship captain discarded port clearance papers that might have shown that he had intended to run a blockade illegally. *Id.* at 529. The Court recognized that the captain had a duty to maintain the documents but held that no adverse inference was due because the captain acted in negligence and not in bad faith. *Id.*

The Supreme Court has not addressed the issue since *The Olinde Rodrigues*. The majority of the lower courts that have considered the issue have held to teachings of *The Pizzaro* and *The Olinde Rodrigues*. *See, e.g., Condrey v. SunTrust Bank of Ga.*, 431 F.3d 191, 203 (5th Cir. 2005). Those courts have not granted adverse inference jury instructions unless the party that destroyed the evidence acted in bad faith. One circuit court required evidence of a desire to suppress the truth before allowing an adverse inference instruction. *See Greyhound Lines, Inc. v. Wade*, 485 F.3d 1032, 1035 (8th Cir. 2007). Another expressly restricted the adverse inference to situations involving the spoliation of evidence in bad faith. *Condrey*, 431 F.3d at 203. Some lower courts have rejected adverse inferences based upon mere negligence. *See Hodge v. Wal-Mart Stores, Inc.*, 360 F.3d 446, 450 (4th Cir. 2004). Poor record-keeping has not been the basis for adverse inference instructions. *See Aramahu v. The Boeing Co.*, 112 F.3d 1398, 1407 (10th Cir. 1997). Even when the destruction is completely unexplained, the Eleventh Circuit has refused to allow the adverse inference in the absence of evidence of bad faith. *Bashir v. Amtrak*, 119 F.3d 929, 931 (11th Cir. 1997).

Modern courts treat the adverse inference as a severe, punitive sanction that is to be used with extreme caution and continue to adhere to the traditional adverse inference doctrine of *The Pizzaro* and *The Olinde Rodrigues* despite advancements in technology. *See Greyhound Lines*, 485 F.3d at 1035. The consensus among the circuits is that courts must focus their inquiries on whether the destruction of evidence indicates a desire to suppress the truth and consciousness of a weak case. *Id.* Mere negligence in discarding evidence does not indicate a desire to suppress the truth or a consciousness of a weak case. *Turner v. Public Serv. Co. of Colo.*, 563 F.3d 1136, 1149 (10th Cir. 2009); *Greyhound Lines*, 485 F.3d at 1035.

The writer reiterates the rule as it has been articulated in the rule explanation, while suggesting the contrary point of view that negligence alone may be sufficient. The counteranalysis that follows concisely explains why a less stringent articulation of the rule is incorrect.

Bad faith, not negligence, is required to support an adverse inference. In one very recent case, a magistrate judge had imposed the sanction on the basis of negligence. *Domanus v. Lewicki*, 742 F.3d 290, 299 (7th Cir. 2014). Ultimately, the circuit court affirmed the sanctions imposed upon the party who had destroyed the evidence. *Id.* The court did so on the basis of a later finding by the district judge in the case that the party had acted in bad faith, however. *Id.* So, the *Domanus* decision is entirely consistent with the rule as expressed and followed by the many circuit courts that have applied it since the Supreme Court issued its decisions in *The Pizzaro* and *The Olinde Rodrigues*.

C. REMEMBER TO SUMMARIZE

When your rule explanation has included more than one paragraph as a result of multiple case descriptions or the inclusion of counteranalysis, your readers are likely to have forgotten the synthesized rule you stated so clearly before the rule explanation. Before turning to application, succinctly summarize the rule that you are about to apply so that readers' minds are focused on that rule and not on the case you have just described. The summary paragraph that follows would fall at the end of the preceding good example:

> ***Good Example***
> In considering whether to permit adverse inferences on the basis of the spoliation of evidence, the courts have drawn a bright line between bad faith and every other state of mind. They have grouped negligence, recklessness, and irresponsibility on one side of that line. On the other side is only conduct actually intended to deprive an adversary of useful information. When a party cannot show that its opponent acted in bad faith in destroying evidence or information, the courts have not permitted juries to infer that the missing evidence would have been favorable. Accordingly, in the absence of evidence of bad faith, a court will not grant an adverse inference jury instruction.

By including a rule summary, you not only remind the reader of the synthesized rule, but you emphasize the aspects of the rule you have focused on in the rule explanation.

D. USING NONMANDATORY AND NONPRECEDENTIAL AUTHORITY

We have said it before, but we will say it once more: you are always on the firmest footing when you are relying on authority from a court whose decisions are mandatory in your jurisdiction and that directly answers the question you are analyzing. You already know that you will not always find that perfect authority. Often, you will be confronted with a dearth of mandatory authority and a range of persuasive authority.

In this section, we will address the use of nonmandatory authority in explaining rules. We will begin with the difficult issue of when and how to use nonprecedential authority and continue with the appropriate use of any nonmandatory authority in a rule explanation.

1. Using Nonprecedential Authority

In recent years, the "publication" and use of unpublished opinions—now more commonly referred to as "nonprecedential opinions"—has become controversial, with some courts forbidding their citation, others allowing them with some restrictions, and one court holding that rules limiting use of unpublished decisions are unconstitutional.[7] The Federal Rules of Appellate Procedure provide that no court may limit the citation of any federal case decided after January 1, 2007. Because the rules about citation of nonprecedential opinions vary from jurisdiction to jurisdiction,[8] the most important thing to do is to consult both the rules of the relevant jurisdiction and the local rules of the relevant court when deciding whether to cite to them.

All U.S. Supreme Court opinions are published, as are virtually all opinions of state supreme courts. State and federal trial courts and intermediate appellate courts, however, currently designate a significant percentage of their opinions as nonprecedential or unpublished. Professor Amy Sloan reported that, in 2007, "84% of opinions issued by the federal courts of appeals are nonprecedential."[9] Actually, because of the availability of opinions on the Internet and on research services such as Lexis and Westlaw, many so-called unpublished decisions are not unpublished in the real sense. Instead, they are decisions that the court has decided to designate as nonprecedential, perhaps because the judges believe that the opinions address routine issues that will not add significantly to the body of law.[10]

The local rules of the various federal appellate courts and of the various state courts treat nonprecedential decisions in a variety of ways. Some courts have promulgated rules that seem to favor the issuance of precedential decisions, while others disfavor their issuance, and still others are silent.[11] Illinois Supreme Court Rule 23, for example, designates categories of appellate court decisions as "opinions," "written orders," and "summary orders."[12] The rule makes clear that only "opinions" qualify as binding precedent, noting that

---

7. *Anastasoff v. United States*, 223 F.3d 898, 899, *vacated as moot on reh'g en banc*, 235 F.3d 1054 (8th Cir. 2000)

8. For example, the Minnesota Rules of Civil Appellate Procedure note that the deciding court determines whether an opinion is precedential or nonprecedential, and they specify that "[n]onprecedential opinions and order opinions are not binding authority except as law of the case, res judicata or collateral estoppel, but nonprecedential opinions may be cited as persuasive authority." Minn. R. Civ. App. P. 136.01(c) (2020).

9. Amy E. Sloan, *If You Can't Beat 'em, Join 'em: A Pragmatic Approach to Nonprecedential Opinions in the Federal Appellate Courts*, 86 Neb. L. Rev. 895, 898 (2008) (citing Statistics Div., Admin. Office of the U.S. Courts, *2006 Annual Report of the Director: Judicial Business of the United States Courts* 52 (2007)).

10. E.g., K. K. DuVivier, *Are Some Words Better Left Unpublished? Precedent and the Role of Unpublished Decisions*, 3 J. App. Prac. & Process 397, 399 (2001).

11. Sloan, *supra* n. 9, at 909-910.

12. Ill. Sup. Ct. R. 23.

written orders and summary orders are "not precedential except to support contentions of double jeopardy, res judicata, collateral estoppel or law of the case."[13] Like the Minnesota rule noted in an earlier footnote, the Illinois Supreme Court has recently amended its rule to allow nonprecedential "orders" to be cited for persuasive purposes, but only if (1) they were issued after January 1, 2021, and (2) counsel provides a copy of the order to all counsel and to the court.[14]

Because a search on a commercial or public legal database may turn up nonprecedential opinions, you must know what the rules are in the jurisdiction in which you are writing. Although of course no court rules govern an interoffice memorandum, you should avoid citing authorities in a memo that you cannot later use in a brief. If local rules forbid citation to unpublished opinions, you should indicate the unpublished status of the opinion—and the legal significance of that status in your jurisdiction—in a parenthetical or a footnote. If you don't know the rules, find out. Check the library, search the court's Web site, or call the clerk of the court. Federal Rule of Appellate Procedure 32.1, for example, mandates that a party who cites any federal "written disposition that is not available in a publicly accessible electronic database" must file and serve a copy of the document with the brief or other document submitted to the court. The comments to the rule indicate that "commercial databases" are considered to be "publicly accessible," so any decision available on Lexis or Westlaw presumably would not need to be filed.

Many courts designate a nonprecedential opinion by putting the word *unpublished* in a parenthetical at the end of the citation. So now you know what the rules are. What is the reality? The answer, like the answer to many questions in law school, is "it depends." Some courts cite routinely to nonprecedential cases, indicating that it is fine for you to do so in memos and briefs. Other courts hardly ever do so. Our first piece of advice here, then, is to find out what the local culture is. Research the current citation customs of the federal and state courts in your jurisdiction. You should also check out the preferences of the members of your law firm—or of influential partners in that firm.

Even if courts and attorneys in your jurisdiction cite routinely to nonprecedential opinions, however, these should never be your first stop. Always prefer precedential to nonprecedential opinions. If you find a nonprecedential opinion that seems appropriate for your

---

13. *Id.* at Ru. 23(1)(e)

14. *Id.* The rule also specifies that the deciding court must label any order with a statement noting that it is "not precedent." It also allows counsel to petition to have an "order" changed to an "opinion."

analysis, try to find a precedential opinion that makes the same point. Use the nonprecedential opinion only if you cannot find a substitute. If there is a "best" time to cite to a nonprecedential opinion, it would be when that opinion is on point and in your jurisdiction; in particular, it is common to see nonprecedential opinions cited because their facts are similar to the facts at issue.

2. "Justifying" Your Use of Nonmandatory Authority

As we said in Chapter 6, mandatory authority is always preferable to persuasive authority for establishing and explaining a rule. Even so, you will sometimes be left without mandatory authority that answers your question, even after a careful search. If your research has not uncovered mandatory authority that adequately identifies or explains a rule, persuasive authority may provide a basis for writing the rule explanation portion of the analysis.

When we talk about persuasive authority here, we are referring to two different categories of court decisions. The first category includes decisions of courts whose decisions could never be mandatory authority in your jurisdiction because of the level or the location of the courts. Decisions by trial courts from inside and outside your jurisdiction are in this category, as are decisions of all courts from outside your jurisdiction. Their decisions may provide useful guidance about the identity and correct application of a rule, but you cannot assume that a court in your jurisdiction will follow them. The second category includes nonprecedential decisions from a court whose precedential decisions are mandatory authority in your jurisdiction. Even though nonprecedential decisions are persuasive rather than mandatory authority, they may be useful in helping you to articulate and explain a rule.

Although you may cite persuasive authority in the rule explanation section of an analysis, be aware that you are violating a reader expectation (that you will be citing to mandatory authorities), and be sure to provide a *justification* for your decision to include that authority. In other words, you must alert readers to (1) the fact that you are using nonmandatory authority and (2) the reason for its inclusion.

The citation alone will tell readers that the authority does not come from a court whose decisions are mandatory authority. Remember that the citation tells readers the source of the authority by naming or otherwise identifying the court. You may safely assume that readers will notice that the authority is persuasive rather than mandatory. The reader will recognize the *fact* that you are using nonmandatory authority. Alerting the reader to the *reason* requires more effort on your part.

Start by explaining to yourself why you are using the persuasive authority. For example, you may be citing a decision of an appellate court from outside your jurisdiction because your local appellate court has never considered the issue. Perhaps you have noticed that your appellate court and the one whose decision you are citing have consistently applied the same general rule in cases involving the claim that you are analyzing. The appellate decision that you are citing provides a definition or a clarification of one sub-rule within that general rule. So, you may explain to yourself that you are using the persuasive authority to fill a gap in the absence of mandatory authority and that you have chosen the particular decision because the two courts have otherwise identified and applied the general rule consistently.

Beginning with the explanation that you have just provided to yourself, you can write a justification for your use of the persuasive authority. It might look something like this:

> The Eighth Circuit has never considered whether a change in job title without a reduction in pay constitutes an adverse employment action for purposes of a retaliation claim under Title VII. The Fifth Circuit, however, which has consistently applied the same general rule for adverse actions as the Eighth Circuit applies, has considered the question and has resolved it in a careful analysis. *See Burger v. Central Apt. Mgt., Inc.*, 168 F.3d 875 (5th Cir. 1999).

From that beginning, the writer may proceed to explain the rule. Readers are alerted to the fact that the authority is the writer's best guess as to what the Eighth Circuit would do with the question and that it is not cited as mandatory authority. The writer has justified the use of the persuasive authority.

E. CONCLUSION

Legal writers have a lot to remember in using case authorities effectively. Remembering the needs of those who will read and use the document will help you to include all of the authorities that are necessary; to give enough information about those authorities, but not too much; and to present that information accurately and in a helpful way. As a legal writer early in your career, take comfort in the truth that your "feel" for legal writing and for tailoring your writing to readers' needs will develop with experience, practice, and some mistakes.

Recall and Review

1. What are the four elements of a case description? I__________, D__________, F__________, and R__________.
2. A good way to make your case descriptions effective is to focus on the relevant p______-________-________.
3. True or False: Before getting into the specifics, you should start a case description by telling the reader what the case *involved*, *regarded*, or *concerned*.
4. Can you explain why it's sometimes hard to be precise when describing the disposition of the phrase-that-pays in a "kick-back" case?
5. True or False: When writing a parenthetical case description, you can disregard the relevant elements of a case description.
6. To avoid misrepresenting the law, you should check the validity of cases you cite in what way(s)?
7. True or False: If an appellate court is reviewing a decision that granted a motion to dismiss, and it reverses and remands that case, the appellate court's decision is a decision on the merits.
8. An analysis of the weaknesses of any interpretation of the rule that differs from the writer's is called c________.
9. True or False: A good case description always makes evident how the court disposed of the issue implicated by the phrase-that-pays.

CHAPTER 12

THE A OF CREXAC

Applying the Rules to Facts and Using Analogies and Distinctions

Now that you have written a well-organized, well-supported, and well-summarized rule explanation, your focus shifts to rule application. In this chapter, we'll examine the A of CREXAC more closely by explaining how to organize the rule application, and also how to use analogies and distinctions to support your application. We will also address the use of counteranalysis in the rule application.

A. ORGANIZING THE APPLICATION

The concept is very simple: apply the rule that you have just explained to your facts. Occasionally, the act is just as simple. A rule may be as basic as "an unsigned will is not valid." Your application of that rule requires little thought about organization or level of detail: "The decedent did not sign the contested will; therefore, it is not valid." Let's be honest, though. The rule is rarely that straightforward. So, we will show you how the organization of your rule explanation can guide you in organizing the application.

In Chapter 10, where we described the parts of the CREXAC formula, we told you that the first step in rule application is to look at the rule that you have just explained and apply that rule to your client's facts. If you have included a helpful rule summary at the end of your rule explanation, that task will be much easier. The opening sentence or paragraph of your application will mirror the rule summary. Watch how it is done in this sample:

> So, the second alternative under the fourth prong of *Ercegovich* is satisfied only if the two employees were similar in all respects that were relevant to the termination or other adverse employment

This paragraph is the rule summary, which, as you know, appears at the end of the rule explanation.

action. *Mitchell*, 964 F.2d at 583. If the employee's claim is based, at least in part, on a supervisor's actions, employees who reported to different supervisors cannot be similarly situated in all relevant respects.

This paragraph begins the rule application; it should articulate the thesis of your application.

Lisa Lagos was similar to Todd North and Jason South in some relevant respects but not in all, as the rule requires. She did not report to the same supervisor, and the actions of her supervisor form a part of the basis for her claim. She will not, therefore, be able to satisfy the second alternative under *Ercegovich*'s fourth prong.

If you are unable to identify the order of the points in your rule explanation, consider these two possible reasons: (1) maybe your rule explanation includes only one point, in which case your application will also include one point; (2) maybe you have focused your rule explanation on the cases you cited rather than on the points that those cases help you establish (if this is true, you are not finished with your rule explanation).

The first paragraph, or thesis, of the application section tracks the rule summary very closely. If the rule summary was carefully written, it incorporates all of the relevant aspects of the rule as you have explained them in the rule explanation. So, if you begin the application with a sentence or paragraph that mirrors the rule summary, you will have a clear thesis for the application section.

The next step in writing the application section is to apply each point you have made about the rule in the rule explanation section to your facts. Unless a different organizing principle is obviously better, you should assume that you will apply those points to your facts in the order in which you have explained them. Notice how the rule application tracks the points of the explanation in this sample:

Explanation

This sentence articulates the rule for this CREXAC unit of discourse.

This sentence is point 1 in which "relevant respects" is clarified.

This sentence is point 2 in which the "same supervisor" aspect of the rule is explained.

To prove disparate treatment in accordance with the second alternative under *Ercegovich*'s fourth prong, an employee must show that she was treated less favorably than an employee who is not part of her protected class and is otherwise similar in all relevant respects. *Ercegovich*, 154 F.3d at 352. Relevant respects are those that relate in some fashion to the basis for the adverse employment action. *See Mickey v. Zeidler Tool & Die Co.*, 516 F.3d 516, 522-23 (6th Cir. 2008). That is, the plaintiff and the employee to whom she compares herself "must have dealt with the same supervisor, [and] have been subject to the same standards." *Ercegovich*, 154 F.3d at 352 (quoting *Mitchell*, 964 F.2d at 583).

This paragraph elaborates in greater depth on the "same supervisor" aspect of the rule because it is the most critical aspect in this analysis.

One district court, applying the "same supervisor" standard from *Mitchell*, considered when differences in supervisor will prevent an employee from proving similarity. *See Duncan v. Koch Air, L.L.C.*, No. Civ. A. 3:04CV-72-H, 2005 WL 1353758, *3 (W.D. Ky. June 2, 2005). Plaintiff Duncan, who was female, was fired for missing work without prior notice. *Id.* at *1. A male employee was not fired for violating the same rule. *Id.* The supervisor who fired Duncan did not make the decision to retain the other employee, however. *Id.* at *3. The court concluded that Duncan could not prove similarity because her claim was based, at least in part, on her supervisor's actions, and the employee to whom she compared herself reported to a different supervisor. *Id.* Because of the difference in supervisors, the differences in the employees' treatment could not be evidence of discrimination. *Id.* (citing *McMillan v. Castro*, 405 F.3d 405, 413-14 (6th Cir. 2003); *Mitchell*, 964 F.2d at 583).

This rule summary successfully incorporates all aspects of the rule as it has been explained and summarizes them in the order in which they were explained. It provides an excellent template for the thesis sentence or paragraph in the application section.

So, the second alternative under the fourth prong of *Ercegovich* is satisfied only if the two employees were similar in all respects that were relevant to the termination or other adverse employment action. *Mitchell*, 964 F.2d at 583. If the employee's claim is based, at least in part, on a supervisor's actions, employees who reported to different supervisors cannot be similarly situated in all relevant respects.

The opening paragraph, or thesis, of the rule application tracks the rule summary, as we established earlier.

Lisa Lagos was similar to Todd North and Jason South in some relevant respects but not in all, as the rule requires. She did not report to the same supervisor, and the actions of her supervisor form a part of the basis for her claim. She will not, therefore, be able to satisfy the second alternative under *Ercegovich*'s fourth prong.

Point 1 of the application tracks point 1 of the explanation.

In the case of Ms. Lagos's selection for termination by Bank Two, the relevant respects were her performance evaluations and years of seniority. Ms. Lagos's seniority was identical to that of Todd North and Jason South. The identity of her supervisor would also be relevant, however, because the supervisor completed the performance evaluations. She was supervised and evaluated by a different vice president, however. Because, in Ms. Lagos's own assessment of events, the determination of which managers to retain turned exclusively on a combination of seniority and performance evaluation scores, those scores are relevant to the comparison between employees required by *Ercegovich*. Ms. Lagos will not be able to establish the requisite degree of similarity because a different vice president evaluated her performance. She cannot show, therefore, that she was similarly situated in every relevant respect to Todd North and Jason South.

Point 2 of the application tracks point 2 of the explanation. The level of depth is also similar because this point is the most critical part of the analysis. Of course, if your case does not have as many legally significant facts, your rule application may be shorter, even for critical issues.

Ms. Lagos acknowledges that North and South likely received superior performance evaluations to hers. In essence, she concedes that she was not similarly situated in that respect, which is quite relevant because performance evaluations factored directly into the formula used to determine who would retain employment.

This final paragraph of the basic rule application elaborates on how the identity of supervisors is relevant in the writer's case.

Once you have completed the process of applying each aspect of the rule, as you have explained it, to your facts, your basic application of the rule is complete. The application section of the CREXAC may not be finished, however. In fact, however simple or complex your application has been, you should always consider adding an analogy or a distinction (maybe even more than one) to support the conclusion that you have reached.

B. ANALOGIES AND DISTINCTIONS

Your application of the rule to your facts has been careful and compelling. You have done all that you can do in your own power to convince readers that your conclusion is correct. You are limited, however, by the fact that *you* are not an authority. So, even at its most convincing, your analysis is only yours, and this limitation is why analogies and distinctions can be so much help to you. An *analogy* allows you to support your conclusion by showing that a court, *an actual authority*, did just what you are suggesting when it was confronted with similar facts. A *distinction* allows you to show that a court, *an actual authority*, did something that is materially different than what you are suggesting when it was confronted with facts that were materially different.

Analogizing and distinguishing relevant authority cases may be a useful part of the application sections of your discussion. By showing the reader the ways in which a case is like or unlike a relevant case, a writer can show the reader that a court will apply the rule in a particular way.

Note that your application section should not *begin* with the analogy or distinction. Instead, begin with an explicit assertion about how the rule applies to your facts. As the example above shows, your application should begin with a sentence that says, in effect, "phrase-that-pays [equals or does not equal] the facts in this case." You should follow that explicit assertion with details about how the relevant aspects of the rule connect to your facts. Analogies and distinctions, when needed, allow you to use the relevant cases to support those assertions in a different way.

Your case analogies and distinctions will be most effective if they are *precise.* Do not analogize a specific fact to a whole case:

Bad Examples

Like *Nini*, Plaintiff alleged no facts in support of her discrimination claim.

Defendant Volpe, like in *Samons*, was the plaintiff's direct supervisor.

This comparison is inapt because one plaintiff, by definition, cannot be "like" a whole case. Make your analogy or distinction specific. Compare defendants to defendants, and other actors and things to their specific counterparts in the authority case. These illustrations make the comparisons explicit:

Good Examples

In the present case, Plaintiff, like the plaintiffs in *Nini* and *O'Hara*, has alleged no facts in support of her discrimination claim.

Defendant Volpe, like the defendant in *Samons*, was the plaintiff's direct supervisor.

Like the landlord in *Aubin*, the plaintiff's landlord refused to answer repeated requests for information about safety precautions.

Unlike the garbage cans in *Rosmarin*, which had been intentionally abandoned and placed at the curb, the heat detected around Defendant's garage had not been "abandoned"; it had escaped without any action on Defendant's part.

These examples also provide details from the client's case that make the analogies vivid. The writer must do more than make the bare statement that "this case is like (or unlike) that case" if readers are to see the connection or the disconnection between the two cases.

Analogies and distinctions are not always needed. A writer should consider including analogies and distinctions in one of two situations: (1) when a point is likely to be especially controversial within the analysis or (2) when the reader needs the direct comparison an analogy or distinction provides to understand the connection between the authority cases and the writer's case. Including analogies or distinctions when they are not needed is likely to prompt an "I get it already" response from the reader. If, in writing an analogy or distinction, a writer feels like the comparison is easy and obvious, the analogy or distinction may not be necessary. On the other hand, where the comparison requires more thought and care, the analogy or distinction is probably necessary because the reader is less likely to have drawn the relevant comparison without the writer's help.

When analogies or distinctions are appropriate, make sure to focus them on the specific people or things that you want to compare. Further, make sure that you provide the details that allow readers to understand both the comparison and the application of law to facts.

At the same time, avoid extraneous details about the comparison case that will distract the reader from the point of the analogy. For example, unless dates, locations, or names are essential to the comparison, exclude them and use legally significant labels. Sometimes, labels like *plaintiff* and *defendant, employer* and *employee*, or *buyer* and *seller* will appropriately indicate the relevant relationships in the case. Your job is to use labels—for both the parties and the other legally significant facts—that highlight the connection (or lack of connection) between the facts in your case and the facts in the authority case.

In the following sample, notice how the analogy begins with an assertion that a fact in the writer's case is similar to a fact in an authority case (the point of the analogy). Then, the writer identifies the facts from the authority case on which the comparison is based and tells how those facts determined the outcome. Next, the writer explicitly identifies the similar (or dissimilar, in the case of a distinction) facts from the current case. Finally, the analogy ends with a mini-conclusion that adds support to the writer's application:

> Ms. Lagos is like the plaintiff in *Duncan*, who could not establish that her employer discriminatorily applied the same rule differently to two different employees because she could not demonstrate that the same supervisor had interpreted and applied the rule to each of them. Ms. Lagos has not suggested that the Bank Two vice president who evaluated her performance also supervised the male employees to whom she compares herself. Accordingly, like the plaintiff in *Duncan*, Ms. Lagos will be stifled in her effort to establish that the termination of her employment resulted from discrimination in her performance evaluations.

When your rule explanation has explained the facts of authority cases in detail, your analogy may sometimes be more succinct. In the following example, the defendant in the case at issue is a fraternity member who is being sued for negligence by a pledge who was injured on pledge night after he was removed from a "drunk room" that had been set up for the pledges in the fraternity house. The defendant then abandoned the pledge while the pledge was unconscious and in a strange place, arguably a breach of duty. In *Hurd* (an authority case described in detail in the rule explanation), the court found that the defendant bus company had breached its duty to a passenger when it dropped the plaintiff off on the side of a busy highway instead of at the park and ride, a location designed to protect passengers from roadside accidents.

> ***Bad Example***
> Like the Columbia Transit Authority in the *Hurd* case, which left Mr. Hurd at the side of the road instead of at the park and ride, Riegert left Kroger alone in a strange second-floor apartment while he was intoxicated.

This example is weak because it uses needless detail and talks in specifics, leaving the reader to figure out the analogy between the authority case facts and the client case facts. The better example uses abstract language that implicitly asserts that the facts in the authority case are the same as the facts in the client's case:

Better Example

Like the defendant transit authority in *Hurd*, Riegert ignored a safety precaution set up to protect someone he owed a duty to and then left that person in a worse position.

The better example highlights the similarities by describing the legally significant facts from the two cases—a park and ride and a "drunk room"—at a level of abstraction that highlights their similarity. The park and ride was set up to protect bus passengers from car accidents, and the drunk room was set up to protect fraternity pledges from harm caused by intoxication, but both were safety precautions set up to protect a person the defendant owed a duty to. By making that connection obvious, the writer demonstrates the similarity of the authority case and the client's case.

If readers agree that the two cases are similar in all material ways, they are more likely to accept your conclusion that the outcomes should be the same. At the very least, the analogy places you on more solid footing than when you stood on your own authority alone.

Unlike an analogy, a distinction uses material differences between the facts in an authority case and the facts in your client's case to support a conclusion that the outcome of your case will be different from the outcome in the authority case. We'll use the drunk room case, but we'll distinguish its facts from the facts in the *McGuffin* case. In *McGuffin*, a court had refused to find that a breach occurred when railroad employees about to close the station for the night had called the police after finding a man unconscious in a shelter on the train platform:

Riegert's behavior is materially different from the behavior of the non-breaching defendant-employees in *McGuffin*. Those employees took several steps to assure the safety of the unconscious man they owed a duty to: they tried to wake him, they called the police for help, and they waited until police arrived before leaving the scene. Indeed, they left the unconscious man in a better position than the position they had found him in. Riegert, in contrast, removed Kroger from the presence of people who were watching over Kroger, and left Kroger totally alone—and intoxicated and unconscious—in a strange place,

The point of the distinction.

The material facts from the authority case.

The distinguished material facts from the writer's case.

The mini-conclusion, which supports the writer's application and the conclusion to this CREXAC unit of discourse.

with no one to attend to his safety. Thus, unlike the plaintiff in *McGuffin*, Kroger will be able to establish the breach element of his negligence claim.

Before we move on, allow us to make a few final points about analogies and distinctions. First, do not try your readers' patience by making overly detailed fact-to-fact comparisons. As noted above, if you have already described the authority case in some detail, you can usually limit the facts in the analogy to just the most significant for the purpose of the comparison. Also, avoid making a comparison that is so short on detail that readers are left scratching their heads. Finally, you are never limited to just one analogy or distinction in a unit of discourse. When an issue is particularly controversial, multiple analogies may support a conclusion in a way that a single analogy would not. On the other hand, use additional analogies or distinctions only if they add something; do not pile on one analogy after another, all making the same essential point. One or two carefully written analogies or distinctions will be helpful enough.

C. COUNTERANALYSIS

A writer's application will always begin with a discussion about how the rule applies to the writer's facts. The careful writer will also, however, be sure to consider how an opposing attorney might apply the rule to the same facts, or to other facts from the same dispute. After considering the opposing attorney's likely application, the writer may choose to include counteranalysis, after the primary application of the rule, to address the opponent's application.

As with counteranalysis in the rule explanation section, the writer will rarely begin the counteranalysis in the application section by stating the opponent's likely position. In other words, a writer need not dignify the opposing application by stating it explicitly. Rather, the writer will keep the focus on the writer's own application while identifying the weakness, incorrectness, or inconsistency in the opposing position. The counteranalysis will almost always be much shorter than the primary application.

Consider the following example. The counteranalysis is in boldface type. Notice that the counteranalysis is shorter than the primary application. This example illustrates a counteranalysis in which a writer highlights the incorrectness of the opposing position:

Good Example
The school district did not act in bad faith when it deleted the emails that the plaintiff has requested in this litigation. The

district has a policy of deleting emails from school-maintained accounts after three months. It has consistently applied that policy by deleting old emails four times per year.

When the plaintiff's attorney requested emails from all district administrator accounts in the course of discovery in this litigation, the district's attorney notified district officials of the need to maintain all emails until the litigation was complete. District officials issued a memorandum to that effect, but the district's information technology staff misunderstood the directive. They continued to follow their regular deletion protocol.

While the district could have done more to ensure that emails were preserved, the actions of the district officials and of the information technology staff reflect negligence, at worst, and not bad faith.

In that sense, the district personnel acted as the defendants had in *Turner*. They were negligent in their responsibility to preserve the evidence, but nothing about their conduct suggests an effort to suppress the truth. *See Turner*, 563 F.3d at 1149. In *Turner*, the court concluded that an adverse inference instruction was improper, and the same result should occur in this case.

If you are referring to an authority that you have already cited and discussed in your rule explanation section, you do not necessarily need to cite it in your rule application section. It may be appropriate to do so where, as here, you want to focus the reader's attention on a specific aspect of an authority case. Note that a "see" citation is appropriate if you are drawing an inference about the meaning of the case.

The writer keeps the focus on the primary application.

The district's personnel did not act in bad faith, even though they knew about this litigation. Knowledge of an obligation to preserve evidence, without more, is insufficient to show bad faith. Any argument that a bad faith finding may be based on mere knowledge lowers the high bar that the courts have set.

Here, the writer suggests the contrary position that destruction of evidence in the face of knowledge of an obligation to preserve it may demonstrate bad faith. The writer does not articulate the contrary position in full. This suggestion is enough to allow the writer to point out the flaw in the position.

Thus, the writer does not say "the plaintiff will argue that the fact that defendant's personnel had knowledge of the litigation shows that they acted in bad faith." Instead, the writer just explains why knowledge of the litigation is not legally significant.

D. CONCLUSION

This detailed discussion of rule application has left you with several things to remember. Eventually, they will become second nature. For now, you may want to keep this checklist handy:

- Always begin by applying the rule to your facts, echoing the rule summary as appropriate.
- Add one or more analogies or disanalogies after the basic application *if* they are needed to lend credibility or clarity to the application of the rule to your own facts.
- Consider adding counteranalysis.

As with other aspects of legal writing, you will develop a "feel" for the level of detail you need to include in rule application, depending on the complexity of the case and the needs of your readers.

Recall and Review

1. True or False: Rule application should begin with a statement that directly applies the phrase-that-pays to the facts.
2. You should consider including analogies and distinctions when the connection or disconnection between the authority case(s) and the client's case is (more/less) obvious.
3. True or False: Effective rule application connects each relevant aspect of the rule to the specific relevant facts of the client's case.

CHAPTER 13

THE PARTS OF A RESEARCH MEMORANDUM

Lawyers write many kinds of analytical documents. One of the best known is a *research memorandum*, which a lawyer in a law practice—usually a junior lawyer—writes for another lawyer in the same practice—usually a senior lawyer. These memoranda are often called *office memoranda* or *office memos*. In the iconic research memorandum, the senior lawyer will ask the junior lawyer to write an analysis of one or more legal issues, to explore them objectively, and to predict how a court in the relevant jurisdiction would resolve them.

If you are asked to write a research memo, your goal should be to write it so effectively that your readers have all the information they need, but no more. This caveat does not mean that the memo should be terse or abrupt. Your analysis should be complete and should provide enough detail that readers can be confident that the analysis is correct. On the other hand, the memo should not discuss irrelevant issues or facts, nor should it trace the development of a legal rule unless that history is at issue in the client's case. In a research memo, your job is not only to provide the answer but to "show your work" in just enough detail so that your readers can understand how you reached the conclusions you did and have confidence in those conclusions.

Typically, if asked to write a research memorandum, you will be given the facts of a client's case, and perhaps some law, and be asked to answer one or more questions. The questions may be broad, as in "Does A have any possible causes of action against B? Would A be successful?" In contrast, you might be asked to write a research memo with a very narrow scope, as in, "Give me all the possible arguments we can use to establish that B is not an employer under Title VII."

In some law practices, research memos are highly stylized documents, with a set of required sections similar to the sections of an appellate brief. If you are asked to write a research memo, you should ask to see a sample so that you know what is expected of you. This chapter will describe sections that appear in typical research memos, and it will presume that you are being asked to analyze the issues objectively.

See Chapter 16 for suggestions about writing effective email and e-memos.

Some supervising attorneys may ask you to submit your research memo in an email message instead of in a more formal hard copy or even an email attachment. Do not let the form of the message suggest that you may take the assignment less seriously. Unless the attorney has asked explicitly only for an *answer*, he or she probably wants at least enough analysis to be confident that your answer is correct. That is the purpose behind the more detailed analysis generally included in the more formal research memo, and you should not forget that purpose just because the attorney asks you to deliver the information in an email.

Because a research memo is a functional document, you will find that many of the sections contain information that also appears in greater or less detail in other sections. This repetition is needed because readers of research memos often skip around within the document, reading sections that they need at the particular time and ignoring others. For example, a reader might read one section before meeting with a client or review several sections before meeting with opposing counsel or drafting a demand letter. Think of your own behavior when you are trying to get information from a website. You may skip around from link to link, trying to find the information that you care about. In a well-designed website, the information at each link would provide sufficient context so that you could understand how that information fits into the larger picture of the information available on the entire site. The authors of the website don't worry about repeating information because they know that few users will read every paragraph at every link of the site. Similarly, even though you may have readers who will read your entire research memo, you should not worry about repeating some information; the repetition helps ensure that you provide sufficient context within each section.

A typical research memo will include the following six or seven components:

1. Caption
2. Question(s) Presented
3. Brief Answer(s)
4. Statutes Involved (if any)
5. Statement of the Case or Statement of Facts
6. Discussion
7. Conclusion

This chapter will address each in turn.

A. CAPTION

The caption is typically a three- or four-line heading that identifies the writer, the recipient, the date, and the subject matter of the document. Some law practices keep a bank of old research memos that they can consult when similar issues arise. Most lawyers keep a bank of their own work. For that reason, your caption should include information that will allow you or other readers to pick up the memo at a later date and use the caption alone to identify the issues that the memo addresses. For example, this caption would *not* be helpful:

Bad Example
To: Senior Partner
From: Junior Associate
Date: January 29, 2008
Re: Cane matter

Within a year or two at most, the subject of the "Cane matter" will probably be forgotten. Instead of using merely the party's name, you should include information that will identify the legal issues; if your law practice has a formal docketing system, you should include the relevant number as well:

Good Example
To: Senior Partner
From: Junior Associate
Date: January 29, 2008
Re: CCDK #08-253; Cane; definition of trespass under Ohio's dog-bite statute

With this caption, a lawyer who is addressing an issue dealing with trespass or with Ohio's dog-bite statute will know that this memo could contain relevant information.

A document design note about captions: the concept of *alignment* is one of the fundamentals of document design.[1] It is obvious that the "To, From, Re, and Date" should all be aligned: that is, their first letters should align vertically. What is less obvious is that aligning the elements after each colon can help the reader to read and digest the information more quickly. Thus, this caption is less effective:

1. Robin Williams, *The Non-designer's Design Book* 50 (3d ed., Peachpit Press 2008).

Bad Example
To: Senior Partner
From: Junior Associate
Date: January 29, 2008
Re: CCDK #08-253; definition of trespass under Ohio's dog-bite statute

In contrast, when the elements are aligned, readers can scan them quickly:

Good Example

To:	Senior Partner
From:	Junior Associate
Date:	January 29, 2008
Re:	CCDK #08-253; definition of trespass under Ohio's dog-bite statute

Alignment is even more useful where, as here, readers probably know the format so well that they will skip the "To, From, Date, Re" on each line to get to the substantive information. Alignment lets the reader find that substantive information much more quickly.

B. QUESTION(S) PRESENTED

In this part of the document, you will articulate the issues that the memorandum will analyze. In some law firms, you will be asked to articulate the question with reference to the specific parties in the case:

> Can Joe Neighbor recover damages for pain and suffering and medical expenses caused by Jim Thurber's dog?

This question does articulate the basic question that the office memo will answer, but it does not give readers enough information about the legal issue that the case presents. Most lawyers, upon reading this question, would think, "Of course he can. Aren't dog owners always responsible for injuries caused by their dogs?" Thus, to make the question more useful to your readers, you should include information about the legal standard and the relevant facts. Further, you might consider using legally significant categories to identify the parties. As with the caption, a question presented that includes names may not be meaningful to future readers. Indeed, because the typical busy lawyer often juggles many cases at the same time, names may not even be meaningful to the lawyer who assigns the memorandum.

As we noted when discussing research questions, an effective format for the question presented is the "under-does-when" format. In this format, the writer essentially asks the following:

> Under relevant law, does legal status exist when legally significant facts exist?

In the "under" part of the question, the writer provides legal context, often by identifying the statute or legal rule at issue. In the "does" part, the writer asks the "core question," that is, the question at the root of this aspect of the controversy. Finally, in the "when" clause, the writer identifies the facts that will help readers to understand how the rule might operate in this case.

Under relevant law: In the "under" part of the question, the writer tells readers the source of the law that will determine the answer to the question. As noted, the purpose of the "under" clause is providing legal context. In some situations, a general reference to the area of law can be sufficient: for example, "Under Ohio election law . . ." or "Under the Fourth Amendment. . . ." More often, however, you and readers will benefit from an "under" clause that specifically mentions the language of the rule at issue: for example, "Under the Fourth Amendment's mandate that searches must be 'reasonable' . . ." or "Under the Ohio election statute that defines a 'residence' as a place where a person's 'habitation is fixed' . . ." Quoting the language at issue (also known as the "phrase-that-pays") is an effective way to focus readers' attention.

Does legal status exist: The "does" part of the question presented is the place where you articulate the core legal question. The "legal status" may be guilt or liability or some other legal consequence, or it may be simply meeting a definition of a term or a part of a relevant test: for example, "Is a person an 'employer' [under Title VII] when . . ." or "is a habitation 'fixed' when . . ."

We must note a couple of important points about the core question. First, it should be a yes-or-no question. Asking a question that is *not* a yes-or-no question often results in an answer that does not resolve the legal controversy. For example, suppose your question presented asks the following:

> ***Bad Example***
> Under Ohio's dog-bite statute, what are the standards about civil versus criminal trespass when an unintentional trespasser is bitten?

Your answer to that question would not reveal whether and how those standards apply to the particular case. Accordingly, your question presented must ask the narrow question or questions whose answer(s) will tell you how the law applies or does not apply in your client's case, as in this example:

> *Better Example*
> Does the language "committing a trespass or other criminal offense" include civil trespass and criminal trespass?

Second, the "does" part need not begin with the word *does*. Two common alternatives are *is* and *can*:

> Under relevant law, is the legal test met when legally significant facts exist?
>
> Under relevant law, can plaintiff recover from defendant when legally significant facts exist?

When legally significant facts exist: As the description implies, the "when" clause tells readers about the facts that are relevant to the core question. Note that the "when" part may not begin with *when*. A common alternative is *includes*:

> Under relevant law, does [phrase-that-pays] include legally significant facts?

When deciding which facts to include in the question, your goal is to be specific enough for the question to be useful, but generic enough to be meaningful to readers unfamiliar with the details of your case. Thinking in terms of legally significant categories can be helpful. For example, if you were asking about whether a fraternity could be liable when one of its pledges was injured after an initiation ceremony, you could use the word *fraternity* rather than *Greek honorary* or *fraternal organization*. The word *fraternity* would be meaningful even to readers who are unfamiliar with the case, and it might help them to understand why liability might or might not result.

Note that the more specific your question is, the more helpful it will be to you—because it will force you to identify the specific issues you are writing about—and to your readers—because they will get a concise snapshot of the legal issue or issues in the case.

Although there are other ways to write questions, we recommend the under-does-when format for a couple of reasons. First, it forces you to identify and articulate the three important elements of the issue: (1) the legal context; (2) the core question, which should be a yes-or-no question; and (3) the legally significant facts. Second, because there may be several legally significant facts, this structure allows you to move complex information to the end of the sentence, which enhances readability.

Thus, you could compose a question presented about the dog-bite statute as follows:

> Under Ohio's dog-bite statute, which exempts dog owners from liability for injuries to persons who are bitten when they are "committing a trespass or other criminal offense" on the dog owner's property, can a person recover damages from a dog owner when (1) he was bitten after entering the dog owner's property uninvited, and (2) he entered the property by mistake, thinking he was entering his brother's home?

One challenge that legal writers face with questions presented is dealing with issues that present multiple sub-issues. It is certainly possible to write a separate question for each sub-issue; on the other hand, reading five or six questions presented for one research memorandum could prove tedious for readers.

For example, in a memo analyzing whether a fraternity brother could be liable to a pledge after a pledge night incident, the writer could draft a separate question for each element (and sub-element) of negligence:

> **Duty:**
> Under South Carolina negligence law, which imposes a duty on persons who affirmatively "take charge" of helpless individuals, does a fraternity brother owe a duty to a pledge when (1) the pledge is unconscious due to extreme intoxication after an initiation event; (2) the pledge is under supervision at the fraternity house; (3) the fraternity brother removes the pledge from the fraternity house; and (4) in answer to the question "You'll take care of him?" the fraternity brother responds, "I've got him"?
>
> **Breach:**
> Under South Carolina negligence law, which states that a person breaches a duty when he or she fails to exercise reasonable care in discharging that duty, does a fraternity brother breach a duty of care to a pledge when (1) the pledge is intoxicated and unconscious at the fraternity brother's apartment; (2) the pledge was removed from the supervision of others; and (3) the fraternity brother leaves the pledge alone in an unfamiliar location while the pledge is still intoxicated and unconscious?
>
> **Causation (legal cause):**
> Under South Carolina negligence law, which provides that legal cause is established when harm is foreseeable from the person's negligent act, is harm to a fraternity pledge foreseeable when the

> drunken, unconscious pledge is left alone in an unfamiliar third-floor apartment with a balcony?
>
> **Causation (actual cause):**
> Under South Carolina negligence law, which provides that actual cause is established when the harm would not have occurred but for the defendant's negligence, is actual cause established when (1) a fraternity pledge is left alone in an unfamiliar third-floor apartment with a balcony, and (2) the pledge falls from the third-floor balcony while left alone?
>
> **Damages:**
> Under South Carolina negligence law, which allows a victim of negligence to recover damages only when he or she has suffered compensable injury, has a fraternity pledge suffered compensable damages when he has fallen from a balcony and been hospitalized for spinal cord injuries?

This set of questions does a good job of laying out the applicable legal standards, the core questions, and the legally significant facts. It would be useful for the *writer* to draft these questions as a way of understanding the issues that the case presents and understanding which facts are relevant to each issue. *Readers*, however, might find it more useful to have a broader snapshot of the case:

> Under South Carolina negligence law, which allows recovery when a defendant has breached a duty and caused compensable harm, can a fraternity pledge recover from a fraternity brother when (1) the pledge was intoxicated and unconscious after participating in initiation activities; (2) the brother removed the pledge from a supervised room at the fraternity house; (3) the brother took the pledge to an unfamiliar third-story apartment with a balcony; (4) the pledge was left unsupervised while still unconscious; and (5) the pledge fell from the balcony and sustained injuries to his spinal cord?

Although this question gives far less detail as to the legal standards, it provides sufficient context for readers to gain a basic understanding of the issues that the case presents. Note that the core question does not ask about the defendant's legal status; instead, it asks about the legal status of the plaintiff: that is, will he be able to recover? This question includes all of the lesser questions within it: to be able to recover, the plaintiff must establish all four elements of negligence. The question asks whether the plaintiff can establish that a defendant has [*breached*] a [*duty*] and [*caused*] [*compensable harm*].

When writing a research memo with multiple sub-issues, you must decide whether your questions should be broad or narrow. Your answer may be different depending on the case, on the custom at your law practice, on your own preferences, or on those of your assigning attorney. For example, if the legal context was something less familiar than basic negligence law, readers might find it helpful to read multiple questions that lay out the legal terrain in more detail. In any event, as noted above, you may find it helpful to *draft* more narrowly focused questions, even if you ultimately decide to include in the research memo only a broadly focused question.

C. THE BRIEF ANSWER

You will not be surprised to learn that in the brief answer, the question presented is answered. Both words in the title of this section are significant: it must *answer* the question presented, and it must be *brief*. The discussion section will provide a thorough analysis of the issues and sub-issues that the case presents. In the brief answer, in contrast, your job is to give readers a succinct overview of how the law applies to the facts.

As noted above, the skeleton of the question presented can be described as follows: "Under relevant law, does legal status exist when legally significant facts exist?" The skeleton of the brief answer has some of these same elements, but it adds some more. Thus, the skeleton of the brief answer could be described as follows:

> Probably yes [or probably not]. Legal status results when these conditions exist. These facts do [or do not] equal these conditions because [succinct reason].

In the memo, the brief answer usually follows the question presented. Not surprisingly, each brief answer should be tied to the relevant question. In the fraternity pledge case, the question presented about duty could be answered as follows:

> **Question Presented:**
> Under South Carolina negligence law, which imposes a duty on persons who affirmatively "take charge" of helpless individuals, does a fraternity brother owe a duty to a pledge when (1) the pledge is unconscious due to extreme intoxication after an initiation event; (2) the pledge is under supervision at the fraternity house; (3) the fraternity brother removes the pledge from the fraternity house; and (4) in answer to the question "You'll take care of him?" the fraternity brother responds, "I've got him"?

Brief Answer:
Probably yes. Here, the pledge was helpless due to his extreme intoxication. A court would probably find that the fraternity brother "took charge" of the pledge when he affirmatively removed him from the supervision of others and impliedly assured the others that he would take care of him. Therefore, he owed the pledge a duty.

Note in particular three features of the brief answer: first, it ties the law to the facts, noting that the brother "took charge" of the pledge when he did certain acts. Second, note that the answer, like the question, speaks in categorical terms about the parties, using descriptive language that is specific only when it would be meaningful to readers who have not read the case file. Third, the answer mentions only facts that have appeared in the question presented.

Some writers do not provide as much detail about the relevant law in the question presented. In that situation, a little more detail about the law should be included in the brief answer, as in this example:

Question Presented:
Under South Carolina negligence law, does a fraternity brother owe a duty to a pledge when (1) the pledge is unconscious due to extreme intoxication after an initiation event; (2) the pledge is under supervision at the fraternity house; (3) the fraternity brother removes the pledge from the fraternity house; and (4) in answer to the question "You'll take care of him?" the fraternity brother responds, "I've got him"?

Brief Answer:
Probably yes. South Carolina negligence law imposes a duty on persons who affirmatively act to "take charge" of helpless individuals. Here, the pledge was clearly helpless due to his extreme intoxication. A court would probably find that the fraternity brother "took charge" of the pledge when he affirmatively removed him from the supervision of others and impliedly assured the others that he would take care of him. Therefore, he owed the pledge a duty.

Note that the brief answer does not mention any cases or statutes that the writer might have relied on to reach the answer. Those sources of law will be addressed in the discussion section. As indicated above, the purpose of the brief answer is merely to end readers' suspense by answering the question presented and by providing sufficient detail so that readers have a basic understanding of why the writer has answered the question in that way.

D. AN OPTIONAL COMPONENT: APPLICABLE ENACTED LAW

The analysis of a legal issue often focuses on the meaning of a word or a phrase in a statute or other enacted law (e.g., a regulation or a constitutional provision). When that is the case, you should always begin your analysis of this language by quoting the relevant portion of the enacted law in the discussion section of the memo. This is true even if the bulk of your analysis will be based on cases that have interpreted that enacted law. It is vital that readers know precisely what the enacted law provides. To further that end, you may *also* choose to reprint relevant sections of enacted law in full in a special section of the research memo. You could place this section either just before the fact statement or just before the discussion section.

In this context, *relevant* means "applicable." If you are analyzing how or whether a statute, regulation, or constitutional provision applies, then that provision should be included in this section. If a statute is comparable to a statute that you are applying, that statute should *not* be included in this section. For example, if you are analyzing the meaning of the word "employer" as it is used in Title VII, you should quote the pertinent provisions of Title VII in this section. Your discussion section might include a discussion and a quotation of similar statutes that also use the term "employer," such as the Age Discrimination in Employment Act, the Americans with Disabilities Act, or the Family and Medical Leave Act. Although those statutes would certainly have "relevance," you are not discussing how they *apply* to your client's case, and so they should not be quoted in the section on relevant enacted law.

Further, note that this section should *not* include case law, even if you believe that the relevant common law rule is very explicit. This section is reserved only for laws enacted by legislative or executive bodies: constitutions, statutory provisions, or regulations.

The section should be titled differently depending on the particular provisions included: for example, "Applicable Constitutional Provisions," "Applicable Regulations," or "Applicable Statutes and Regulations." If a lengthy statute is at issue—for example, the Americans with Disabilities Act—it is appropriate to quote only the section or subsection that is at issue.

The following example contains both constitutional provisions and a statutory excerpt:

Good Example

APPLICABLE STATUTORY AND REGULATORY PROVISIONS

Ohio Revised Code § 4511.19 forbids operating a vehicle under the influence of alcohol and other drugs, and it provides in pertinent part as follows:

> No person shall operate any vehicle, streetcar, or trackless trolley within this state, if, at the time of the operation, any of the following apply:
>
> * * *
>
> (b) The person has a concentration of eight-hundredths of one per cent or more but less than seventeen-hundredths of one per cent by weight per unit volume of alcohol in the person's whole blood.

Ohio Rev. Code Ann. § 4511.19 (A)(1)(b) (Westlaw, current through Files 1 to 78 and 80 to 93 of the 130th GA (2013-2014)).

The Ohio Administrative Code regulates the method for withdrawing blood for evidence collection, and it provides in pertinent part as follows:

> In the course of providing emergency medical treatment and at the request of a law enforcement officer, an advanced emergency medical technician or paramedic may withdraw blood as provided under sections 1547.11, 4506.17, and 511.19 of the Revised Code. The advanced emergency medical technician or paramedic shall not respond to the request to withdraw blood for the purpose of evidence collection unless the advanced emergency medical technician or paramedic is also responding to a request for emergency medical treatment and transport of the patient to a health care facility. A clinically competent patient may refuse transport.

Ohio Admin. Code Ann. § 4765-6-06(D) (Westlaw current through Mar. 23, 2014).

Be sure to follow appropriate citation rules.

E. STATEMENT OF FACTS

Now that you have given readers a basic understanding of the legal issues and their resolution, it is time to describe the facts in a little more depth. In the statement of facts, the writer gives a well-organized presentation of the legally significant facts and the relevant background facts. You should have four goals when writing the statement of facts:

1. to describe the facts in appropriate detail,
2. to provide sufficient context,
3. to use an effective organizing principle, and
4. to be accurate.

1. Provide Appropriate Detail

In general, the fact statement should include an appropriate "universe of facts" for the research memo. With rare exceptions, any fact that is even referred to in any other part of the memo should be included in the fact statement and should be presented within an appropriate context. As indicated above, the statement of facts should include both legally significant facts and relevant background facts.

Legally significant facts are relatively easy to identify. After you have written your discussion section, consult the A part of the CREXAC formula—in which you have applied the law to the facts—and note which facts you have referred to when applying the law to the facts in each CREXAC unit of discourse. Any fact referred to in the rule application goes into your statement of facts.

Next, you must determine which relevant background facts should be included. The relevant background facts are the facts that you need to tell the story. They put the legally significant facts into a context that allows readers to understand what happened when and where, and how the facts relate to each other. Often, but not always, they are facts that would or might be put into evidence if the case goes to trial, through testimony, exhibits, or documents. In the fraternity house case, for example, it is probably not legally significant that the pledge went to sleep on a couch rather than a bed or the floor. In testimony, however, the fraternity brother would probably explain that he put the pledge on the couch in the living room. Thus, that detail is appropriate to include in the fact statement.

While it is probably better to be over- rather than underinclusive, you should certainly avoid going too far when writing your fact statement. Remember that your readers are busy lawyers. They will be reading the statement of facts with suspicious eyes, perking up at any detail you include. Including one or two details that are not referred to in your discussion section is not a problem. If you include too many irrelevant details, however, your readers will feel as if you are wasting their time. Every time you include a specific date or time within a fact statement, for example, you signal to readers that there is something important about that date or time. Often, what is significant is not the date or time, but the relationship between that date or time and other dates or times in the case. If this is the situation, you should be sure to "do the math" for readers so that they can see the relationships. In addition, it may be appropriate to summarize certain information.

This example contains some inappropriate details:

Bad Example

At 8:00 p.m., the pledges were given a one-quart "baby bottle" full of unspecified alcoholic beverages. At approximately 8:30 p.m., the brothers began a drinking game to encourage the pledges to finish the bottles. At 9:00 p.m., after all the pledges had finished the first bottle, they were given the next one-quart baby bottle. At 9:30 p.m., when this bottle was finished, they were walked over to the Chi Omicron sorority house, where they were required to sing songs to the members of the sorority. At 10:30 p.m., they were taken back to the fraternity house and each given a third one-quart bottle of champagne. Several of the pledges, but not all of them, finished these bottles.

This paragraph gives readers details in an inefficient way, sending the signal that certain times in the evening are crucial to the legal issue. Instead, what is crucial is the amount of time that passed, and that information is what the fact statement should provide:

Good Example

At 8:00 p.m., the pledges were given a one-quart "baby bottle" full of unspecified alcoholic beverages. Over the next two and a half hours, each pledge consumed two to three quarts of this alcohol. During this time, the pledges were walked over to the Chi Omicron sorority house. . . .

In the following example from an employment law case, the writer suggests that all of the plaintiff's job changes are important details, when his claim is based only on his employer's failure to promote him in 2020:

Bad Example

The defendant first hired Plaintiff Salaam as a front desk host in 2009. In 2010, at Mr. Salaam's request, the defendant transferred him to the hotel's fitness center attendant position. Then, in 2013, Mr. Salaam applied for and was given a position in the accounting department. He worked in accounting for seven years before becoming a night auditor. In 2020, Plaintiff Salaam applied for a promotion to the position of human resources manager. Instead of promoting Mr. Salaam, the defendant hired a white external applicant.

A reader will assume that the writer has included only necessary facts and, therefore, will try to keep track of all of the job changes.

The extraneous details will distract the reader from the smaller set of relevant facts.

The most common culprits in these overinclusive fact statements are dates and irrelevant events that complete a chronology. Writers may believe that they *must* include those details to avoid giving the reader an incomplete picture. Instead, they overtax the reader's short-term memory with unnecessary information.

Thus, when drafting your fact statement, be sure to include sufficient and necessary details and to put those details in a form that will send accurate signals about the significance of the information.

2. Provide Sufficient Context

It is tempting to tell the "story" of the facts in a once-upon-a-time manner, starting at the beginning and going through until the end:

Weaker Example

Statement of Facts
On January 25, 2007, Joe Neighbor came to Columbus to attend a family funeral. He was headed for his brother's home, at 2369 Spring Grove Lane. He had never been to his brother's home before, however, and he became confused while driving. He inadvertently ended up on Spring Brook Lane, and when he pulled in the driveway of 2369, he was not at his brother's home but at the home of James Thurber.

Readers who were unfamiliar with the facts would be in suspense at this point, perhaps wondering, "What will happen to Joe? Who is this James Thurber fellow?" This suspense may distract readers from noticing important legally significant facts. You may be thinking that readers should already know the issues because they will have read the question presented and the brief answer. Remember, however, that not all readers read all the elements of a research memo at the same time, nor do they always read them in order. Further, in some firms the standard format is to begin the research memo with the statement of the facts, in which case readers would have no idea at all what the issues might be. Accordingly, it is a good idea to begin the fact statement with one or two sentences of context:

Better Example

Statement of Facts
Our client, James Thurber, is being sued by Joe Neighbor for damages suffered when Thurber's dog, Muggs, bit Mr. Neighbor

> on the leg. The bite occurred when Mr. Neighbor entered Mr. Thurber's home by mistake.
>
> On January 25, 2007, Mr. Neighbor came to Columbus to attend a family funeral. He was headed for his brother's home, at 2369 Spring Grove Lane. He had never been to his brother's home before, however, and he became confused while driving. He inadvertently ended up on Spring Brook Lane, and when he pulled in the driveway of 2369, he was not at his brother's home but at the home of James Thurber.

Because the writer has provided context, the reader can concentrate on the legally significant details about Mr. Neighbor's mistaken trespass.

Suspense is the enemy of effective legal writing. Prevent unneeded suspense by providing sufficient context in the first paragraph of your fact statement.

3. Use an Effective Organizing Principle

The most common way to organize a fact statement is chronologically, and indeed, chronological order is often the most effective way to present information. You should at least consider, however, whether a topical organization might be appropriate. In the fraternity case, for example, it might seem logical to recite the facts chronologically, beginning with the arrival of the pledges at the fraternity house and proceeding through the evening and the next morning until the accident. Certain facts would not fit well into this organization, however. For instance, it is significant that the fraternity had a supervised room set up for the pledges and that the two brothers assigned to supervise that room were on duty until well after noon the next day, two hours after the accident. If you use a strictly chronological organization, you might need to begin the story weeks or months before the accident, when the fraternity made its plans. Further, while describing the accident at the apartment building, you might find yourself writing something like "meanwhile, back at the fraternity house. . . ."

An example of a fact statement organized primarily by topic is included at the end of this chapter.

Instead, it might be more effective to think of a topical organization. One topic could be "Pledge Night," another could be "The Accident," and another topic could be "The Fraternity's Safety Measures." Within each section, you could include a paragraph or two in chronological order about that topic. The information within the "safety measures" topic, for example, might be a paragraph or two describing how the fraternity had decided to set up the supervised room (which may have occurred weeks before the events of hell night) and the details about the supervision provided in that room on hell night and on the day of the accident.

Whether you choose a topical or chronological organization, you should consider using headings to signal your organization. With a topical organization, the headings are obvious. With a chronological organization, you might label the most significant categories of time. For example, in the fraternity house case, the "Pledge Night" and "The Accident" headings would be appropriate even if you were using a chronological organization.

4. Be Accurate

As you know, legally significant facts are facts that affect or could affect the outcome of a legal issue. Therefore, it is crucial to be as accurate as possible in describing the facts. If you do not know with confidence that a fact is true, make sure that your description of it makes your uncertainty clear. For example, if you are including a fact because your client or a potential witness told you or someone else of that fact, put that information in that person's "mouth":

> According to Mr. Thurber, Mr. Neighbor screamed at the dog before the dog bit him.

If all of your facts come from one source, you need not use this technique with every sentence. Instead, note the source within the fact statement:

> *Good Example*
> Our client, James Thurber, is being sued by Joe Neighbor for damages suffered when Thurber's dog, Muggs, bit Mr. Neighbor on the leg. The bite occurred when Mr. Neighbor entered Mr. Thurber's home by mistake. Mr. Thurber related the following facts to me in an interview.

In addition to being accurate about the facts you have, you may also wish to note facts that you do not have. Take this step only if legally significant facts are unknown, as in the following example:

> *Good Example*
> Mr. Neighbor claims that he entered Mr. Thurber's house by mistake. Mr. Thurber called the police after the incident; it is unknown whether Mr. Neighbor was charged with criminal trespass.

Do not go overboard with these techniques. Readers will be distracted if you constantly qualify your statements ("A man claiming to be Joe Neighbor came to our offices today") or if you include a long list of unknown facts.

5. Test Yourself

A writer who is very familiar with the facts in an analysis may not be in the best position to evaluate the statement of facts. After all, the writer does not need the statement of facts; the statement is written for the reader. To test the organization, detail, and context in the statement of facts, the writer should consider setting aside the draft version for some period of time after writing it. Then, the writer should read it in isolation from the rest of the analysis and attempt to experience the facts as a reader, who is not familiar with the facts, would experience them. Does the organization advance comprehension? Is appropriate context given? Are all necessary details provided? Does the statement of facts avoid distracting and unnecessary information?

F. DISCUSSION

The discussion section will not be addressed in detail in this chapter. As noted in Chapter 10, the discussion section typically consists of multiple CREXAC ("Prove") and/or CRAC ("Clarify") units of discourse that analyze the issues and sub-issues that the case presents. Chapter 14 will discuss how to write appropriate introductory material for the sections and subsections within the discussion. If you wish to have some idea of what that introductory material might include, consult the sample memo at the end of Chapter 14.

G. CONCLUSION

The conclusion should generally be no longer than a paragraph or two. In the conclusion, you should summarize the connection-conclusions that you have drawn throughout the discussion section. The conclusion is different from the brief answer in that the conclusion may use specific names instead of legally significant categories; nevertheless, you should not be surprised if there is some overlap. Just as you should consult the application piece of the CREXAC or CRAC formula when drafting your fact statement, you should consult the "connection-conclusion" piece when drafting your conclusion.

A good guideline to follow when drafting your conclusion is "no surprises." Generally, everything in the conclusion section should repeat or summarize information that has come before. The only exception to this guideline occurs if you have been asked to do more than analyze the legal issues. For example, if you have been specifically asked to recommend a course of action, then it would be appropriate to include this "new" information within the conclusion. Otherwise, however, the conclusion should simply be an adaptation of the connection-conclusions that have appeared earlier in the document.

H. ANNOTATED SAMPLE MEMORANDUM

An annotated sample memorandum appears at the end of Chapter 14. The annotations in italics highlight the principles addressed in this chapter; the other annotations highlight the principles from Chapter 14 and identify the elements of the CREXAC units of discourse in the discussion.

Fact Statement Organized Primarily by Topic

Brown, Green & White (BG&W) is a law practice. It is seeking damages from The Billing Company ("TBC") for breach of a service agreement.

From February 2017 until September 2020, The Billing Company ("TBC") performed billing services for BG&W under a billing services agreement (the "Agreement"). The Agreement provided that TBC would keep seven percent of all monies collected from BG&W's corporate clients and ten percent of all monies collected from BG&W's individual clients. The Agreement further provided that TBC would keep twenty percent of all monies collected on past-due accounts, as defined in the Agreement.

In September 2020, Byron Brown, a principal in BG&W, discovered from Deerhart Implements, one of Brown's corporate clients, that TBC had been inflating amounts owed by Deerhart Implements to BG&W and retaining the excess. BG&W inquired of other clients and learned that TBC had been inflating amounts owed by many of BG&W's clients.

BG&W canceled the Agreement and now seeks damages from TBC for breaching the Agreement, which specifically required TBC to collect from clients no more than the clients owed BG&W. The Agreement further provided that TBC would pay to BG&W any monies collected from overcharges, inadvertent or otherwise, to BG&W's clients.

The amounts by which TBC overcharged each of BG&W's clients are documented in the Damages Appendix, which is attached to this motion. Those amounts are summarized here:

1. Corporate Client Overcharges

BG&W has ongoing relationships with many corporate clients. While the Agreement was in force, TBC overcharged seven of those clients in the following amounts, as the Damages Appendix documents fully:

Client	Total amount overcharged
Basic Computing	$24,272.83
Brendan Accounting Services	$8,766.65
Deerhart Implements	$4,008.23
Ehrle Heating and Cooling	$7,550.00
Mound City Automotive	$6,220.85
Nussle Business Services	$10,364.22
Windows Are We	$3,567.26

Those amounts do not include overcharges to corporate clients whose accounts were past due.

The total amount by which TBC overcharged BG&W's corporate clients is $64,750.04. Of that amount, TBC collected $51,012.76, as the Damages Appendix documents fully.

2. Individual Client Overcharges

TBC also overcharged many of BG&W's individual clients, as the Damages Appendix documents fully. The amounts by which TBC overcharged individual clients may be summarized by annual totals:

Year	Total amount overcharged
2017	$40,336.92
2018	$56,250.74
2019	$52,387.65
2020	$39,269.83

Those amounts do not include overcharges to individual clients whose accounts were past due.

The total amount by which TBC overcharged BG&W's individual clients is $188,245.14. Of that amount, TBC collected $128,439.66, as the Damages Appendix documents fully.

3. Past-Due Accounts Overcharges

TBC inflated amounts owed by all clients whose accounts were past due, as the Damages Appendix documents fully. The amounts by which TBC overcharged corporate and individual clients whose accounts were past due may be summarized by annual totals:

Year	Total amount overcharged
2017	$22,418.78
2018	$28,590.01
2019	$31,177.36
2020	$24,841.17

The total amount by which TBC overcharged BG&W's clients whose accounts were past due is $107,027.32. Of that amount, TBC collected $45,807.30, as the Damages Appendix documents fully.

As of the date of this motion, TBC has not paid to BG&W any of the monies collected in excess of amounts owed by clients. The total amount of overcharges collected by TBC as of the date of this motion is $225,259.72.

Recall and Review

1. A good format for questions presented is the U________ -D____________-W__________ format.
2. To identify the legally significant facts that must appear in the statement of facts, consult the __________ portions of the CREXAC units of discourse in the Discussion section.
3. Because readers might read the statement of facts without having read the question presented, you should begin the statement of facts with a sentence or two of ___________.
4. Two main methods of organizing the fact statement are c_________ and t_________.
5. The Conclusion section of the office memo should be based on the _____________ portions of the CREXAC units of discourse from the Discussion section.
6. When writing the question presented, use _____________ instead of names to refer to the parties.

CHAPTER 14

THE PARTS OF A RESEARCH MEMORANDUM (PART B)

Including Context Cues for Legal Readers

Context is what helps you store information in your brain. Whenever you get a new piece of information, you subconsciously try to slot it into place, to relate it to a piece of information that you are already aware of and familiar with. Lack of context is why the first few months of law school are so difficult: you keep getting new information, but you often have nothing to attach it to. When reading legal documents, readers without sufficient context may jump to the wrong conclusion and slot information into the wrong place. While they may be able to correct the error eventually, they will spend some time being confused, which is not an experience they relish.

Thus, your job at the beginning of the discussion section *and* at each transition point between units of discourse is to provide context cues that set the stage in two ways. First, you must identify the ultimate question that your memo will answer and provide the "legal backstory" for that question. Your readers must understand, in general terms, the area of law that your memo will be addressing and the context in which the issue is currently arising. Second, you must provide a roadmap to the analysis so that your readers understand how many points you will be discussing, the order in which you will be discussing those points, and your position on those points. In this chapter, we will introduce the umbrella section and headings as the two most powerful tools in this stage-setting process.

A. THE UMBRELLA

Linda Edwards has used the term "umbrella paragraphs" to describe the combination of introductory material and roadmaps that appears—or should appear—at the beginning of most discussions of legal

Placement of Umbrellas

I. **Main Point of Discussion Section**
Main Umbrella [legal backstory relevant to A, B, & C and roadmap foreshadowing A, B, & C]
   A. **[CREXAC analysis of point A]**
   B. **Mini-umbrella** [legal backstory relevant to 1 & 2 and mini-roadmap foreshadowing 1 & 2]
      1. **[CREXAC analysis of point 1]**
      2. **[CREXAC analysis of point 2]**
   C. **[CREXAC analysis of point C]**

Figure 14.1

issues.[1] In introductory material, the writer generally includes any information that is needed to provide context, that is common to all of the subpoints, or that will connect the subpoints to the writer's thesis. One way of thinking of the legal backstory (i.e., the introductory material that comes before the roadmap in the umbrella) is moving readers from what is known to what is unknown. Figure 14.1 shows where the umbrellas should appear; generally, any time you break a section down into further subsections, you should provide some sort of introduction and roadmap. Note that the illustration refers to the umbrella that "covers" the whole discussion section as the "main umbrella"; an umbrella for a discussion section that is divided into subsections is referred to as a "mini-umbrella."

Sometimes the legal backstory and roadmap can be combined in a one-paragraph umbrella; at other times, you may need two or three paragraphs for the umbrella. As will be illustrated below, you should also provide sufficient context at the beginning of each CREXAC unit of discourse. This context can often be provided merely by stating the conclusion and the rule; indeed, one function of the "rule cluster" is to move readers from a general rule to the specific rule at issue.

Exercise 14.1

Presume that you are about to read the discussion section of an office memo analyzing the public policy exception to the employment at will doctrine. Read the three sample umbrellas below. What aspects of the umbrellas are more useful? What aspects are less useful?

---

1. Linda Holdeman Edwards, *Legal Writing: Process, Analysis, and Organization* 134-146 (5th ed., Aspen 2010).

Example A

Our client was terminated from his employment after complaining about smoking in the workplace, and he would like to sue based on the public policy exception to the employment at will doctrine. There are four elements to the tort of wrongful discharge in violation of public policy: (A) the clarity element; (B) the jeopardy element; (C) the causation element; and (D) the overriding business justification element. *McGuffin v. Smith*, 101 N.E.2d 104, 108 (Ohio 2010). This memorandum will address each in turn.

Example B

The general rule is that an employer may terminate an employee for any reason. *McGuffin v. Beazley*, 102 N.E.2d 101, 106 (Ohio 2011). There are several statutory exceptions to this requirement, however, and there is at least one common law exception: the public policy exception. *Id.* The public policy exception to the employment at will doctrine allows a terminated employee to recover damages from the employer if the employee was terminated for reasons that violate public policy. *E.g., Smith v. Beazley*, 104 N.E.2d 105, 107 (Ohio 2011). The plaintiff must establish four elements: that a clear public policy existed (the clarity element); that the termination would jeopardize that public policy (the jeopardy element); that the termination was causally related to the public policy (the causation element); and that the employer had no legitimate justification for the termination (the overriding business justification element). *McGuffin v. MacGyver*, 99 N.E.2d 999, 1004 (Ohio 2009). The first two elements are questions of fact, and the second two are questions of law. *Id.*

A court would likely rule in favor of the plaintiff if this case were to go to trial. The plaintiff is likely to be able to prove the clarity, jeopardy, causation, and business justification elements.

Example C

The general rule in Ohio has been that an employer may terminate an employee for any reason. *McGuffin v. Beazley*, 102 N.E.2d 101, 106 (Ohio 2011). Although statutory exceptions have existed for decades, *id.*, few common law exceptions have been recognized. In 1995, however, a plaintiff challenged his termination when he was fired for asking to have child support payments deducted from his paycheck. *McGuffin v. Greeley*, 44 N.E.2d 55, 57 (Ohio 1995). At that time, the court recognized the new tort of wrongful discharge in violation of public policy. *Id.* The court recognized four elements of that tort, and the elements have evolved over

> the ensuing decades. *McGuffin v. MacGyver*, 99 N.E.2d 999, 1002 (Ohio 2009).
>
> At first, for example, only statutes could form the basis for the clarity element. *Greeley*, 44 N.E.2d at 56. More recently, however, courts have allowed a variety of expressions of public policy to satisfy the basis for this "sufficiently clear public policy" element. *E.g., Ralph v. Lee*, 106 N.E.2d 107, 109 (Ohio 2011). The plaintiff must establish four elements: that a clear public policy existed (the clarity element); that the termination would jeopardize that public policy (the jeopardy element); that the termination was causally related to the public policy (the causation element); and that the employer had no legitimate justification for the termination (the overriding business justification element). *MacGyver*, 99 N.E.2d at 1004.

If you had to choose only one of the samples, which one would you choose? Which one did the best job of providing context? What was good about it? Of the ones that you did not choose, what prevented you from choosing them? Look at the examples you did not choose: was there anything about them that you found to be helpful to you as a reader?

Many legal writers mistakenly believe—consciously or unconsciously—that they do not need to provide their readers with an introduction within the discussion section. These writers believe that their readers should know enough from having read the question presented, brief answer, and the statement of facts, and that they can figure out how this case fits in the scheme of things. And on one level they may be right; many lawyers could figure things out, with enough time. But good legal writing doesn't make readers figure things out: it provides them with the information they need when they need it. And at the beginning of the discussion section, legal readers need two things: they need to know what's already happened, and they need to know what's coming. You must write the legal backstory to tell them what has already happened in the law and a roadmap to tell them what's coming in the discussion section.

1. What's Already Happened: The Legal Backstory

By "what's already happened," we are not talking just about the facts of the case (although certainly, legal readers do need this information, which you have no doubt supplied in the fact statement). We're talking about what has already happened "in the law." Where did this issue come from? How has it been spending its time? If the law is a seamless web, what part of the web are we looking at right now? To explain what has happened "so far," you need to provide the legal backstory, as succinctly as possible and with citations as appropriate.

By providing the legal backstory, you give readers vital context for the roadmap and the discussion that follows. If you are explaining whether a plaintiff can show that a defendant breached a duty of care, don't dive into the breach analysis, presuming that readers know how it is relevant to the plaintiff's claim. Instead, set the discussion in the context of the elements of negligence. Likewise, if you are explaining that the assumption of risk defense to a negligence claim does not apply, make sure that you start by stating what the assumption of risk defense is. Further, if there is a split in the authorities, don't make readers figure that out five pages later; tell that important detail right away.

In general, in the backstory, you should move your readers from what is already known about the rule at the root of the controversy in the document (or the section of the document) to what is unknown: the specific controversy that you are addressing in the document. Sometimes you will need a few sentences to move readers from the root to the narrow issue; at other times, the issue will be the rule at the root of the controversy. Providing the rule at the root of the controversy and moving readers to the narrow legal issue prepares them for the roadmap, which should follow the backstory. In one of the samples above, for example, the writer explained the general rule about employment at will and then described the exception to it, rather than just diving into a discussion about the exception.

Broadly stated, readers should be able to glean four elements from the legal backstory:

1. The legal rule that is at the root of this analysis, or, for a mini-umbrella, this part of the analysis. Many legal analyses are about the meaning of a particular word or phrase within a constitutional provision, statute, or legal rule. Even when there is a thick layer of judicial gloss on the original rule—as there is, for example, on the First Amendment—you should still note (or quote) the pertinent part of the First Amendment before moving to the concept of, for example, the existence of a chilling effect in a particular case. If a common law rule is at the root of the controversy, you should articulate that common law rule. If your discussion addresses an exception to or subpart of a more general common law rule, you should first articulate that general rule. If the overarching rule for your discussion is a statute, the elements of the statute may be part of the legal backstory, and you should include some reference to them in your umbrella for the entire discussion.

2. How the legal issue in this case (or section of the discussion) relates to the rule at the root of the controversy. After stating the rule that is at the root of your controversy, move from that rule to the rule

The Fourth Amendment is at the root of this controversy. This basic requirement of the Fourth Amendment is "known."

The writer moves readers from considering *all* Fourth Amendment law to considering Fourth Amendment law relevant to searches conducted via dog sniff, telling us what is "known" about rules regarding this kind of search.

In this sentence, the writer both tells us the issue that this document will answer (what is unknown) and shows us how the issue relates to the rule at the root of the controversy: it is a facet of Fourth Amendment law as it relates to dog-sniff searches.

or sub-rule currently at issue. The concept of the "rule cluster" that was discussed earlier may be appropriate here, as there may be a direct progression from one rule to the next. In contrast, the legal issue in your case may be a sub-part of the main rule. In general, think of moving from what is known to what is unknown. For example,

> The Fourth Amendment provides that all "searches" must be reasonable. When defining the term "search," courts have held that a dog sniff of the exterior of a car is not a search if it is conducted during a legitimate police stop. *King*, 432 F.3d at 684. Our client has asked us to determine whether he will be able to successfully challenge a dog sniff that occurred when police walked a dog down a street and had the dog sniff every parked car.

Readers will be able to understand the relationship between the Fourth Amendment and the client's dog-sniff question because the writer moved from the broad Fourth Amendment rule to the narrower rule about dog-sniff searches to the question of whether police can conduct a "dog-sniff search" of a row of parked cars.

3. ***The question that this part of the document is answering.*** If you are writing the backstory for the whole discussion section, you can talk about the question that the whole document is answering. If you are providing backstory for just one part of the discussion, focus on that part alone. One way to provide this information is by describing what your client wants to know, as in, "our client has asked whether he had a legal duty to protect a fraternity brother who became intoxicated after a 'pledge night' ceremony." This part of the umbrella will usually overlap with item two (the relationship between the issue and the rule at the root of the controversy). In addition, or in the alternative, you may have announced that question at the beginning of the umbrella, as the writer did in Sample A above.

4. ***Information about the current status of that issue in the relevant jurisdiction, if needed.*** This last provision is a catch-all provision. You must decide whether there is any more information that readers need to know about the current status of the rule. In Example B above, for example, the writer told readers which issues were questions of law and which were questions of fact. You might need to point out that there is a split among the courts as to an issue. It might be appropriate to point out that sister states or sister circuits have adopted a particular rule but that your particular jurisdiction has not yet done so. On the other hand, you may not need to add any information at this point.

It is important to be honest in the legal backstory. For example, if there is a split in the circuits, it might be tempting to point out only that certain other courts have decided the case in your client's favor. Remember, however, that your job in a memorandum is not to paint a rosy picture for your readers; rather, you should give an *accurate* picture of the current state of the law and of how you believe a court would apply the law to the facts. Your credibility will suffer if your readers have to find out the truth on their own—and particularly if they have to discover it in a conversation with opposing counsel.

The umbrella below is another version of an umbrella that a writer would include at the beginning of a discussion section about wrongful discharge in violation of public policy. It is annotated to show where the writer is accomplishing the goals of the umbrella:

Good Example

Our client, Steve Johansen, wants to know whether he can recover damages from Cedar Publishing for being discharged after complaining about violations of state antismoking law. Generally, at-will employees can be discharged for any reason or for no reason. *Painter v. Graley*, 639 N.E.2d 51, 55 (Ohio 1994). Nonetheless, Ohio courts recognize an exception to the general rule when the discharge violates public policy. *Id.* at 55-56. Such a claim for wrongful discharge in violation of public policy is brought in tort and is commonly known as a "Greeley claim." *Greeley v. Miami Valley Maint. Contractors, Inc.*, 551 N.E.2d 981, 987 (Ohio 1990). *See also Avery v. Joint Twp. Dist. Mem'l Hosp.*, 286 F. App'x 256, 260 (6th Cir. 2008).

The writer articulates the question that the document is designed to answer.

The writer articulates the general rule that is at the root of the controversy: the rule about when someone can recover damages for wrongful discharge.

The writer shows how the controversy in the current case relates to the general rule: the memo will address *one* cause of action that an at-will employee can use to recover damages.

Although Johansen believes he was fired for complaining about a legal violation, he cannot recover under Ohio's whistleblower statute because he did not comply with its specific requirements and because the antismoking statute is not classified as a criminal statute. *See* Ohio Rev. Code Ann § 4113.52 (Westlaw current through Mar. 9, 2010) (employee must orally notify his supervisor of the alleged statutory violation and then file a written report with the supervisor); Ohio Rev. Code Ann. §§ 3794.02, 3794.09 (Westlaw current through Mar. 9, 2021) (providing the imposition of "civil fines" for violation of the Act).

The writer is moving into the roadmap part of the umbrella, and he begins by describing a *tell* issue that the memo will not address. Note that it is not always appropriate to *begin* the roadmap in this way, but it is here, where the issue that is not being addressed does not relate directly to the rules that *are* being addressed.

To prevail upon a claim for wrongful discharge in violation of public policy, an employee must prove four elements:

1. That clear public policy existed and was manifested in a state or federal constitution, statute, or administrative regulation, or in the common law (the clarity element).
2. That dismissing employees under circumstances like those involved in the plaintiff's dismissal would jeopardize the public policy (the jeopardy element).
3. [That] [t]he plaintiff's dismissal was motivated by conduct related to the public policy (the causation element).

The writer lays out the four points he will be addressing, in the order in which he will address them.

4. [That] [t]he employer lacked overriding legitimate business justification for the dismissal (the overriding justification element).

Painter v. Graley, 639 N.E.2d 51, 57 n.8 (Ohio 1994) (citation omitted). The first two elements are questions of law to be decided by the court, whereas the last two elements are questions of fact to be decided by the jury. *Collins v. Rizkana*, 652 N.E.2d 653, 658 (Ohio 1995).

The writer articulates his position on the relevant issues.

Given the facts from the interview, Johansen can probably prove that his discharge was in violation of public policy and thus be able to recover damages from Cedar Publishing.

An umbrella for subsections within the discussion—i.e., a "mini-umbrella"—may be much shorter. The following example of a legal backstory comes from a memorandum that analyzes a negligence cause of action. In the main umbrella, the writer had laid out the four-part test for negligence in the relevant jurisdiction (duty, breach, proximate cause, and damages). In this mini-umbrella, the writer sets out the backstory for the proximate cause analysis, which will be divided into two parts:

Good Example

The writer articulates the rule regarding proximate cause, which is at the root of the controversy surrounding the causation element.

The writer lays out the two points that she will address in this section, in the order in which she will address them.

The writer establishes her position on the issues that will be addressed in this section.

C. Proximate Cause

In South Carolina, proximate cause requires proof of both causation in fact and legal cause. *Hurd v. Williamsburg Cnty.*, 611 S.E.2d 488, 492 (S.C. 2005). Causation in fact is proved by showing that the plaintiff's injuries would not have occurred "but for" the defendant's breach of duty. *Id.* Legal cause is proved by showing that the plaintiff's injuries were the foreseeable or the natural and probable consequences of the defendant's negligence. *Id.* at 493. Kroger can likely establish both elements of proximate cause: but for Riegert's breach of duty, Kroger would not have sustained his injuries, injuries that were foreseeable in light of his intoxicated condition.

By referring specifically to the proximate cause element, the writer has ensured that readers will be able to understand what rule is at the root of the controversy for this part of the analysis. The status of the rule is not controversial, and so the writer merely relates the two parts of her analysis to the causation rule.

Whether your legal backstory is simple or complex, providing it will go a long way toward helping readers to understand the rest of the analysis.

2. What's Coming Next: The Roadmap

The roadmap follows the legal backstory. It may be only a sentence, but a paragraph is often required to provide complete guidance to the reader. A good roadmap will foreshadow exactly what's going to happen in the discussion section. Roadmaps are important because they help confirm, and sometimes establish, readers' expectations for the document. A good roadmap tells readers the points the writer will and will not be addressing. Obviously, there are dozens of points you will *not* be addressing; include those points in the roadmap only if readers would expect that you would be addressing the point. A good roadmap will also reveal the writer's position on the points to be addressed in the relevant sections or subsections. By writing an effective roadmap, the writer tells readers how far this part of the document extends—how many points does the writer talk about before stopping?

In addition, an effective roadmap lays out the document's large-scale organization by telling readers the order in which the writer will address the main points. Even a poorly organized document will be easier to understand if the writer has provided a good roadmap.

It is tempting to skip this step, but providing this material makes your memo more effective by reducing readers' suspense. If readers see a Roman "I" heading, followed immediately by an "A" heading, for example, they do not know how many subheadings will follow or how the subheadings connect to the writer's main point. By writing a backstory and a roadmap, the writer provides connections for readers so that links between the different parts of the document are obvious.

Although many writers are familiar with the law review style of roadmap paragraphs (e.g., "this article will address three issues"), roadmaps in briefs and memos can and should be more sophisticated. A simple technique is to provide the legal backstory and then focus the roadmap on what one party or the other must prove or what the decision maker must find,[2] as in the following example:

Good Example

I. Can Kroger hold Riegert liable?

Our client, Larry Kroger, wants to know whether he can hold Peter Riegert liable for negligence for removing Kroger from a supervised area and then abandoning him while Kroger was known to be severely intoxicated. In order to recover, Kroger must first establish that he was injured due to Riegert's negligence by proving four elements: (1) that Riegert owed Kroger a legal duty

The writer articulates the question that the document will answer.

The writer articulates the rule at the heart of the analysis. In some situations, readers might be confused by the incorporation of a client's facts into the rule. Here, however, doing so is more acceptable because the rule is a familiar one.

2. *See* Laurel Currie Oates, Anne M. Enquist & Kelly Kunsch, *The Legal Writing Handbook* 581-583 (3d ed., Aspen 2002).

of care; (2) that Riegert failed to discharge that duty; (3) that Kroger suffered a compensable injury; and (4) that Riegert's actions proximately caused the injury. *See McGuffin v. Town of Summers*, 455 S.E.2d 8, 8 (S.C. 1993). Even if Kroger establishes these elements, however, Riegert will not be held liable if he can establish that Kroger's comparative negligence outweighs Riegert's own negligence. *See Slavin v. Blemberg*, 599 S.E.2d 1215, 1218 (S.C. 1997).

The writer refers to a second rule that underlies the analysis: the rule of comparative negligence.

Given the facts in the current situation, there is no question that Kroger has suffered a compensable injury. As the discussion below indicates, it is likely that Kroger will be able to establish duty, breach, and causation as well. Furthermore, although Riegert may assert the doctrine of comparative negligence as a defense, it is unlikely he will succeed in proving that Kroger is more than 50 percent negligent. Consequently, it is likely that Kroger will be able to hold Riegert liable.

The writer articulates a point that the memo will not be addressing (i.e., a *tell* issue).

The writer identifies the points the memo will address, and the order in which they will be addressed. Note how the writer focuses on what Kroger and Riegert will each have to prove. Note also that the writer reveals her position on the outcome of each of the issues.

Although the writer in the example above chose not to use enumeration (perhaps because there had been other sentences with enumeration in the backstory), enumeration almost always makes roadmap paragraphs more effective. The user's eye is drawn to numbers on a page, and the reader needs to do less work to understand how the points relate to each other. The previous roadmap paragraph could be enumerated with a few simple changes:

Better Example of Roadmap

Given the facts in the current situation, there is no question that Kroger has suffered a compensable injury. As the discussion below indicates, it is likely that Kroger will be able to recover because (1) Kroger can establish that Riegert owed him a duty; (2) Kroger can establish that Riegert breached the duty; (3) Kroger can establish that Riegert's breach of duty caused Kroger harm; and (4) Riegert will not be able to establish that Kroger is more than 50 percent negligent. Consequently, it is likely that Kroger will be able to hold Riegert liable.

Here, the writer articulates a point that the memo will not be addressing (i.e., a *tell* issue).

In most circumstances, the writer could use the phrase "Kroger can establish" in an introductory clause and avoid repeating it three times. However, because the fourth piece of the analysis focuses on something that *Riegert*, rather than Kroger, must prove, the repetition is needed for the sake of clarity.

Two kinds of mistakes are particularly common in umbrella sections. First, writers sometimes fail to include needed citations in the backstory because they believe that "general" rules do not need citation:

Bad Example

Our client, Steve Johansen, wants to know whether he can recover damages from Cedar Publishing for being discharged after complaining about violations of state antismoking law. Generally,

> at-will employees can be discharged for any reason or for no reason. Nonetheless, Ohio courts recognize an exception to the general rule when the discharge is in violation of public policy. Such a claim for wrongful discharge in violation of public policy is brought in tort and is commonly known as a "Greeley claim." *Greeley v. Miami Valley Maint. Contractors, Inc.*, 551 N.E. 2d 981, 987 (Ohio 1990).

This paragraph lacks needed citations; the statements about when at-will employees can be discharged and about the exception to the general rule should both be followed by citations.

The second kind of common mistake in umbrella sections is that the writer gives too much detail. For example, if a section of the analysis is going to be divided into subsections, details about the rules relevant to those subsections should not be included in the main umbrella. Likewise, if certain aspects of the backstory are relevant to only one part of the discussion section, they should generally be saved for that part of the discussion:

> ***Bad Example***
> Our client, Larry Kroger, wants to know whether he can hold Peter Riegert liable for negligence for removing Kroger from a supervised area and then abandoning him while Kroger was known to be severely intoxicated. In order to recover, Kroger must first establish that he was injured due to Riegert's negligence by proving four elements. First, he must establish that Riegert owed Kroger a legal duty of care. *See McGuffin v. Town of Summers*, 455 S.E.2d 8, 8 (S.C. 1993). Generally, a person does not owe a duty to another person, but a person may assume a duty under a variety of circumstances. *Id.* at 10. In this case, Kroger can establish that Riegert voluntarily assumed a duty to care for Kroger while Kroger was helpless. *See Enns v. Montague*, 403 S.E.2d 101, 103 (S.C. App. 1988). In South Carolina, an intoxicated person is considered helpless. *Id.* at 104.
>
> Second, Kroger must establish that Riegert failed to discharge that duty. *See McGuffin*, 455 S.E.2d at 10. Third, Kroger must establish that he suffered a compensable injury. *See id.* Fourth, Kroger must establish that Riegert's actions proximately caused the injury. *See id.* In South Carolina, proximate cause requires proof of both causation in fact and legal cause. *Hurd v. Williamsburg Cnty.*, 611 S.E.2d 488, 492 (S.C. 2005). Causation in fact is proved by showing that the plaintiff's injuries would not have occurred "but for" the defendant's breach of duty. *Id.* Legal cause is proved by showing that the plaintiff's injuries were the foreseeable or the

natural and probable consequences of the defendant's negligence. *Id.* at 493. Even if Kroger establishes these elements, however, Riegert will not be held liable if he can establish that Kroger's comparative negligence outweighs Riegert's own negligence. *See Slavin v. Blemberg*, 599 S.E.2d 1215, 1218 (S.C. 1997).

Given the facts in the current situation, there is no question that Kroger has suffered a compensable injury. As the discussion below indicates, it is likely that Kroger will be able to recover because (1) Kroger can establish that Riegert owed him a duty; (2) Kroger can establish that Riegert breached the duty; (3) Kroger can establish that Riegert's breach of duty caused Kroger harm; and (4) Riegert will not be able to establish that Kroger is more than 50 percent negligent. Consequently, it is likely that Kroger will be able to hold Riegert liable.

The example above contains too much information about the causation and duty elements. Because the section of the memo addressing causation will later be divided into two subsections, the backstory regarding those subsections should be saved for that umbrella, illustrated above.

Further, the information regarding the duty element relates only to that element, and so need not be included in the main umbrella. Instead, it can be included in the "duty" section, where the writer articulates the rule governing when a person assumes a duty. As was noted in Chapter 10, the articulation of a rule may need to begin with a general rule and then move to a specific rule. Likewise, if a rule includes a *tell* issue, the writer may need to incorporate that *tell* into the rule paragraph. Here is an example of using *tell* issues to provide context at the beginning of a discussion section:

Good Example

A. Did Riegert have a duty of care to Kroger?

It is likely that Kroger will be able to establish that Riegert had a duty to Kroger to act with due care. Generally, a person does not have a duty to act unless a statute, contract, relationship status, property interest, or some special circumstance creates a duty to act. *McGuffin v. Humboldt Cnty. Dep't of Corrections*, 374 S.E.2d 910, 913 (S.C. App. 1988) (defendant corrections department had no special duty to protect prisoners from each other). A duty to act can be created, however, if a person "takes charge" of another who is "helpless" to aid or protect himself or herself adequately. *Carson v. Adgar*, 486 S.E.2d 3, 6-7 (S.C. 1997) (citations omitted). The *Carson* Court adopted the Restatement position that an intoxicated person is helpless. *Id.* (citing Restatement (Second) of Torts § 324 cmt. b (1965)). When the police found Kroger, he had a blood-alcohol concentration of .12, and his blood-alcohol concentration was presumably higher when Riegert had taken him home several hours earlier. Hence, a court would likely find that Kroger was helpless. Further, Riegert's actions indicate that he "took charge" and thus assumed a duty.

Admittedly, a rule paragraph is not the same as an umbrella; an umbrella generally shows how different rules relate to one another, while a rule paragraph is generally focused on just one rule. Nevertheless, a rule paragraph, like an umbrella, does provide readers context.

B. USING HEADINGS EFFECTIVELY IN A LEGAL MEMORANDUM

The author Elmore Leonard is well known for his advice to writers. He once said, "I try not to write the parts that people skip." This is fruitless advice for legal writers. Legal writing is functional writing, and your readers will constantly be looking for the information that they want and need, and looking to skip the information that they don't want or need. We are guessing that you will skip parts of this book as you scan through, looking for information that you need as you work on a particular section of your document. Legal readers are grateful to legal writers who provide context cues that act as signals for readers and make it easy to find the parts they need and to skip the parts they don't. Headings are the most useful signals for this purpose. You must decide when to include headings and what information to include in them.

1. When to Include Headings

Your headings should signal the large-scale structure of your document. In general, you should provide a heading for each CREXAC unit of discourse, and you may also want to provide headings for CRAC units of discourse. If several CREXAC units of discourse work together to make one larger point, you should provide a heading that signals that relationship.

For example, suppose that you were representing someone who was suing her employer for violating the rule against wrongful discharge in violation of public policy and for retaliating against her in violation of Title VII. A memorandum analyzing these causes of action would likely be broken into two large sections, and each of those two large sections would be broken into smaller sections. Both the substance and the enumeration of your headings should signal these relationships:

I. Wrongful Discharge in Violation of Public Policy
  A. Clarity Element
  B. Jeopardy Element
  C. Causation Element
    1. Causation in Fact
    2. Legal Cause
  D. Overriding Business Justification
II. Retaliation in Violation of Title VII
  A. Activity Protected Under Federal Law
  B. Adverse Employment Action
  C. Connection Between Protected Activity and Adverse Action

These headings signal that the wrongful discharge claim has four elements and that one of those elements (the causation element) has two elements itself. Likewise, it signals that there are three relevant elements to the retaliation violation under Title VII. Of course, if any of these elements were *tell* issues—that is, if they were so clear that you did not need to discuss them—you would not need to have headings for them because you would have dealt with them in the umbrella between the Roman numeral and the first-listed element.

2. How to Write a Heading in a Research Memorandum

As noted above, the purpose of headings is to help readers find the information that they are interested in and to skip the information that they are not interested in. To help readers navigate your documents, your headings should echo language that you used in your roadmap, which in turn should echo language that courts use to talk about the element. You may wish to signal the outcome of your discussion, using language such as "Plaintiff cannot establish the clarity element" rather than just "the clarity element." We advise, however, that you keep your headings as short as possible; aim for one line of text, and almost never go beyond three lines. Legal readers are impatient and want to scan headings to get the gist of what you are talking about.

This discussion uses "elements" to refer to subparts within a discussion section. The same guidelines apply to "factors" tests, and they apply any time that you break a legal discussion into multiple CREXAC units of discourse.

One caveat about headings relates to the text that immediately follows the heading. You must write the heading to signal readers about the topic under discussion, but you must *also* include a signal in the text that immediately follows. In other words, do not treat the heading as if it is the first words or the first sentence in the paragraph. This advice may not make sense to you. You may wonder why readers can't connect the heading to the text. Yes, readers can make that connection, but not all readers read both the heading and the text. You must write the heading and the accompanying text to accommodate three kinds of readers: (1) readers who read only headings (make sure the heading provides the information that they need to understand what the section covers); (2) readers who read headings and text (make sure the text does not exactly repeat the heading); and (3) readers who skip the headings when they are reading the text (make sure that the first sentence of the paragraph makes sense without the heading). Thus, this combination of heading and text is not appropriate:

Bad Example

C. The Causation Element
This element requires the plaintiff to establish . . .

This combination of heading and text is more appropriate:

Better Example

C. The Causation Element
To establish causation, the third required element, the plaintiff must . . .

The better combination of heading and text signals the content in both the heading and the first sentence. Further, the better combination reminds readers that causation is the third required element. This reminder may seem ridiculous to the person who has been working on the memo for days and who can recite the needed elements backward and forward. But that simple, extra signal, telling readers "the third required element is causation," is a very welcome reminder to tired readers who are juggling four or five different cases on any given day and who need signals like that to keep focused.

3. The Sentence Heading

In most persuasive writing (motion memos and appellate briefs) and some predictive writing (office memos and research memos), headings take the form of sentences that provide concise synopses of the discussions that follows. These sentence headings serve two purposes: (1) they act as a part of the roadmap for the entire analysis, and (2) they allow readers to get the gist of a section or an analysis without reading it.

You may wonder why you would want to make it easier for readers to skip part of your analysis. Think of it this way: readers will skip whether you make it easier for them or not. They will search for the part of the discussion that addresses the point that most interests them.

By including a sentence-long synopsis of the section, you encourage readers to spend at least a few seconds thinking about a point that they are otherwise inclined to skip. Does that make you feel better about writing the sentence heading?

The sentence heading should be a synopsis, or very short version, of the analysis that follows, so it should include something about the rule (such as the phrase-that-pays for the section) and the legally significant facts. In this example, the writer has incorporated important information about the rule, the legally significant facts, and the outcome of the application of the rule to the legally significant facts:

> *Good Example*
> B. Having failed to identify a male employee who was similarly situated in all relevant respects, Ms. Lagos cannot succeed in proving that Bank Two chose managers for termination in a manner that reflected disparate treatment.

The writer has provided a mini-analysis for skimming readers in a way that the following example does not:

> *Less Than Optimal Example*
> B. Ms. Lagos was not similarly situated.

The writer of the second example might as well have just provided the label "similarly situated" because the heading does nothing more than act as a title for the section. Titles alone can be effective as part of a roadmap, but they do not serve the mini-analysis purpose as carefully written sentence headings do. If a writer has written all of the sentence headings with care, readers can read just the headings and comprehend the basic points of the writer's entire analysis.

C. ANNOTATED SAMPLE MEMORANDA

Two annotated sample memoranda appear below. In the first sample, the annotations in italics highlight the principles from Chapter 13; the other annotations highlight the principles from this chapter and identify the elements of the CREXAC units of discourse in the discussion. The second sample illustrates the same principles in a different legal and factual context. Study the second sample and its annotations when you are ready to consider variations in the manner in which the principles from these chapters apply.

Memorandum

To: Partner
From: Associate
Date: January 14, 2013
Re: Lisa Lagos's allegations of sex discrimination (disparate treatment; reduction 1.
in force) against Bank Two

2.

Question Presented

3.

Under Title VII, is Lisa Lagos likely to succeed on a Title VII claim for sex discrimina- 4.
tion against Bank Two stemming from the Bank's decision to terminate her employment in a 5.
reduction in force when that decision is based on past performance evaluations, Ms. Lagos has
no evidence of discriminatory motive, and the male managers who were retained had better
evaluations from different supervisors?

Brief Answer

6.

Probably not. A plaintiff who claims sex discrimination in the termination of her employ- 7.
ment as part of a reduction in force must (A) introduce direct evidence of discriminatory
motive or (B) show that her employer treated her less favorably than male employees who
were similar to the plaintiff in all relevant respects. Ms. Lagos has not identified evidence of
discriminatory motive, and she compares herself to male employees who performed different 8.
jobs, had better evaluations, and reported to a different supervisor; therefore, she is unlikely
to succeed on her Title VII claim.

Facts

9.

Our client, Lisa Lagos, was recently terminated from her job as a manager at Bank Two; the termination occurred as part of a reduction in force. Male managers with similar seniority were not terminated, and Ms. Lagos wants to know whether she can recover damages for sex discrimination.

10.

Ms. Lagos, Todd North, and Jason South were all managers at Bank Two in November 2010, when Bank Two decided to reorganize by reducing the number of managers it employed. The Bank stated that it would retain the most highly compensated managers because compensation was the best measure of seniority and merit. The Bank consistently based raises in pay for managers on the managers' scores on annual evaluations. Because all managers

1. *Note that caption elements are aligned, and that the "Re:" line includes identifying detail.*

2. *The "under" clause identifies the relevant law.*

3. *Although this question uses the party's name, some readers may prefer legally significant categories (e.g., "a female employee").*

4. *The legal status identified in the "does" clause is the legal status of successfully bringing a Title VII claim.*

5. *The "when" clause contains the legally significant facts. The writer may need to include some detail here; placing the facts at the end of the sentence makes it easier to accommodate that kind of detail.*

6. *The brief answer begins with a direct answer to the question presented.*

7. *The brief answer may include relevant information about the relevant law, if that information did not appear in the question presented.*

8. *The brief answer connects the facts from the "when" clause to the legal status.*

9. *The fact statement begins with context.*

10. *The facts are organized around the events that gave rise to the claim; the writer does not follow a strict chronological order.*

started at the same salary, increases in salary reflected only evaluation scores. The difference in pay between two managers who were hired at the same time, as Ms. Lagos, Mr. North, and Mr. South were, could be explained solely by differences in evaluation scores.

From the time of her hiring, Ms. Lagos had worked as a manager in the Commercial Lending Department of Bank Two. She reported to the Vice President of Commercial Lending, who was responsible for her annual evaluations. All of the managers in Commercial Lending were women. Ms. Lagos supervised only nonprofessional employees who tended to turn
11. over at a high rate. Her evaluation scores were perfect with the exception of "Employee Management," in which she annually received the second highest possible score. The stated reason for the lower score in "Employee Management" was her failure to retain employees. Bank Two terminated Ms. Lagos's employment in the reduction in force in November 2010.

Mr. North and Mr. South came to Bank Two on the same day as Ms. Lagos did. They had the same education and experience as Ms. Lagos had at the time of their hiring. From the time of their hiring, Mr. North and Mr. South worked as managers in the International Transactions Department, where they supervised only professional employees. In Bank Two's culture, professional employees turned over very infrequently. All of the managers in International Transactions were men. Mr. North and Mr. South reported to the Vice President of International Transactions, who was responsible for their annual evaluations.

In the reduction in force, both Mr. North and Mr. South retained their jobs. Ms. Lagos assumes that Mr. North and Mr. South received perfect scores annually in their evaluations, including in the category of "Employee Management."

Ms. Lagos believes that Bank Two has discriminated against her by terminating her job while it retained male managers at the same level of seniority. She acknowledges that the male managers to whom she compares herself probably had better performance evaluations than hers because their employee retention scores were better. She complains that that quality of her
12. employees negatively impacted her employee retention score in a way that the male managers were not impacted. Nevertheless, she has not indicated that she has other information about the way that Bank Two carried out the reduction in force that would suggest that Bank Two chose the method it used in order to eliminate female managers.

<u>Discussion</u>

13. Ms. Lagos probably will not be able to establish a Title VII claim on the sole basis of the termination of her employment.

14. In the Sixth Circuit, the analysis of a Title VII disparate treatment claim follows the standard outlined in *Mitchell v. Toledo Hospital*, 964 F.2d 577 (6th Cir. 1992). The Circuit

11. *These details are not legally significant in that they do not alter the analysis. They do, however, provide context, and they help readers to understand why plaintiff believed that she had been treated unfairly and perhaps illegally.*

12. *Note that the fact statement identifies "missing" legally significant facts.*

13. The umbrella section begins here.

14. The legal backstory begins here.

added flexibility to the standard six years later in *Ercegovich v. Goodyear Tire & Rubber Co.*, 154 F.3d 344 (6th Cir. 1998). The Sixth Circuit still applies the *Ercegovich* test today. It requires the following showing by a plaintiff in a disparate treatment action: (1) the plaintiff is a member of a protected class; (2) the plaintiff was otherwise qualified for the position in question; (3) the plaintiff suffered an adverse employment action; and either (4a) the plaintiff can produce direct evidence of discrimination or (4b) the plaintiff can demonstrate that comparable similarly situated nonprotected employees were treated more favorably. *Id.* at 350; *see also DiCarlo v. Potter*, 358 F.3d 408, 415 (6th Cir. 2004). 15.

16. Title VII includes women as a protected class along with racial minorities. *See* 42 U.S.C. § 2000e-2. Accordingly, the Title VII cases in the racial context are equally applicable in the context of alleged sex discrimination. *See, e.g., Taylor v. Union Inst.*, 30 F. App'x 443, 447 (6th Cir. 2002). 17.

18. Ms. Lagos will be able to satisfy the first three prongs of the Title VII claim as set forth in *Ercegovich*, 154 F.3d at 350. As a woman, she is a member of a class of employees protected from discrimination by Title VII, satisfying the first prong. 42 U.S.C. § 2000e-2. Bank Two, having given her very favorable performance evaluations each year of her employment, is unlikely to deny that she was qualified to retain a management position, satisfying the second prong. The termination of her employment was an adverse employment action, satisfying the third prong. *Mitchell*, 964 F.2d at 582 (termination of employment is an adverse employment action). The success of Ms. Lagos's claim based upon the termination of her employment will depend upon her ability to satisfy the fourth prong of the test set forth in *Ercegovich*.

19. Ms. Lagos's claim is likely to fail to the extent that it is based upon the termination of her employment at the end of 2010. In order to prove discrimination under Title VII, an employee must (a) produce direct evidence of discrimination or (b) demonstrate that comparable similarly situated nonprotected employees were treated better. *Ercegovich*, 154 F.3d at 350; *see also DiCarlo*, 358 F.3d at 415. Ms. Lagos will probably not be able to establish a Title VII violation relating to the termination of her employment under either the direct evidence alternative *or* the similarly situated nonprotected employees model.

20. A. Lisa Lagos cannot succeed under the direct evidence alternative because she has not identified such evidence

21. Unless discovery would uncover direct evidence of discrimination in the manner in which Bank Two carried out the restructuring, Ms. Lagos is not likely to succeed under the first alternative of prong four of the *Ercegovich* test. She has not indicated that she has such evidence now.

15. The legal backstory ends here. The legal backstory is unusually complex in this memorandum. It will often be much simpler (and, therefore, shorter).

16. The roadmap begins here. It includes matter that will apply in all of the subsections that follow, the discussion of *tell* issues, and guidance about the issues that the discussion will address in full CREXAC units of discourse.

17. This clarification of a point of law applies to all of the discussion that follows, so it is included in the umbrella section and is not repeated in each subsection of the discussion.

18. In this paragraph, the writer eliminates three *tell* issues very briefly.

19. This paragraph tells what is coming in the subsections of the discussion.

20. This subhead is effective because it incorporates something about the relevant rule and the legally significant facts.

21. Conclusion–Thesis.

22. In order to prove a claim using direct evidence in the reduction in force context, a plaintiff must introduce evidence that tends to show that the employer intentionally singled out members of the protected class for discharge. *Geiger v. Tower Automotive*, 579 F.3d 614,
23. 624 (6th Cir. 2009). The plaintiff in *Geiger* identified several inferences that suggested that his employer may have been motivated by age-based animus in the decision to terminate his employment in a reduction in force. *Id.* The court held, however, that the plaintiff could not rely on inferences but must introduce direct evidence that itself proved that an impermissible and discriminatory motive was behind the employer's choices. *Id.* Inferences will not suffice to establish impermissible motive, therefore, and a discrimination plaintiff in the reduction in force context must introduce direct evidence of such a motive. *Id.*

24. Ms. Lagos does not claim to have direct evidence of an impermissible motive, so she cannot establish the fourth prong using such evidence. Ms. Lagos has not stated that she believes that Bank Two carried out the restructuring intentionally in such a way as to target women for discharge. None of the facts she has presented suggests that additional discovery is likely to uncover direct evidence of such a motive. In short, she does not state that she has direct evidence that would tend to show that Bank Two actually singled out female managers for discharge in the reduction in force or provide a reason to believe that such evidence exists.
25. Accordingly, Ms. Lagos will be unable to establish a Title VII claim on the basis of the first alternative under the fourth *Ercegovich* prong. Her claim must proceed, if at all, under the second prong.

26. B. Having failed to identify a male employee who was similarly situated in all relevant respects, Lisa Lagos cannot succeed in proving that Bank Two chose managers for termination in a manner that reflected disparate treatment

27. Ms. Lagos has not suggested that she can identify a male manager who was similarly situated in all relevant respects and was treated more favorably in the reduction in force. She will, therefore, probably not be able to satisfy the second alternative under the fourth *Ercegovich* prong.

28. In order to prove disparate treatment in accordance with the second alternative under *Ercegovich*'s fourth prong, an employee must show that she was treated less favorably than an employee who is not part of her protected class and is otherwise similar in all relevant respects. *Ercegovich*, 154 F.3d at 352. That is, the plaintiff and the employee to whom she compares herself "must have dealt with the same supervisor, [and] have been subject to the same standards." *Id.* (quoting *Mitchell*, 964 F.2d at 583). Relevant respects are those that relate in some fashion to the basis for the adverse employment action. *See Mickey v. Zeidler Tool & Die Co.*, 516 F.3d 516, 522-23 (6th Cir. 2008).

22. Rule.

23. Explanation.

24. Application.

25. Connection-conclusion (notice that this C serves as a connection between this subsection and the discussion as a whole and includes a clear transition to the next subsection).

26. This subheading also incorporates the relevant rule and legally significant facts.

27. Conclusion.

28. Rule. This R includes three sentences. The writer has not determined which part of this R is the Rule and which part could have been part of the EX (or omitted altogether).

29. One district court, applying the "same supervisor" standard from *Mitchell*, considered when differences in supervisor will prevent an employee from proving similarity. *See Duncan v. Koch Air, L.L.C.*, No. Civ.A. 3:04CV-72-H , 2005 WL 1353758, *3 (W.D. Ky. June 2, 2005). Plaintiff Duncan, who was female, was fired for missing work without prior notice. *Id.* at *1. A male employee was not fired for violating the same rule. *Id.* The supervisor who fired Duncan did not make the decision to retain the other employee, however. *Id.* at *3. The court concluded that Duncan could not prove similarity because her claim was based, at least in part, on her supervisor's actions, and the employee to whom she compared herself reported to a different supervisor. *Id.* Because of the difference in supervisors, the differences in the employees' treatment could not be evidence of discrimination. *Id.* (citing *McMillan v. Castro*, 405 F.3d 405, 413-14 (6th Cir. 2003); *Mitchell*, 964 F.2d at 583).

So, the second alternative under the fourth prong of *Ercegovich* is satisfied only if the two 30.
employees were similar in all respects that were relevant to the termination or other adverse employment action. *Mitchell*, 964 F.2d at 583. If the employee's claim is based, at least in part, on a supervisor's actions, employees who reported to different supervisors cannot be similarly situated in all relevant respects.

Ms. Lagos was similar to Mr. North and Mr. South in some relevant respects but not 31.
in all, as the rule requires. She did not report to the same supervisor, and the actions of her supervisor form a part of the basis for her claim. She will not, therefore, be able to satisfy the second alternative under *Ercegovich*'s fourth prong.

In the case of Ms. Lagos's selection for termination by Bank Two, the relevant respects were her performance evaluations and years of seniority. Ms. Lagos's seniority was identical to that of Mr. North and Mr. South. The identity of her supervisor would also be relevant, however, because the supervisor completed the performance evaluations. She was supervised and evaluated by a different vice president, however. Because, in Ms. Lagos's own assessment of events, the determination of which managers to retain turned exclusively on a combination of seniority and performance evaluation scores, those scores are relevant to the comparison between employees required by *Ercegovich*. Ms. Lagos will not be able to establish the requisite degree of similarity because a different vice president evaluated her performance. She cannot show, therefore, that she was similarly situated in every relevant respect to Mr. North and Mr. South.

Ms. Lagos acknowledges that Mr. North and Mr. South likely received superior performance evaluations to hers. In essence, she concedes that she was not similarly situated in that respect, which is quite relevant because performance evaluations factored directly into the formula used to determine who would retain employment.

29. Explanation.

30. This rule summary is helpful because the rule explanation is somewhat complex and includes multiple sources.

31. Application (this application includes all of the aspects of the rule that were part of the explanation and a supporting analogy).

Ms. Lagos is like the plaintiff in *Duncan*, who could not establish that her employer discriminatorily applied the same rule differently to two different employees because she could not demonstrate that the same supervisor had interpreted and applied the rule to each of them. 2005 WL 1353758, *3. Ms. Lagos has not suggested that the Bank Two vice presidents in question acted in concert to ensure that she received poorer performance evaluations than her male colleagues. Accordingly, like the plaintiff in *Duncan*, Ms. Lagos will be stifled in her effort to establish that the termination of her employment resulted from discrimination in her performance evaluations.

32. Because she cannot demonstrate that Bank Two treated her less favorably in the restructuring than male employees who were similarly situated in all relevant respects, Ms. Lagos will not be able to prove a claim of discrimination under Title VII on the basis of the termination decision itself. That decision was based upon seniority and performance evaluation scores. Ms. Lagos has not suggested that Bank Two chose those metrics or applied them in a discriminatory fashion. Accordingly, her claim based upon the reduction in force will fail.

<u>Conclusion</u>

Ms. Lagos is not likely to be able to establish that Bank Two discriminated against her in violation of Title VII when it terminated her employment because she does not have direct evidence of discriminatory animus and she cannot identify a male employee who was similarly situated in all relevant respects and whom Bank Two treated more favorably in the reduction in force.

32. Connection-conclusion.

Memorandum

To: Partner
From: Associate
Date: June 22, 2021
Re: Rufus McNeil's wrongful termination claim against Sports-R-Us Publications

Question Presented

Can a former employee prove a claim for wrongful discharge in violation of West Montana public policy when he alleges that his employer terminated his employment because he reported his employer's failure to enforce a COVID-19 workplace mask requirement but the person who decided to terminate him did not know about the report? 1. 2. 3.

Brief Answer

No. The former employee will not prove the clarity element of a wrongful termination claim because he has not identified a West Montana public policy requiring employers to enforce workplace COVID-19 mask requirements. He will not prove the causation element of the claim because he cannot prove that the person who decided to terminate his employment was motivated by his report. Because he cannot prove the clarity and causation elements, he will also fail to prove the jeopardy and overriding justification elements. 4. 5. 6.

Relevant Statutes 7.

The West Montana Chemical Protection Act, W.M.C. § 442(c) (West 2021), provides, in relevant part, that "[n]o employer shall discharge or in any manner discipline any employee because such employee has filed any complaint or instituted or caused to be instituted any proceeding under or related to this chapter. . . ."

At § 454(a)(1), the Act requires that an employer "furnish to each of his employees a place of employment which is free from chemical hazards that are likely to cause death or serious physical harm to employees[.]"

The Act defines "chemical hazards," in § 440(e), to exclude "biological agents and infectious diseases."

1. This clause, like the "does" clause in the first sample, identifies the legal status necessary to prove the claim.

2. Like the "under" clause in the first sample's question presented, this clause identifies the relevant law.

3. Here, the writer identifies the legally significant facts.

4. The brief answer begins with the direct answer to the question presented. In this sample, the writer expresses great confidence in the answer by omitting any hedging words ("probably," "likely," "may").

5. Here, and in the next two sentences, the writer identifies relevant information about the relevant law that was not included in the question presented.

6. The writer connects the legally significant facts from the question presented to the legal status.

7. The writer has chosen to include relevant statutes before beginning the analysis to avoid extensive quoting from the statutes in the analysis.

Facts

8. Our client, Sports-R-Us Publications, Inc., has been named a defendant in a lawsuit filed by its former employee Rufus McNeil. Sports-R-Us hired McNeil as an at-will employee at its Morningside, West Montana, location in May of 2014. During the course of his employment, all of McNeil's employee evaluations were "mostly average," according to Sports-R-Us. Sport-R-Us discharged McNeil during the business downturn caused by the COVID-19 pandemic because his job performance was unsatisfactory as compared to that of other Sports-R-Us employees. The COVID-19 pandemic had reduced Sport-R-Us's need for reporters to cover sporting events, and Sports-R-Us's regional manager, Cody Calvin, chose McNeil for discharge. McNeil claims, however, that Sports-R-Us discharged him because of his complaints about lax enforcement of the facial mask policy at Sports-R-Us's workplace in Morningside.

9. To help prevent the spread of the COVID-19 virus, Sports-R-Us began requiring its employees to wear masks covering their mouths and noses while on company premises on March 23, 2020. Mr. McNeil alleges over several paragraphs in his complaint that another employee, Harper Slack, began at that time to stand outside near the main entrance of the Morningside location without a mask. Because this main entrance was used by "most or all employees," McNeil alleges that most employees passed within a few feet of Ms. Slack, placing them "and the general public at risk of contracting the COVID-19 virus." Mr. McNeil claims that, by allowing Ms. Slack's behavior, Sports-R-Us violated § 454(a)(1) of the West Montana Chemical Protection Act.

Mr. McNeil alleges that he told his supervisor, Marla Guy, "[o]n at least three occasions" that permitting Ms. Slack's behavior violated the West Montana Chemical Protection Act. McNeil then made a report to the West Montana Health and Safety Administration ("WMHSA") on April 24, 2020, regarding Sports-R-Us's alleged "failure to prevent Harper Slack from standing just outside its main entrance without wearing a mask."

McNeil does not allege that Cody Calvin knew of his complaints either to WMHSA or to Ms. Guy before terminating his at-will employment. McNeil acknowledges in his complaint that, when he asked Calvin "whether the termination of his employment related to his WMHSA complaint," Calvin told him that his job performance had been unsatisfactory and that Calvin had been unaware of the WMHSA report when he chose McNeil for discharge. Still, McNeil alleges that Calvin discharged him "without a sound business reason" and because of his complaints about alleged "violations of the law in Defendant's workplace."

Rufus McNeil claims that Sports-R-Us wrongfully terminated his employment in violation of West Montana public policy. He cites W.M.C. § 442(c) as the source of the public policy against "terminating employees for complaining about dangerous conditions, including air contaminants, in and around a workplace."

8. The fact statement begins with context.

9. Some of these facts are not directly relevant to the claim. The writer includes them to provide context for the facts that are legally significant.

Analysis

Rufus McNeil will not succeed on his claim for wrongful termination in violation of West 10.
Montana law because he has not alleged facts that would prove two of the required elements
of his claim. In West Montana, either party may terminate at-will employment at any time 11.
for any reason. *Barnes v. Jacoby*, 152 N.W.3d 871, 874 (W. Mont. 2020) (citation omitted).
West Montana recognizes an exception to the at-will employment doctrine and a tort claim
for wrongful termination in violation of public policy. *Id.* (citing *Beecher v. Colorado Valley
Snowmobiles, Inc.*, 35 N.W.3d 439, 446 (W. Mont. 2015)). To bring a successful claim for 12.
wrongful termination in violation of West Montana public policy, a plaintiff must prove the
following four elements:

> (1) a clear public policy existed and was manifested either in a state or federal constitution, statute or administrative regulation or in the common law ("the clarity element"), (2) dismissing employees under circumstances like those involved in the plaintiff's dismissal would jeopardize the public policy ("the jeopardy element"), (3) the plaintiff's dismissal was motivated by conduct related to the public policy ("the causation element"), and (4) the employer lacked an overriding legitimate business justification for the dismissal ("the overriding-justification element").

Id. (citation omitted). The clarity and jeopardy elements are questions of law, and the 13.
causation and overriding-justification elements are questions of fact. *Id.*

Mr. McNeil will not be able to prove the clarity element of his claim because his 14.
WMHSA complaint did not relate to a *clear* public policy, as the West Montana Supreme Court has defined that phrase. He will also fail to prove the causation element of his claim because he acknowledges that Cody Calvin did not know about his WMHSA complaint when he terminated McNeil's employment. Because he cannot prove clarity or jeopardy, McNeil will not be able to prove jeopardy or the lack of an overriding business justification, and his claim will fail.

1. The Clarity Element

Mr. McNeil will not be able to prove the clarity element of his claim because he has not 15.
identified an *actual* public policy embodied in a federal or state statute or regulation or West 16.
Montana common law. The public policy that McNeil has identified, enforcement of employee 17.
mask-wearing requirements against COVID-19, is not embodied in the only source he has 18.
identified, W.M.C. § 442(c) and is, therefore, not a *clear* public policy.

10. The umbrella section begins here.

11. These two sentences are the legal backstory.

12. Here, the writer identifies the overall rule that governs the relevant claim.

13. This sentence informs the reader of a point of law that relates to all elements of the claim. The umbrella section is usually the best location for information of that type.

14. The roadmap begins here. It tells the reader what is coming in the separate subsections of the analysis to follow.

15. The conclusion-thesis begins here. We call it the conclusion-thesis because it includes the thesis for the analysis that follows.

16. Here, the writer identifies a phrase-that-pays for this subsection of the analysis. The word "actual" is italicized to emphasize its relevance in the governing rule.

17. In this sentence, the writer tells how the phrase-that-pays interacts with the legally significant facts.

18. These are the legally significant facts.

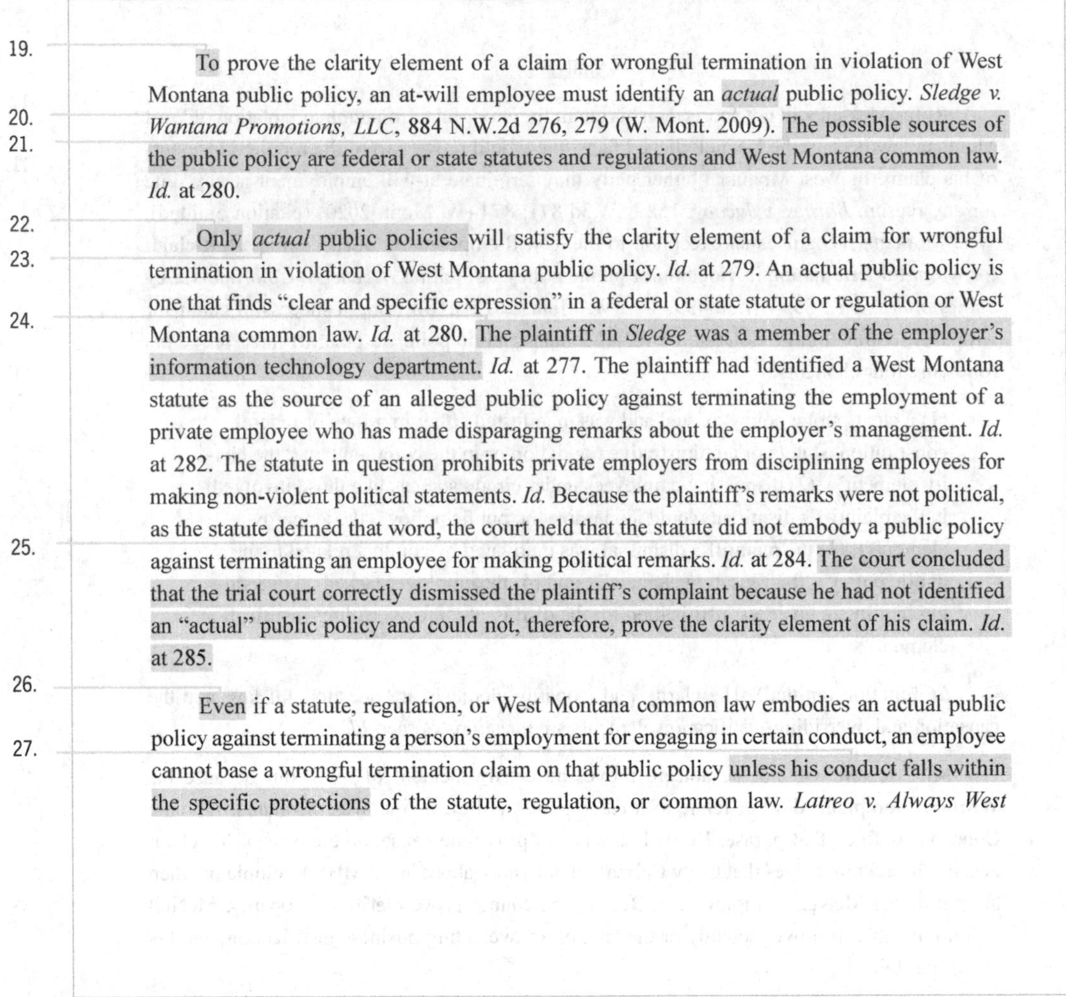

19. To prove the clarity element of a claim for wrongful termination in violation of West Montana public policy, an at-will employee must identify an *actual* public policy. *Sledge v.*
20. 21. *Wantana Promotions, LLC*, 884 N.W.2d 276, 279 (W. Mont. 2009). The possible sources of the public policy are federal or state statutes and regulations and West Montana common law. *Id.* at 280.

22. Only *actual* public policies will satisfy the clarity element of a claim for wrongful
23. termination in violation of West Montana public policy. *Id.* at 279. An actual public policy is one that finds "clear and specific expression" in a federal or state statute or regulation or West
24. Montana common law. *Id.* at 280. The plaintiff in *Sledge* was a member of the employer's information technology department. *Id.* at 277. The plaintiff had identified a West Montana statute as the source of an alleged public policy against terminating the employment of a private employee who has made disparaging remarks about the employer's management. *Id.* at 282. The statute in question prohibits private employers from disciplining employees for making non-violent political statements. *Id.* Because the plaintiff's remarks were not political, as the statute defined that word, the court held that the statute did not embody a public policy
25. against terminating an employee for making political remarks. *Id.* at 284. The court concluded that the trial court correctly dismissed the plaintiff's complaint because he had not identified an "actual" public policy and could not, therefore, prove the clarity element of his claim. *Id.* at 285.

26. Even if a statute, regulation, or West Montana common law embodies an actual public
27. policy against terminating a person's employment for engaging in certain conduct, an employee cannot base a wrongful termination claim on that public policy unless his conduct falls within the specific protections of the statute, regulation, or common law. *Latreo v. Always West*

19. This paragraph identifies the governing rule. The writer has identified two components of the rule.

The following rule explanation elaborates on each component.

20. Here, the writer identifies the actual public policy component of the rule.

21. This sentence identifies a second component of the rule. In the following rule explanation, the writer has not elaborated on this component of the rule but has interjected a component that is not part of this rule statement. A reader who expects the component identified in this sentence to be a part of the analysis will be troubled by its absence.

22. The rule explanation begins here. In this paragraph, the writer explains the *actual public policy* component of the rule. Notice that the first sentence of this paragraph of rule explanation is focused on the rule, not on the case from which it derives. This rule focus alerts the reader to the fact that the paragraph is about the rule and not a case.

23. The thesis sentence identifies the relevant phrase-that-pays.

24. This sentence includes information about the authority case that is not relevant to the issue the court considered and resolved. It will distract the reader, as the case description is less focused on relevant case information than it could be.

25. In this last sentence of the paragraph, the writer tells the reader explicitly how the phrase-that-pays derives from the case the writer has described.

26. This thesis sentence focuses on the component of the rule that is the subject of the paragraph, rather than on a case.

27. Here, the writer identifies the phrase-that-pays for the component of the rule that is the subject of this paragraph of rule explanation. You may notice that this phrase-that-pays is not included in the rule statement above. Its absence may cause surprise to some readers when they reach this portion of the rule explanation. The relationship between this phrase-that-pays and the rule may not be clear.

Montana, Inc., 14 N.W.3d 522, 529 (W. Mont. 2014). Plaintiff Latreo sued his employer for 28.
terminating his employment after he had protested its chemical disposal in the West Montana 29.
River. *Id.* at 524. Latreo identified a regulation and a statute as the sources of the public policy
on which he based his claim. *Id.* at 525. The regulation prohibited the disposal of specifically
listed chemicals in the waterways of West Montana; the statute prevented employers from
disciplining employees who complained about or protested violations of the regulation. *Id.*
The problem for Mr. Latreo was that the chemical in question was not listed in the regulation.
Id. Applying the rule from *Sledge*, the court held that the *regulation* did not embody the public 30.
policy that Latreo had identified. *Id.* at 528. Then, the court took one more step and held that
the *statute* did not embody a public policy against terminating the employment of a person
who protested the disposal of chemicals that were not listed in the regulation. *Id.* at 528. So, the
court concluded that the public policy on which Mr. Latreo based his claim was not an *actual* 31.
public policy embodied in either the regulation or the statute. *Id.* at 529.

To prove the clarity element of a wrongful termination in violation of West Montana
public policy claim, then, a plaintiff must identify an *actual* public policy that is embodied in 32.
a federal or state statute or regulation or West Montana common law. A plaintiff may identify
a public policy preventing employers from disciplining employees for complaining about
or protesting certain employer conduct, as defined by statute, regulation, or common law;
however, if the employer conduct of which the plaintiff complained did not fall within the
specific protection of the policy, the employee has not identified an *actual* public policy.

Mr. McNeil has not identified an actual public policy. The statute on which he relies 33.
for the mask enforcement policy, W.M.C. § 454(a)(1), does not require employers to enforce 34.
a mask policy to prevent the spread of COVID-19. In fact, the definitional section of the
WMHSA explicitly excludes "biological agents and infectious diseases" from the definition
of "chemical hazard." In other words, the WMHSA does not govern biological agents or
infectious diseases in the workplace. If an actual policy requiring West Montana employers to
enforce COVID-19 mask requirements exists, Mr. McNeil has not identified the source for it. 35.

28. Note that some readers may find it easier to absorb case descriptions if the parties in the authority cases are labeled by legally significant categories (e.g., employer and employee) rather than by names.

29. In this sentence of the case description, the writer identifies the relevant issue. The relevant facts are in the next three sentences.

30. These two sentences include the relevant reasoning.

31. Here, the writer identifies the relevant disposition. You may notice that the writer has not connected the phrase-that-pays, *conduct falling within the specific protection*, to the case description. The case description would be more effective if the writer had done so.

32. In this paragraph, the writer summarizes the rule. The word "then" signals to the reader that this is a rule summary. The two sentences of the summary remind the reader of the two relevant phrases-that-pay.

33. In this first paragraph of application, the writer applies the first phrase-that-pays. The writer has identified the phrase-that-pays, *actual public policy*, in the first sentence of the paragraph, so the reader will not have to guess which component of the rule is the subject of the paragraph.

34. The relevant issue in this subsection of the analysis is a question of law, as the writer has indicated in the umbrella section. The language of the statutes is, therefore, the legally significant fact to which the writer applies the rule in this paragraph and the next. Chapter 11 discusses rule application in the context of a question of law in greater depth.

35. The final sentence of this application paragraph explicitly connects the phrase-that-pays to the writer's conclusion.

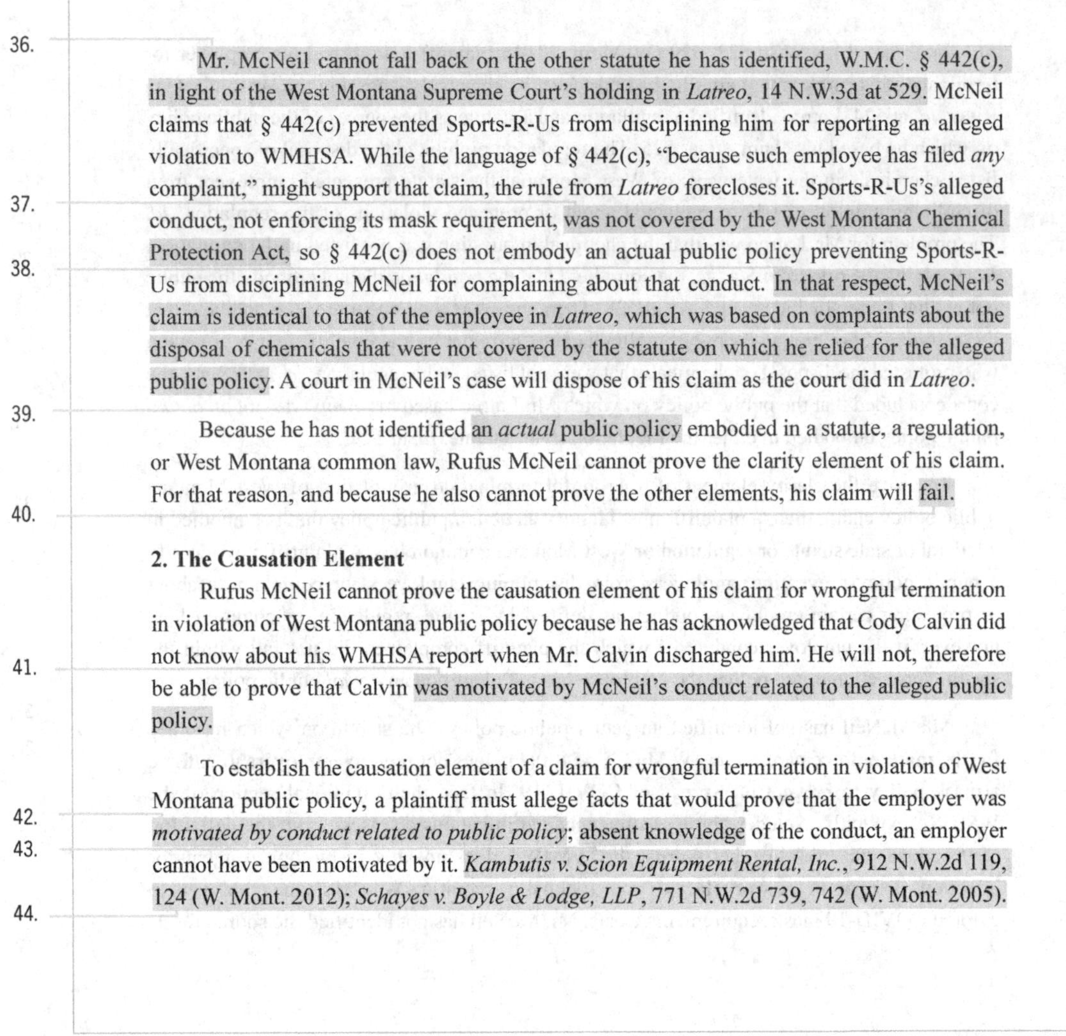

36. Mr. McNeil cannot fall back on the other statute he has identified, W.M.C. § 442(c), in light of the West Montana Supreme Court's holding in *Latreo*, 14 N.W.3d at 529. McNeil claims that § 442(c) prevented Sports-R-Us from disciplining him for reporting an alleged violation to WMHSA. While the language of § 442(c), "because such employee has filed *any* complaint," might support that claim, the rule from *Latreo* forecloses it. Sports-R-Us's alleged
37. conduct, not enforcing its mask requirement, was not covered by the West Montana Chemical Protection Act, so § 442(c) does not embody an actual public policy preventing Sports-R-
38. Us from disciplining McNeil for complaining about that conduct. In that respect, McNeil's claim is identical to that of the employee in *Latreo*, which was based on complaints about the disposal of chemicals that were not covered by the statute on which he relied for the alleged public policy. A court in McNeil's case will dispose of his claim as the court did in *Latreo*.

39. Because he has not identified an *actual* public policy embodied in a statute, a regulation, or West Montana common law, Rufus McNeil cannot prove the clarity element of his claim. For that reason, and because he also cannot prove the other elements, his claim will fail.
40.

2. The Causation Element

Rufus McNeil cannot prove the causation element of his claim for wrongful termination in violation of West Montana public policy because he has acknowledged that Cody Calvin did not know about his WMHSA report when Mr. Calvin discharged him. He will not, therefore
41. be able to prove that Calvin was motivated by McNeil's conduct related to the alleged public policy.

To establish the causation element of a claim for wrongful termination in violation of West Montana public policy, a plaintiff must allege facts that would prove that the employer was
42. 43. *motivated by conduct related to public policy*; absent knowledge of the conduct, an employer cannot have been motivated by it. *Kambutis v. Scion Equipment Rental, Inc.*, 912 N.W.2d 119, 124 (W. Mont. 2012); *Schayes v. Boyle & Lodge, LLP*, 771 N.W.2d 739, 742 (W. Mont. 2005).
44.

36. This sentence, which begins the application of the second component of the rule, would be more helpful to the reader if the writer had included the relevant phrase that pays, *conduct falling within the specific protection.*

37. Here again, the application would be more effective if the writer had used the phrase-that-pays instead of this phrase with similar meaning. The writer could have replaced these words with "did not fall within the specific protection of the West Montana Chemical Protection Act."

38. The writer has precisely identified the aspects of the case that are the reason for the analogy and, in the next sentence, tells the reader how that analogy supports the writer's conclusion.

39. In this conclusion, the writer reminds the reader that this phrase-that-pays determines the outcome.

40. In this second sentence of the connection-conclusion, the writer connects the conclusion of this subsection to the broader analysis.

41. Here, the writer identifies the phrase-that-pays for this subsection, *motivated by conduct related to the public policy.*

42. The writer has italicized the phrase-that-pays to give it emphasis.

43. In the second half of the rule statement, the writer identifies a secondary phrase-that-pays.

44. The rule expressed in the two halves of the sentence derives from two authority cases. It is a synthesized rule. The rule explanation will elaborate on both components, ideally using the phrases-that-pay identified in this statement of the rule.

To prove causation, a wrongful termination plaintiff must prove that the employer was 45.
motivated by a negative reaction to the employee's conduct; motivation requires *knowledge* of the conduct. *Id.* For example, where an employee was discharged after having filed a report with OSHA, the West Montana Supreme Court explained that the plaintiff had to demonstrate that her employer knew about her OSHA report before deciding to terminate her and that knowledge of the report motivated the employer's actions. *Id.* at 742-43. The court affirmed a lower court's decision to grant summary judgment to the employer because, although the employer was aware that a report had been made to OSHA, the evidence did not establish that 46.
the employer knew that the plaintiff had made the report. *Id.* at 741-42.

Having acknowledged in his complaint that Cody Calvin did not know about McNeil's 47.
WMHSA report when he decided to discharge him, McNeil will not be able to prove the causation element of his claim. McNeil alleges that Marla Guy knew that he had complained to WMHSA, but he also unequivocally alleges that Cody Calvin made the decision to terminate his employment. He has not alleged that Guy was involved in any fashion in the decision, so any animus on her part could not have affected Calvin, even indirectly. Without knowledge of the report, Calvin could not have been motivated by it.

Accordingly, McNeil will not be able to prove the causation element of his claim, just as 48.
he will not be able to prove the clarity element.

3. The Jeopardy and Overriding Justification Elements 49.

Rufus McNeil cannot prove the jeopardy and overriding justification elements of his claim because those elements are dependent on the success of the clarity and causation elements. Therefore, he will not be able to prove any of the elements of his claim for wrongful termination in violation of West Montana public policy.

To prove the jeopardy element of a wrongful termination claim, a plaintiff must identify 50.
a clear public policy that was jeopardized by the plaintiff's termination. *Barnes*, 152 N.W.3d at 874. To prove the lack of an overriding justification, the plaintiff must first prove that conduct related to the public policy caused the termination of employment.

45. The rule explanation begins here. The writer has combined the explanation of the two components of the rule in one paragraph and has informed the reader of that choice by including both phrases-that-pay in the first sentence. The writer has italicized both phrases-that-pay.

46. This case description is short on relevant details. Some readers may find that it does not say enough about the authority case to convince them that it supports the writer's version of the rule. Others may appreciate the omission of extraneous details.

47. The writer applies both components of the rule in this single application paragraph but has neglected to include the motivated phrase-that-pays in the first sentence. Readers will not be certain until the final sentence of the paragraph that the writer has applied the entire rule in this one paragraph.

48. This sentence is the writer's connection-conclusion.

49. In this subsection, the writer includes a very concise CRAC analysis of the remaining two elements.

50. These two sentences include the writer's rule for this CRAC analysis. This version of the rule may be complete, but the writer has not included a citation to authority for the second sentence. A reader will not be convinced that the law supports the sentence.

51. As is set out above, Mr. McNeil cannot identify a clear West Montana public policy requiring COVID-19 mask enforcement in the workplace; therefore, he cannot prove that his termination jeopardized that policy. Moreover, because McNeil cannot prove that his conduct related to a clear public policy caused his termination, he cannot prove that Sports-R-Us lacked an overriding justification for the termination.

Simply put, Mr. McNeil cannot prove the jeopardy and overriding justification elements of his claim *because* he cannot prove the clarity and causation elements.

Causation

52. For that reason, and those above, his claim will fail on every element.

51. In this CRAC analysis, the writer has omitted a rule explanation, likely on the belief that the rule is sufficiently clear and obviously governs the outcome of the issues presented by the two remaining elements. Had the writer included a citation to support the second sentence of the rule, the amount of rule information would have satisfied most readers.

52. This conclusion to the overall analysis is just about as concise as it could be. Some readers may find it to be terse; others will appreciate its brevity.

Recall and Review

1. The umbrella paragraph(s) are made up of two elements: the ________ and the ___________.
2. Readers understand new information better if the new information is preceded by information that provides ________________.
3. The legal backstory should include contextual information that moves the reader from what is _________ to what is ________________.
4. True or False: Roadmaps should not include numbers because numbers are distracting.
5. True or False: Anytime a document divides a section into subsections, the writer should include an umbrella between the section heading and the first subsection heading.

CHAPTER 15

CITING, QUOTING, PARAPHRASING, AND WHEN NOT TO WORRY ABOUT PLAGIARIZING

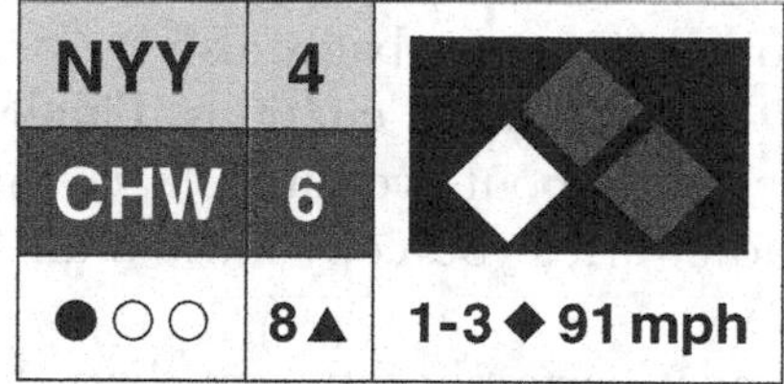

Figure 15.1

Can you identify the error in the scoreboard on the left? If you are a baseball fan, the answer is almost certainly yes. The scoreboard on the left uses "1-3" for what baseball players call "the count," i.e., the count of how many balls and strikes have been called on the current batter. In baseball scoring, balls are always listed before strikes. A player is out if he reaches three strikes, so a count of 1-3 is impossible.

If you're not a baseball fan, you may be thinking, "Who cares? Can't people figure it out by watching the game or listening to the announcers? Why do they always have to be in that order?"

Can you identify the error(s) in this (fictional) legal citation?

> *McGuffin v. Gordon*, (9th Cir.) 202 P.2d 234, 235 (2021).

If you are an experienced legal reader, you will note that the court indicator (9th Cir.) is in the wrong place; it should be in the same parenthetical with the date. Further, the reporter (Pacific, Second Series) publishes only state court decisions, while the Ninth Circuit is a federal court. Therefore, a case from the Ninth Circuit could never be published in the Pacific Reporter.

Here is a correct citation, indicating that the Supreme Court of Nevada issued the decision: *McGuffin v. Gordon*, 202 P.2d 234, 235 (Nev. 2021).

If you are an inexperienced legal reader, we hope you are not saying, "Who cares? Can't they figure it out by reading the opinion?" You recognize that the reader is relying somewhat on the information in the citation and doesn't want to have to read the opinion to find out what court decided it.

All rights and wrongs of both baseball scoring and legal citation boil down to two things: conventions and expectations. Baseball players and legal readers need to have confidence that scores and cites will meet their expectations by following the conventions of communication. Both scoreboards and legal citations convey a lot of information in a small amount of space. They do this by using accepted abbreviations and by organizing the information in a certain way.

If you have done any kind of academic writing (and we're guessing you have, even if it was only a term paper in high school), you have some concept of citations (which you may have thought of as "references"). You may have included citations internally, perhaps in parentheses; you may have used footnotes or endnotes; or you may have attached a bibliography to your document. You probably also learned some rules about when and how to include those citations. Finally, you have probably internalized some rules about avoiding plagiarism charges, about when you have to quote (after you copy more than X words) and when you can paraphrase.

The rules in legal writing are almost certainly different than the rules you've learned in the past. In this chapter, we're going to address some of the common questions that legal readers and legal writers face when they use authorities:

1. How do I read a citation? Can't I just bleep over it?
2. How much should I quote and how much should I paraphrase?
3. When and how do I incorporate citations into my writing?

While your analysis is (we hope) useful to legal readers, it is no better than the authority on which it is based. For that reason, we cannot overstate the important role that effective citation plays in the presentation of a legal analysis. A legal writer's job is not finished until the writer has determined that the document uses quotations and paraphrases effectively and has inserted every necessary citation, in the proper place and in the correct form.

In this chapter, we will first address how to "read" the citations that you are bombarded with in your casebooks and your research. Next we will explain how to use quotations and citations, particularly of language from court opinions. Finally, we will explain when and how to incorporate effective citations into your writing. The rules are fussy, we know. But taking care with quotations and citations is worthwhile: your readers will have more confidence in your legal analysis if you fulfill their expectations about how to use and cite to legal authorities.

A. HACKS FOR READING CASE CITATIONS

The baseball scoreboard pictured above tells readers a lot more than just the count of balls and strikes. The scoreboard reveals what inning it is, which team's ballpark is hosting the game (the "home team"), and which team is up to bat. In the same way, a case citation reveals immediately whether the case is from a federal or state court, when it was decided, and which court decided it. All of these elements are vital for a reader who wants to assess whether the cited material could be a mandatory authority for the current issue. Figure 15.2 shows a case citation with its parts labeled.

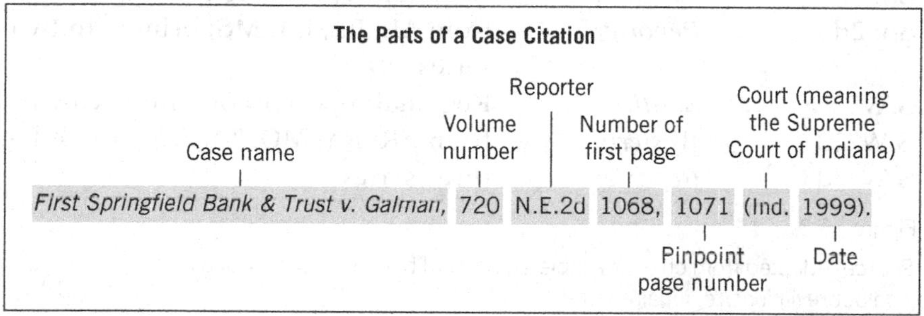

Figure 15.2

We know that it's tempting to skip case citations. The numbers and abbreviations look incomprehensible. Trust us, though: you need to learn how to skim them, because you need some of that information to better understand what you are reading. The case name, obviously, gives readers and writers a way to refer to and remember the case. The reporter abbreviation (N.E.2d) shows the book that "reported" the opinion, and it's preceded by the volume number of the reporter and followed by the numbers of the page on which the case begins and the page to which the writer is citing ("pinpoint"). You will need the pinpoint page if you are looking up the case, but otherwise you can bleep over those numbers.

Further, if the first-listed party is a state or commonwealth, as in *Nevada v. Beazley*, there is a strong chance that the case is a criminal case.

If the opinion is "published" only online and not in a book, the abbreviations used will reveal that fact to the reader. Citation guides contain rules for citing to materials found in the major databases or other online sources.

The reporter abbreviation, however, is meaningful right away. Experienced legal readers know that so-called "regional reporters" publish the precedential opinions of state trial and appellate courts. The regional reporters and their abbreviations are shown in Figure 15.3.

Abbreviation	Title	Description/Coverage
A. A.2d A.3d	*Atlantic Reporter*	Regional reporter containing cases from CT, DE, D.C., ME, MD, NH, NJ, PA, RI, VT; printed in three series
N.E. N.E. 2d	*North Eastern Reporter*	Regional reporter containing cases from IL, IN, MA, NY, OH; printed in two series
N.W. N.W. 2d	*North Western Reporter*	Regional reporter containing cases from IA, MI, MN, NE, ND, SD, WI; printed in two series
P. P.2d P.3d	*Pacific Reporter*	Regional reporter containing cases from AK, AZ, CA, CO, HI, ID, KS, MT, NV, NM, OK, OR, UT, WA, WY; printed in three series
S.E. S.E. 2d	*South Eastern Reporter*	Regional reporter containing cases from GA, NC, SC, VA, WV; printed in two series
So. So. 2d	*Southern Reporter*	Regional reporter containing cases from AL, FL, LA, MS; printed in two series
S.W. S.W. 2d S.W. 3d	*South Western Reporter*	Regional reporter containing cases from AR, KY, MO, TN, TX; printed in three series

Figure 15.3

Source: Adapted from chart available at: https://libguides.law.gonzaga.edu/legalabbreviations/regionalreporters.

If a case is a precedential decision from a Federal Court, it will likely appear in one of three reporters, as indicated in Figure 15.4.

Note that the decisions of some specialty courts, like bankruptcy courts and tax courts, appear in specialty reporters

Abbreviation	Title	Description/Coverage
F. Supp. F. Supp. 2d F. Supp. 3d	*Federal Supplement*	National reporter containing precedential opinions from all of the United States District Courts, printed in three series
F. F.2d F.3d	*Federal Reporter*	National reporter containing precedential opinions from all of the United States Courts of Appeal, printed in three series
U.S.	*United States Reports*	Reporter containing all opinions of the United States Supreme Court.

Figure 15.4

Source: Adapted from chart available at https://libguides.law.gonzaga.edu/legalabbreviations/federalreporters

Thus, if you look at a citation and see that it has regional geographical abbreviations like the ones in Figure 15.3, you can be confident that the writer is citing to a state court opinion. If it is in F. Supp. 2d or F.3d, you know it is a Federal opinion. The next important piece of information comes from the parenthetical. The parenthetical tells you the year of the decision; this information is obviously meaningful, because recent decisions may have more weight than older decisions. Second, for all cases but United States Supreme Court decisions, the parenthetical indicates the court that decided the case.

Don't try to predict the coverage by the names of the reporters, since many of them were named before all 50 states had joined the union. E.g., Illinois is in the *North Eastern Reporter*, and Wisconsin is in the *North Western Reporter*. The geography is about as useful as the geography of baseball divisions.

The *United States Reports* publish only decisions of the United States Supreme Court. Thus, if you see that a case citation includes that abbreviation, you already know it is a decision of the United States Supreme Court.

Some fussy rules govern how to abbreviate the deciding court in a parenthetical, but we'll give you a couple of hacks for reading citations. First, if it's a regional reporter, and the only abbreviation is an abbreviation for a state name (e.g., Conn. or Mont.), then the decision is the decision of the highest court in the state. As for federal decisions, the biggest hack is the name of the reporter: the F. Supp. series publishes only trial court opinions (i.e., those of the United States District Court). The F. series (F., F.2d, and F.3d) publishes only appellate court decisions (i.e., from the federal circuit courts). The abbreviation in the parenthetical will give you the state that the district court appears in (and the division, if needed) or the number of the circuit.

This information can help you as you research because it can allow you to quickly assess which of the cited opinions might serve as mandatory authority for your issue. Let's presume you are reading the opinion of an intermediate appellate court and it cites two cases as authority for the rule it has articulated:

> An insurance company's obligation to represent its insured depends on the allegations of the underlying complaint and the provisions of the insurance policy. *Jenkins Insurance Co. v. Chester–West Co.*, 611 N.E.2d 1083, 1095 (Ill. App. Ct. 1999); *McGuffin v. Consolidated Insurers, Inc.*, 555 N.E.2d 143, 149 (Ill. 1995).

Simply by looking at the parentheticals, you can tell that *McGuffin* came from the Illinois Supreme Court (the highest court in Illinois), while *Jenkins* is from a lower court. Thus, you know to click on *McGuffin* to seek mandatory authority from the highest court for your issue.

Likewise, reading cites can help you to assess your sources when researching. Many broad searches will bring back results from courts of last resort, intermediate appellate courts, and trial courts. If you are searching for Sixth Circuit opinions, for example, you may also retrieve opinions from federal trial courts in Ohio, Tennessee, Kentucky, and Michigan. Noting the F. Supp. in the citation is one way to be alerted to that problem.

We know it's never fun to read citations. By understanding how they work, however, you can skim them quickly and effectively to pick up vital information.

B. USING QUOTATIONS EFFECTIVELY WHILE AVOIDING PLAGIARISM CONCERNS

As you do your research, you're no doubt looking for support for the assertions you want to make in your memo. In your earlier research projects, you may have provided that support by inserting long quotations from your source material. That method is rarely effective in legal writing. It's true that quotations can very effectively provide support to a writer's assertions. But in legal writing, you should usually paraphrase rather than quote language from cases, and you can often paraphrase language from statutes. Quotation marks draw readers' attention, and you want to save that special attention for important statements. Generally, follow these three guidelines for quoting in legal writing:

1. Use direct quotations when you are stating rules or other language at issue; when you are justifying a conclusion you have drawn about the meaning of a case, statute, or other authority; or when the language is both unique and relevant.
2. On most other occasions, paraphrase the relevant language. You may combine paraphrases and quotes to highlight the most significant language.
3. Whether you are quoting or paraphrasing, be sure to provide appropriate citations.

Writers' problems with quotations, especially from cases, tend to fall into the two categories of "not enough" and "too much." Some writers drop quotations into their writing without giving readers enough information about the case. Without sufficient context, the quotation is meaningless. Other writers give readers too much quoted language, leaving readers to complete the writer's job of sifting through the language and sorting out its meaning. That kind of quoting may also suggest that the writer does not understand the authority well enough to describe or explain it *or* that the writer has not been willing to invest the mental resources necessary to describe or explain the authority in the writer's own clear way. Finally, don't use constant quoting as a way to avoid plagiarism charges; citations to paraphrased statements are usually just as effective.

1. Insufficient Context

Legend has it that Marie Antoinette once said, "Let them eat cake!" Marie sounds like a pretty nice person—unless you know the context of her remark. She sounds a lot less friendly once you learn that she supposedly said it while looking down at the peasants in the street who were crying for bread.

Keep Marie in mind when you are tempted to drop a pithy quotation from an obscure case into the middle of your rule explanation section. If your readers don't know what that court was looking at—that is, the issue, the rule, and the facts—when it made that statement, they can't begin to understand the significance of the quotation without looking the case up. And because many readers don't take the time to read all of the cases cited in the documents they read, the quotation may have a negative impact: readers will be annoyed at being given insufficient or misleading information.

Thus, when using a quotation from a case, be sure you have provided readers with the context required to understand its significance. Do not drop a quotation into your analysis like a chocolate chip into batter:

> *Bad Example*
> The Alaska Supreme Court has noted that "durational residency requirements are more susceptible to constitutional infirmity than laws that distinguish residents from nonresidents." *Heller v. State, Dep't of Revenue*, 314 P.3d 69, 78 (Alaska 2013).

This isolated quotation with an unaccompanied citation would not fill readers with confidence about the validity of your "durational residency" analysis. When it comes to "durational residency," for example, it may well make a difference whether a court is analyzing the right to vote, the right to serve as a political candidate, or the right to receive state benefits. Instead of giving only an isolated quotation, include the details that will give context for the quotation:

> *Good Example*
> In analyzing whether the State can impose residence requirements before allowing eligibility for the Alaska Permanent Fund Dividend, the Alaska Supreme Court distinguished between "bona fide residency requirements" that advance state goals and residency requirements that needlessly burden newcomers to a state. *See Heller v. State, Dep't of Revenue*, 314 P.3d 69, 77 (Alaska 2013). Even so, the court admitted that "durational residency requirements are more susceptible to constitutional infirmity than laws that distinguish residents from nonresidents." *Id.* at 78.

If you are not including a textual case description, you can include (short) quotations in parentheticals:

Good Example

In analyzing whether the State can impose residence requirements before allowing eligibility for the Alaska Permanent Fund Dividend, the Alaska Supreme Court distinguished between "bona fide residency requirements" that advance state goals and residency requirements that needlessly burden newcomers to a state. *See Heller v. State, Dep't of Revenue*, 314 P.3d 69, 77, 78 (Alaska 2013) (finding valid a Dividend-related requirement but admitting that "durational residency requirements are more susceptible to constitutional infirmity than laws that distinguish residents from nonresidents").

By making a quotation part of a coherent case description, you increase the odds that the quotation will convince readers that the case stands for the proposition you say it does.

2. Too Much Quoted Language

Some writers are so enamored with the court's language, or so insecure over their understanding of the law, that they hate to paraphrase. Instead, they simply provide paragraph after paragraph of excerpted quotes and let readers determine the significance of the quoted language. "Overquoting" creates two problems. First, the writer is not doing his or her job. The writer is not supposed to provide the raw material to readers and let them sort out what it all means. The writer's job is to research the law, synthesize the available information, and write up the analysis in a way that allows readers to understand the situation with a minimum of effort.

The second problem is related to the first. Readers who are constantly asked to consume and digest lengthy quotations may lose the thread of the analysis. As a practical matter, many readers (including some law students) skip long quotations. Attorneys reading legal memos may skip long quotations because they know that the quotations say nothing directly about the client's case; instead, these quotations discuss other cases, which readers must somehow connect to the current case. Writers who overuse long quotations frequently do so because they have not figured out that connection and thus cannot make the connection within the discussion. They compensate by giving readers background reading; with luck and lots of work, the readers may use these quotations to reach the conclusion that the writer espouses. Because the writer, not the reader, is supposed to do the work, it is usually ineffective to use lengthy quotations.

In the following example, the writer is trying to explain the rule about qualified immunity by citing information from *Snider v. Jefferson*

State Community College. The writer is trying to illustrate that a rule is not a "clearly established constitutional right" (the phrase-that-pays) if no holdings from mandatory courts had addressed that *specific* legal issue *at the time that the behavior occurred*:

Bad Example

In 2003, the Eleventh Circuit found that the rule that same-sex sexual harassment violated equal protection rights was not "clearly established." *Snider v. Jefferson State Cmty. Coll.*, 344 F.3d 1325, 1327-30 (11th Cir. 2003). That court reasoned in part as follows:

> The Supreme Court has only considered the issue of same-sex sexual harassment in the context of a Title VII action against a private employer. *See Oncale*, 523 U.S. 75, 118 S. Ct. 998, 140 L. Ed. 2d 201. In the pertinent 1998 decision, the Supreme Court pointed out that the state and federal courts had taken a "bewildering variety of stances" on same-sex sexual harassment under Title VII. *Id.* at 1002. The Supreme Court concluded that, although male-on-male sexual harassment in the workplace was "assuredly not the principal evil Congress was concerned with when it enacted Title VII . . . statutory prohibitions often go beyond the principal evil to cover reasonably comparable evils. . . ." *Id.* Because *Oncale* involved a Title VII action against a private employer, the issue of whether same-sex harassment also violated the Equal Protection Clause was not considered by the Supreme Court. *Oncale,* 523 U.S. 75, 118 S. Ct. 998, 140 L. Ed. 2d 201.
>
> Although some people may well have reasonably guessed earlier that same-sex sexual harassment was a violation of the Equal Protection Clause, the answer was debatable, not free from cloudiness and truly settled, before our 2003 decision—with its six-page explaining opinion—in *Downing*, 321 F.3d 1017; and officials cannot be "expected to predict the future course of constitutional law." *Wilson v. Layne*, 526 U.S. 603, 119 S. Ct. 1692, 1701, 143 L. Ed. 2d 818 (1999) (quoting *Procunier v. Navarette*, 434 U.S. 555, 98 S. Ct. 855, 860, 55 L. Ed. 2d 24 (1978)). Neither the Supreme Court's decision in *Oncale*, 523 U.S. 75, 118 S. Ct. 998, 140 L. Ed. 2d 201, nor our decision in *Fredette*, 112 F.3d 1503, provided clear notice to government officials that same-sex sexual harassment violated the Equal Protection Clause.

We have preserved the court's original citations, but you should not always imitate a court's use of citations; courts do not always follow the same citation rules that writers must follow (e.g., here, the court uses parallel citations that the rules do not require).

Id. at 1329 (footnote omitted). Therefore, court holdings that address the same issue in a nonconstitutional context do not "clearly establish" the rule, nor do holdings that occur after the behavior had occurred.

Readers who skipped the quotation would not understand the basis for the writer's analysis. Even readers who read the quotation would have to figure out for themselves the significance of the quoted language. If you are tempted to use a lengthy quotation, try one of two tactics to help ensure that your readers will understand your message.

The most obvious solution is to shorten the quotation. Consider what language you absolutely need to quote. Don't bother quoting language that conveys information that you can convey in your own words just as effectively. To determine which language you should quote, underline the language that is (a) significant to your analysis, (b) necessary to establish your point, and (c) will be much less effective if paraphrased. And be ruthless when doing so:

> The Supreme Court has only considered the issue of same-sex sexual harassment in the context of a Title VII action against a private employer. *See Oncale*, 523 U.S. 75, 118 S. Ct. 998, 140 L. Ed. 2d 201. In the pertinent 1998 decision, the Supreme Court pointed out that the state and federal courts had taken a "bewildering variety of stances" on same-sex sexual harassment under Title VII. *Id.* at 1002. The Supreme Court concluded that, although male-on-male sexual harassment in the workplace was "assuredly not the principal evil Congress was concerned with when it enacted Title VII . . . statutory prohibitions often go beyond the principal evil to cover reasonably comparable evils. . . ." *Id.* Because *Oncale* involved a Title VII action against a private employer, the issue of whether same-sex harassment also violated the Equal Protection Clause was not considered by the Supreme Court. *Oncale*, 523 U.S. 75, 118 S. Ct. 998, 140 L.Ed.2d 201.
>
> Although some people may well have reasonably guessed earlier that same-sex sexual harassment was a violation of the Equal Protection Clause, the answer was debatable, not free from cloudiness and truly settled, before our 2003 decision—with its six-page explaining opinion—in *Downing,* 321 F.3d 1017; and <u>officials cannot be "expected to predict the future course of constitutional law</u>." *Wilson v. Layne*, 526 U.S. 603, 119 S. Ct. 1692, 1701, 143 L.Ed.2d 818 (1999) (quoting *Procunier v. Navarette*, 434 U.S. 555, 98 S. Ct. 855, 860, 55 L.Ed.2d 24 (1978)). Neither the Supreme Court's decision in *Oncale*, 523 U.S. 75, 118 S. Ct. 998, 140 L.Ed.2d 201, nor our decision in *Fredette*, 112 F.3d 1503, provided clear notice to government officials that same-sex sexual harassment violated the Equal Protection Clause.

Then, revise, quoting only the underlined material (after removing the underlining), and paraphrasing of the rest of the quotation into your analysis:

Good Example

Courts will consider at least two facts when determining whether a constitutional right may be "clearly established" for purposes of qualified immunity of public officials. *Snider v. Jefferson State Cmty. Coll.*, 344 F.3d 1325, 1327-30 (11th Cir. 2003). First, the ruling must be a holding as to a constitutional right; a holding that same-sex sexual harassment is actionable under Title VII, for example, will not "clearly establish" that it is actionable under the Equal Protection Clause. *Id.* at 1329. Second, the relevant ruling must exist at the time of the alleged behavior: "officials cannot be 'expected to predict the future course of constitutional law.'" *Id.* (citations omitted). Therefore, court holdings that address the same issue in a nonconstitutional context do not "clearly establish" the rule, nor do holdings that occur after the behavior had occurred.

You will notice that the period is inside the quotation marks. In American English, commas and periods belong inside quotation marks. If you have seen them outside the quotation marks, you were probably reading British English.

In the alternative, you may decide that the lengthy quotation is absolutely necessary. If so, promote its effectiveness by articulating the conclusions you want readers to draw from it and putting those conclusions into the body of your analysis. We recommend using what we call an *NPR Introduction* before the quotation.

An NPR Introduction focuses readers' attention on the point the writer is using the quotation to prove or establish. We call it that because NPR newscasters (like all newscasters) constantly introduce little snippets of reporting, interviews, or public events. In much the same way, a long quotation is a little snippet of an opinion or another legal document. Legal writers, unfortunately, often give readers unfocused introductions like "the court noted" or, as in the previous illustration, "the court reasoned." In contrast, newscasters almost never give introductions like "the president said" or "the senator noted." Instead, they give the audience some context and essentially tell it what to listen for when it hears the quoted language.

The illustration below is from a broadcast in which a reporter for the *Marketplace* program heard on NPR set up a quotation by a history professor about the use of executive orders to accomplish a president's objectives when those objectives are not likely to be shared by a majority of Congress. The quotation mentions executive orders by Abraham Lincoln and Harry Truman. The language leading up to the quotation prepares readers by mentioning that presidents have used executive orders "throughout history." This language may pique listeners' interest; in any event, it states directly what is implied in the quotation—that executive orders are not unusual:

Good Example
[NPR:] President Obama vowed to make climate change a priority and on Tuesday he's giving a speech explaining how he's going to do it. But with Congress divided on the issue of climate change, the President is expected to tackle the issue through an executive order.

Presidents can order federal employees and agencies to enact regulations without approval from Congress, says Allan Lichtman, a history professor at American University. He says, throughout history, presidents have used executive orders to make their mark.

[ALLAN LICHTMAN:] The Emancipation Proclamation by Abraham Lincoln was in effect an executive order. Harry Truman used an executive order to desegregate the armed forces.[1]

In the same way, you should prepare your audience for a long quotation by stating the conclusion you want them to draw from it:

Good Example
The *Snider* court observed that although it is now clear that same-sex sexual harassment violates constitutional rights, officials would have had to "guess" about its constitutionality until a 2003 decision settled the issue:

> Although some people may well have reasonably guessed earlier that same-sex sexual harassment was a violation of the Equal Protection Clause, the answer was debatable, not free from cloudiness and truly settled, before our 2003 decision—with its six-page explaining opinion—in *Downing,* 321 F.3d 1017; and officials cannot be "expected to predict the future course of constitutional law." *Wilson v. Layne*, 526 U.S. 603, 119 S. Ct. 1692, 1701, 143 L. Ed. 2d 818 (1999) (quoting *Procunier v. Navarette*, 434 U.S. 555, 98 S. Ct. 855, 860, 55 L. Ed. 2d 24 (1978)). Neither the Supreme Court's decision in *Oncale*, 523 U.S. 75, 118 S. Ct. 998, 140 L. Ed. 2d 201, nor our decision in *Fredette*, 112 F.3d 1503, provided clear notice to government officials that same-sex sexual harassment violated the Equal Protection Clause.

Id. at 1329. Therefore, court holdings that occur after the behavior had occurred cannot have "clearly established" the constitutional right at the time of that earlier-occurring behavior.

---

1. Queena Kim, *Marketplace, Forget Congress: How Obama Can Fight Climate Change Solo*, http://www.marketplace.org/topics/sustainability/forget-congress-how-obama-can-fight-climate-change-solo (June 25, 2013) (includes audio).

Use an NPR Introduction to help readers get the most out of lengthy quotations. The focused introduction will direct readers' attention as they read the quotation and make it easier for them to understand its point. Even if readers do skip the quotation, you still will have articulated your point by placing the quotation where readers can see it and in a way that they can better understand it.

In an objective document, your goal with an NPR Introduction is merely to provide objective preparation for the content of a quotation. In a persuasive document, you might want to use the introduction to advance your analysis in some way.

3. When Not to Worry About Plagiarism

Many students "learn" early in their academic careers that they can use a certain magical number of exact words from a source without quoting and citing. We're not going to give you examples of that; we're just going to tell you that this rule doesn't apply in legal writing. The first point to remember is that you need to cite to material from a source regardless of whether you have quoted or paraphrased the material. The second point is a little more nuanced: you have to develop an understanding of when you need to quote specific language and when you can use that same language without quotation marks (in either event, the material would contain a citation). And of course, in an academic setting, you should never submit the work of others as your own.

Of course, you already know the foundational rules about acknowledging sources: Whenever you use the words or ideas of another writer, acknowledge the original source. Never copy from a court opinion, a law review article, or any other material without citing the source properly. If you use the exact words of a source, you should generally use quotation marks in addition to citing the source. If you put ideas or information from a source into your own words, you should not use quotation marks, but you should always cite the source.

Now we shift to the nuance. In legal writing, it is sometimes acceptable to use exact words *with citation but without quotation marks*, for example, when (1) you are stating a short proposition of law that is not at issue, (2) you are restating a short proposition of law that you have previously quoted, or (3) you are stating case facts that the court described in straightforward language. However, in this situation, it is particularly important that each sentence must have a citation. Note also that any uniquely-phrased thought should be in quotation marks if you are using the unique phrasing.

Section C below will provide examples of when to cite and when not to cite.

Further, while it might, on rare occasions, be acceptable to copy a short sentence word for word without quotation marks and with citation, copying more than one sentence word for word without quotation marks would almost always constitute plagiarism, even with citations. Further, it would rarely be effective or appropriate—stylistically or substantively—to copy even one sentence word for word without quoting it.

The concept of copying ideas can be more problematic. If an idea is well established and widely known, you may discuss your own opinions about the idea without citing to the source of the idea. Of course, if you are writing to a court, even well-established propositions of law should be cited to provide meaningful authority to the court. Further, if you are a law student writing a law review article, your analysis would be better supported if you were to cite to meaningful authority for the foundation of your analysis. As a law student, you are a relative newcomer to the discipline of the law; therefore, it may be hard for you to judge whether you are writing about an idea whose existence must be cited or an idea that is so well established that citation is not necessary. If you are in any doubt, you should cite the idea. And, of course, you must always provide a citation if you use, imitate, or discuss any person's opinions or analysis of the idea.

You should not worry about plagiarism if you are writing a memo and using case authorities to articulate analysis, so long as you are citing to those authorities in your work. You should worry about plagiarism if you are copying professional briefs (or sections of those briefs) and claiming them as your own, or if you are writing a law review article and talking about the ideas of others without citing the sources of those ideas.

Professional briefs are readily available online. Using them in a legal writing course without permission of your professor can result in plagiarism charges. Attorneys sometimes use these materials in practice, but they may face malpractice claims if they do not adapt the materials appropriately for their clients or if they submit false invoices for time they did not spend writing. Because the quality of briefs online varies drastically, we recommend using them sparingly, if at all.

If you are ever unsure about whether or not you are plagiarizing, or if you are having difficulties with an assignment, talk with your professor or faculty advisor before turning in the assignment, or drop a footnote or sidebar expressing your concerns.

C. EFFECTIVE CITATIONS

This section will address when to cite, as well as common concerns about incorporating citations in your documents.

1. When to Cite

The first challenge for many legal writers is figuring out when citations are necessary. Generally, you *must* include a citation at the end of every sentence in which you state a legal proposition, refer to a new authority, or quote or paraphrase information from a court opinion or other source. One of the few occasions on which you may *omit* a citation is when you have already analyzed an authority and are applying that authority's rule to your facts. For example, the statement that "the *McGuffin* rule applies here" does not need a citation in a discussion in which the writer has already introduced and cited *McGuffin*.

Some legal propositions are so basic that they may seem self-evident. If you are asking a court to apply such a legal principle to your client's case, however, you should cite an authority that controls in that court's jurisdiction. The following, for example, would not be appropriate in a memorandum about Illinois tort law:

Bad Example
It is well known that to recover damages for negligence, a plaintiff must establish duty, breach, causation, and injury.

If a legal proposition is well established, it should be easy for the writer to find and cite appropriate authority:

Good Example
To recover damages for negligence, a plaintiff must allege and prove that the defendant owed a duty to the plaintiff, that defendant breached that duty, and that the breach was the proximate cause of the plaintiff's injuries. *First Springfield Bank & Trust v. Galman*, 720 N.E.2d 1068, 1071 (Ill. 1999).

Legal writing is referenced writing, and readers expect frequent citation. You can use short citation forms and effective sentence structures to keep your writing readable, but you must include citations whenever you state a legal proposition, refer to an authority for the first time, or quote or paraphrase material from a source. This means that within the rule explanation section, for example, every sentence may have a citation after it. Many of the citations may appear in shortened forms, but readers will still expect and need citations.

2. Distinguishing Between Authorities and Sources

Although this text often refers to all cases, statutes, and the like as "authorities," the reality is that some are only "sources": they contain information that the court may find interesting and relevant, but the source has no *authority* over the court that could eventually decide the client's case. Too many legal writers also fail to make this distinction, and they annoy and frustrate courts by their imprecise use of citations.

We do not mean to imply that you may cite only to cases written by courts whose decisions are mandatory authority for you. Rather, you should recognize that a citation has at least three different possible meanings, some of which may overlap. The citation may mean simply, "I am not the person who first said or thought of this statement." This kind of citation is used to give appropriate credit to the originator of an idea and to avoid charges of plagiarism. A citation may also mean,

"Here is the source of the law, facts, or policy I just mentioned, so you can find it if you want." This kind of citation—and its accuracy—is very important for judges and their clerks. Finally, a citation can mean, "This statement is *the law*." This citation is very important for legal writers because it is used to justify and support legal analysis.

Unfortunately, the same citation forms are used for all three of these categories, so a legal writer must be sure that the text makes the distinction. If the writer says nothing, readers' instincts are to presume that a cited statement is authoritative, and readers may be startled or frustrated when they look at the citation and realize that the cited case (or other source) is not authoritative.

Writers who quote or paraphrase relevant legal assertions from law review articles and nonmandatory courts must make the necessary distinction by introducing the material with a phrase indicating that an authoritative court did not make the statement. Here are two examples from some analysis of an issue that could be argued before the Illinois Supreme Court; see whether you can identify how they might mislead readers:

> ***Bad Examples in Case Before Illinois Supreme Court***
> When courts must analyze the validity of a dog-sniff search, "the proper standard" to determine its validity is "reasonable suspicion." Robert M. Bloom & Dana L. Walsh, *The Fourth Amendment Fetches Fido: New Approaches to Dog Sniffs*, 48 Wake Forest L. Rev. 1271, 1294 (2013).
>
> When it enacted the Telephone Consumer Protection Act, "the intention of Congress" was not to preempt state laws, but rather "to regulate the telecommunications industry concurrently with the states." *Sussman v. I.C. Sys., Inc.*, 928 F. Supp. 2d 784, 789 (S.D.N.Y. 2013).

In both of these examples, the statements are relevant legal assertions that are followed by a citation and are not preceded by a qualifier. In both situations, readers would instinctively presume that the citation provides authority for the validity of the statement and would be frustrated to see the nonauthoritative citation following the statement. To avoid this problem, simply use qualifying language that reveals that the source is not authoritative. Generally, the best way to do this is to mention or refer to the source; you need not announce to the court that a particular source is not authoritative:

> ***Bad Examples***
> Although not authoritative, commentators have noted that when courts must analyze the validity of a dog-sniff search, "the proper

> standard" to determine its validity is "reasonable suspicion." Robert M. Bloom & Dana L. Walsh, *The Fourth Amendment Fetches Fido: New Approaches to Dog Sniffs*, 48 Wake Forest L. Rev. 1271, 1294 (2013).
>
> A persuasive court has found that when the Telephone Consumer Protection Act was enacted, the "the intention of Congress . . . was not to preempt state laws, but rather to regulate the telecommunications industry concurrently with the states." *Sussman v. I. C. Sys., Inc.*, 928 F. Supp. 2d 784, 789 (S.D.N.Y. 2013).

Your readers—whether your supervisors, coworkers, judges, or clerks—know that commentators and the decisions of nonauthoritative courts are only persuasive authority. The best way to make them aware of the nonauthoritative nature of the statement is to succinctly reveal the source in text. If possible, you should also justify the use of the source, i.e., give readers a reason to find value in the statement:

> ***Good Examples***
> Commentators have argued that when courts must analyze the validity of a dog-sniff search, "the proper standard" to determine its validity is "reasonable suspicion." Robert M. Bloom & Dana L. Walsh, *The Fourth Amendment Fetches Fido: New Approaches to Dog Sniffs*, 48 Wake Forest L. Rev. 1271, 1294 (2013). The commentators compared dog sniffs to a *Terry* stop, concluding that. . . .
>
> A district court in the Second Circuit analyzed a report of the Federal Communications Commission before concluding that "the intention of Congress in enacting the [Telephone Consumer Protection Act] was not to preempt state laws, but rather to regulate the telecommunications industry concurrently with the states, which 'have a long history of regulating telemarketing practices.'" *Sussman v. I.C. Sys., Inc.*, 928 F. Supp. 2d 784, 789 (S.D.N.Y. 2013) (citing *In re Rules & Regulations Implementing the Tel. Consumer Prot. Act of 1991*, 18 F.C.C. Rcd. 14014, 14060 (2003)).

Note that giving readers a reason to find value does not have to be an elaborate production. In the first example, the writer tries to increase the value of the source by tying its assertion to an analogous type of search. In the second example, the writer tells readers why they should care about this nonauthoritative source by stating that the court used relevant authority to reach its conclusion. Of course, citing to a mandatory authority is almost always preferable. When other citations are necessary, however, a good legal writer does not try to hide the use of nonmandatory authority, but instead uses effective writing techniques to try to increase the value of nonmandatory sources.

3. Where to Cite

As noted previously, citations in legal documents will sometimes be citations to sources rather than citations to authorities. For this reason, writers should place their citations in text in almost all situations. Use footnotes for citations only on rare occasions. Placing citations in text allows readers to identify immediately which citations are and are not authoritative citations. Readers' immediate need to understand a source's validity makes it more important for memo and brief writers to place citations in text than it is to preserve the supposed ease of reading that citation-free text allows. Readers will be more annoyed by having to search for footnoted information than by having to visually jump across the citation in the text.

E.g., footnotes may be appropriate when a string citation is necessary. This chapter will address string cites below.

4. Using Effective Sentence Structures to Accommodate Citation Form

Incorporating citations into text is the best way to promote easy identification of the value of your authority. You will help your readers, however, if you use effective sentence structures to accommodate citations. Many writers instinctively introduce a new case by beginning a sentence with a long-form citation:

> ***Bad Example***
> In *Bombard v. Fort Wayne Newspapers, Inc.*, 92 F.3d 560, 563 (7th Cir. 1996), the court held that a "qualified individual with a disability" is defined as "an individual with a disability who, with or without reasonable accommodation, can perform the essential functions of the employment position that such individual holds or desires."

This sentence is difficult to read because the citation takes up a lot of space within the sentence. Furthermore, this structure puts too much emphasis on the citation and not enough emphasis on the substance of the sentence. To solve this problem, some writers mistakenly separate the case name from the rest of the citation:

> ***Bad Example***
> In *Bombard v. Fort Wayne Newspapers, Inc.*, the court held that a "qualified individual with a disability" is defined as "an individual

with a disability who, with or without reasonable accommodation, can perform the essential functions of the employment position that such individual holds or desires." 92 F.3d 560, 563 (7th Cir. 1996).

This "separated long-form" or "split cite" structure is not optimal. Although some citation rules may condone this separation, it can confuse readers, who could be expecting a long-form citation because they do not recall reading about the case earlier. The best way to write a readable sentence and still use correct citation form is to put the citation in a separate citation sentence:

Good Example
A "qualified individual with a disability" is defined as "an individual with a disability who, with or without reasonable accommodation, can perform the essential functions of the employment position that such individual holds or desires." *Bombard v. Fort Wayne Newspapers, Inc.*, 92 F.3d 560, 563 (7th Cir. 1996).

Thus, instead of focusing the attention in your sentence on the citation, you focus it on the rule itself or, if appropriate, on the court that made the statement:

Good Example
The Seventh Circuit has defined "qualified individual with a disability" as "an individual with a disability who, with or without reasonable accommodation, can perform the essential functions of the employment position that such individual holds or desires." *Bombard v. Fort Wayne Newspapers, Inc.*, 92 F.3d 560, 563 (7th Cir. 1996).

A writer relying on non-mandatory authority for the same definition would give the reader a reason to find value by including the following language at the beginning of the sentence: "A district court applying the ADA's 'qualified individual with a disability' language defined the phrase as 'an individual who, with or without reasonable accommodation, can perform' the position's essential functions." *Poe v. Waste Connections US, Inc.*, 371 F. Supp. 3d 901, 909 (W.D. Wash. 2019) (citing 42 U.S.C. § 12111(8)).

Putting citations at the end of the sentence lets the citation do its work of telling readers the name of the case, the court, and the year of decision, but keeps it from intruding on the sentence itself. Including a case name alone in your sentence is appropriate only if you have already cited the case in full in that same discussion:

Good Example
The Seventh Circuit has defined "qualified individual with a disability" as "an individual with a disability who, with or without reasonable accommodation, can perform the essential functions of the employment position that such individual holds or desires." *Bombard v. Fort Wayne Newspapers, Inc.*, 92 F.3d 560, 563 (7th Cir. 1996). In *Bombard,* the court identified a two-part test for determining whether that definition is satisfied. *Id.*

Thus, structure your sentences so that all citations, and particularly long-form citations, can be placed in their own citation sentences. You can accomplish this goal by keeping the focus on the substance of the cited material rather than on the citation.

5. Avoiding String Citations

Judges are almost uniformly against the use of string citations. As Judge Boyce Martin notes, "When I read a lengthy string cite in a brief or slip opinion, I often find that I have lost the gist of the argument after fighting through line after line of gobbledygook."[2] Admittedly, string citations are useful on rare occasions. For example, if you need to illustrate a trend in the law, give a brief overview of a still-developing area of law, or establish that multiple authorities in a variety of jurisdictions have followed or not followed a particular rule, a string citation may be appropriate. We make two warnings about string citations: first, most cases you write memos or briefs for will not present any of these situations, so presume that you will not need a string cite. Second, the longer the string cite, the less likely it is that anyone will look at any of the cases cited in it.

When a string citation is unavoidable, put as much information as possible into the sentence preceding the string cite. Most readers would have to struggle to pick up any information in phrases and clauses interspersed among the citations. One problem with a string citation is that it inevitably creates a very long sentence, and, psychologically, readers try to keep that sentence "going" in their brains. A sentence with text and citations interspersed is probably the hardest thing for readers to read:

> ***Bad Example***
> A "long-standing" exception to the warrant requirement allows searches incident to arrest and permits not only the seizure of items from the arrestee's person but the search of any container found on or near the arrestee as well, allowing courts to uphold the search of a closed cigarette package on the arrestee's person in *United States v. Robinson,* 414 U.S. 218, 233-34 (1973); to uphold the search of a cell phone incident to arrest, *United States v. Finley,* 477 F.3d 250, 259 (5th Cir. 2007); to uphold the search of a cell phone incident to arrest, despite questioning the permissibility of a more invasive search, *United States v. Flores-Lopez,* 670 F.3d 803, 810 (7th Cir. 2012); to uphold the searches of closed and open

2. Boyce F. Martin, Jr., *Judges on Judging: In Defense of Unpublished Opinions*, 60 Ohio St. L.J. 177, 193 (1999).

suitcases near the arrestee on a bed, *United States v. Andersson*, 813 F.2d 1450, 1455 (9th Cir. 1987); to uphold the searches of a flannel bag within reach of the arrestee, *United States v. Punzalan*, CR 07-00075, 2014 WL 702383, *5 (D. Guam Feb. 24, 2014); to allow a search of a laundry bag and rolling suitcase, and of a hair gel bottle inside suitcase of gang member arrested at a train station, *People v. Cregan*, 2014 IL 113600 (Ill. Feb. 21, 2014); to uphold the search of a purse thrown to the ground by a person arrested on suspicion of prostitution, *People v. Hoskins*, 461 N.E.2d 941, 945 (Ill. 1984).

To make this information easier to digest, write a sentence informing readers of the significance of the cases and then end it with a period. In that sentence, do your best to include all of the information that is common to all of the cases, so that any parenthetical information can focus on the differences between them. Depending on the circumstances, the string citation could be placed in a footnote; even if it is in the text, using this technique will make the citation string easier for readers to comprehend:

Better Example
Under a "long-standing" exception to the warrant requirement, courts have allowed searches incident to arrest and permitted not only the seizure of items from the arrestee's person but the search of a variety of containers found on or near the arrestee as well. *United States v. Robinson*, 414 U.S. 218, 233-34 (1973) (closed cigarette package on arrestee's person); *United States v. Finley*, 477 F.3d 250, 259 (5th Cir. 2007) (cell phone); *United States v. Flores-Lopez*, 670 F.3d 803, 810 (7th Cir. 2012) (cell phone for its phone number only); *United States v. Andersson*, 813 F.2d 1450, 1455 (9th Cir. 1987) (open and closed suitcases near arrestee); *United States v. Punzalan*, CR 07-00075, 2014 WL 702383, *5 (D. Guam Feb. 24, 2014) (flannel bag in reach of arrestee); *People v. Cregan*, 2014 IL 113600 (Ill. Feb. 21, 2014) (laundry bag, rolling suitcase, and hair gel bottle in arrestee's possession); *People v. Hoskins*, 461 N.E.2d 941, 945 (Ill. 1984) (purse thrown to ground by arrestee).

The best solution is one that avoids the string citation entirely. If you are using the string citation to point out the well-established fact that many courts have already agreed with a legal rule, you may be able to use a parenthetical to accomplish the goal of the string cite. Often, one of the most recent cases in a string will have addressed the fact that the rule is well established and may have cited most or all of the other cases. In that situation, you may tell readers that the cases exist and give them access to those cases by citing only the most recent one:

Good Examples
Several courts have interpreted claims of discrimination based upon the plaintiff's status of being "Hispanic" as being a national origin discrimination claim. *E.g., Beltran v. Univ. of Tex. Health Sci. Ctr. at Houston,* 837 F. Supp. 2d 635, 640 (S.D. Tex. 2011) (citing cases).

Indeed, every court of appeals to consider a facial constitutional challenge to FISA—whether for due-process or Fourth Amendment purposes—has upheld the statute. *See U.S. v. El-Mezain,* 664 F.3d 467, 567 (5th Cir. 2011) (citing cases from the D.C., Sixth, Eighth, and Ninth Circuits); *United States v. Abu-Jihaad,* 630 F.3d 102, 120 (2d Cir. 2010) (citing cases from the First, Fourth, Sixth, Seventh, and Ninth Circuits, as well as numerous district court authorities).

These citations support accurate statements—that "several" courts or "every court" has decided a certain type of case in a certain way—and because they cite to decisions that cite the multiple decisions referenced, they allow readers to find all those decisions if needed.

Of course, you must use this method with care. It cannot be used unless the text of your analysis accurately reflects what the cited case has said about the list of cases cited. Furthermore, you should not use this method if information from each authority is important to your analysis. When this method is appropriate, however, you will be able to simultaneously avoid a string cite and give readers access to multiple authorities that support your analysis.

6. Cases That Cite Other Cases

Figure 15.5 includes examples of citations that include parenthetical information beyond court and date.

A citation dilemma for many legal writers is what to do when citing an excerpt of a case that has quoted another case. Traditionally, citation rules have encouraged writers to cite the original source, as the writer does in the following example:

Bad Example
It is a "bedrock principle" that federal courts are of limited jurisdiction. *Alcala v. Holder,* 563 F.3d 1009, 1016 (9th Cir. 2009) (citing *Gary v. Curtis,* 44 U.S. (3 How.) 236, 244 (1845)).

Although this guideline may be appropriate for law review articles and other publications, it is not always the best rule for writing memos and briefs. In this situation, it is doubtful that readers need to know about an 1845 case that is the origin of the concept.

Of course, a legal writer may need or want to cite the original source to give added credence to a discussion of a case decided by a nonmandatory court. In the example below, from a petitioner's brief to the United States Supreme Court, the writer is discussing a Second Circuit case that applied *Williams v. Taylor*, a significant U.S. Supreme Court case that had been previously cited in that same section of the brief:

> ***Good Example***
> A federal court may not grant habeas simply because, in its independent judgment, the "relevant state-court decision applied clearly established federal law erroneously or incorrectly." *Fuller v. Gorczyk*, 273 F.3d 212, 219 (2d Cir. 2001) (quoting *Williams*, 529 U.S. at 411). The *Fuller* court applied that standard and found that a court's analysis was not valid because it "did not adequately identify why" it found a decision affirming a defendant's conviction to be objectively unreasonable. *Fuller*, 273 F.3d at 212.

Noting that the Second Circuit based its decision on U.S. Supreme Court authority may give that decision more weight in a brief written to the U.S. Supreme Court. Thus, if knowing the origin of the cited language could affect readers' understanding of your analysis, identify that source. This situation does not occur regularly in legal writing; generally, if the origin of the language is significant, the writer should go to the original source and cite that authority in addition or instead. It is only when the relationship between the two sources is significant—as it is when an on-point nonmandatory court applies a rule from a mandatory court—that readers are likely to be interested in the origin of the quoted language.

In most other situations, however, readers who look at the citations supporting an analysis want to know only that a valid court made that statement in a relevant case. They usually have little or no interest in the original source of particular words or phrases. If the cited opinion is a valid authority for that quote, it matters only that an authoritative court made the statement in its majority opinion and that the statement is not dicta. Even if that court misinterpreted the original language, what matters is that the court believed that the language was appropriate to apply to the set of facts that was before it. Thus, determine whether your readers would better understand your analysis if they knew the original source of the quoted language. If knowing the source would not improve readers' understanding, you can omit the citation, so long as you inform readers that you are doing so:

Good Example
It is a "bedrock principle" that federal courts are of limited jurisdiction. *Alcala v. Holder,* 563 F.3d 1009, 1016 (9th Cir. 2009) (citation omitted).

Substituting the "citation omitted" parenthetical phrase for the full citation will allow those who wish to track the original language the opportunity to do so. Most readers, however, will be grateful that you have not cluttered the brief with irrelevant citations.

These are examples of just some of the instances in which a writer provides additional case information in a parenthetical.

1. To show that the cited authority cites another authority for the proposition

   Moeller v. Qualex, Inc., 458 F. Supp. 2d 1069, 1071 (C.D. Cal. 2006) (citing *Pareto v. F.D.I.C.*, 139 F.3d 696, 699 (9th Cir. 1998)).

   If the writer had previously cited *Pareto* in the same document

   Moeller v. Qualex, Inc., 458 F. Supp. 2d 1069, 1071 (C.D. Cal. 2006) (citing *Pareto v. F.D.I.C.*, 139 F.3d at 699).

2. To show that the cited authority quotes another authority

   Bronson v. Hitchcock Clinic, 677 A.2d 665, 667 (N.H. 1996) (quoting *Thompson v. The H.W.G. Group*, 664 A.2d 489, 490 (N.H. 1995)).

   If the writer previously cited *Thompson* in the same document

   Bronson v. Hitchcock Clinic, 677 A.2d 665, 667 (N.H. 1996) (quoting *Thompson v. The H.W.G. Group*, 664 A.2d at 490).

3. To show that the cited portion of an authority is a concurring opinion

   United States v. Davis, 825 F.3d 1014, 1029 (9th Cir. 2016) (Christen, J., concurring).

4. To show that the cited portion of an authority is a dissenting opinion

   United States v. Davis, 825 F.3d 1014, 1031 (9th Cir. 2016) (Bea, J., dissenting).

5. To show that a court of appeals decision was delivered *en banc* (by all active members of the court rather than a smaller panel)

United States v. Davis, 825 F.3d 1014, 1019 (9th Cir. 2016) (en banc).

Figure 15.5

7. The Importance of Pinpoint Citations

A pinpoint citation is a citation to the specific page on which quoted or cited language appeared. Some legal writers use the phrases *pin cite* or *jump cite* to mean the same thing. You must include a pinpoint citation *every time* you cite to a case. The best time to insert pinpoint citations is in your initial outline or draft; the small cost of doing it then will be well worth the substantial saving of not having to relocate the precise page later.

Do not convince yourself that you are citing the case only "generally" and thus do not need to include a citation to the specific page. If you want your readers to be able to verify that the authorities you cite stand for the propositions you say they do, you must make it incredibly easy for them to find the law that is the source of your analysis. If you cite a case for its main holding, find the page on which the court articulated that holding: that is the pinpoint page. Even if you are citing the first page of the opinion (a rare event, because many reporters fill the first page with headnotes and other editorial information), you must still provide a pinpoint citation:

Good Example
McGuffin v. Wood, 101 F.3d 115, 115 (6th Cir. 2015).

Think of your readers whenever you are making a citation decision. Whenever you can make it easier for them to understand your analysis by putting a little more information into the document, you should do so.

8. Summary

The practical legal writer has a lot to remember when trying to use case authorities effectively. Remembering the needs of those who will read and use the document will help you to (1) include all of the authorities that are necessary; (2) give enough information about those authorities, but not too much; (3) present that information accurately and in a helpful way; and (4) cite that information in a way that provides sufficient information without needlessly intruding on the text.

D. HOW TO CITE

The mechanics of citation are often confounding to beginning legal writers. One way to simplify the process is to begin by asking whether

Short-form citations include *id.* citations and the shortened form of the full citation. An *id.* citation is appropriate only when the reference is to the most recently mentioned authority.

Long-form citations are sometimes called full citations. *Full* suggests that the citation includes all of the necessary identifying information about the authority. Within a document, only one full citation to any particular authority is necessary.

For example, many state courts now require citation to a paragraph number rather than a page number. This method of citation may spread to national cites, but it has not done so as of this writing.

you have cited the authority before in the same document. If not, you need a long-form citation. If so, you need a short-form citation. Once you have determined which form you need, your task is to include the necessary components for that form as outlined in the following sections. Note that the guidelines below describe what we might call national requirements, as illustrated in the major citation guides. It is common for states to develop their own citation rules. While these rules are often similar to national rules, be sure you know what rules your assigning attorney expects you to follow before submitting a document within your firm.

1. Long-Form Case Citation

The typical long-form case citation includes five elements:

(a) ***The case name***. For most cases, the name of the case consists of one name on each side of the *v.* Do not use a party's first name (unless it is part of a corporate name, e.g., "Larry King, Inc.") and do not use more than one party's name, even when there are multiple plaintiffs and defendants. Never use *et al.* in a case citation. Case names should be underlined or italicized. Some writers mistakenly underline or italicize an entire citation, whether to a case or a statute, because they have seen entire citations underlined in hypertext on a Web site or another online resource. Statutory citations are *never* italicized or underlined; in cases, *only* the case name (e.g., *Smith v. Jones*) should be italicized or underlined. Because the eye is drawn to underlined words more than to italicized words, we recommend underlining in memos and briefs.

(b) ***Where the case and the information cited to can be found***. This element is the most important part of the citation for readers who are actually looking up a case that you've cited. Provide the volume of the reporter, the designated reporter abbreviation, and the page on which the case begins.

(c) ***The pinpoint citation***. With every cite, you should include the specific page to which you are citing. If you have accessed the case online, locating the pinpoint page will require you to look for the asterisked numbers running through the case. Your pinpoint page number is the one immediately before the spot where the relevant text appears. For example, figure 15.6 is an imaginary screenshot from *Gardea v. JBS USA, LLC*, 915 F.3d 537 (8th Cir. 2019). If you

2. Qualification

In order to show that he is a qualified individual under the ADA, Gardea must prove that he was able "to perform the essential functions of the position, with or without reasonable accommodation." Hill v. Walker, 737 F.3d 1209, 1216 (8th Cir. 2013) (quotation omitted). Essential functions of the position are "the fundamental job duties of the employment position the individual with a disability holds or desires." 29 C.F.R. § 1630.2(n)(1). Accommodations are not reasonable if an employer "can demonstrate that the accommodation would impose undue hardship on the operation of the business." 42 U.S.C. § 12112(5)(A). An employee must show that an accommodation is "reasonable on its face." U.S. Airways, Inc. v. Barnett, 535 U.S. 391, 401, 122 S.Ct. 1516, 152 L.Ed.2d 589 (2002).

***542** As the district court found, lifting is an essential function of the maintenance mechanic position. The record shows that mechanics must have the ability to lift objects weighing up to 100 pounds, carry ladders and motors in excess of 40 pounds, and frequently perform lifting between 10 and 50 pounds. (JA at 27, ¶¶ 25-27, 517-518, 560.) Gardea does not directly dispute that lifting is an essential function, but rather challenges the frequency with which heavy lifting is required in his position. However, "a task may be an essential function even if the employee performs it for only a few minutes each week." Minnihan v. Mediacom Commc'ns Corp., 779 F.3d 803, 812 (8th Cir. 2015). The record shows that heavy lifting is commonplace in the maintenance mechanic position. Therefore, the lifting of objects heavier than Gardea can lift is an essential function.

Gardea also alleges that his lifting restriction could have been reasonably accommodated because (1) assistance from other mechanics was available and (2) the use of lift-assisting devices was available.

First, assistance from other mechanics is not a reasonable accommodation. "'[A]n accommodation that would cause other employees to work harder, longer, or be deprived of opportunities is not mandated' under the ADA." Id. at 813 (quotation omitted). Because Gardea's lifting limitations are so restrictive, he would require assistance lifting many commonplace objects involved in his job, including all ladders and machinery. The record reflects that certain storage areas are too small for two people to perform a lift, and other mechanics are not always available to assist others in lifting objects. (JA at 28, ¶¶ 32-33.) Because this accommodation would require JBS to extensively change its practices and work environment, **it is unreasonable.**

Figure 15.6

were writing about the court's conclusion that the accommodation requested by the employee was unreasonable (bolded in Figure 15.6), you would look for the asterisked number that appears most immediately before that text. In this instance, the number is *542. That number follows closely after 537, which you know to be the first page of the case in the Federal Reporter, 3d series. So, "542" is your pinpoint page.

(d) ***The year of decision***. This element is the simplest: put the year of the decision into parentheses. Even readers who aren't fussy about minor citation form errors care deeply when you leave the date of decision out of a long-form citation. Because the date of a decision affects its current validity, readers always want to know the year in which authority cases were decided.

(e) ***Which court decided the case***. Although court information is not needed when citing to decisions of the United States Supreme Court (because the U.S. Reports publishes only decisions of the U.S. Supreme Court), citations to cases of any other court will need this information in the date parenthetical.

Knowing which court decided the case is vital for readers who want to determine whether a case is controlling. Therefore, even readers who are not fussy about citation form want to know which court decided the case. Make sure to include this important element in your citation.

Good Examples
Martinez v. Reed, 101 U.S. 101, 105 (2001).

Ohio v. Sampson, 101 N.E.2d 122, 128 (Ohio 2006).

Prendergast v. Hagen, 101 F. Supp. 2d 122, 128 (N.D. Ohio 2010).

Sanders v. Wood, 101 N.E.2d 122, 128 (Ohio Ct. App. 2001).

2. Short-Form Case Citation

The most basic guideline for short-form citations is that you should omit the date and court information and use an "at" before the page number. Otherwise, use of short form depends on context.

If you are citing again to the *last-cited and last-mentioned* authority, you may use the *id.* form. *Id.* replaces the name of the case, the volume of the reporter, and the abbreviation of the reporter. Thus, if you cited again to the case of *Martinez v. Reed* immediately after you had cited it the first time, you could use the following short form if you were citing to a different page in the opinion:

Id. at 107.

If you were citing to the same page, you would use *Id.* alone. If you were citing to an already cited opinion, but (a) you have cited to or *mentioned* another authority in the meantime *or* (b) there is any doubt that readers will know to which authority you are referring, use a short form that identifies the name of the case. Make sure to use an identifiable case name; if one of the parties is a governmental entity, for example, use the name of the other party in the short-form cite. If you were citing again to *Ohio v. Sampson*, but there had been an intervening cite, use either of the following formats:

Sampson, 101 N.E.2d at 125.

Ohio v. Sampson, 101 N.E.2d at 125.

Note that it is *never* appropriate to use *supra* when citing cases in a brief, nor is it appropriate to use a case name cite without including reporter information. Thus, the two examples below are both wrong:

Supra, usually after an author's name, is acceptable in citations in academic legal writing, including law review articles, to indicate that the source has been cited earlier within the same document.

Bad Examples
Prendergast, *supra*, at 126.

Sanders at 135.

3. Citing Nonmajority Opinions

Unless your citation indicates otherwise, readers will presume that you are citing a majority opinion. Thus, when you cite a plurality opinion, a concurrence, a dissent, and so on, you must indicate as much in a parenthetical after the citation. This is true even when you have mentioned the type of opinion cited in your text; it's also true for both long-form and short-form citations. Thus, the following citations are all correct:

Martinez v. Reed, 101 U.S. 101, 125 (2006) (plurality opinion).

Id. at 155 (Williams, J., dissenting).

Sanders, 101 N.E.2d at 135 (Moyer, C.J., concurring in part and dissenting in part).

4. Statutory Citations

The first thing to remember when citing statutes is to consult the appropriate charts in *ALWD* (Appendix 1) or the *Bluebook* (Table T.1). Look up the jurisdiction that you are citing and check the recommended method. Note that although the *Bluebook* illustrates statutory citations using large and small capitals, Rule 2.1 advises writers to use this convention mostly in law review articles. As ALWD's illustrations make clear, use the simpler style of capital and lowercase letters when citing statutes in other materials, such as memos and briefs.

The second thing to remember about statutory citations is that for long-form statutory citations, you must include a date for the statute, and the date required is the date of the version of the statute that you are looking at. If you obtained the statutory language from a book and/or pocket part (supplement) that the language appears in, you must indicate the date(s) of the book(s). If you obtained the statutory language from a database, you must consult the "currentness" link to indicate how current the statutory language is.

Thus, a correct citation to a statute that appears partially in a bound volume dated 2014 and partially in a pocket part dated 2015 would be as follows:

> Okla. Stat. tit. 19, § 222.22 (2014 & Supp. 2015).[3]

If the entire statute appeared in the pocket part (or at least the entirety of the writer's reference), the citation would be as follows:

> Okla. Stat. tit. 29, § 122.22(h) (Supp. 2015).

If the language cited appeared entirely in the bound volume, the citation would be as follows:

> Okla. Stat. tit. 15, § 111.22(a) (2014).

When citing to statutory language that you have obtained from a computer database, consult the language at the top of the page (for LexisAdvance) and the "Currentness" link (for WestlawNext) to find the appropriate information for the date parenthetical. Note that this information may be somewhat lengthy:

> Okla. Stat. Ann. tit. 8, § 111 (West, WestlawNext current with emergency effective provisions through Chapter 168 of the Second Regular Session of the 54th Legislature (2014)).

---

3. Note that the supplements to the United States Code are numbered; thus, you might have a cite like this: 29 U.S.C. § 122 (Supp. III 2009).

Note also that different databases may include statutes at slightly different levels of currency:

> 42 U.S.C.S. § 1983 (LexisAdvance, current through PL 113-101, approved 5/9/21).

> 42 U.S.C.S. § 1983 (West, WestlawNext, current through P.L. 113-93 (excluding P.L. 113-79) approved 4-1-21).

> Ohio Rev. Code Ann. § 4511.19 (LexisAdvance, current through Legislation passed by the 130th General Assembly and filed with the Secretary of State through File 94 Annotations current through April 14, 2021).

> Ohio Rev. Code Ann. § 4511.19 (West, WestlawNext current through Files 1 to 94 and Statewide Issue 1 of the 130th GA (2021-2022)).

Further, be aware that although your instincts may be to provide the date of enactment or amendment, that information is not required. You may decide to add this information, however, if you think it is relevant to your analysis:

Local culture can also affect citation methods. If there is no controversy about which version of the statute you are citing (e.g., if it has not been recently amended), it may be appropriate to list the database and the current year as the date.

> Okla. Stat. tit. 19, § 222.22 (2009 & Supp. 2021) (effective Feb. 27, 1987).

The final thing to remember about citing statutes is that you can use a short form to refer to statutes. The statute cited in the first example above could be cited later in the discussion by title and section number, as in "tit. 19, § 222.22," or simply by section number, as in "§ 222.22."

Note that you should never start a sentence with an abbreviation or a symbol. If you wish to open the sentence with a short-form reference to a statute, spell out the first word, e.g., "Title 19, § 222.22, provides . . ." or "Section 222.22 provides. . . ."

C. CONCLUSION

Although the customs and rules for statutory citations may seem annoying and needlessly fussy, it is worth taking the time to follow them. You may annoy or distract your readers if you fail to follow correct citation form; more important, you may hurt a client's case if you fail to include citations when they are needed or expected.

Recall and Review

1. What kinds of decisions are published in the Pacific Reporter (P.2d), Atlantic Reporter (A.2d), Southern Reporter (So. 2d), and other regional reporters?
2. True or False: Decisions published in F. Supp. 3d are mandatory authority to the trial courts in their respective jurisdictions.
3. True or False: A pinpoint cite is not necessary for long-form case citations.
4. For long-form citations to decisions from all courts other than the United States Supreme Court, what information needs to appear in the parenthetical?
5. Whenever you quote or paraphrase information from a source, you should include what at the end of the quotation or the sentence (for paraphrased material)?
6. What must you include as part of any case citation to material from a dissenting opinion?

CHAPTER 16

CORRESPONDENCE & EMAIL

Lawyers write letters. They also write professional emails. They do these things even though formal correspondence in other areas of life seems to be a dying practice. Lawyers are not simply bucking the trend by persisting in their use of written correspondence. Their continued reliance on a form that may seem overly formal for our casual culture serves at least three important purposes.

First, lawyers recognize the need for precision and care in their work on behalf of clients. Tweets and text messages are usually inadequate for the task of explaining complex matters to clients or to other lawyers. The need for precision dictates the medium for communication.

Second, as you have already learned, legal material is often difficult to absorb in one pass. A letter or a detailed email allows readers to reread dense portions.

And third, a lawyer's correspondence will survive the present legal matter and, in most cases, the lawyer-client relationship. When memories of conversations have faded, the written record, in the form of correspondence, will remain. So, when lawyers put information or advice for their clients into written form, they document that information for all time.

As a lawyer, you will probably write many more letters and emails than you will briefs and memos. We hope that we have already convinced you that a lawyer who is preparing a document for filing in a court must take care to consider and address the needs and expectations of the intended readers. The same is true of a lawyer who is preparing correspondence.

The audience for a lawyer's correspondence will often be a client or another lawyer. The needs and expectations of those two audiences will vary significantly in at least two ways. First, the emotional needs of a client, who is personally invested in a matter, are likely to be very different from those of another lawyer. This distinction is true whether that lawyer is opposing counsel, a representative of a client, or an ally. Even within the category of "client," the emotional needs will depend on the financial stake, the nature of the matter, and the emotional content of the matter at hand. Second, the need of the audience for detail and depth in the explanation of legal subject matter will depend on the level of sophistication of the audience and the purpose of the correspondence. A letter to a corporate client with in-house counsel is likely to include depth and legal language, while a letter for a client who is a juvenile is likely to include just a few conclusions with a clear and simple explanation of any advice.

In this chapter, we will identify some of the important considerations you should keep in mind as you prepare correspondence. You will notice that these considerations call on your psychology and communication skills as much as they call on your legal knowledge. In fact, we find that first-year law students, who are just beginning the transition from human being to lawyer, are often more adept than lawyers at drafting correspondence that satisfies the needs and expectations of their audiences.

Exercise 16.1

Before you read further, review the following two letters. The client, Lisa Lagos, is a former bank supervisor with no legal training. Her brother is a senior lawyer in the writer's office who has asked the writer to research an employment law issue and then write a client letter to Ms. Lagos. The purpose of the letter is to advise Ms. Lagos, who has been fired from her job, as to whether she should file a lawsuit based on some form of wrongful termination. Place yourself in the client's position and try to gauge your responses to the letter's content and tone. Which letter would best fulfill the needs of this particular client?

Letter A

Dear Ms. Lagos,

I have completed my research and preliminary analysis of the question you posed to Mr. Smith, your brother, whether you have a claim against Bank Two relating to the termination of your employment at the end of last year. Specifically, I looked at whether Bank Two discriminated against you on the basis of your gender when it terminated you. Unfortunately, the news I have to convey is not good news.

As I understand the facts, Bank Two hired you, along with two male managers, on the same date. The Bank assigned the two male managers to positions in a department with low turnover, while it assigned you to a position supervising unskilled employees who turn over frequently. The Bank apparently expressed belief that women are more effective managers of unskilled workers. Then, the Bank criticized you for the higher turnover rate. This criticism took the form of lower evaluation scores in the area of "Employee Management." Those lower scores resulted in a lower salary over time. When the Bank reduced the number of managers at the end of 2010, it used salary as a measure of seniority and effectiveness and terminated your employment because your salary was lower than those of the two male managers whom the Bank hired along with you. The only relevant difference among the three of you in terms of education, experience, seniority, and salary was a result of the Bank's initial placement of you in a department with high turnover.

In *McDonnell Douglas*, the United States Supreme Court established a test for claims of discrimination in employment. That test would apply to your claim against Bank Two. A plaintiff must show that (1) she is a member of a protected class, (2) she applied for and was qualified for a job, (3) she was not selected, and (4) the employer kept the position open and continued to look for candidates with the same qualifications as the plaintiff had. The Supreme Court offered further guidance in how to apply this standard in *McDonald v. Santa Fe Trail Transp. Co.* The standard provided in *McDonnell Douglas* was not meant to be any "indication of any substantive limitation of Title VII's prohibition of racial discrimination." Rather, the four elements were designed to "demonstrate how the racial [or gender-based] character of the discrimination could be established in the most common sort of case." Thus, the Supreme Court created a general standard that the circuit courts could tailor and adapt to the exigencies of their cases.

In our circuit, the analysis of a claim like yours follows the *Ercegovich v. Goodyear Tire & Rubber Co.* standard, which requires the following: (1) the plaintiff is a member of a protected class; (2) the plaintiff was otherwise qualified for the position in question; (3) the plaintiff suffered an adverse employment action; and either (4a) the plaintiff can produce direct or statistical evidence of discrimination or (4b) the plaintiff can demonstrate the comparable similarly-situated non-protected employees were treated better.

Title VII includes women as a protected class, so you can satisfy the first part of the *Ercegovich* standard. Bank Two gave you very favorable performance evaluations each year of your employment, so you are very likely able to prove that you were qualified for a management position. The termination of your employment was an adverse employment action. In short, you would probably be able to prove the first three parts of the *Ercegovich* standard. The problem with your claim is with the fourth part of that standard.

The fourth part of the *Ercegovich* standard requires that you either produce direct or statistical evidence of discrimination or show that you were treated differently than male employees who were similarly-situated in every material respect. As I understand the facts, you do not have direct or statistical evidence of discrimination. That is, you have no evidence that directly shows that Bank Two terminated your employment because you are a woman or that it wanted to eliminate women from management positions. I am also unaware of any statistics showing that Bank Two structured the terminations so as to eliminate women. So, you will succeed in establishing discrimination only if you can show that you were treated differently from male employees who were similarly-situated in every relevant respect.

Relevant respects are those that relate in some fashion to the basis for the adverse employment action. In your situation, the relevant respects were seniority and salary. Your seniority was the same as that of the two male managers whom Bank Two hired on the same date. You concede that your salary was different, however. Even if the reason for the difference was lower evaluation scores, you cannot prove your claim, because you had a different supervisor, and that supervisor gave you the evaluation scores. In that circumstance, the identity of your supervisor is relevant, and because the identity of your supervisor is different from that of the two male managers, you cannot show that you were similarly-situated in every relevant respect.

A better basis for a claim of discrimination would have been your initial assignment, which, as I understand the facts, appears to have been based on assumptions about women and men as managers. Those assumptions are based on stereotypes, and stereotypes should not be used to place female employees in less advantageous positions. Unfortunately, the governing law requires that you make a claim about an act of discrimination within 300 days of that act or the first adverse consequences of the act. In your case, that would have been within 300 days of your hiring or of your first evaluation and ensuing salary increase. Those events occurred much longer than 300 days ago, so any claim based upon them would be too late.

My advice to you is to move on from this dispute. I do not believe that a claim against Bank Two for discrimination would be successful. If you believe that I have misunderstood any of the facts that form the basis for that advice, please do not hesitate to let me know. I am sorry that the news is not better.

Very truly yours,

S.A. Student

Letter B

Dear Ms. Lagos,

Your brother asked me to do some research in order to determine whether you might have a claim for sex discrimination against Bank Two. The basis for your claim would be one of two actions by Bank Two. The first was your initial placement in Commercial Lending supervising unskilled workers, and the second was the termination of your employment as part of Bank Two's contraction at the end of 2010. I am afraid that my research and preliminary analysis leave me skeptical about the likely success of any such claim. I do have some lingering questions, however, and I invite you to follow up on this note with any additional information that you believe would change the analysis. If anything about my explanation is unclear, please call me. I want to be certain that the explanation and my advice are clear.

The critical facts as I understand them are that Bank Two used stereotypes about women and men to determine where managers would be placed. So, when Bank Two hired you and two men with identical credentials and experience on the same day, it placed you in a position supervising unskilled workers who apparently required more nurturing. The Bank placed the two men in positions supervising an educated, stable workforce, whom, the Bank apparently assumed, would benefit from the more analytical and less nurturing style of a male manager. You performed as well as the male managers, but your employees turned over as was their wont, and you received lower scores in one category of evaluation. Your supervisor marked you down one level for failing to retain your unretainable employees, while the vice president supervising the male managers gave them top marks for retaining the employees who did not turn over frequently anyway. That unfair scenario resulted in a lower salary increase every year for you and, ultimately, in the termination of your employment when Bank Two decided that salary was an effective way to determine which managers to retain.

The standards governing claims of sex discrimination in employment are well-established. After an act of discrimination occurs, an employee has 300 days to file a claim of discrimination with the Equal Employment Opportunity Commission. That requirement will prevent you from bringing a claim relating to your initial placement and the resulting salary disparity. Those events took place more than 300 days ago, and a claim based upon them now would be untimely. You still have time to file a claim based upon the termination of your employment, however.

In order to succeed on that claim, you would be required to prove a number of things. I am convinced that you will be able to prove that, as a woman, you are protected by anti-discrimination law; that you were qualified for a management position; and that the termination of your employment was adverse to you. Each of those is a required part of the standard, but I will not focus on them because Bank Two is very likely to agree that you satisfy them. The critical inquiry in your case will be the requirement that you identify direct or statistical evidence of discrimination *or* that you can prove that you were treated less favorably than male employees who were similarly situated to you in all of the respects related to the ultimate termination of your employment.

To satisfy the first alternative, you would be required to introduce direct evidence of discrimination, such as a statement by a decision-maker at Bank Two that the contraction was designed to eliminate female managers or that the elimination of female managers was a desirable effect, or statistical evidence demonstrating that such an intent must have motivated the decisions about the contraction. Bank Two is too sophisticated to make such statements or to clumsily apply the standard in such a way that statistical evidence would be available. So, that alternative is likely unavailable to you. Please correct me if I am missing something important here from the facts.

The second alternative would require that you identify at least one male employee who was similar to you in all respects relating in any way to the termination of your employment and whom Bank Two treated more favorably. The relevant respects in your case would be seniority and performance evaluations because those are the measures that determined retention of managers. While you were equally senior as the two managers whom Bank Two hired along with you, their performance evaluations were slightly better. The reason for the difference is grossly unfair, but it makes them dissimilar in one relevant respect. Unfortunately, you cannot even claim discrimination in the manner in which you were evaluated because you had a different supervisor, and the courts have said that the identity of the supervisor must be the same where the supervisor's actions or decisions form the basis for an adverse employment action. Because the supervisors' evaluations of you and the two male employees played a role in the ultimate decision to terminate your employment, the identities of the supervisors are relevant. Because the identities of the supervisors are different, you can succeed under this alternative only if you can prove that someone else actually dictated the scores for all three of you. Correct me if I am wrong, but I do not believe that that is the case.

I wish I could advise you to bring suit against Bank Two. The Bank treated you abysmally, obviously. Unfortunately, the law and the courts' decisions interpreting it are not on your side. I would not advise you to sue. Again, please let me know if any part of this analysis or advice is based upon erroneous or incomplete information.

Very truly yours,

P.S. Student

How did you react to the two letters? Did you find the level of detail in each to be appropriate? Was the detail more or less than most nonlegally trained readers would desire or comprehend? What about the level of sophistication of the legal analysis? How easily would a nonlawyer understand the content? Finally, how did you view the tone of the letters? Was it too cold, too emotionally removed, too emotional, too strident? Give examples from the letters that support your responses.

We hope that this quick exercise demonstrated some of the balances that a lawyer must strike in drafting any correspondence. Level of detail, level of sophistication, and tone and emotional content are all essential components in most correspondence. The balance with respect to each of those factors will be different in nearly every letter because each recipient will be different. Let's examine each of those considerations more closely.

A. LEVEL OF DETAIL

As a first-year law student, you have probably already had the experience of reading a legal analysis that was so detailed that you eventually gave up trying to retain all of the information it included. You have probably also had the experience of jumping to the end of a document to try to find a conclusion that would help you make sense of all that you were reading. You may have wished that the writer had summarized more of the information, provided the conclusion first, or edited out more of the tangential information. If you have had any of these experiences, you will have an idea of how readers feel when trying to decipher a typical letter from a typical lawyer.

1. Where the Writer's Needs and Readers' Needs Diverge

As lawyers, we recognize that legal questions are rarely answered in a simple sentence. The answers to some of the most basic legal questions usually include caveats, exceptions, and qualifiers. We know that leaving out even one of these details can cause a legal analysis to be misleading or at least incomplete. So, as careful lawyers, we err on the side of including everything that may ever become relevant. This is helpful, even critical, to *our* understanding of the whole legal picture.

Guess what? Readers will (almost) never be able to absorb all of the information that we could provide about a legal question. Readers without legal training will be especially befuddled by the recitation of numerous exceptions, caveats, and qualifiers to general rules. Even other lawyers who have not been as laser-focused on the question as we have, will eventually feel their eyes glaze over. Obviously, in spite of our strong compulsion to be complete and completely accurate, we do not serve our *readers'* needs when we draft legal correspondence to satisfy *our* need for thoroughness and accuracy.

So, a lawyer must balance accuracy and completeness with readers' tolerance for detail. By putting yourself in readers' places, you have an understanding of their need for conclusions. "I just want the bottom line," you can almost hear a client say. And the bottom line is what you should provide. Your judgment about how much of the underlying detail readers will want and can absorb will dictate the level of detail you include *after you provide a conclusion*, but you must begin with a conclusion.

2. As Usual, Begin with a Conclusion

We have already written about the importance of beginning with a conclusion in written legal analysis. The paradigm holds true for correspondence as well. Readers, who are looking for answers to legal questions or for suggested plans of action, will be unable to focus on your message until they reach those answers or suggestions. No matter how detailed the underlying analysis may be, you should be able to express the outcome in a sentence or two. Begin there.

If you have a hard time articulating your conclusion(s), save space at the top, and write that part of the letter after you have composed the rest of the letter.

The conclusion is the response to the specific question or request that you are answering in the written correspondence. In your analysis of that question or request, you may have examined a number of issues. Take a moment to think about the question or request from the recipient's point of view before you write the conclusion. What question does the recipient expect you to answer? Your opening conclusion should respond to that specific question.

After carefully setting out the conclusion or bottom line, you may, but will not always, add an explanation. Your letter or email will probably include an invitation to readers to contact you to discuss your conclusion. If it does, do not write the explanation as though it were the final word from you to the readers about your answer or advice. Rather, include enough detail to inspire confidence in readers that you have a sound basis for the conclusion or the advice. In many instances, the explanation may be as simple as "the law does not permit you to take the action you want to take" or "your claim is consistent with Ohio law." In other instances, a bit more detail may be required to establish a basis for confidence that your analysis has been complete and that a compelling explanation exists, even if it is not included in the correspondence. Of course, if you cannot guarantee your answer 100 percent, you may need to use limiting language of some kind, even in your short answer. You must do this even when you include an invitation for follow-up, for the simple reason that your readers may not accept your invitation.

As we will explain below, the custom when writing formal opinion letters is to include formal "caveats" that warn readers of the limits of the letter, including the fact that no letter can guarantee a legal result.

Thus, for example, you might say, "My research indicates that the actions you propose are consistent with Ohio law. I will be glad to meet with you to explain my analysis further." This answer gives readers some confidence in the answer, but the use of the word "indicates" also signals that the answer is not an ironclad guarantee.

On rare occasions, your purpose may be to convince your readers of a legal conclusion and to avoid further communication. In a letter asking someone to cease and desist some behavior, for example, you may choose to include a high level of detail in order to communicate the soundness of your position in the letter itself. Those occasions will be rare because you will rarely write with the goal of ending communication.

In every instance, the purpose for writing the correspondence and your knowledge of the intended audience will dictate the level of detail you choose to include. One of your tasks before writing, therefore, will be the psychological exercise of identifying your purpose and your audience.

3. The Formal Opinion Letter Exception

Lawyers are sometimes called upon to provide a formal opinion about a legal question. A private lawyer may prepare such a letter for a client, but, more often, a government lawyer will prepare such a letter to advise a public client, such as an executive-level government officer, about the legality of a contemplated action. The purpose of a formal opinion letter is to set out the basis for a legal conclusion, or opinion. That purpose dictates a much greater level of detail than is typical in correspondence to a client.

When the purpose of the letter is to provide the legal basis for an opinion, the writer must include information relevant to every nuance of the question posed. The writer satisfies readers' needs only by providing an explanation that is detailed enough to convince readers that the lawyer has understood the question and considered every relevant aspect of the question.

A lawyer who prepares a formal opinion letter must still, of course, be mindful of readers' need for an understandable explanation. When the lawyer explains the basis for the opinion, however, the analysis may be very complex and may include numerous caveats and qualifiers. Therefore, the lawyer is wise to begin with an explicit acknowledgment of that complexity. Readers, no matter how sophisticated, may reach cognitive overload when reading your explanation. You can lessen some of your readers' frustration if you acknowledge at the outset that the explanation will be complex and assure readers (1) that you have tried to make the information as understandable as possible

The word *cognitive*, obviously, refers to thinking. When we have too many pieces of new information to think about, we may suffer from "cognitive overload." Using headings and other reader signals can help readers to deal with cognitive overload by giving them a way to connect that new information to other information, and a way to find information that they wish to reread.

and (2) that formal opinion letters are normally complicated because they explore every relevant issue and sub-issue. We suggest an explicit warning like this:

> The purpose of this letter is to explain the basis for my opinion. Before I begin, let me explain a few features that are common to all opinion letters. First, to explain fully how the law would apply to your proposed action, this letter discusses not only the question you raised but also a number of questions that relate to that question. Second, the letter will also include a number of caveats and qualifiers. These qualifiers are standard in formal opinion letters of this type because the answer to a legal question is rarely a simple "yes" or "no," and understanding these qualifiers will help you to understand my opinion. Of course, if you have any questions about any aspect of this letter, you may contact me for clarification.

The fact that the opinion letter is generally prepared for more legally sophisticated readers does not excuse the writer from the other considerations that relate to lawyer correspondence. The most sophisticated legal readers like clarity, simplicity, and thoughtful organization at least as much as average readers do. The considerations that follow apply with equal force to opinion letters and to ordinary correspondence.

B. LEVEL OF SOPHISTICATION

Legalese usually refers to two kinds of language. One kind is needlessly complex language such as "said document," instead of "the contract," or "heretofore" instead of "earlier." This kind of language confuses everyone.

The other kind of language that may be confusing is *jargon*, a term used for specialized language within any given field. When one lawyer is communicating with another lawyer, it's fine to use jargon. But when lawyers are communicating with nonlawyers, they should avoid jargon when possible, and define it when not possible.

Have you noticed that your vocabulary has changed since you began law school? You may not have noticed the transformation because everyone at school is speaking this new language, but your nonlaw friends will notice right away.

You may remember that we said that new law students are usually more adept at written communication than experienced lawyers are. The primary reason for this phenomenon is that they recently spoke the language of nonlawyers. They remember most of that language, even if they don't speak it regularly anymore. Retaining your ability to communicate in your original language will make you a better communicator in many aspects of your law practice, correspondence among them.

One of the chief complaints that laypeople make about lawyers is that they speak a specialized language, often called *legalese*. Some lawyers are probably showing off when they use language that laypeople cannot understand. More often, however, lawyers are merely thoughtless when they confuse laypeople by using legal terms that are not widely understood outside legal environments. A word like *tort*, which is well understood by anyone who has spent a week or two in law school, is virtually unknown to nonlawyers. Countless other words that lawyers use routinely are foreign to nonlawyers. Take a moment to think of some. In short order, you have probably identified ten or more such words.

The problem with most legal correspondence is that most lawyers don't pause and think about their language the way you just did. Lawyers who do not stop to consider what words or phrases require translation into English may spend hours carefully crafting a letter that their readers won't understand.

A lawyer who doesn't think about readers provides this conclusion to a client who no longer wishes to go through with the purchase of a house:

> ***Bad Example***
> The seller's breach allows you to rescind the purchase agreement.

This lawyer believes that the letter or email will be received with great joy. Instead, the client goes straight to *dictionary.com* to find the definitions of "breach" and "rescind." Had the lawyer paused for a second to think about the language, the client would have been met with this happy news:

> ***Better Example***
> The seller didn't fix the roof within the time allowed, so you don't have to buy the house.

The amount of translation required will vary depending upon the sophistication of your readers, but you should not overestimate *any* reader's tolerance for legalese. You are now legally trained, but you may notice how quickly you feel like a layperson again the next time you receive a letter advising you that you are entitled to participate in a class action. Even legally trained readers crave translation. Don't make readers work harder than is necessary to figure out what you are saying in your correspondence.

Sometimes, you will find that your answer or advice is complicated in spite of your efforts at using clear language. Even after you have pared out all of the nonessential information, you may be concerned about your readers' ability to make sense of the information. In those instances, your writing task is not complete until you have organized the information in the most comprehensible way, using roadmaps, transitions, and organizational signals.

Consider these two excerpts from letters in which two lawyers attempt to explain to a potential client why they will not represent her:

Excerpt 1

After careful consideration of the law and the facts of your situation, I have decided to decline representation. Your concerns relate to the fact that you were not permitted to participate on the company softball team. You believe that your employer discriminated against you because you are a woman. The softball team was comprised mostly of men. You acknowledge, however, that you were permitted to try out for the softball team. Other women were also permitted to try out, and two made the team. In addition, some men who tried out for the team were not permitted to participate. You will not, therefore, be able to show that women were treated differently from men in the selection of players for the company softball team. The law requires you to show that you, as a woman, were treated differently from men in one or more of the terms or conditions of your employment, and you probably cannot show different treatment.

Participation on a softball team is probably not a term or condition of your employment anyway. Terms and conditions of employment are aspects like work assignments, eligibility for benefits, and payment for overtime. Participation on the softball team appears to have been purely voluntary and not connected in any way to compensation, work assignments, or benefits. You will probably not be able to convince a court that any discrimination in the selection of players for the softball team would relate to a term or condition of employment.

You cannot prove discrimination on the basis of actions by a coworker that were not sponsored, authorized, or endorsed by the employer (the company). The coach of the softball team was one of your coworkers. He made the team selections apart from any work assignment. The players were all laborers, like you, and the company's management was not involved in the selection of the coach or the players. The company did not sponsor the team or contribute to it in any way. Because the company did not take the action you are complaining about, you cannot make a claim against the company for that action.

Excerpt 2

I have carefully reviewed the facts as you presented them to me. I believe that they are as follows, but I invite you to let me know if I have missed something. One of your coworkers

> formed a softball team. The team used your employer's name, but the company did not sponsor the team, appoint the coach, or participate in the management of the team in any way. The coach held tryouts and selected twelve men and two women for the team. He rejected two men and two women, including you. You believe that he engaged in sex discrimination in the selection of the team, and you would like to sue your employer for the discrimination.
>
> The law does not support your claim, and I have decided that I cannot represent you. My reasons can be summarized as follows:
>
> (1) You cannot claim employment discrimination because participation on the softball team was not a part of your employment; your employer did not sponsor the team or participate in the selection of the coach or the players.
>
> (2) Even if the employer had sponsored the team, players were not compensated for participating, and participation on the team did not affect their employment in any way; participation was not a term or condition of the employment relationship.
>
> (3) Even if participation had been a term or condition of employment and the employer had selected the players, both male and female employees were allowed to try out and participate for the team, and some women were selected for the team; therefore, you are not likely to prove that women were treated less favorably than men in the selection process.

Which of these formulations is more likely to be understood by readers? For most readers, the organization of the second excerpt, which breaks the explanation into smaller bits with transitions and mini-explanations, allows for greater comprehension. The psychological concept of *cognitive load* and the graphic concept of *white space* explain the difference.

The first letter requires readers to digest several pieces of information at once. Each piece of information fills a part of readers' cognitive space. We know that our brains have only so much available room at any given time. In fact, research shows that we can retain only one to three pieces of new information at a time. After we have encountered one to three pieces of new information, our brains stop absorbing. We have exceeded maximum *cognitive load*, which is a way of conceptualizing the "weight" of the information that fills our brains. (Are you surprised to learn that cognitive load explains most of your stress during your first few weeks of law school?)

The second excerpt eases cognitive load by allowing readers to absorb only one piece of new information at a time. By using transitions to form connections between the pieces of information, the second excerpt allows readers to "chunk" some of the information. Chunking is the joining of two or more pieces of information into one, keeping more cognitive space available.

Research also demonstrates that readers of complex material benefit from white space on the page or screen. These white spaces are like breaths for the reader. Although every page will have white space in the margins and between words, most readers need more white space than the margins provide. When legal readers turn a page and see no white space beyond the margins, not even a paragraph break, they experience intellectual suffocation. Conversely, readers who see significant white space are like the actor in the asthma commercial who breathes easier after using her inhaler. They believe that they will have sufficient mental oxygen to understand the material on that page. In correspondence, as in every other form of legal writing, you should consider the way the page appears as well as the substance of your writing.

C. TONE AND EMOTIONAL CONTENT

As a writer of legal correspondence, you will have a relationship of some kind with nearly every recipient of every letter or email. The tone and emotional content of your correspondence will vary significantly, depending upon the nature, duration, and desired future of that relationship. Some aspects of tone will be consistent, however, and we will begin with those.

1. Communicating Your Professionalism

In all of your correspondence, you want to communicate that you are a professional. Professionalism encompasses a number of concepts, and we intend to include several of them in our use of the word here. Specifically, we intend to include the concepts of (1) professional care and competence and (2) civility.

a. Professional care and competence

A professional exercises care in all tasks. By *care*, we mean concern, interest, and attention. If you have agreed to undertake any legal task, even one that leads you to decide not to represent a potential client, you must exercise the caution and diligence of one who cares about the matter and who is sufficiently interested to be thorough and attentive. The recipient of your correspondence will not have confidence in anything else you say if you have not convinced the recipient that you have been careful in your consideration of the matter.

The first step in communicating appropriate professional care is *taking* appropriate professional care. In practice, this may mean rejecting a client if you cannot devote sufficient care; if you are receiving an assignment from a supervisor, you must sometimes develop that caring attitude based not on your personal feelings but on your feelings of professionalism alone. If you are sufficiently interested to be focused and diligent, your care will likely be evident in your correspondence. You should still express it explicitly.

The simplest way to tell a recipient of your correspondence that you have been careful is to explain what you have done before drafting the correspondence. The following fictional examples highlight the effectiveness of a simple recitation of the writer's efforts in communicating appropriate care.

> **Sample 1**
> I am sorry to inform you that you have no chance of succeeding on your claim.

> **Sample 2**
> I am sorry to have to inform you that I believe that you have no chance of succeeding on your claim. Let me briefly explain the basis for this conclusion. I have carefully considered the facts as you presented them to me. I have read every case in which a person has made a claim based on similar facts. I have looked at similar claims in other states, and I have looked at statutes that relate to the situation. In all of my research, I have not uncovered a case in which a claim based on similar facts has been successful. I am certain that none of the relevant statutes will be helpful to you.

The recipient of the first sample is far more likely to think "Why should I believe you?" than is the reader of the second sample. The second writer has communicated sufficient information about the underlying investigation of the claim to assure most readers that the writer has been careful.

We have focused on correspondence to clients and potential clients, but the same consideration applies in correspondence to other attorneys, whether they are allies or opponents. If a lawyer doubts that another lawyer has been diligent in the analysis of a legal matter, the recipient will discount the advice or demand included in correspondence. As in correspondence to a client, a lawyer allays concerns about professional care by actually exercising it.

b. Civility

The breakdown in civility in the legal profession has cost lawyers a great deal of credibility and respect over the past few decades. This breakdown has been the focus of substantial attention from within and outside the profession. Civility is one of the basic requirements of any professional person, and we believe that it is the default mode of most law students at the beginning of their legal lives. Unfortunately, as some lawyers become more experienced, their civility erodes, probably due to many factors. Rather than identifying all of these factors, we want to identify two important reasons to resist that erosion of civility: self-preservation and legacy.

Every act of incivility costs a lawyer something. The lawyer may not be aware of the cost at the time, or ever, but acts of incivility are, by definition, witnessed by someone. If that observer is a client, the client is far less likely to engage with the lawyer in the future. If the observer, or target, is opposing counsel, that observer is far less likely to facilitate a friendly and mutually agreeable resolution of a legal dispute. Likewise, that opposing counsel will be less likely to agree to deal amicably with any of the small problems that arise in the course of a legal dispute, such as the need to postpone a meeting or a hearing. Whoever the target of the incivility, the uncivil lawyer will have lost some income or benefit without being aware of the loss. We are convinced that, over time, lawyers who are routinely uncivil are less successful and have fewer favorable professional relationships. They are also more likely to experience uncivil behavior directed at them. Their losses are real, even if they are not obvious.

We have already observed that a lawyer's correspondence creates a long-lasting record of the lawyer's professional communication. The endurance of that record serves important purposes, including the preservation of the lawyer's exact words if they are ever called into question. The endurance of that record is also a reason to consider carefully the civility of anything you commit to writing. An intemperate sentence, while satisfying when you write it, may embarrass you down the road, when the emotion that spurred you to write it has long since passed.

2. Setting a Tone

When we began this chapter, we described letters and emails as formal communication. The word *formal* is sometimes used as a synonym for *unemotional* or *emotionally detached*, and you may assume from our use of it here that we are suggesting that your formal communication should be unemotional in tone. You would be right to a point but with one big caveat. Formal professional correspondence is rarely the place for expressions of high emotion. It is completely appropriate, however, to acknowledge the recipient's emotions and to write with a warm and inviting tone when needed.

High emotion and reason are rarely companions, and in your professional communications you are conveying reason. You hope to incite reason, as well, whether you are writing to a client, to opposing counsel, or to another interested audience. Even when you know that emotion is present in the matter your correspondence addresses, your goal is to allow reason to carry the day. This hope does not mean, however, that you should ignore the emotion in the situation.

A lawyer who is preparing a letter to a client in a routine business transaction will rarely have to give much thought to the client's emotional state. The task is much more delicate, however, for a lawyer in a custody dispute, a discrimination action, or a disagreement about the division of property. In each of these examples, the lawyer knows that the client is likely to have strong emotions about the situation. Those emotions are unlikely to be factors in the lawyer's analysis, but the client will often be unable to separate the emotion from the legal aspects of the conflict. The lawyer cannot, therefore, ignore the emotional content of the situation altogether.

In most situations, the lawyer can dignify the emotion in a situation by naming it near the beginning of the correspondence. A sentence like this is not unusual within the first paragraph of the letter:

> I know that this has been a difficult year for you, and I am sorry that you have had to revisit your father's death on so many occasions.
>
> The final year of your employment was a very trying time for you, and I know that you are eager to bring the conflict to a conclusion.
>
> Family disagreements are never pleasant, and I understand why you are reluctant to engage in litigation about this matter.
>
> I am sorry to have to deliver disappointing news.

The lawyer is not trying to take the place of a therapist. At the same time, however, the client will often be better able to absorb advice after having had the emotion of the situation acknowledged.

In any letter, a friendly greeting and a generally warm tone will put the recipient at ease. Correspondence that is so emotionally detached as to be cold or clinical, on the other hand, is less likely to engender open communication and a sense of trust between the writer and the recipient. So, if your purpose in writing the correspondence is to engender open communication, you should choose a tone that suggests openness. If, on the other hand, your purpose is just to deliver information, a more clinical tone may be best.

D. SPECIAL CONSIDERATIONS FOR EMAIL AND E-MEMOS

Many lawyers now send informal or even formal correspondence using email.

While the substance of a message should be the same whether it is in paper or digital form, email correspondence presents some concerns that do not exist with hardcopy messages. The first concern is that there are too few barriers between your foot and your mouth. It is frighteningly easy for you to send an ill-advised message. With a hardcopy document, you must write it, print it, and sign it; it is typical to reread or at least skim the letter before signing it. These natural barriers slow down the communication process and may have the benefit of making you think over a fit of temper that spilled out onto paper. With an email, in contrast, you can hit the "Send" button as soon as you finish the thought. What's worse, you may send a message inadvertently, as an automatic reaction to a ringing telephone or a knock on the door.

The second concern is that it is very easy to send an email to a whole group of the wrong persons or to the very worst wrong person. You may be a member of several email lists; some of those lists may have a default setting of "Reply Only to Sender," while others may default to "Reply All." It is easy to forget about these defaults when you are in a hurry to send a message to a friend or colleague; if you are not careful, you may send a private message to dozens or hundreds of people. Further, many email systems try to read our minds and anticipate who we are sending a message to. If we type in "Ma . . ." it will try to fill in the gaps, scanning through your most recently sent messages to guess at the recipient. Mary Beth once received an email full of insults about another professor; it was intended for a student's significant other, whose name also began with *M*. She informed the student of the mistake and received an abject apology. We note that she never ratted out the student or forwarded (or showed) the email to the professor in question.

With these and other concerns in mind, we offer the following guidance.

1. Decide Whether Email Is the Best Medium for the Message

First, recognize that people are not excited to receive emails. Email is something they have to deal with: the email may give them a task they have to complete or a request they have to respond to. Even junk email has to be deleted, or at least its subject skimmed as the reader scrolls past it. Accordingly, if your email can be handled over the phone or in person, don't send it.

2. Consider How Best to Protect Attorney-Client Privilege

Above, we discussed the problem of accidentally sending emails to the wrong person, or to a whole group instead of to its intended recipient. In practice, of course, you may at times need to send an email to a larger group, if several people are working on a project. You may also want to secretly send Person B an email that was sent to Person A, so that Person B can know what's going on between you and Person A. Take care when doing so.

First, sometimes group emails (the bane of many a lawyer) don't need to be group emails anymore. You may disengage or rename a group email if (1) you wish to address a related issue that doesn't concern the whole group, (2) you see people listed on an address line without understanding why they are included, or (3) you want to address an issue that isn't relevant to the original purpose of the email.

First, send an email only to those who need to have the information, and inform them of any change, either in the subject line of the email or at the beginning of the email, e.g., "Private to you" or "Private to Monte and MB." If you are concerned about new names in the address line, make that clear, e.g., "I wanted to check with you because I'm not sure why Monte Smith and Mary Beth Beazley were added here." Even if the whole group needs to receive the email, change the subject line if the conversation has morphed into a new area. You will make friends of those who have to read all of the emails about one topic immediately but who can skip emails about other topics.

If you are primarily directing the email to one person but including a few others to keep them in the loop, you may indicate that method in a salutation, e.g., "Dear Monte (and CC MB & Jess FYI):" A salutation like this one shows Monte that he is the primary recipient, and signals to MB and Jess that they may need to skim it for some other reason.

"CC" is a retronym; it's an abbreviation for "carbon copy." In typewriter days, typists put a sheet of carbon paper between two sheets of typing paper. The typewriter keys made an imprint of carbon on the second sheet, creating an instant—though highly smudgeable—copy. Note that if you inserted the carbon paper backwards, you ended up with a mirror image copy on the back of the first page, and nothing on the second. And yes, Mary Beth did that at least once during the 1970s.

You may have noticed the "BCC" option in your email system. This abbreviation stands for "blind carbon copy," and it allows you to copy someone on an email without the other recipients knowing about it. Most practicing attorneys who we consulted don't use this option. A wrong mouse maneuver or keystroke could turn a BCC into a CC. If you want another person to see an email, wait until you've sent it and then forward a copy from your "Sent" mailbox.

Likewise, take care when you forward messages. First, obviously, make sure that you are not destroying attorney-client privilege or creating some other problem. Second, read the entire message before sending. If you see something at the start of a message that you want to share with another, don't forward the whole message unless you are certain that the entire message is appropriate for sharing. Once a message goes out with your name at the bottom (or on the address list, at least), it's published forever.

Finally, and perhaps most importantly, consider privacy issues such as attorney-client privilege. The rules on these issues can vary by jurisdiction and can change over time, so the main thing we will tell you is to be careful. In general, attorney-client privilege exists only between an attorney and a client, so if non-clients are included on an email, the information in that email is no longer privileged. Likewise, if the client forwards that email to someone else, the client will destroy the privilege as to that information. Accordingly, scrutinize the recipient and CC list of any email to a client. Note that just typing the word "privileged" at the top of the page does not confer attorney-client privilege on information that is shared beyond an attorney and a client. Instead, make sure your client understands the concept of "privilege," and label any messages in a way that reminds the client of this requirement, e.g., "To Preserve Attorney-Client Privilege, Do Not Forward."

When writing any significant message, you should leave the address blank while you are writing (or delete the address if you are replying to a significant message). Obviously, this advice doesn't apply when you are responding to a scheduling request for a luncheon meeting. A blank address line provides two advantages: first, it ensures that you will not send the message unconsciously—it sets up a barrier to communication that may encourage you to consider the content of your message. Second, it forces you to look at the address and may prevent you from sending a private message to an email list. Take care when you put that address back in: make sure that the message goes to the right person(s).

3. What to Include and Not to Include in an Email

In general, professional emails should include only information that needs to be preserved in written form for some reason. When you write an email, you may be creating evidence, whether you intend to do so or not. Thus, emails should never include information that you would not like to see brought forward as evidence or in the newspaper. And the fact that the email is sent "privately" is meaningless. You may intend a message for one person, but that person may or may not have your best interests at heart; further, that person may not have your good judgment. And, of course, deleting an email from your mailbox does not really make it disappear, as you no doubt know from a variety of well-publicized scandals and lawsuits. Anything that you send in an email can someday show up as evidence.

If you need to share information that you do not want to put in the email, suggest in the email that you talk on the phone or in person so that you can provide the necessary details. Note that you should *talk* about these details. Do not put sensitive information into text messages, because texts are as discoverable as emails are. Likewise, if your correspondent doesn't answer when you call, don't leave the sensitive information on voicemail—some voicemail systems transmit messages as emails, and then we are back where we started.

4. Tone in Emails

We addressed tone generally above, and all of that advice applies to emails. Note, however, that sometimes people forget to self-police tone when sending email. When sending a letter, it is easy to recognize the formal requirements of the correspondence. When the message is within the body of an email, however, it may be easy to forget to follow the same requirements of tone, formality, and professionalism. In general, do not let the medium of the letter influence your writing decisions. You should not be casual in writing an email just because it is sent electronically rather than printed on watermarked letterhead. Rather, your writing decisions should be guided by your relationship with readers, the sophistication of those readers, and the goal of the message.

Our general advice is that you should send only compliments via email. Obviously, this statement is hyperbole; you will use email for many things besides sending compliments. Perhaps this advice would be better worded as "never send an insult" or "never rant" over email. You never know where that email will go after it gets to its first recipient; make sure that it will not embarrass you no matter who sees it.

5. Organization and Level of Detail

As noted above, people are rarely excited to receive work emails. Almost certainly, their first thought, consciously or unconsciously, is "what do I have to do?" If you are responding to the question of another, the recipient's first thought is "so what's the answer?" Your job when drafting and designing your email is to answer these questions as quickly as possible.

If you are making a request or a demand—especially one with a deadline—it may be appropriate to put the gist of that request in the email subject header:

Re: Request for Information needed by February 4 for Voehl case

If you are responding to a request for information or a report, put specifics into the subject line that will allow the recipient to distinguish your "information" from the information sent by others:

Re: Answer to Venzor: elderly driving question

In an opening paragraph, include bullet points that tell the reader the purpose of the email, noting particularly what kind of response or action you're asking for, if any. Don't write this opening until after you've finished the substance of the email, for the obvious reason that you won't know what you're saying until after you've written the message. If you are asking someone to meet a deadline, put that information in a prominent place at the beginning of the message, perhaps as part of a formal "re" message within the body of the email, underlined and in bold-faced type.

As noted above, your relationship with the reader should dictate the email's tone, so begin with an appropriate opening sentence, and then follow with a numbered list, as in this example:

The format shown here is one that might be appropriate in informal memos, sometimes called "e-memos" (for the obvious reason that they are sent by email).

Dear Priscila—

Hope your week is going well. I'm writing in response to your question about what steps our client can take to get his elderly father to stop driving. A more detailed answer follows, but the gist is:

(1) There's no governmental agency that he can call that will check a senior's driving skills upon the request of a family member. I verified this answer with employees at three relevant agencies and with the Outreach Director at the Vanita Department of Aging.

(2) Van. Rev. Code § 123.12(c) allows a "doctor or medical caretaker" to recommend testing a driver's abilities due to concerns about a driver's "cognitive or physical fitness." The license can be pulled only if the driver fails tests conducted by the local Bureau of Motor Vehicles. This step may be an option if our client has a good relationship with his father's doctor.

(3) The local AAA office offers Senior Driving Education courses. The person I talked to there said that many participants voluntarily opt out of driving after the course.

I hope these points (and the details below) answer your questions. Feel free to follow up further, but otherwise no need to reply unless you need more information from me. Thanks again for the opportunity to work on this project.

Best,

Biff

Analysis of relevant information about when a driver's license can be taken away involuntarily:

(1) No governmental agency in this state allows a family member to request a check on a senior's driving skills.

* * * *

This email gives a very succinct answer up front, and it relieves the writer of a need to respond. The level of detail in the rest of the message, of course, will depend on the complexity of the issues and the writer's relationship with and knowledge of the recipient of the email.

One warning about level of detail in emails. Many readers of email want to have it both ways. They want the email to be succinct and to the point, but they want it to provide enough information so that they can be confident that the answer is correct. Further, they expect the writer to have the depth of knowledge needed to answer any follow-up questions the recipient may have. This problem is one reason we still teach law students to write formal office memos. Even if your reader doesn't want to *see* the level of detail that appears in a formal office memo, you must still *have* that level of knowledge and understanding.

To help give your reader confidence that your answer is correct, try to write your answer as a statement of a legal issue, with those three parts: legal context, answer to core question, and legally significant facts. When you provide the legal context, include any relevant statute numbers, and in your accompanying note, indicate that you understand how the major cases in the jurisdiction back up your conclusion (and, of course, be ready to provide those case names and succinct, focused case descriptions on request). Be explicit in your brief answer, and include enough factual detail to show that you understand how the law and the facts relate to each other. If you are giving the reader bad news, soften it in some of the ways recommended in earlier sections. Likewise, support your answer with reference to statutes and other authorities. In the example above, note how the writer supported his "no agency can help" response by noting that he had consulted three state agencies and the State Department of Aging. In this way, the writer spreads the blame for the bad news.

6. Email as E-Memo

As we noted earlier in this text, formal office memos are written less frequently in this century than the last, although they are far from extinct.[1] The traditional memo is often replaced by the so-called e-memo, a one- to two-page document submitted via email, often with a short turnaround time. As Professor Desnoyer's research shows, the

---

1. *See, e.g.*, Brad Desnoyer, *E-Memos 2.0: An Empirical Study of How Attorneys Write*, 25 Legal Writing: J. Legal Writing Inst. 213, 261-62 (2021) (noting that more than half of attorneys surveyed write 1-5 traditional memos per year, while about 10 percent write more than 30 per year); *see also* Kirsten K. Davis, *"The Reports of My Death Are Greatly Exaggerated": Reading and Writing Objective Legal Memoranda in a Mobile Computing Age*, 92 Or. L. Rev. 471 (2014).

requirements for e-memos vary, depending on such things as the size of the firm and the preferences of the attorney asking for the e-memo.[2]

In our opinion, the skills needed for an effective e-memo are a combination of the skills needed for effective research, effective analytical writing, effective correspondence, and effective email. As with effective research, you must be able to identify the relevant legal issues, identify applicable statutes and cases, and understand how the law applies to the facts. As with effective analytical writing, you must be able to identify reader needs and expectations. Further, you must be able to succinctly articulate issues, provide accurate and concise case descriptions, and clearly apply law to facts. As with correspondence, you must identify the appropriate tone in which to convey your findings and convey your analysis without needless detail. Finally, as with email, you must be aware of the medium so that you write, organize, and design the message for ease of reading and navigation.

If you are asked to write any kind of document while on the job, try to get your hands on one or more samples of the document so that you can get an idea of reader expectations and local culture as to that document. This recommendation is particularly relevant for in-house documents, whether they are formal memoranda or informal e-memos. While we do not recommend any particular e-memo format, you may find it helpful to read Professor Desnoyer's article (cited in footnote 1). It includes samples of different formats, as well as the reactions of practicing lawyers who reviewed the various formats.

7. Document Design

As you know from your own experience, reading a letter in hard-copy form is different than reading it in digital form. Likewise, reading a letter on a computer screen or tablet is different than reading it on a phone. If a person receives a hard copy of a long letter, it's easy to flip through a few pages and look at the last paragraph to get the bottom-line answer. Scrolling through a document on a phone makes this process much more difficult. This reality is why we recommend that you start with the answer, and that you place that answer in an obvious place in the message.

The fact that people read emails on a variety of platforms means that your paragraphs must be short, with double-spacing between paragraphs. Further, you should include headings that make your message easy to navigate. In the example above, the writer listed three points that would be addressed in detail below. If the reader cared only about the third point, she could scroll through the message looking for that heading, which should be underlined and in bold-faced type to make it easy to find.

Think about design issues when responding, as well. If the sender has asked you a set of questions, it may be best to insert your responses after each question. Be sure to signal, however, where your responses begin and end. Because formatting from one platform may not survive in another platform, you may not be able to use color or other fancy design features to set off your responses. At the least, you should

---

2. Desnoyer, *supra*. n. 1, at 227.

create new paragraphs for your responses. You may want to begin each answer with the word **Answer:** or **My answer:** or use asterisks or some other method to make them stand out. Likewise, in some messages, it may be necessary to signal the end of your response, e.g., ****End of this answer.**

8. Etiquette

The rules on etiquette vary according to time and place. Nevertheless, a few pieces of advice may make your emails more palatable. Using a salutation and a signature (beyond your generated signature block) is one way to develop or to reinforce the relationship you have with the reader. Always be sure to check the spelling of the first and last names of your recipients. As teachers, we know that most first names have alternate spellings (e.g., Kristin or Kristen? Matthew or Mathew?); be sure you are using the right alternate. And last name spelling should be easy to discern from the email address or from prior correspondence.

Monte has received emails addressed to Monty (they usually get his last name right), while Mary Beth frequently sees her last name misspelled directly beneath an email address that includes its correct spelling. While we don't hold grudges over these misspellings, they are needless distractions.

If you are asking for information from someone, do whatever you reasonably can to make their task easier. That may mean reminding them of the document where certain information resides within a huge case file (especially if you have that knowledge handy because you have been working with that file for weeks). If you are asking someone to review a document, perhaps note particular concerns (e.g., "I'm especially interested in your feedback on Section B.2"). When trying to set up a schedule, it's a bit imperious to ask for someone else's availability without giving yours first (especially if you are asking a supervisor). Instead, say, e.g., "I'm glad to meet about this next week. My best availability is on Monday and Wednesday afternoon and Thursday morning. I look forward to hearing from you."

Finally, it's almost always worthwhile to send a quick thank you to anyone who has given you information or responded in some other way. In this way, you support your relationship with the writer and let the writer know that the message has been received. If your correspondent has devoted significant time to helping you, your message can go into more detail; otherwise, it may be fine to send one of the automatic messages that some programs now generate.

We don't mean to scare you too much about email (although we do want to scare you a little). We just want you to realize that the messages you send as a professional are much more significant—and can have much more impact—than the messages you send as a student. When in doubt, ask yourself, "How would I feel if my boss or my mentor saw this message?" If either or both of those people wouldn't like your email message, it's time to revise or delete.

E. SUMMARY

Although each individual letter will probably be shorter than any office memo or brief that you write, it can represent an extremely important aspect of your practice. Take care when you decide whether to write a letter, when you decide what information to include in the letter, and when you decide how to write the letter. Doing so will allow you to do a better job for your clients and for your career.

Recall and Review

1. When sending an opinion letter, it is important to include ___________ that describe the limits of the letter.
2. True or False: The purpose of the letter or the task being requested should appear at the end of the letter so the body of the letter can justify the purpose before presenting it.
3. You should take care before sending emails because emails and texts, like any written information, can be submitted in court as ___________.
4. When sending a lengthy email message, be sure to include numerous ___________ to ease navigation.
5. True or False: Lawyers should consider psychological issues when writing letters and emails.
6. Including ___________ in letters and emails gives readers mental breathing space.
7. When sending an email to a client, the lawyer must make sure the client understands how to preserve a___________ -c___________ privilege.

CHAPTER 17

THE *WRITING* PART OF LEGAL ANALYSIS AND WRITING

Clarity, Precision, Simplicity, and Everything Else that Makes Legal Writing Readable

By now, we have spent a significant amount of time focused on the analysis part of legal analysis and writing. Analysis includes the legal substance of the document and its organization around a framework that meets the needs of its likely readers. The document's organization is one of two tools you will use to ensure that readers glean exactly the meaning from the document that you intend. The other tool is careful writing, writing that is crafted to convey your analysis without impeding readers' comprehension. Careful writing avoids incoherence, imprecision, or unnecessary complexity.

You will hear lawyers talk about *clarity* in writing. We understand *clarity* to refer to invisibility: just as clear glass is invisible, clear writing never stands in the way of a complete understanding of the writer's message. This type of clarity incorporates concepts of precision, simplicity, and usage, which all contribute to readability. When a writer achieves that state of maximum readability, we say that the writing is like butter.[1] We glide right through it.

We will break the concept of clarity into three subconcepts: precision, simplicity, and usage. *Precision* describes the state of your writing when you have said exactly what you mean and nothing else. *Simplicity* describes the state of your writing when the sentence and paragraph structures contribute to comprehension. *Usage* is "everything else."

Admittedly, this chapter encompasses some points about grammar and punctuation. We expect that you already know a lot about these subjects, so we will keep our focus on the issues that are particularly troublesome for legal writers.

A. WHAT DO YOU MEAN, EXACTLY?

Precision encompasses a number of concepts, all of which contribute to the communication of exactly the message you want to deliver as a

1. To be completely honest, we say "buttah" (an old *Saturday Night Live* reference; before your time).

writer. One simple way of thinking about precision is that it is the clear identification of who did what to whom. You may be thinking, "Oh, this is like subject and verb," and you would be right. But that's not all it is. Some of these precision concepts may be familiar to you, but we will try to help you see them in a new way. They include identifying the actor, choosing the best verb to identify the action, and putting the actor and the action at or near the front of the sentence.

1. Identifying the Actor

In the following sentence, who is the actor?

There is one way that disability can be proven even when it does not exist.

How would you know? As frequent readers of English, we expect to find the actor, or subject, near the beginning of a sentence. The first noun in this sentence is "way," but it doesn't seem to be doing anything. The next possibility, "disability," is also just hanging about, waiting to be proven. The verbs in the sentence don't help much either. "Is" accompanies "way" but tells us only that a way exists. "Can be proven" accompanies "disability," but disability is not the actor; it is being acted upon. It also does not "exist," as we are told by the time we reach the end of the sentence. The answer, of course, is that the actor is absent from the sentence. We don't know who is trying to prove that a disability exists.

Many smart lawyers commit the crime of failing to include the actors in their sentences. The problem is not that these sentences are utterly incoherent. Rather, these sentences inconvenience readers and slow down the reading process because readers have to figure out what is happening in the sentence. By not including some information, the writer has given up some control over the message and left open the possibility that readers will fill in the wrong information.

Even where the identity of the actor is unmistakable from the context of the sentence or surrounding sentences, leaving the actor out of the sentence, or placing the actor at the end of the sentence, slows readers' comprehension by preventing them from moving through the sentence in a linear fashion. *Linear reading* means reading that begins with the first word in a sentence and continues through the words in order without having to double back to an earlier point in the sentence to put the pieces together. You cannot read the following sentence in a linear fashion: "It is likely that several of the factors will be found by the court to be satisfied." Sentences beginning with *it is* and *there is/are* usually suffer from a lack of clarity that prevents readers from moving through them in a linear fashion. Readers are forced to go more slowly and to do more of the work of interpretation.

Compare for yourself. As you read the following sentences, judge how efficiently you are able to discern the writer's message. Which sentence makes its meaning clear to you more quickly?

A. There is likely enough circumstantial evidence to raise an issue, beyond a preponderance, that Lash regarded Nutt's weight as disabling.

or

B. Mr. Nutt will probably be able to show, through circumstantial evidence, that Lash regarded Nutt's weight as disabling.

We are guessing that you answered B. As you see, Sentence B begins with a subject-verb combination, allowing readers to move through the sentence in a linear fashion.

A construction that interferes with both clarity and linear reading is *passive voice*. When writers use passive voice, they often obscure the identity of the actor and, once again, prevent readers from moving through the sentence in a linear fashion. Consider this example:

> Several factors are used to determine whether customer confusion is likely.

The action is described by the verb "used," but readers must guess at the identity of the user. The actor is clear in the following version, and readers can move through the sentence in a linear fashion:

> The court will use several factors to determine whether customer confusion is likely.

As our examples illustrate, the culprit in many unclear sentences is the vague *it is* or *there is/are* construction or the passive voice (or both). The solution is almost always to begin the sentence with the actor, identified precisely, and to follow immediately with the action. If you can communicate the action with an active verb rather than with a form of *to be*, do so.

Sometimes, the solution also includes breaking the sentence into multiple sentences that precisely identify actors and actions. Consider this example, in which the second sentence defies linear reading:

> Larry Lash indicated that the newer hires had more energy. It can safely be inferred that the only reason Lash would believe that is Mr. Nutt's weight, as his record of being in the top one-third for efficiency shows that it is not true that the new hires had more energy.

Notice how breaking the sentence into shorter sentences enhances precision and readability:

> Larry Lash indicated that the newer hires had more energy. Mr. Nutt had been consistently efficient, among the top one-third of performers. Nutt's weight is the only possible explanation for Lash's assessment.

The meaning of the paragraph is the same, and the second version is shorter. Nothing is lost, and precision is gained.

Editing to eliminate *it is* and *there is/are* constructions is easy because the Find or Search function in your word-processing software will allow you to identify every such construction in your document. You can then rewrite the sentences following the actor-action-object format that promotes linear reading.

Editing for passive voice is not quite as easy. The best way to find passive-voice sentences that rob your writing of precision is to identify the verb in each sentence or clause and then to identify the actor associated with each verb. If the actor is the subject, the verb is in the active voice. Note that often, a passive voice verb needs a *to be* verb to function, so looking for a *to be* verb partner can help you to identify a passive construction. For example, the clause "the defendant hit the plaintiff" is written in active voice. The subject, *defendant*, is doing the hitting, and there is no *to be* verb. To make it passive, you would write, "the plaintiff was hit by the defendant," *or* "the plaintiff was hit." Note that for each passive example, the subject is *the plaintiff*, and the plaintiff is not doing any hitting. Further, the verb, *hit*, has a *to be* partner.

If the actor is not the subject of the sentence or clause, but you have identified the actor precisely, you may or may not choose to rewrite the sentence with the actor as the subject. Usually, you should rewrite the sentence to promote linear reading unless another consideration outweighs the linear-reading goal. If you have not clearly identified the actor, you must rewrite the sentence.

2. Identifying the Action

Our approach to editing may give rise to the false impression that identifying the actor precisely is the key to precision. In reality, the action is even more important. Three separate considerations guide the writer's choices in describing the action in a sentence: the first is choosing the verb that precisely describes the action; the second is avoiding a form of *to be* as often as possible; and the third is avoiding nominalizations.

In legal writing, the primary actors are parties (often through their lawyers) and courts. Their actions are precisely described by two sets of verbs. Those two sets of verbs do not often overlap. Parties argue, contend, move, request, assert, and claim, among other actions. Courts hold, find, reason, opine, rule, decide, and conclude, among other actions. Part of your job as a legal writer is to choose the verb that most precisely describes the action.

Is or another form of *to be* is rarely the best verb. The forms of *to be* are not the best verbs because the only "action" they indicate is the action of existing. Accordingly, they do not create a picture in readers' minds. They don't suggest any conduct that might help readers to determine what is happening in a sentence. The two primary culprits in the overuse of forms of *to be* are (1) *it is* and *there is/are* constructions and (2) passive voice. Neither of these constructions will be an obstacle to precision in *your* writing because you have read the preceding discussion.

Nominalizations are another impediment to precise verb use. A nominalization is a verb masquerading as a noun. Turning a verb into a noun does not violate any rules of grammar, but it does slow down readers' comprehension of the information in that word. For example, the word *decision* is a nominalization of the verb *decide*. When you turn the verb *decide* into the noun *decision*, you lessen its impact:

> The court decided that the defendant had violated the statute.
> The court made a decision that the defendant had violated the statute.

Note the difference between the verb form and the noun form within these sentences:

> The committee failed to complete its assignment.
> A failure by the committee resulted in the noncompletion of the assignment.
> The school may require students to follow a dress code.
> The school may impose requirements as to student dress.

You can often find nominalizations by looking for words that end in *-ment* or *-ion*. In the alternative, review your sentences (particularly overlong sentences) and circle just the verbs. When you find sentences in which all of the verbs are weak words without a lot of concrete meaning—e.g., *was*, *is* (or other *to be* verbs), *had*, *made*, *occurred*, *existed*—you should look for "hidden verbs" in the nouns or noun phrases in that sentence.

When deciding whether to revise, ask yourself whether you want to emphasize the verb or the noun. Sometimes, a nominalization may be the better choice. First, a nominalization may be more efficient. For example, it's more efficient to say *election* than to say *when voters elected the candidates*. Second, you may want to deemphasize certain negative information, and you can accomplish that goal by slowing readers' comprehension. Usually, however, you will have no reason to use nominalizations. When that is the case, identify your hidden verbs, find the actors who are *verbing* or "doing" the action of the verbs, and create a stronger, more easily comprehensible sentence.

When looking for nominalizations, you might find a sentence like this:

> The interference with the attempt to call an attorney constituted a violation of *Miranda*.

Once you identify the hidden verbs ("interfere," "attempt," and "violate"), you can work on making the sentence clearer:

> [Someone] interfered with [someone's] attempt to call an attorney and violated [that person's] *Miranda* rights.

Revising to avoid nominalizations provides a hidden benefit: you may realize when information is missing from the sentence. Thus, your next step might be to include some of the missing information:

> Officer Olson violated Mr. Jobe's *Miranda* rights when she prevented him from calling his attorney.

Thus, knowing how nominalizations can affect your writing can help you to make your points more explicitly when clarity is your goal and to blunt your message when it is to your advantage to do so.

B. KEEP (OR MAKE) IT SIMPLE

The concept of simplicity encompasses a variety of writing techniques and strategies for eliminating unnecessary complexity. They include closely watching the length of paragraphs and sentences, maintaining parallelism, and using effective transitions.

1. Size Matters

Lawyers tend to write long sentences and long paragraphs because they have long and complicated ideas to express. They forget that readers may grow weary and need the brief mental break that a period or a new paragraph provides. Long sentences are not always bad, and legal readers can often understand them better than other readers can; however, if you find that you frequently write sentences that are more than two lines long, you should scrutinize those sentences to see whether you can break them up into more manageable pieces.

A common cause of long sentences is the long participial opening:

> *Bad Example:*
> Attempting to demonstrate that grouping conditional intent and specific intent together is an established principle in criminal law, the court cited . . .

You can cure this type of long sentence by turning the opening clause into its own sentence:

> *Better Example:*
> The court attempted to demonstrate that grouping conditional intent and specific intent together is an established principle in criminal law. It did this by citing . . .

Another common culprit is including too many subordinate clauses or even one long one:

> *Bad Example:*
> This case, therefore, is similar to *Ohio v. Robinette*, in which this Court reversed a judgment for a defendant and found that the scope of a detention was no broader than necessary when defendant was stopped for a speeding violation and was asked for permission to search his car for drugs. 519 U.S. 33, 38 (1996).

As in the previous example, the solution is to reach for a period instead of a comma:[2]

> *Better Example:*
> This case, therefore, is similar to *Ohio v. Robinette*, 519 U.S. 33, 38 (1996). In *Robinette*, this Court reversed a judgment for a defendant and found that the scope of a detention was no broader than necessary. *Id.* The defendant in *Robinette* had been stopped for a speeding violation and was asked for permission to search his car for drugs. *Id.*

---

2. *See generally* Theodore Bernstein, *The Careful Writer* 314 (2d ed., Free Press 1995).

This is not to say that long sentences can never be effective sentences. To make a long sentence more effective, the writer should get to the verb quickly, place subjects close to verbs and verbs close to objects, and properly coordinate compound subjects, verbs, and objects.[3] Properly constructed, a long sentence can be the best vehicle with which to convey important information.

Strong writers pay attention to paragraph length as well as sentence length. Long paragraphs do not give readers opportunities to pause to digest ideas. Readers may pause by stopping midparagraph, but if they do, they may not pause where writers want them to. Writers can control the size and contents of the bites that readers take by breaking paragraphs frequently and at the most opportune spots.

Strategic writers create frequent paragraph breaks for at least two reasons. First, each paragraph break inserts white space. Second, each paragraph break potentially recaptures readers' attention.

White space on a page does not affect the substance of a document, but it makes that substance easier to read and to understand. Legal readers rarely read documents straight through from beginning to end; without sufficient white space, they may have a difficult time finding the section of the document they are most interested in. White space is also important for psychological reasons. A document with adequate white space is more appealing than a document where the words are crammed together on the page. White space on the page makes readers more willing to read the document, and to keep reading, while lack of white space encourages readers to postpone reading the document until another time—perhaps forever.

Each paragraph break provides a new opportunity for a thesis sentence as well, and thesis sentences are the best chance to catch readers' attention with a new idea or with new information about an old idea. Many legal readers skim by reading just the first sentence of each paragraph. If you write only two paragraphs in a subsection of analysis, busy or lazy readers may read only two sentences. Even careful readers will pay more attention at the beginning of the paragraph, so keeping paragraphs short is always worth the effort.

2. Unparalleled Simplicity

Parallelism is "the use of similar grammatical form for coordinated elements."[4] In lay terms, this means to use similar grammatical form for elements joined by conjunctions (e.g., *and*, *or*, or *but*) and by *either/*

---

3. *See* Joseph M. Williams, *Style: Ten Lessons in Clarity and Grace* 185-209 (5th ed., Longman 1997).

4. Anne Enquist & Laurel Currie Oates, *Just Writing* 221 (2d ed., Aspen 2005).

or or *neither/nor*. The next sentence violates the parallelism rule; the first word in each coordinated element is italicized:

> ***Bad Example:***
> The court found that the defendants had *interviewed* the plaintiff, *collected* his personal information, and *were* sharing it with others.

As a general rule, you should be able to grammatically connect the word or phrase that appears just before the first coordinated element with each of the coordinated elements. Thus, "the defendants had interviewed" and "the defendants had collected" are both phrases that make grammatical sense. But "the defendants had were sharing it with others" does not make sense. Revise to use parallel grammatical forms for each of the coordinated elements. In other words, all should be past-tense verbs, all should be participles, or all should be nouns:

> ***Better Examples:***
> The court found that the defendants had *interviewed* the plaintiff, *collected* his personal information, and *shared* it with others.
>
> The court found that the defendants were *interviewing* candidates, *collecting* their personal information, and *sharing* it with others.
>
> The court found that the defendants had violated the rights *of the plaintiff*, *of his family*, and *of all of those candidates* whom they had interviewed.

Repeating an introductory word—as we did in the last example above—emphasizes the parallelism and often makes the sentence easier for readers to understand. This repetition is not a grammatical requirement, but we recommend that you use it when drafting to identify where each element begins. In the alternative, use enumeration or make a slash mark while drafting so that you can identify what pieces of your sentence need to be parallel. Using this technique can also be helpful because it makes it easier to find errors by using the test that we described above: connect the opening of the sentence with each of the coordinated elements and make sure that these elements connect grammatically.

Work on making the key words in the phrases parallel; not every single word has to be in the same grammatical form. For example, each coordinated element could start with the same part of speech—a noun, an adjective, a preposition, and so on. Sometimes, as Enquist and Oates note, matching just the endings of key words will create parallelism.

Some bad and good examples follow. The first word in each of the coordinated elements is italicized:

Bad Example
It appears the court may have *deviated* from the presumptive child support figure, erroneously *based* its decision on the former wife's purported monthly deficit in the event the child support significantly decreased, and incorrectly *finding* that the husband needed to increase payments.

If the writer breaks out the coordinated elements and tries to match each to the rest of the sentence, the error becomes clear:

It appears the court may have	deviated from the presumptive child support figure,
It appears the court may have	erroneously based its decision on the former wife's purported monthly deficit in the event the child support significantly decreased, and
It appears the court may have	incorrectly finding that the husband needed to increase payments.

Once the elements are separated, it is clear that "finding" should be replaced with "found":

Better Example:
It appears the court may have *deviated* from the presumptive child support figure, erroneously *based* its decision on the former wife's purported monthly deficit in the event the child support significantly decreased, and incorrectly *found* that the husband needed to increase payments.

Sometimes, solving the parallelism problem is not the only way to fix the sentence. Once again, check the coherence of the sentence by connecting each of the coordinated elements with the appropriate subject, verb, or object:

Bad Example:
In the past, the defendant had been found guilty of *assault with a deadly weapon* in connection with an automobile accident, *reckless endangerment* in a separate incident in which he caused an automobile accident, and *was also found guilty of selling drugs in violation of the Drug Abuse Prevention and Control Act*.

Once again, the best way to identify problems is to match up each coordinated element with the subject:

In the past, the defendant had been found guilty of	*assault with a deadly weapon* in connection with an automobile accident,
In the past, the defendant had been found guilty of	*reckless endangerment* in a separate incident in which he caused an automobile accident, and
In the past, the defendant had been found guilty of	*was also found guilty of selling drugs in violation of the Drug Abuse Prevention and Control Act.*

You can fix this sentence in two ways. One is to fix the match-ups:

In the past, the defendant had been found guilty of	*assault with a deadly weapon* in connection with an automobile accident,
In the past, the defendant had been found guilty of	*reckless endangerment* in a separate incident in which he caused an automobile accident, and
In the past, the defendant had been found guilty of	*selling drugs in violation of the Drug Abuse Prevention and Control Act.*

Another way to fix the sentence is to give the third coordinated element—different in character from the other two—its own sentence:

> In the past, the defendant had been found guilty of assault with a deadly weapon in connection with an automobile accident and reckless endangerment in a separate incident in which he caused an automobile accident. He had also been found guilty of selling drugs in violation of the Drug Abuse Prevention and Control Act.

Be on the lookout for parallelism problems in any long sentence; look for uses of *and, or, neither,* and *nor* as signals that you may have coordinated elements that need review.

3. Making Effective Transitions

Most writers learn at an early age that they are supposed to provide "transitions" in their writing because, without transitions, writing doesn't "flow." Unfortunately, the transition repertoire of most writers is limited to words like *although, therefore, in contrast*, and the ubiquitous *however*. These mechanical or generic transitions are not wrong, and, in fact, they are useful to signal a shift in point of view (*in contrast, on the other hand*) or to tell readers how new information relates to old information (*furthermore, therefore*). But the best writers do not rely exclusively on generic transitions. Instead, they use a variety, including substantive ("echo") transitions and orienting transitions.[5]

Substantive transitions, as their name implies, are transitions that are based on the substance of the sentence. Rather than imposing a mechanical transition, the writer provides a transition by repeating a word or phrase from a previous sentence in the new sentence. In the following example, the substantive transition words are underlined:

> Nevertheless, the police had information that the only thing Chandler was reeling in was money for himself. This information was corroborated by Chandler's failure to inform the police where and when he was selling cocaine and by his flight from the police after his sale of crack cocaine to Detective Harper on March 10.

Note that "this" alone might be confusing. If the writer had said "This is corroborated by . . .," readers would have had to stop and figure out what "this" referred to. The word "this" should almost always be followed by the noun or noun phrase that you are referring to.

Sometimes, a substantive transition uses a label that is implicit in the previous sentence, as in this example from a fictional court opinion (the transition is underlined):

> The court must next decide whether the defendant can satisfy the *Jackson* test. This issue need not detain us for long.

Although the word "issue" does not appear in the first sentence, that sentence describes an issue, so the writer uses the phrase "this issue" as a substantive transition to begin the next sentence. Perhaps obviously, you should take care when using this technique so that you do not needlessly confuse readers. (Did you notice that "this technique" described what was implicit in the previous sentence?)

5. *See* Laurel Currie Oates, Anne Enquist & Kelly Kunsch, *The Legal Writing Handbook* 575-86 (2d ed., Aspen 1998); *see also* Joseph M. Williams, *Style: Ten Lessons in Clarity and Grace* 102-06 (5th ed., Longman 1997) (discussing the concept of "flow" in writing).

Finally, writers use *orienting transitions* to place their readers at a particular location. That location may be a physical (or jurisdictional) location, a temporal location, or an intellectual location:

Orienting transitions based on physical locations:
In Vermont, plaintiffs must . . .
A defendant in the Ninth Circuit may refuse . . .

Orienting transitions based on temporal locations:
In 2014, the legislature refused to . . .
Early that morning, the defendant had . . .
At 7:30 a.m., the defendant's wife placed the first phone call.

Orienting transitions based on intellectual locations:
The petitioner claims . . .
The U.S. Supreme Court has held . . .
In *Heller*, the defendant . . .
The plaintiff never argued that . . .

The best transitions occur naturally (as many do) or are added during the editing process. We advise against consciously trying to add transitions as you write: that way lies madness.

C. WE'LL CALL IT "USAGE"

Most lawyers follow most of the foundational grammar and punctuation rules, so we don't teach grammar and punctuation. But we do teach "usage." Some usage issues are particularly common to lawyers, and we will touch briefly on those here. In the next section, we will identify some of the most common grammatical errors that lawyers and law students make.

1. Avoiding Misplaced Modifiers

To find misplaced modifiers, look for opening clauses with "missing" information. These clauses often use gerunds or *-ing* verbals:

When selling cocaine on a street corner . . .
Although under arrest . . .

Next, evaluate whether the sentence meets readers' expectations. Generally, readers expect that the first noun following the clause supplies the missing information. If the noun supplies the "wrong" information, you have a misplaced modifier:

> *Bad Example:*
> Although under arrest, the Court noted that the defendant was not in handcuffs at the time.

To fix the problem, rewrite the opening clause to include the missing information *or* rewrite what comes after the opening clause to put the missing information immediately after the opening clause:

> *Better Examples:*
> Although under arrest, the defendant was not in handcuffs at the time, according to the court.
>
> The Court noted that although the defendant was under arrest, he was not in handcuffs at the time.

If you tend to misplace your modifiers, scrutinize any sentence with an opening clause. That's not the only place they can be found, but they like to hang out there.

2. Point of View and Positions of Emphasis in a Sentence

Readers subconsciously pay more attention to information in certain positions in a sentence or in a document. Accordingly, make sure to control the information that you put in those positions of emphasis. One common position of emphasis is the subject position of the sentence. As often as possible, you should fill that position with the person or concept that is the "star" of the document, or at least of that portion of the document. When writing a statement of facts, for example, you may wish to describe the fact scenario from the point of view of your client, if doing so would allow your readers to see the case in a more positive light.

When writing a letter or other document that might describe rights and responsibilities, you might wish to use a different point of view depending on your strategy. If you wish to emphasize the benefits that one party will receive, you might put that person in the subject position ("Upon completion of the contract, *you* will receive . . . *You* will be obligated only to . . ."). On the other hand, if you wish to stress all that your client is doing, you might put your client in that position of emphasis ("The buyer will accomplish three things before the closing date. First, the buyer will . . . Second, the buyer will . . ."). Using a consistent point of view can be a subtle but effective method of telling readers how significant certain parties are.

3. Use of Pronouns

Perhaps obviously, pronouns always have the potential of slowing reader comprehension. They force the reader to contemplate, even for a nanosecond, to whom or what the pronoun refers, and to mentally sync that information. We are not saying that you should never use pronouns; we *are* saying to use them carefully, and to focus on your use of pronouns as you edit and polish your documents.

Any time you have more than one person or thing in a sentence, pronouns can be confusing:

> *Bad Example:*
> Officer Strelow then frisked Beal. He felt an object in his pocket that he recognized as a pair of keys; in his other pocket, he felt what he described as a soft bulge that felt like tissue.

Although the reader might be able to figure out that *he* refers to Officer Strelow and that *his pocket* refers to Beal's pocket, it's better to revise and substitute nouns for pronouns as needed:

> *Better Example:*
> Officer Strelow then frisked Beal. Strelow felt an object in Beal's pocket that he recognized as a pair of keys; in the other pocket, he felt what he described as a soft bulge that felt like tissue.

Note that this example uses pronouns, but that all of them refer to the same person. Further, the better example substitutes "the" for "his." This method is a common and effective technique for avoiding pronoun use.

When referring to generic singular people, it is easy to avoid both singular *they* and the sometimes clumsy *he or she* with simple revisions. One way to edit is to change singular nouns to plural:

> Rule 11-507 NMRA (recognizing the privilege of a legal voter to refuse to disclose his or her vote).

> Rule 11-507 NMRA (recognizing the privilege of legal voters to refuse to disclose who they voted for).

> The state agrees that a defendant moving for relief under section 1203.4(a)(1)2 is entitled as a matter of right to the statute's benefits upon a showing that he or she has fulfilled the conditions of probation for the entire period of probation.

> The state agrees that defendants who move for relief under section 1203.4(a)(1)2 are entitled as a matter of right to the statute's

> benefits upon a showing that they have fulfilled the conditions of probation for the entire period of probation.

If the singularity of the generic person is crucial to the meaning of the sentence—or the law—try repeating the noun, substituting "the" for "his or her," or even removing the pronoun as possible. Note these examples and possible revisions:

> By participation in a civil conspiracy, a coconspirator effectively adopts as his or her own the torts of other coconspirators within the ambit of the conspiracy.
>
> By participation in a civil conspiracy, a coconspirator effectively adopts the torts of other coconspirators within the ambit of the conspiracy.
>
> By participation in a civil conspiracy, a coconspirator effectively becomes responsible for the torts of other coconspirators within the ambit of the conspiracy.
>
> A losing primary contestee can achieve his or her objective—i.e., effective reversal of the trial court's judgment—without establishing the merits of his or her appeal.
>
> A losing primary contestee can achieve the original objective—i.e., effective reversal of the trial court's judgment—without establishing the merits of the appeal.
>
> The trial court ultimately concluded a person acts wrongfully if he or she either acts intentionally and unreasonably, or acts while knowing or having reason to know he or she lacks authorization.
>
> The trial court ultimately concluded a person acts wrongfully if the person either (1) acts intentionally and unreasonably, or (2) acts without authorization while knowing or having reason to know of that lack.

These techniques can help you avoid singular *they* when referring to generic people. When referring to people who use *they/them* pronouns, however, it is appropriate and important to use singular *they*. You may wish to note its use in a footnote or in text, as courts often do. Many readers, however, will understand the use of singular *they* in this context without explanation, particularly if the person is referred to with the gender-neutral honorific *Mx.* Use plural verbs with singular *they*, just as you do with singular *you*:

> If you are coming to my place for our date tonight, please bring ice cream.

> Mx. Drozd concedes their sixth and seventh claims for relief, and therefore those claims against the City of Portland should be dismissed. They are also conceding their eighth claim, but only as to the individual defendants.

We hope that this short section on usage increases your awareness of potential writing issues as you write and revise your documents.

D. COMMON ERRORS

To err is human. Lawyers and law students are human. They err. When they write, they commit a variety of grammatical errors, many of which are idiosyncratic. We know that we said that we would not be talking about grammar, but some errors are sufficiently common among the legal writing population that we feel compelled to spend some space telling you about them so that you can avoid them.

1. Semicolons

Effective use of semicolons separates sophisticated writers from unsophisticated ones; it's worth taking a little time to learn to use them properly. Here are a few basic semicolon rules:

An *independent clause* is a *clause* (i.e., subject + verb) that can stand on its own as a sentence.

1. Use a semicolon to separate independent clauses *not* joined by a coordinating conjunction.

The most common coordinating conjunctions are *and*, *or*, *but*, *yet*, and *for*.

> *Good Example:*
> We do not have any evidence that the defendant and Mr. Otsego began their relationship while the defendant was still married; we do know, however, that they married the day after the defendant's divorce was final.

Writers often use semicolons to imply a relationship between the points made in each of the two independent clauses. In the previous example, the writer is implying something about the relationship between the defendant and Mr. Otsego.

A *conjunctive adverb* does more than make the connection between two parts of a sentence: it also tells readers something about the relationship between the two parts of the sentence. Common conjunctive adverbs are *therefore*, *accordingly*, and *furthermore*, but there are many others.

2. Use a semicolon when two independent clauses are joined with a conjunctive adverb.

> *Good Example:*
> The parties refused to meet to reach an agreement; therefore, Judge Byers required them to attend a court-supervised mediation session.

Note: Do not assume that every conjunctive adverb separates two independent clauses and therefore needs a semicolon; instead, realize that conjunctive adverbs can also appear in many other sentence structures.

3. Always use semicolons to separate items in a series when one or more of the items has internal commas.

Good Example:
The plaintiff has owned homes at 288 Newspaper Street, Milan, Michigan; 4992 Kinnickinnic Place, Milwaukee, Wisconsin; and 1659 N. High Street, Columbus, Ohio.

You may use a couple of different techniques to search for semicolon problems. If you use too *many* semicolons, use the Find feature on your computer to search for and scrutinize your semicolons. If you use commas where semicolons belong, first, train your reader's "ear" by reading about and doing exercises on semicolon use. Second, scrutinize your longer sentences and/or your lists.

2. Commas

Although the simple little comma arrives on the punctuation scene with the baggage of many rules, only three of the most common problems are addressed here. Two rules concern when you should use a comma, and the other rule concerns when you should not use a comma.

1. Use commas between items in a series of more than two items. Make sure to put a comma before the conjunction, as in "constitutions, statutes, *and* regulations."

Some writers eliminate the comma after the second-to-the-last item in a series (in our example, after "statutes"), but legal writers should never eliminate this comma: missing commas in wills, contracts, and statutes have resulted in needless litigation to settle a grammatical question that became a legal issue. In legal writing, make sure to include the comma before the conjunction.

The comma before the conjunction is commonly known as "the Oxford comma." We like the Oxford comma and recommend it for all legal writers, and we don't care how you happen to feel about Oxford as an institution or a location.

Bad Example:
You should review the relevant constitutions, statutes and regulations.

Good Example:
You should review the relevant constitutions, statutes, and regulations.

Bad Example:
Mr. Khan interviewed the client, researched the relevant issues and drafted the complaint.

Good Example:
Mr. Khan interviewed the client, researched the relevant issues, and drafted the complaint.

2. Place a comma before a coordinating conjunction separating two independent clauses.

When a coordinating conjunction creates a compound noun or verb, the sentence has only one independent clause, and no comma is necessary before the conjunction.

Good Examples:
Mr. Khan interviewed the client and researched the relevant issues.

Maria walked into the courtroom and then greeted the judge.

However, when the two parts of the sentence are independent clauses, they should be separated with a comma.

Good Examples:
Mr. Khan interviewed the client, and he researched the relevant issues.

Maria walked into the courtroom, and then she greeted the judge.

For most people, the hard part about using this comma properly is correctly identifying an independent clause. Usually, you can identify an independent clause by looking for an independent subject and a verb, as long as the clause is not introduced by a subordinating conjunction. In the sentence "Maria walked into the courtroom and then greeted the judge," a verb (*greeted*) follows the "and," but there is no separate subject for that verb; the subject from the first, independent, clause carries over into the second, dependent, clause. However, in the sentence "Maria walked into the courtroom, and then she greeted the judge," you find a separate subject (*she*) for the verb (*greeted*) in the second clause, which means that it is an independent clause. Although this rule is not foolproof, it can help you separate the dependent clauses from the independent clauses.

A *subordinating conjunction* is a conjunction that introduces a dependent clause (i.e., a clause that cannot stand on its own as a sentence). Common subordinating conjunctions are *when*, *if*, *how*, and *where*. Once again, however, the list is a long one.

3. Unless a clause intervenes, do *not* put a comma between a subject and a verb.

Bad Example:
The Fair Use Doctrine, allows some minor copyright infringement in certain circumstances.

Good Examples:
The Fair Use Doctrine allows minor copyright infringement in certain circumstances.

The Fair Use Doctrine, which is the focus of many a law school exam question, allows minor copyright infringement in certain circumstances.

3. Quotation Marks with Other Punctuation

The question of whether to put the comma or period inside or outside the quotation marks plagues many legal writers. Lawyers use quotation marks often, so it's important for you to understand the simple rule that governs the placement of the punctuation in the United States: the comma or period goes inside the quotation marks.

Good Examples:
The court concluded that "a demotion with loss of pay is an adverse action."

Under the *Guidelines,* three types of engineering satisfy the science-background requirement: "genetic engineering," biomechanical engineering," and "chemical engineering with an emphasis on biochemical."

The period or comma belongs inside the quotation marks whether it is part of the quoted material or not.

4. More Guidance on Common Writing Issues

This short section on common problems is by no means comprehensive. If you have problems that are not covered here, you may wish to consult Anne Enquist & Laurel Currie Oates, *Just Writing* (4th ed., Aspen 2013); Mary Barnard Ray & Jill J. Ramsfield, *Legal Writing: Getting It Right and Getting It Written* (5th ed., West 2010); or Theodore Bernstein, *The Careful Writer* (2d ed., Free Press 1995).

Recall and Review

1. A writer promotes clarity in legal writing by using linear, s_______ -v_________-o_________ sentence structures when possible.
2. True or False: Readers understand information in nouns more easily than they understand information expressed in verbs.
3. In the sentence "The defendant punched the plaintiff," the verb "punched" is in _________ voice.
4. Good legal writers use the __________ comma in lists of more than two items to express themselves clearly, to promote precision, and to avoid needless controversy.
5. Repeating a word from one sentence early in the following sentence is a good way to use a ___________ ("*echo*") transition.

INDEX